PERSPECTIVES AND PROGRESS
IN
MENTAL RETARDATION

City Hall, Nathan Phillips Square, Toronto, Ontario.
(*Courtesy of Government of Ontario, Ontario House, London*)

PERSPECTIVES AND PROGRESS IN MENTAL RETARDATION

*Sixth Congress
of the International Association
for the Scientific Study of Mental Deficiency (IASSMD)*

Volume II

BIOMEDICAL ASPECTS

Edited by

J. M. Berg, M.B., B.Ch., M.Sc., F.R.C.Psych., F.C.C.M.G.

Technical Editor
Jean M. de Jong

University Park Press
Baltimore

UNIVERSITY PARK PRESS
International Publishers in Medicine and Human Services
300 North Charles Street
Baltimore, Maryland 21201

Typeset by Maryland Composition Company, Inc.

Manufactured in the United States of America by The Maple Press Company

Library of Congress Cataloging in Publication Data
International Association for the Scientific Study
of Mental Deficiency. Congress (6th : 1982 : Toronto,
Canada)
Perspectives and progress in mental retardation.

Includes indexes.
Contents: v. 1. Social, psychological, and educational
aspects — v. 2. Biomedical aspects.
1. Mental deficiency—Congresses. I. Berg, J. M.
II. De Jong, Jean M. III. Title. [DNLM: 1. Mental
retardation—Congresses. W3 IN12T 6th 1982p / WM 300
I611 1982p]
RC569.9.I57 1982   362.3   83-14621
ISBN 0-8391-1952-6 (v. 1)
ISBN 0-8391-1953-4 (v. 2)

CONTENTS

SECTION I: EPIDEMIOLOGY AND SURVEYS

SECTION II: PRENATAL ENVIRONMENTAL HAZARDS

CONTENTS OF VOLUME I

SECTION V: EDUCATION AND TRAINING

SECTION VI: DEINSTITUTIONALIZATION AND COMMUNITY LIVING

PREFACE

The sixth Congress of the International Association for the Scientific Study of Mental Deficiency took place in Toronto from August 22nd to 26th, 1982. The remarkable interest in the subject is reflected by the fact that the Congress attracted 1,100 fully registered participants and their associates from many disciplines and from 60 countries. As Professor Hans Olof Åkesson and Dr. Robert McClure each indicated, in their opening presidential remarks and closing banquet address, respectively, it was a great opportunity to exchange ideas and information between workers from widely varying cultural milieus and socioeconomic circumstances; indeed, such a beneficial exchange was a hallmark of the Congress.

Some 500 presentations were made on many aspects that constitute the intricate mosaic of mental retardation, and 426 of these presentations were submitted for consideration for publication in the Proceedings. Financial and other practical exigencies precluded the publication of more than two volumes of Proceedings. This necessitated the inevitable exclusion of many worthy papers, which are listed by title and authors' contact addresses in the first of these volumes. The editor is indebted to the members of the editorial board (listed on page xviii) and the following additional panel of reviewers for graciously and generously assisting in the delicate selection process: Dr. J. Corbett, Dr. C. Cunningham, Dr. S. Einfeld, Dr. M. Feldman, Dr. J. Hogg, Dr. C. Kiernan, Dr. V. Markovic, Professor M. Partington, Dr. D. Reeves, Dr. C. A. Rubino, Dr. B. S. Scott, Dr. P. E. Sylvester, Professor M. W. Thompson, and Dr. A. Wellman. Their advice, individually and collectively, was invaluable, although such exclusion of papers as may be considered injudicious should be attributed to the editor, who personally read, and made the final decision on, every submission.

The papers accepted for publication fell conveniently, as in previous Congresses, into two main categories that provided the subtitles for each volume (Volume I—Social, Psychological and Educational Aspects; Volume II—Biomedical Aspects), under the overall heading of Perspectives and Progress in Mental Retardation. The division of each volume into subsections was undertaken for ease of reference and does not necessarily follow the order of oral presentation at the Congress itself. In making the selections for these proceedings, particular weight was given to papers that were considered to be of scientific interest, in keeping with the crucial component in the name of the Association under whose aegis the volumes are published.

It is a pleasure to express here special gratitude to two admirable ladies without whose enormous help and support the editor's task would have been well nigh impossible. Mrs. Jean de Jong, the technical editor, once again brought her wide-ranging talents and experience to bear, with characteristic grace and goodwill, in organizing and shepherding the editorial process through its multiple phases; only those who have been associated with her in similar contexts could know how large a debt is owed to her by the Association and the editor. Ms. Marika Korossy gave unstintingly of her time in facilitating the process, also with the characteristic good natured competence from which the editor had benefitted greatly in more than a decade of work together. The pleasant and efficient collaboration of the production editor, Ms. Megan Barnard Shelton, and her associates at University Park Press also is gratefully acknowledged. It would be remiss not to thank as well my wife, Eva, for her patient tolerance during the countless hours devoted to the present undertaking.

J. M. Berg
Toronto, Canada

Officers of the
International Association
for the Scientific Study
of Mental Deficiency:
1979–1982

President: H. O. Åkesson, Psychiatric Department III, Lillhagen's
Hospital, S-422 03 Hisings Backa 3, Sweden
President-Elect: G. A. Roeher, 21 Colwick Drive, Willowdale, Ontario
M2K 2G4, Canada
Honorary Past Presidents: H. A. Stevens, 128 West Main, Evansville,
Wisconsin 53752, United States
A. D. B. Clarke, Psychology Department, The University, Hull, HU6
7RX, England
M. J. Begab, University Park Press, 300 North Charles Street, Baltimore,
Maryland 21201, United States
Vice-Presidents: I. Wald, Instytut Psychoneurologiczny, Al. Sobieskiego
1/9, 02-957 Warsaw, Poland
C. G. A. de Jong, Bartimeushage, Centre for Multiply Handicapped, P.B.
87, 3940 Doorn, The Netherlands
Honorary Officers: A. Shapiro, B. E. Cohen
Secretary: D. A. Primrose, The Royal Scottish National Hospital, Larbert,
Stirlingshire FK5 4EJ, Scotland
Treasurer: A. Dupont, Institute of Psychiatric Demography, Aarhus
Psychiatric Hospital, 8240 Risskov, Denmark

Officers of the
International Association
for the Scientific Study
of Mental Deficiency:
1982–1985

President: G. A. Roeher (*due to his untimely death, the President-Elect has
become President*)
President-Elect: A. Dupont, Institute of Psychiatric Demography, Aarhus
Psychiatric Hospital, 8240 Risskov, Denmark
Honorary President: H. A. Stevens, 128 West Main, Evansville, Wisconsin
53752, United States
Vice-Presidents: C. G. A. de Jong, Bartimeushage, Centre for Multiply
Handicapped, P.B. 87, 3940 Doorn, The Netherlands
R. J. Andrews, Commonwealth Schools Commission, P. O. Box 34,
Woden, Canberra ACT 2606, Australia
Honorary Vice-Presidents: A. D. B. Clarke, M. J. Begab
Secretary: M. Mulcahy, Medico-Social Research Board, 73 Lower Baggot
Street, Dublin 2, Ireland
Treasurer: A. H. Bernsen, Demographic-Genetic Research Department,
8240 Risskov, Denmark
Honorary Officers: S. Krynski, A. Shapiro, B. Cohen, J. Veerman, I. Wald
Honorary Secretary: D. A. Primrose

Congress Organized by the
International Association
for the Scientific Study
of Mental Deficiency
in Association with the
Local Organizing Committee

Local Organizing Committee
Honorary Chairman: William B. Bremner
Chairman: Mrs. Louise Stuart, C.M.
Vice-Chairmen: Peter Cekuta, Helen Honickman, John McCrea, Margot
Scott, Dolly Tarshis
Members: Diane Anderson, Shirley Barron, Henry Botchford, Robin
Chetwyn, David Courtin, Shirley Crombie, Vince Gillis, John Haddad,
Shirley Ingram, Jack Pulkinen, Mike Solomonides, Steve Wace, Shirley
Walker

Scientific Program Committee
Chairman: G. A. Roeher
Members: H. O. Åkesson, M. J. Begab, J. M. Berg, A. Blanchet, C. G.
A. de Jong, G. C. J. Magerotte, A. H. Neufeldt, J. Pelletier, D. A.
Primrose

Proceedings Editor
J. M. Berg

Co-Hosts
The Canadian Association for the Mentally Retarded
The National Institute on Mental Retardation
The American Association on Mental Deficiency—Region VI and Ontario
Chapter

IASSMD Congress Publications

Proceedings of the First Congress (Montpellier, 1967):

Editor: Barry W. Richards
October 1968   982 pages
Distributor: editor, St. Lawrence's Hospital,
          Caterham, Surrey CR3 5YA, England

Proceedings of the Second Congress (Warsaw, 1970):
Editor: David A. A. Primrose
December 1971   774 pages
Distributor: Swets & Zeitlinger, B.V., Heereweg
          347B, Lisse, The Netherlands

Proceedings of the Third Congress (The Hague, 1973):
Editor: David A. A. Primrose
April 1975   2 volumes   875 pages
Distributor: editor, The Royal Scottish National
          Hospital, Larbert, Stirlingshire
          FK5 4EJ, Scotland

Proceedings of the Fourth Congress (Washington, D.C. 1976):
Research to Practice in Mental Retardation
Editor: Peter Mittler
July-September 1977   3 volumes   1718 pages
Publisher: University Park Press, 300 N. Charles
          Street, Baltimore, Maryland 21201,
          United States

Proceedings of the Fifth Congress (Jerusalem, 1979):
Frontiers of Knowledge in Mental Retardation
Editor: Peter Mittler
April 1981   2 volumes   870 pages
Publisher: University Park Press, 300 N. Charles
          Street, Baltimore, Maryland 21201,
          United States

Proceedings of the Sixth Congress (Toronto, 1982):
Perspectives and Progress in Mental Retardation
Editor: Joseph M. Berg
December 1983   2 volumes   960 pages
Publisher: University Park Press, 300 N. Charles
          Street, Baltimore, Maryland 21201,
          United States

PROCEEDINGS OF THE SIXTH CONGRESS
OF THE INTERNATIONAL ASSOCIATION
FOR THE SCIENTIFIC STUDY
OF MENTAL DEFICIENCY

Toronto, Canada August 22nd–26th, 1982
The Sheraton Centre

**Perspectives and Progress
in
Mental Retardation**

Published in two volumes:
Volume I: Social, Psychological, and Educational Aspects
Volume II: Biomedical Aspects

Edited by
J. M. Berg, M.B., B.Ch., M.Sc., F.R.C.Psych., F.C.C.M.G.
Professor of Psychiatry and of Medical Genetics,
University of Toronto
Director of Genetic Services and Biomedical Research
Surrey Place Centre, 2 Surrey Place
Toronto, Ontario M5S 2C2, Canada

Editorial Board:

DEDICATION

Professor G. Allan Roeher died tragically in an airplane accident on 2nd June 1983. He was, at the time, President of the International Association for the Scientific Study of Mental Deficiency. As President-Elect of this Association and Chairman of its Congress Programme Committee, he gave unstintingly of his many talents and his time to ensure the success of the 6th Congress from which these Proceedings are derived. He was devoted, for many of his 58 years, to the welfare of mentally handicapped persons and their families to the great benefit of all concerned. His wise counsel will be sorely missed. As a small token of the well-deserved esteem in which he was widely held, the two volumes of PERSPECTIVES AND PROGRESS IN MENTAL RETARDATION are respectfully dedicated to his memory.

SECTION I
Epidemiology and Surveys

PERSPECTIVES AND PROGRESS IN MENTAL RETARDATION
Volume II—Biomedical Aspects
Edited by J. M. Berg
Copyright © 1984 by I.A.S.S.M.D.

SURVIVAL RATES AND CAUSES OF DEATH AMONG PERSONS WITH NONSPECIFIC MENTAL RETARDATION

D. S. Herbst and P. A. Baird

*Department of Medical Genetics, University of British Columbia,
6174 University Boulevard, Vancouver, British Columbia V6T 1W5,
Canada*

Deaths among persons with nonspecific mental retardation in the 1952–65 birth cohort in British Columbia were ascertained from community sources through the British Columbia Health Surveillance Registry. Direct causes of death were obtained from death registrations in the British Columbia Ministry of Health. Life tables listing the death rates and probabilities of survival were constructed with respect to age group and level of retardation. The rate of death among persons 1 to 24 years of age who were mentally retarded was higher than the general population death rate. The probability of survival decreased with increasing severity of retardation. The main causes of death were different from those in the general population, with respiratory infections being the most common. Accidents, congenital anomalies, and diseases of the central nervous system were the second, third, and fourth most common causes of death, respectively. Certain associated conditions, such as cerebral palsy, epilepsy, and hydrocephalus, were identified as contributing to deaths from specific causes.

Mortality among institutionalized mentally retarded residents has been investigated in a number of studies (Kramer et al., 1957; Tarjan et al., 1958; Pense et al., 1961; Heaton-Ward, 1968; Richards and Sylvester, 1969; Åkesson and Forssman, 1972; Roboz, 1972). Because mortality

---

Supported by grant No. 30(80-1) of the British Columbia Health Care Research Foundation.

rates and information on the causes of death in these studies are based on institutional data, they may not be applicable to cases of mental retardation in the general population. With the current trend toward deinstitutionalization, the institutionalized population must obviously be changing, so information from these studies is likely to be outdated and may not be applicable even to present-day institutionalized cases.

We felt it would be beneficial to investigate mortality in a birth cohort of mentally retarded persons who have been ascertained from community sources and whose retardation is not due to a determined specific cause. If the cause is known, mortality and survival information is often available: life tables and mortality information have been published for distinct types of retardation such as Down's syndrome (Forssman and Åkesson, 1965, 1967; Fabia and Drolette, 1970; Deaton, 1973; Gallagher and Lowry, 1975; Öster et al., 1975). Specific prognoses with general indications of probability for survival can be deduced for persons with specific biochemical disorders associated with mental retardation, such as the Lesch-Nyhan syndrome (Nyhan, 1973) or the mucopolysaccharidoses (Spranger, 1972).

In this report we present life tables with survival probabilities and death rates and the causes of death for those who have died among the nonspecifically mentally retarded in the 1952–65 birth cohort in British Columbia, for which other epidemiological information is already available (Herbst and Baird, 1983).

METHODS

The British Columbia Health Surveillance Registry (HSR) is the source of information on cases in the 1952–1965 birth cohort. This registry has been ongoing since 1952 with continual ascertainment of mental retardation cases, currently from over 80 sources in the province. It is felt that ascertainment is maximum for cases born during 1952–65 inclusive in British Columbia. HSR records up to the end of 1978 were used to investigate mortality of the nonspecifically mentally retarded in this birth cohort. (At that time the *International Classification of Diseases, Adapted, Eighth Revision* was being used by the HSR to classify disabilities and by British Columbia Vital Statistics to classify causes of death.) Mental retardation was regarded as nonspecific if it was *not*: 1) following infections or intoxication; 2) following trauma or physical agents; 3) associated with disorders of metabolism, growth, or nutrition; 4) associated with gross brain disease; or 5) associated with chromosomal abnormalities. All cases of retardation associated with neural tube defects and muscular dystrophy were also omitted.

The HSR records whether a registrant is currently alive or, if deceased, the age at death, which is obtained from or confirmed by British Columbia death records. Only mental retardation cases in the birth cohort who died after 1 year of age and by year-end 1978 were included in the study. The direct cause of death was obtained from the death certificates of the British Columbia Department of Vital Statistics, Ministry of Health. Access to death registrations and data from the HSR was permitted only under strict conditions of confidentiality.

Mortality rates were calculated and life tables constructed that were specific for age and level of retardation according to current methodology (Statistics Canada, Catalogue No. 84-532). Causes of death were analyzed with respect to age at death, sex, level of retardation, and selected associated neurological conditions. For comparison, age-specific life tables for the British Columbia population during 1975–77 produced by Statistics Canada (Catalogue No. 84-532) were used. Age-specific tabulations of the causes of death for the British Columbia population between 1952 and 1978 were obtained from *Vital Statistics of the Province of British Columbia*, Report Nos. 81 to 107 (British Columbia Ministry of Health, 1952–1978).

RESULTS

Life Tables

Of the 2,333 persons with nonspecific mental retardation in the 1952–65 birth cohort, 254 were deceased by year-end 1978. Of the dead, 16 had been mildly retarded (IQ 52–67), 14 had been moderately retarded (IQ 36–51), 24 had been severely retarded (IQ 20–35), 98 had been profoundly retarded (IQ < 20), and 102 had had an unspecified level of retardation. Life tables that include mortality rates and that are specific for age group and level of retardation are presented in abbreviated form in Table 1. In constructing these tables, the number of cases alive at the start of each age interval (O_x) was determined by taking into consideration the birth year and the age either at the end of the ascertainment period (year-end 1978) or at death. Death rates (Q_x) and probabilities of survival (P_x) were not differentiated by sex because no significant sex differences were observed. Cases at the mild and moderate levels of retardation were combined because of the small numbers in each group and because there were no apparent differences between them.

Death Rates

The average death rate for those ages 1 to 19 with nonspecific mental retardation was 0.007 per year, which was 11 times higher than the

Table 1.   Abbreviated life tables for individuals with nonspecific mental retardation in the 1952–65 birth cohort from information ascertained by year-end 1978

Level of mental retardation	Age group	$O_x{}^a$	$D_x{}^b$	$W_x{}^c$	$Q_x{}^d$	$P_x{}^e$
Mild-moderate	1–4	1125	1	—	0.0002	1.0
	5–9	1124	4	—	0.001	0.999
	10–14	1120	11	109	0.002	0.996
	15–19	1000	8	383	0.002	0.986
	20–24	609	6	457	0.003	0.977
	25–26	146	0	146	0	0.962
Severe	1–4	286	5	—	0.004	1.0
	5–9	281	4	—	0.003	0.983
	10–14	277	10	39	0.008	0.969
	15–19	228	3	101	0.003	0.933
	20–24	124	2	93	0.005	0.918
	25–26	29	0	29	0	0.897
Profound	1–4	320	22	—	0.017	1.0
	5–9	298	33	—	0.022	0.931
	10–14	265	30	35	0.024	0.828
	15–19	200	12	83	0.015	0.733
	20–24	105	1	73	0.003	0.679
	25–26	31	0	31	0	0.669
Unspecified	1–4	602	47	—	0.020	1.0
	5–9	555	32	—	0.012	0.922
	10–14	522	12	51	0.005	0.869
	15–19	460	7	161	0.004	0.848
	20–24	292	4	210	0.004	0.834
	25–26	78	0	78	0	0.817
All levels	1–4	2333	75	—	0.008	1.0
	5–9	2258	73	—	0.006	0.968
	10–14	2185	63	234	0.006	0.937
	15–19	1888	30	728	0.004	0.909
	20–24	1130	13	833	0.004	0.892
	25–26	284	0	284	0	0.877

[a] O_x = number of cases alive at start of age group interval.
[b] D_x = number of deaths in interval.
[c] W_x = number of alive withdrawals during interval.
[d] Q_x = Average death rate per year.

$$Q_x = \frac{D_x}{(O_x - \frac{1}{2} W_x)n}$$

where n = number of years in interval.
[e] P_x = cumulative probability of survival at start of interval:
$$P_x = (1 - Q_{x-1})(P_{x-1})$$

British Columbia general mortality rate for the same age group. After subdividing the sample with respect to the level of retardation, the rate for those at the mild-moderate level (0.001) was twice as high as the general population rate. For those at the severe and profound levels, the rates of 0.005 and 0.020 were 7 times and 31 times as high, respectively. As shown in Table 1, these rates (Q_x) varied slightly with respect to age group within each level of retardation.

A major proportion (102 of 254) of the dead individuals were registered with an unspecified level of retardation. The mean age at death of 7 ± 5 years for this group was less than the mean ages at death for the specified levels, which were 9 ± 5 years for the profoundly retarded, 10 ± 6 years for the severely retarded, and 14 ± 6 years for the mildly-moderately retarded. The younger mean age at death suggests that many of these individuals died before the level of retardation could be properly assessed.

Survival Rates

The probability of survival to age 20 for those with nonspecific mental retardation who reached at least 1 year of age was 89.2%, compared to 98.8% for the general population. These probabilities varied considerably with respect to the level of retardation. Among those who were mildly-moderately retarded, 97.7% were expected to reach age 20. Of those severely retarded, 91.8% were expected to survive to that age, and only 67.9% of those profoundly retarded would likely reach that age. In Table 1, the probabilities of survival (P_x) to ages 5, 10, and 25 are also given.

The frequencies of four conditions associated with nonspecific mental retardation—microcephalus, hydrocephalus, cerebral palsy, and epilepsy—were investigated. As shown in Table 2, the frequencies of all of these conditions were higher among those persons who had died than among those who were still alive at year-end 1978. We have shown elsewhere that the frequencies of these conditions increased with the severity of the retardation (Herbst and Baird, 1983). More persons surviving to the end of 1978 had none of these associated conditions than did those who had died.

Causes of Death

The direct causes of death were retrieved for 249 of the 254 cases recorded as dead in the birth cohort, by hand searching the death certificates in the vital statistics records of the British Columbia Ministry of Health. The registry information was rechecked for those 5 cases whose death certificates were not found, and it was determined that

Table 2.   Number of persons with nonspecific mental retardation and selected associated conditions in the 1952–65 birth cohort who were alive or dead at year-end 1978

Condition	Number alive[a] (n = 2,079)	Percent of cases alive	Number dead[a] (n = 254)	Percent of cases dead
Microcephalus	67	3.2	33	13.0
Hydrocephalus	71	3.4	36	14.2
Cerebral palsy	426	20.5	99	39.0
Epilepsy	465	22.4	90	35.4
None of these associated conditions	1,234	59.4	72	28.3

[a] Some cases have more than one associated condition, and therefore are counted more than once.

these persons were indeed dead, but that the death certificates could not be retrieved for various reasons.

The direct causes of death for the 249 persons are classified in Table 3 according to the major groups of diseases or conditions given in the *International Classification of Diseases, Adapted, Eighth Revision.* Because there were no major differences in causes of death between males and females, the data for both sexes were combined. The frequencies of deaths due to these causes in this nonspecific group varied considerably from the frequencies in the general population. For the years between 1952 and 1978 inclusive, in the 1–24 age group of the British Columbia population, the first four causes of death were: 1) accidents (65.3%); 2) neoplasms (9.2%); 3) respiratory infections (5.9%); and 4) congenital anomalies (4.4%).

The age-specific death rates for the four main causes of death among the nonspecifically mentally retarded are shown in Table 4. Respiratory infection, mainly pneumonia, was the most common cause of death among all age groups. The rates of death from respiratory infections were relatively constant in the younger age groups (approximately 400/100,000) and showed a decrease to 84/100,000 for those 20–24 years of age. For years 1952 to 1978, respiratory infection in the general population has been consistently listed among the four main causes of death only for the 1–4 age group. In that age group there has been a gradual decline in the rate of death due to respiratory infections, from 22.2/100,000 in 1952 to 2.2/100,000 in 1978. No such decrease during this time period was noticeable for those with nonspecific mental retardation.

The rates of death due to congenital anomalies, mainly hydrocephalus and heart defects, among the nonspecifically mentally retarded

Table 3. Number of deaths among those with nonspecific mental retardation in the 1952–65 birth cohort at year-end 1978, classified by cause of death

Cause of death[a]	Number of deaths	Percentage
1. Respiratory infection (e.g., pneumonia)	140	56.2
2. Accidents		
Aspiration of food	15	
Fires (burns or smoke asphyxiation)	5	
Drowning	6	
Other	9	
Total	35	14.1
3. Congenital anomalies		
Hydrocephalus	11	
Heart defects	8	
Other	3	
Total	22	8.8
4. Central nervous system diseases		
Epilepsy	10	
Meningitis/Encephalitis	5	
Total	15	6.0
5. Other infections (excluding pneumonia and meningitis)	8	3.2
6. Neoplasms	6	2.4
7. Digestive system diseases	6	2.4
8. Urinary system diseases	5	2.0
9. Circulatory system diseases	4	1.6
10. Ill-defined conditions	4	1.6
11. Endocrine, metabolic, or nutritional diseases	3	1.2
12. Diseases of the blood	1	0.4

[a] Numbered in descending order of frequency.

in the 1–4 and 5–9 age groups were nine times and seven times higher, respectively, than the same-age rates in the general population. Congenital anomalies remained an important cause of death among the mentally retarded in the older age groups, whereas its rate gradually decreased in the general population. The death rates associated with congenital anomalies showed little variation over time between 1952 and 1978 for both the mentally retarded and the general population.

Accidents of various types was the fourth most common cause of death for the 1–4 age group among those with nonspecific mental retardation, and was the second most common after respiratory infections for the 5–9, 10–14, and 15–19 age groups, whereas in the general population of the same ages it was the leading cause of death. In com-

Table 4. Death rates for the four main causes of death by age group among those with nonspecific mental retardation

Age group	Cause of death[a]	Number of deaths	Percentage of all deaths in age group	Age specific death rate (per 100,000)
1–4 (n = 74)	1. Respiratory infections	41	55	439
	2. Congenital anomalies	10	14	107
	3. Central nervous system diseases	7	9	75
	4. Accidents	4	5	43
5–9 (n = 72)	1. Respiratory infections	45	63	398
	2. Accidents	13	18	115
	3. Central nervous system diseases	3	4	27
	3. Congenital anomalies	3	4	27
10–14 (n = 61)	1. Respiratory infections	34	56	329
	2. Accidents	11	18	106
	3. Congenital anomalies	5	8	48
	4. Other infections	2	3	19
	4. Neoplasms	2	3	19
	4. Central nervous system diseases	2	3	19
	4. Digestive system diseases	2	3	19
15–19 (n = 30)	1. Respiratory infections	17	57	223
	2. Accidents	4	13	52
	3. Congenital anomalies	3	10	39
	4. Other infections	2	7	26
20–24 (n = 12)	1. Respiratory infections	3	25	84
	1. Accidents	3	25	84
	3. Central nervous system diseases	2	17	56
	3. Digestive system diseases	2	17	56

[a] Listed in decreasing order of frequency within age groups; duplicate numbers indicate equivalent frequency.

paring age-specific rates of death due to accidents, an increase of four times and three times over the population rate was observed for the 5–9 and 10–14 age groups, respectively. In the 1–4, 15–19, and 20–24 age groups, the death rates were approximately the same as those in the general British Columbia population. Approximately one half of the accidental deaths among the general population in the 1–24 age group were due to traffic-related incidents, but that was not the case for those with nonspecific mental retardation. In this group, aspiration of food was the cause of 15 of the 35 accidental deaths. Again, no significant trends in the rates of death due to accidents were apparent during the study period.

The number of deaths due to the four main causes are differentiated by level of retardation in Table 5. The number due to respiratory infections increased with the severity of the retardation. A major proportion (37%) were in the unspecified category in which the mean age of death was younger. Accidents were the leading cause of death at the mild-moderate level, and were in second place at the other levels of retardation.

An associated neurological condition (microcephalus, hydrocephalus, cerebral palsy, or epilepsy) can be an important factor in the cause of death, as is apparent in Table 6. Respiratory infection, which was common in all groups, was the most likely cause of death in the multiply handicapped individuals and those with only cerebral palsy associated with mental retardation. Accidents were most common for those without any of these conditions. Congenital anomalies causing deaths were mainly hydrocephalus and heart defects. Those dying from heart defects were usually in the category without any of the associated neurological conditions. Deaths in the central nervous system disease group were mainly seizure related or due to status epilepticus, and therefore these cases were listed in the epilepsy only or the multiply handicapped group. Deaths of the three persons in the group with mental retardation only were due to meningitis or encephalitis. The numbers of individuals dying from other causes were too small to make a valid comparison with the population death rates.

DISCUSSION

The probabilities of survival differentiated by mental retardation level in the life tables are useful information for those professionals counseling families caring for a nonspecifically mentally retarded child. Other investigations have shown that the mentally retarded have a higher risk of death than someone in the general population (Richards and Sylvester, 1969; Åkesson and Forssman, 1972) and this study con-

Table 5. Number of deaths differentiated by the main causes of death and the level of mental retardation

Level of mental retardation	Cause of death				
	Respiratory infections	Accidents	Congenital anomalies	Central nervous system diseases	Other
Mild-moderate (n = 28)	5	8	5	1	9
Severe (n = 24)	14	5	1	0	4
Profound (n = 97)	68	7	6	4	12
Unspecified (n = 100)	53	15	10	10	12
Total (n = 249)	140	35	22	15	37

Table 6. Number of deaths differentiated by the main causes of death and certain associated neurological conditions

Associated condition	Cause of death				
	Respiratory infections	Accidents	Congenital anomalies	Central nervous system diseases	Other
Microcephalus only ($n = 13$)	7	2	0	0	4
Hydrocephalus only ($n = 20$)	7	1	11	0	1
Cerebral palsy only ($n = 43$)	31	5	0	0	7
Epilepsy only ($n = 38$)	21	6	1	5	5
Two or more of above conditions ($n = 64$)	46	5	1	7	5
None of these conditions ($n = 71$)	28	16	9	3	15
Total ($n = 249$)	140	35	22	15	37

firms that finding. Because the probability of survival decreases with increasing severity of retardation, special care must be given to those who are severely or profoundly retarded.

Respiratory infection, mainly pneumonia, was identified as the most common cause of death among those with nonspecific mental retardation. Therefore, all respiratory infections among these individuals should be treated early and aggressively. Other investigators have found that respiratory infection is the main cause of death among institution residents and have suggested that early admission is an important contributing factor for deaths due to this cause (Kramer et al., 1957; Tarjan et al., 1958; Roboz, 1972). However, even with the current trends toward deinstitutionalization in British Columbia, respiratory infection remains an important cause of death for all those with nonspecific mental retardation.

Immobilization, whether because of young age, association with cerebral palsy, or the delayed mobility of the severely and profoundly retarded, is likely to restrict proper expansion of the lungs and limit coughing and clearing of the nasal passages. This restriction will in turn contribute to the risk of death from respiratory infections. Therefore, very young children, those with cerebral palsy, and those with severe and profound mental retardation are at greater risk of dying from such infections.

Even though rates of death due to accidents for some age groups within the retarded population are about the same as those in the general population, they are increased three- to fourfold for those 5 to 14 years of age. Such an increase has not been noted in other studies (Richards and Sylvester, 1969), probably because institutional, rather than community, sources were used for ascertainment. A number of different types of accidents led to death, with aspiration of food being the most common among the mentally retarded. Obviously, many deaths due to these types of accidents can be prevented with better supervision.

The increased rates of death due to congenital anomalies and central nervous system diseases that were apparent for those with nonspecific mental retardation are mainly related to specific congenital or neurological conditions—hydrocephalus, heart defects, and epilepsy. Mentally retarded individuals with these conditions definitely have an increased risk of death.

REFERENCES

Åkesson, H. O., and Forssman, F. 1972. Mortality in patients with mental deficiency. In: D. A. A. Primrose (ed.), Proceedings of the Second Congress of IASSMD, Warsaw, pp. 87–93. Swets and Zeitlinger, Amsterdam.

British Columbia Ministry of Health. 1952–1978. Vital Statistics of the Province of British Columbia, Report Nos. 81 to 107. British Columbia Ministry of Health, Victoria, British Columbia, Canada.

Deaton, J. G. 1973. The mortality rate and causes of death among institutionalized mongols in Texas. J. Ment. Defic. Res. 17:117–122.

Fabia, J., and Drolette, M. 1970. Life tables up to age 10 for mongols with and without congenital heart defect. J. Ment. Defic. Res. 14:235–242.

Forssman, H., and Åkesson, H. O. 1965. Mortality in patients with Down's syndrome. J. Ment. Defic. Res. 9:146–149.

Forssman, H., and Åkesson, H. O. 1967. Note on mortality in patients with Down's syndrome. J. Ment. Defic. Res. 11:106–107.

Gallagher, R. P., and Lowry, R. B. 1975. Longevity in Down's syndrome in British Columbia. J. Ment. Defic. Res. 19:157–163.

Heaton-Ward, W. A. 1968. The expectation of life of mentally subnormal patients in hospital. In: B. W. Richards (ed.), Proceedings of the First Congress of the International Association for the Scientific Study of Mental Retardation, Montpellier, p. 939. IASSMD, Royal Scottish National Hospital, Larbert, Scotland.

Herbst, D. S., and Baird, P. A. 1983. Nonspecific mental retardation in British Columbia as ascertained through a registry. Am. J. Ment. Defic. 87:506–513.

International Classification of Diseases, Eighth Revision, Adapted for Use in the United States. United States Department of Health, Education and Welfare, P.H.S. No. 1693. U.S. Government Printing Office, Washington, D.C.

Kramer, M., Person, P. H., Jr., Tarjan, G., Morgan, R., and Wright, S. W. 1957. A method for determination of probabilities of stay, release, and death, for patients admitted to a hospital for the mentally deficient: The experience of Pacific State Hospital during the period 1948–1952. Am. J. Ment. Defic. 62:481–495.

Nyhan, W. L. 1973. The Lesch-Nyhan syndrome. Annu. Rev. Med. 24:41–60.

Öster, J., Mikkelsen, M., and Nielsen, A. 1975. Mortality and life-table in Down's syndrome. Acta Paediatr. Scand. 64:322–326.

Pense, A. W., Patton, R. E., Camp, J. L., and Kebalo, C. 1961. A cohort study of institutionalized young mentally retarded children. Am. J. Ment. Defic. 66:18–22.

Richards, B. W., and Sylvester, P. E. 1969. Mortality trends in mental deficiency institutions. J. Ment. Defic. Res. 13:276–292.

Roboz, P. 1972. Mortality rate in institutionalized mentally retarded children. Med. J. Aust. 1:218–221.

Spranger, J. 1972. The systemic mucopolysaccharidoses. Ergeb. Inn. Med. Kinderheilkd. 32:165–265.

Statistics Canada. Life Tables, Canada and Provinces, 1975–1977. Catalogue No. 84-532.

Tarjan, G., Wright, S. W., Kramer, M., Person, P. H., Jr., and Morgan, R. 1958. The natural history of mental deficiency in a state hospital. I. Probabilities of release and death by age, intelligence quotient and diagnosis. Am. J. Dis. Child. 96:64–70.

PERSPECTIVES AND PROGRESS IN MENTAL RETARDATION
Volume II—Biomedical Aspects
Edited by J. M. Berg
Copyright © 1984 by I.A.S.S.M.D.

RELATIVE CONTRIBUTION OF MEDICAL AND SOCIAL FACTORS TO SEVERITY OF HANDICAP IN MENTALLY RETARDED CHILDREN

M. Ort and B. Cooper
*Zentralinstitut für Seelische Gesundheit, D-6800 Mannheim 1, J 5,
Federal Republic of Germany*

Preliminary findings are reported from a cross-sectional survey of school-age mentally retarded children and their families in Mannheim, West Germany. Strong associations were found between degree of neurological impairment, level of formal intelligence, and severity of functional handicap. The findings provided no evidence that children from low social status families are more severely handicapped than others, if the relative degree of neurological and intellectual impairment is held constant. However, the low-status families suffer from a relative excess of social problems that increase the difficulty involved in coping with their children's handicaps.

This paper reports some preliminary findings from an epidemiological study of mentally retarded children and their families in Mannheim, an industrial city in West Germany with a population of about 300,000. The present study follows up an earlier prevalence survey in Mannheim (Cooper et al., 1979; Liepmann, 1979) and is devoted to a more detailed investigation of the nature and severity of the children's handicaps,

The research reported in this paper formed part of a collaborative research project in the Special Research Programme 116 (Psychiatric Epidemiology) at the University of Heidelberg, supported by a grant from the Deutsche Forschungsgemeinschaft (German Research Association).

17

the associated family problems, and the interrelations between these factors.

DESIGN AND METHOD

The survey sample consisted of all mentally retarded children of German nationality between 7 and 16 years of age who were residents of Mannheim on the census day, October 1, 1978. Those children living in institutions more than 100 km distant from the city were excluded from the detailed inquiry, because earlier experience had shown that their investigation would be uneconomical in relation to the additional gain in information.

The method of data gathering consisted of five steps:

1. Information was sought from a variety of agencies, the most important being the city's public health department. All case notes and records were scrutinized, and a summary made of the medical, psychometric, and social data.
2. A simple standard medical examination of the child was carried out and an assessment made of the degree of central nervous system involvement. The examination, developed specifically for use with severely handicapped children, generates a weighted total score. Comparisons of score distributions for criterion groups of brain-damaged and physically normal children, examined in a preliminary study, indicated the following categories:

Neurological impairment (NI) score	Degree of damage
0–19	Normal: no evidence of brain damage
20–49	Borderline: brain damage possible or probable
50+	Severe abnormality: brain damage certain or highly probable

3. The children were examined individually with the aid of a psychometric test battery (TBGB), which has been standardized on a large representative sample of mentally retarded children in West Germany (Bondy et al., 1971). The subtests used were the Columbia Mental Maturity Scale, Peabody Picture Vocabulary Test, Dotting Test of Fine Motor Function, and Raven's Coloured Progressive Matrices.
4. A German translation of the Schedule of Children's Handicaps, Behaviour and Skills (HBS), developed by Wing and Gould (1978), was used to conduct informant interviews. For children living at

home, the parents or nearest relatives acted as informants; for those in institutional care, the staff members in closest contact with the children were the informants. For this preliminary analysis, an overall rating of the severity of handicap, based on the SSL and SPI scales of Kushlick et al. (1973), has been derived from the interview data.

5. The family of each child was visited and interviewed, using an adaptation of the Standardized Interview to Assess Social Maladjustment and Dysfunction (Clare and Cairns, 1978). A number of indices were derived from the interview data in order to assess, first, the problems of child care and management associated with the child's handicaps and, second, any coexisting, nonspecific family disadvantage.

PRELIMINARY FINDINGS

The response to the inquiry was generally satisfactory. In only six instances (2.8%) was permission to examine a child refused by the parent or guardian. Medical examination could be completed in 189 cases (88.3%), psychological assessment in 194 (90.6%), informant interviews in 201 (93.9%), and family interviews in 188 (87.9%). Highly significant associations were found between the severity of the child's functional handicaps and both his/her level of formal intelligence and the degree of his/her neurological impairment. Severe degrees of handicap were found mainly among children who had NI scores above 20, or IQ scores below 50, or both.

The next step was to examine the relationship of these variables to features of the child's family and social background. For the purpose of this preliminary analysis, an index of social class based on parental occupational prestige (Moore and Kleining, 1960) was taken as a crude indicator of the type of family environment. The numbers of families in the upper and middle class categories are small, because Mannheim is a predominantly working class community, but, even when compared with this background population, the mentally retarded children were found to be drawn disproportionately from the lowest social status groups.

No significant association was found between social class and the severity of the child's handicaps, despite the fact that the lower class children had on average somewhat higher IQ scores and were less often neurologically impaired than those from the higher-status families. These findings (which are similar to those of the earlier Mannheim survey) are most readily explained by a selective tendency for children of low intelligence to be designated as mentally retarded if they come

Table 1.   Severity of functional handicap, according to neurological impairment (NI) score and social class of family (n = 214)

| Severity of functional handicap | NI score 0–19 (normal) | | NI score 20+ (impaired) | | |
	Social classes I–IV (%)[a]	Social classes V, VI (%)[a]	Social classes I–IV (%)[a]	Social classes V, VI (%)[a]	Not examined
Mild or moderate	78.6	71.8	27.3	23.9	5
Marked	21.4	16.9	27.3	31.0	1
Severe	—	11.3	45.4	45.1	6
Total	100.0	100.0	100.0	100.0	
No. of children	14	71	33	71	12
No. not rated	1	3	1	1	7

[a] Social class rankings according to Moore and Kleining (1960).

from a lower social class background. The sample contained very few children from middle or lower-middle class families who had been so designated in the absence of conspicuous neurobiological abnormality.

In Table 1, the distribution of severity of functional handicap according to social class category is shown for children with and without neurological impairment. No general association can be demonstrated between the two variables; however, there is a small subgroup of children from the lower class families who are severely functionally handicapped, although they have no apparent neurological damage. In Table 2, a corresponding analysis of severity of handicap is shown in which the children have been divided into two main groups, according to level of formal intelligence. Within each group, no appreciable difference was found in severity of handicap between children drawn from the higher and lower social status categories.

Table 2.   Severity of functional handicap, according to level of formal intelligence and social class of family (n = 214)

| Severity of functional handicap | IQ < 50 | | IQ ≥ 50 | |
	Social classes I–IV (%)[a]	Social classes V, VI (%)[a]	Social classes I–IV (%)[a]	Social classes V, VI (%)[a]
Mild or moderate	17.8	21.0	70.9	69.4
Marked	28.6	27.4	20.8	21.2
Severe	53.6	51.6	8.3	9.4
Total	100.0	100.0	100.0	100.0
No. of children	28	62	24	85
No. not rated	3	4	—	3

[a] Social class rankings according to Moore and Kleining (1960); social class was unknown in 5 cases.

The findings provide no evidence, therefore, that mentally retarded children from low social status families are more severely handicapped than others in their general level of functioning, if the relative degree of neurological and intellectual impairment is held constant. This conclusion was supported by the results of a stepwise multiple regression analysis in which severity of functional handicap was treated as the dependent variable. Whereas 50% of the total variance could be accounted for by the NI score alone, addition of a number of other explanatory variables, including social class of the family, increased this total to only 58%. Similar findings were obtained when the index of severity of handicap was replaced by an index of severity of child-care problems, derived from the family interview. This index was, as might be expected, positively correlated with severity of functional handicap ($r = 0.56$) and with degree of neurological impairment ($r = 0.46$), but not with social class ($r = -0.02$). When the score distributions were examined, no association was found between social class and severity of child care problems, either for children with neurological deficits or for those without.

Although the special problems of child care thus appeared to be largely independent of family social status, it was found at interview that very many of the families, and especially those in the lowest status groups, presented severe social difficulties, such as unemployment, poor housing conditions, chronic ill health or disability of one or both parents, alcoholism, and psychiatric disturbance. These difficulties, although not directly linked with the presence of a mentally retarded child, often appeared crucial in determining the family's ability to cope with this problem and, in consequence, the quality of help and support the child received from his/her family. An index of social disadvantage, based on information from the family interview, was found to correlate positively with social class ($r = 0.46$), but to be unrelated to the severity of the retarded child's handicaps or of specific child care problems. In Table 3, the score distribution for this index, according to social class, is set out for children in the two main IQ categories.

These findings are difficult to interpret without a suitable basis of comparison. For this reason, a control study is now being undertaken in which a matched sample of children drawn from normal schools in Mannheim is being investigated by the same methods as those used with the mentally retarded sample. In Table 4, distributions for the index of social disadvantage are shown for families of the first 41 matched pairs. From these preliminary data, social problems of the kind represented in the index appear to be characteristic not so much of families with retarded children as of all those in the lowest status groups. There is some suggestion of an additional loading of social

Table 3.   Degree of social disadvantage, according to social class and level of formal intelligence ($n = 214$)

Index of social disadvantage	IQ ≥ 50		IQ < 50	
	Social classes I–IV (%)[a]	Social classes V, VI (%)[a]	Social classes I–IV (%)[a]	Social classes V, VI (%)[a]
0, 1 (none or slight)	43.5	25.6	76.0	44.8
2, 3 (moderate)	52.2	32.9	16.0	27.6
4+ (severe)	4.3	41.5	8.0	27.6
Total	100.0	100.0	100.0	100.0
No. of children	23	82	25	58
No. not rated	1	6	6	8

[a] Social class rankings according to Moore and Kleining (1960); social class was unknown in 5 cases.

problems in the retarded children's families, which cannot be explained by social class alone. However, it should be noted that the social classification used here discriminates poorly in the lower socioeconomic range, and that more sensitive measures are required.

DISCUSSION

The survey findings indicate that the degree of severity of a retarded child's handicaps is determined very largely by his/her primary impairments and relatively little by his/her current family situation. They yield no evidence that retarded children from lower social class homes in Mannheim suffer from an excess of secondary, socially induced handicaps that compound their difficulties. However, this conclusion must be seen as tentative for a number of reasons. Data collection is still incomplete and so far only rather crude measures have been applied in analyzing the interview data. It may be that more detailed and

Table 4.   Degree of social disadvantage, according to social class (families of mentally retarded and of control group children)

Index of social disadvantage	Mentally retarded children		Controls	
	Social classes I–IV[a]	Social classes V, VI[a]	Social classes I–IV[a]	Social classes V, VI[a]
0, 1 (none or slight)	4	12	4	19
2, 3 (moderate)	4	10	4	8
4+ (marked or severe)	0	11	0	6
Total	8	33	8	33

[a] Social class rankings according to Moore and Kleining (1960).

refined analyses will reveal forms of handicap that are more strongly influenced by family and social factors.

The implications of this study are more directly relevant to service provision than to questions of etiology. A number of earlier studies have investigated the burden on the family represented by the presence of a mentally retarded child (Fowle, 1968; Tizard and Grad, 1971; Carr, 1974). This approach may be, in some respects, an oversimplification of the social problem. It is generally accepted that milder forms of retardation are highly concentrated among lower social status groups of the population. Evidence from epidemiological research into the social class distribution of the more severe forms of retardation is conflicting and the possibility cannot yet be ruled out that here also there is a relative excess in the lower status groups.

The widespread provision of special schools for the mentally retarded in many developed countries has no doubt served to mitigate the worst effects of social deprivation and to reduce secondary handicaps. At the same time, efforts directed solely toward the education of mentally retarded children are unlikely to achieve their full effectiveness as long as the families in which these children live remain characterized by a high loading of social pathology and disadvantage. Provision of special education needs to be complemented by the offer of systematic social help and support to those families identified as belonging to this category.

REFERENCES

Bondy, C., Cohen, R., Eggert, D., and Lüer, G. 1971. Testbatterie für geistig behinderte Kinder (TBGB). Beltz, Weinheim.

Carr, J. 1974. The effect of the severely subnormal on their families. In: A. M. Clarke and A. D. B. Clarke (eds.), Mental Deficiency: The Changing Outlook, pp. 807–839. Methuen, London.

Clare, A. W., and Cairns, V. E. 1978. Design, development and use of a standard interview to assess social adjustment and dysfunction in community studies. Psychol. Med. 8:589–604.

Cooper, B., Liepmann, M. C., Marker, K., and Schieber, P. M. 1979. Definition of severe mental retardation in school-age children: Findings of an epidemiological study. Soc. Psychiatry 14:197–205.

Fowle, C. M. 1968. The effect of the severely mentally retarded child on his family. Am. J. Ment. Defic. 73:468–473.

Kushlick, A., Blunden, R., and Cox, G. 1973. A method of rating behaviour characteristics for use in large-scale surveys of mental handicap. Psychol. Med. 3:466–478.

Liepmann, M.C. 1979. Geistig Behinderte Kinder und Jugendliche. Eine Epidemiologische, Klinische und Sozialpsychologische Studie in Mannheim. Huber, Bern.

Moore, H., and Kleining, G. 1960. Das soziale Selbstbild der Gesellschaft in Deutschland. Köln Z. Soz. Sozialpsychol. 12:86–119.

Tizard, J., and Grad, J. C. 1971. The Mentally Handicapped and their Families. Maudsley Monograph No. 7. Oxford University Press, London.

Wing, L., and Gould, J. 1978. Systematic recording of behaviour and skills of retarded and psychotic children. J. Autism Child. Schizophr. 8:79–97.

PERSPECTIVES AND PROGRESS IN MENTAL RETARDATION
Volume II—Biomedical Aspects
Edited by J. M. Berg
Copyright © 1984 by I.A.S.S.M.D.

PATTERNS OF DISABILITY IN A MENTALLY RETARDED POPULATION BETWEEN AGES 16 AND 22 YEARS

S. A. Richardson,[1] H. Koller,[1] M. Katz,[1] and J. McLaren[2]
[1] *Albert Einstein College of Medicine, 1300 Morris Park Avenue, Bronx, New York 10461*
[2] *Medical Research Council, Institute of Medical Sociology, Aberdeen, Scotland*

A population of mentally retarded persons ages 16 to 22 years living in a British city is described in terms of moderate and severe single and multiple disabilities (epilepsy, behavior disturbance, communication disorders, limb disabilities, and incontinence). Disabilities were examined for subsets of the population who had different career paths through mental retardation services in the postschool period of 16 to 22 years of age. These paths were long-term residential care, long-term day care, short-term services in day and/or residential care, and no services. Differences in patterns of disabilities for the subsets are examined and other factors are discussed that influence forms of services received.

Few epidemiological studies of mental retardation provide any information on other disabilities (for exceptions, see Kushlick and Blunden, 1974; Abramowicz and Richardson, 1975). Even fewer researchers have presented this information in terms of the ways various types of disabilities combined in individuals (for an exception, see Bernsen, 1981). Abramowicz and Richardson (1975) expressed concern about the scarcity of data on disabilities associated with mental retardation.

This study was supported by the Foundation for Child Development, the William T. Grant Foundation, the Easter Seal Research Foundation, the National Institute of Child Health & Human Development (Grant No. HD07970), the Social Science Research Council of the United Kingdom, and the Scottish Home and Health Department.

Such information is necessary to gain a better understanding of people who are mentally retarded and to provide useful data for planning services for them.

The purpose of this paper is to examine a number of different disabilities in a population of young people who are mentally retarded, and to relate the patterns of disabilities to severity of retardation and to different histories of mental retardation services the young people experienced in the period after school leaving age.

METHODS

The study population was selected by identifying everyone born from 1951 through 1955 who was a resident of a British city in 1962 and had been placed in a special school, training center, or hospital for retarded children before 16 years of age, as well as a few severely retarded children who were entirely cared for by their parents. Detailed descriptions of their evaluation, classification, and placement can be found in Birch et al. (1970). A follow-up of these young people was carried out as they reached age 22, and comprehensive interviews were conducted separately with the young adults and their parents. In addition, information about the study subjects was obtained from records kept by schools, courts, residential institutions, and social workers.

Two hundred twenty-one subjects met the study requirement of having been placed in a mental retardation facility in childhood, and follow-up interviews with both parent and young adult, or at least one of the two, were obtained for 192 of the 221 subjects. The 29 subjects lost to follow-up included 10 who had died, two who were not traced, two who were living too far away to be followed, and 15 where both young adult and parent refused to be interviewed.

The IQ levels used in this paper were based on scores obtained when the subjects were 7 to 10 years of age. For approximately three-fifths of these subjects, scores on the Wechsler Intelligence Scale for Children (WISC) were used. For the remaining subjects, to whom the WISC had not been administered, scores on the Terman-Merrill revision of the Stanford-Binet Intelligence Scale and Moray House Picture Test of Intelligence were used. The children who were given the WISC were also given the Terman-Merrill and Moray House examinations. By comparing the WISC with the other test scores for these subjects, we ascertained the differences between tests. For children not given the WISC, the other test scores were adjusted to be equivalent to the WISC. Subjects with IQs below 50 were not all given individual intelligence tests. The levels of mental competence of most of these subjects were estimated on the basis of direct behavioral observation, history of competence, and level of functioning. Where examination scores were available for these subjects, they were used.

The information on the disabilities and the postschool career paths followed by the study subjects was obtained from the follow-up interviews with the young adults and their parents, observation schedules completed by the interviewers, and agency records.

Classifications of Disabilities

One of our concerns in the study was the functional consequences of impairment. Therefore, medical classifications were generally inappropriate, because most were developed to determine etiology, diagnosis, and treatment. Our classifications of disabilities were guided by the extent to which their presence caused disturbances and difficulties in the everyday lives of the young people. The age period examined in this paper is 16 to 22 years, the 6-year period after leaving school. Only disabilities rated as moderate or severe and present in the postschool period are included in this paper. The following are the disabilities examined and their definitions.

Epilepsy   A severity measure was based on the proportion of time between ages 16 and 22 when there were seizures; the frequency and severity of seizures within that time; whether anticonvulsant medication was given; and the side effects of medication (Richardson et al., 1981).

Behavior Disturbance   The overall behavior disturbance during the period from ages 16 to 22 was rated on a 5-point scale from mild to severe based on the amount of time and degree to which the problem impaired the persons' ability to function in the activities expected of them and on the evidence of concern about the behavior by the persons themselves, their families, or some authorities. Three types of behavior disturbance were considered in assigning the severity ratings: 1) emotional disturbance; 2) aggressive conduct disorder, and 3) antisocial behavior (Koller et al., 1983).

Communication Disorders   The overall severity rating of communication disorders was based on the most severe of the following three components:

1.   Visual disabilities
     Severe—Legally blind, or registered as blind
     Moderate—Blind in one eye or markedly impaired vision not correctable with glasses
     Mild—Sight in both eyes but with a visual disability not marked but not correctable with glasses
2.   Deafness

Severe—Complete or almost complete hearing loss

Moderate—Hearing loss not severe or mild or where proficiency in lipreading overcomes severe deafness

Mild—Difficulty in hearing some people, may have to ask some people to speak louder

3.   Speech defects: Severe, moderate, and mild ratings of speech being slurred or unclear or containing a lisp or other impediment were based on observations made after an interview several hours in length

Limb Disabilities

1.   Upper limbs

Severe—Limited use of both upper limbs; help needed in tasks requiring use of upper limbs

Moderate—Full use of one upper limb and severely limited in use of the other; disabilities not defined as mild or severe

Mild—Able to perform most activities requiring the upper limbs, but difficulties with tasks requiring moderate manual dexterity

2.   Lower limbs

Severe—Severely restricted in ambulation; requires help to move about

Moderate—Some limitations in getting about, tires easily; may require a walking stick or crutches, but with their use moves about in the community

Mild—Some degree of awkwardness or clumsiness in moving about, has a limp or unusual gait, but moves about in the community with little difficulty; some difficulty in strenuous activities such as sports requiring running, climbing, or jumping

Incontinence

Severe—Inability to control urinary or bowel function during the day, or both day and night

Moderate—Inability to control urinary or bowel function at night only

Career Paths through Mental Retardation Services

For the postschool period, four different career paths related to mental retardation services were identified:

Residential—Care in institutions for mentally retarded people for all or most of the postschool period

Day services—Daily attendance at Senior Training Centers for mentally retarded adults 5 days a week for all or most of the postschool period

Table 1.   Distribution of each disability by IQ for total study population

Type of disability	IQ^a					
	<20	20–49	50–59	60–69	70+	Total
No moderate or severe disability	0	5 (20%)	20 (44%)	27 (39%)	17 (40%)	69 (36%)
Epilepsy[b]	5 (45%)	4 (16%)	5 (11%)	5 (7%)	1 (2%)	20 (10%)
Behavior disturbance	4 (36%)	8 (32%)	15 (33%)	25 (36%)	20 (48%)	72 (38%)
Communication disorders[b]	10 (91%)	14 (56%)	14 (31%)	14 (20%)	11 (26%)	63 (33%)
Limb disability	5 (45%)	6 (24%)	2 (4%)	5 (7%)	0	18 (9%)
Incontinence	2 (18%)	2 (8%)	1 (2%)	3 (4%)	0	8 (4%)
Total in IQ subset[c]	11	25	45	69	42	192

[a] Percentages sum to more than 100 because multiplicity of disabilities is not taken into account.

[b] Percentages for these disabilities may be slight underestimates because evidence was incomplete or missing for six subjects on epilepsy and for 24 subjects on communication disorders.

[c] Totals are less than vertical sum of column because multiplicity of disabilities is not taken into account.

Short-term services—Services in either residential or day care for one-third or less of the time in the 6 years since leaving school. This ranged from a few weeks to 2 years

No services—No mental retardation services were received during the postschool period.

RESULTS

We would expect that a person's history of mental retardation services in the postschool period would be related both to the severity of retardation and to the presence or absence of other disabilities. Behavior disturbance and communication disorders at a moderate or severe level were present in over one-third of those who were mentally retarded. These two forms of disability were more than three times as frequent as epilepsy, limb disabilities, and incontinence (Table 1). Within the mentally retarded population, epilepsy, communication disorders, limb disabilities, and incontinence were all more frequent among individuals with IQs below 50. For epilepsy there was a consistent stepwise increase for each degree of severity, but for the remaining disabilities there was no consistent gradient between IQ categories of 50 and above. No relationship existed between behavior and severity of IQ (Table 1).

The combinations of disabilities in each mentally retarded person were related to severity of retardation (Table 2). Three or more disabilities as defined for this paper occurred only among those with an IQ of less than 60. They showed a stepwise increase below an IQ of 60, with 6% found in those with IQs of 50–59, 16% in the IQ subset 20–49, and 45% in those with IQs below 20. Communication disorders as a single disability increased with severity of retardation. Behavior disturbance as a single disability was more common among those with mild retardation. The most frequent patterns of disability were behavior disturbance alone (24%), communication disorders alone (16%), and behavior and communication disorders combined (7%).

Least is known about the characteristics of those who received no further mental retardation services after leaving school. They made up half of the total population of mentally retarded young people. None had IQs under 50 and the largest subset was those with IQs between 60 and 69. Thirty-six percent had a single disability other than intellectual impairment and 4% had two disabilities (Table 3).

Of those persons who received short-term services none had IQs below 50, but they did have lower IQs than those who received no services in the postschool period. The predominant disability in this group was behavior disturbance alone, which occurred in 59% of all cases (Table 3). For persons in long-term services, the only difference in IQ level between those in day and in residential services was for those with IQs below 50. More individuals with IQs below 20 were in residential care, and more of those with IQs of 20–49 were in day care. Only those in long-term care had three or more disabilities (Table 3).

Influence of Behavior Disturbances

The main difference between the pattern of disabilities among those in day and in residential care was that behavior disturbance was present significantly more often among those in residential care ($\chi_1^2 = 4.77$, $P < 0.05$). There was virtually no difference between those individuals not in services and those in long-term services in the frequency of behavior disturbance alone, but those in long-term residential care more often had behavior disturbance in combination with other disabilities (43%) than those in day services (13%) or those not receiving services (9%). Moreover, examination of data not given here shows that the behavior disturbance of persons in residential services was more likely to have been severe compared to those in day care or those who received no services, for whom the behavior disturbance was more likely to be moderate.

Table 2. Patterns of disability by IQ for total study population

Disabilities[a]	<20	20–49	50–59	60–69	70 +	Total	
No moderate or severe disabilities		5 (20%)	20 (44%)	27 (39%)	17 (40%)	69 (36%)	
Single disability							
E			1 (2%)	1 (1.4%)		2 (1%)	
B	3 (27%)	4 (16%)	8 (18%)	21 (30%)	13 (31%)	46 (24%)	
C		6 (24%)	7 (16%)	9 (13%)	5 (12%)	30 (16%)	42%
L				1 (1.4%)		1 (0.5%)	
I				1 (1.4%)		1 (0.5%)	
Two disabilities							
EB	1 (9%)			1 (1.4%)	1 (2%)	3 (1.5%)	
EC	1 (9%)		1 (2%)	1 (1.4%)		3 (1.5%)	
EL		1 (4%)		1 (1.4%)		2 (1%)	
EI		1 (4%)		1 (1.4%)		2 (1%)	
BC		1 (4%)	5 (11%)	1 (1.4%)	6 (14%)	13 (7%)	16%
BL				1 (1.4%)		1 (0.5%)	
BI				1 (1.4%)		1 (0.5%)	
CL	1 (9%)	3 (12%)		2 (3%)		6 (3%)	
Three disabilities							
ECL		1 (4%)	1 (2%)			2 (1%)	
EBC	1 (9%)	1 (4%)	1 (2%)			3 (1.5%)	
BCL		1 (4%)				2 (1%)	4.5%
BCI		1 (4%)				1 (0.5%)	
CLI	1 (9%)					1 (0.5%)	
Four disabilities							
EBLI			1 (2%)			1 (0.5%)	
EBCL	1 (9%)					1 (0.5%)	1.5%
ECLI	1 (9%)					1 (0.5%)	

[a] E = epilepsy, B = behavior disturbance, C = communication disorder, L = limb disability, I = incontinence.

31

Table 3. Patterns of disabilities by services received for total population in the postschool period

Disabilities[a]	None	Short-term services[b]	Long-term day care	Long-term residential
No moderate or severe disabilities	55 (54%)	4 (18%)	10 (22%)	
Single disability				
E	1 (1%)		1 (2%)	
B	20 (20%)	13 (59%)	8 (17%)	5 (22%)
C	14 (14%)	1 (4.5%)	11 (24%)	4 (17%)
L	1 (1%)			
I		1 (4.5%)		
Two disabilities				
EB	2 (2%)			1 (4%)
EC	1 (1%)	1 (4.5%)		1 (4%)
EL		1 (4.5%)	1 (2%)	
EI			1 (2%)	1 (4%)
BC	6 (6%)	1 (4.5%)	3 (7%)	3 (13%)
BL			1 (2%)	
BI	1 (1%)			
CL			4 (9%)	2 (9%)
Three disabilities				
ECL			2 (4%)	
EBC			1 (2%)	2 (9%)
BCL				2 (9%)
BCI				1 (4%)
CLI			1 (2%)	
Four disabilities				
EBLI				1 (4%)
EBCL			1 (2%)	
ECLI			1 (2%)	

[a] E = epilepsy, B = behavior disturbance, C = communication disorder, L = limb disability, I = incontinence.

[b] Day and residential combined.

Influence of Gender

There was a significant difference ($\chi_1^2 = 7.91$, $P < 0.01$) in the sex distribution of those in long-term day and residential care (Table 4). Males comprised 74% of those in long-term residential care and 35% of those in day care. Approximately equal numbers of males were in residential and day care, but five times as many females were in day programs as were in residential care. All males in residential care who had three or four disabilities were behaviorally disturbed. There were no females in residential care who had more than two disabilities, but there were three in day care. Five of the six females in residential care (83%) and

Table 4. Patterns of disabilities by sex for those in long-term residential and day care during postschool period

Disabilities[a]	Residential Males	Residential Females	Day center Males	Day center Females
No moderate or severe disabilities			2 (13%)	8 (27%)
Single disability				
E				
B	2 (12%)	3 (50%)	1 (6%)	8 (27%)
C	4 (24%)		5 (31%)	6 (20%)
L				
I				
Two disabilities				
EB		1 (17%)		
EC	1 (6%)			
EL				1 (3%)
EI	1 (6%)			1 (3%)
BC	2 (12%)	1 (17%)	1 (6%)	2 (7%)
BL				1 (3%)
BI				
CL	1 (6%)	1 (17%)	4 (25%)	
Three disabilities				
ECL			1 (6%)	1 (3%)
EBC	2 (12%)			1 (3%)
BCL	2 (12%)			
BCI	1 (6%)			
CLI				1 (3%)
Four disabilities				
EBLI	1 (6%)			
EBCL			1 (6%)	
ECLI			1 (6%)	
Total	17 (74%)	6 (26%)	16 (35%)	30 (65%)

[a] E = epilepsy, B = behavior disturbance, C = communication disorder, L = limb disability, I = incontinence.

12 of the 30 females in day care (40%) had behavior disturbance, alone or in combination with other disabilities. The comparable figures for males were 10 out of 17 in residential care (59%), and two out of 16 in day care (13%). Put another way, almost half the females and slightly more than a third of the males receiving some type of long-term services had moderate or severe behavior disturbance, but only two out of 12 males (17%) who had behavior disturbance lived at home and attended a day center, compared to 12 out of 17 of the females (71%).

Reasons for Institutional Placement

The presence of behavior disturbance in young adults who were in residential care does not necessarily mean that the behavior disturbance was the reason for the placement. To examine the reasons for the institutional placements, we combined those persons placed in residential care for both short and long periods. Of the 22 young adults who received short-term services (Table 3), seven were in residential care. When we examined the reasons for the institutional placement of the 30 subjects (23 males and seven females) admitted on both long- and short-term bases, behavior disturbance was found to be the primary reason for 77% of all placements (23 persons). Of the remaining seven (23%), all but one were males.

The presence of other disabilities among these seven subjects was insufficient to provide clues to the reasons for placement in institutional care, because there were other young people with similar or greater multiplicity and severity of disabilities who were living at home. The major reason for placement was the unwillingness or inability of the family to cope with them. Four of the seven first entered an institution in early childhood: two were abandoned by their parents before 2 years of age, and two were placed at ages 3 and 4 because the parents were unable to manage. In one of the latter cases, the doctor suggested placement. All four of these children evidenced signs of either Down's syndrome or cerebral palsy before placement. Of the three remaining placements, one was due to parental neglect, one was because the family made frequent moves between Britain and abroad and the relocations caused problems, and one occurred when the stepfather remarried after the death of the mother on the condition that the stepson be removed from the home. The ages of placement of these three subjects were 12, 14, and 21 years, respectively. Despite this, the median age of those who were placed in residential institutions because of behavior disturbance was 14 years, compared to $5\frac{1}{2}$ years as the median age of those placed for other reasons.

Summary

There were associations between IQ, multiplicity of disability, type of service received, and gender. There was a progression of greater multiplicity of disability across the four career paths of no services, short-term services, long-term day care, and long-term residential care. Long-term institutional placement most often occurred because of behavior disturbance, often combined with other disabilities. These placements more often occurred in adolescence or the young adult years. Placement of those who did not manifest signs of behavior disturbance after age 16 appears to have been influenced by the early identification of cerebral palsy or Down's syndrome and inability of the family to manage or cope. These placements were more often made at younger ages than the placements of those with behavior disturbance.

DISCUSSION

The work reported in this paper originated because of our concern for obtaining a broader view than has been available of the individual characteristics, including disabilities, of a mentally retarded population. We believe that learning more about mentally retarded people is important both for planning services and for epidemiological research. In the longitudinal study we have carried out, a major interest was in the consequences of disability for retarded people and their families during the periods of childhood, adolescence, and young adulthood.

Classifications must be tailored to the purposes for which they are to be used, and we found that the existing classifications did not deal with the disabling consequences of impairments. For example, a frequently used classification within the field of mental retardation is Down's syndrome, but this gives little information on the functional status of the individual. Using our classifications, we found that communication was the predominant moderate to severe disability among seven young adults with Down's syndrome. Only one person with Down's syndrome had more than one of the disabilities we classified, and only one, the same person, had moderate or severe behavior disturbance. If such findings are not unique to this population and were generally known earlier, they might have given pause to those who used to recommend early institutional placement for children with Down's syndrome. Another commonly used classification is cerebral palsy, but, again, this provides little information on the functional status across a number of disabilities. This led us to develop the classifications that have been described.

In the midst of the development of our classifications, the World Health Organization (1980) published for trial purposes an *International Classification of Impairments, Disabilities and Handicaps*, which has influenced our work. The distinctions between impairment, disability, and handicap are important, and in this paper we have focused on disability, which is defined as "any restriction or lack (resulting from an impairment) of ability to perform an activity in the manner or within the range considered normal for a human being" (World Health Organization, 1980). We believe there are good reasons for the development of a set of disability classifications appropriate for children and adults who are mentally retarded; one is that they would facilitate systematic comparisons between epidemiological studies and another is that they would provide important practical knowledge for planning services. For the purposes of this paper, we found it necessary to combine some of the disabilities and to reduce the number of severity categories. However, we plan to use the full range of classifications and severity in other analyses.

When we compared the behavior disturbance of young adults in the two types of long-term care, we found that those in residential institutions frequently had behavior disturbance and multiple disabilities. Fewer individuals in long-term day care had behavior disturbance, and, when present, it was usually less severe and unaccompanied by other disabilities. The striking difference in the proportions of males and females with behavior disturbance in long-term day care suggests that behavior disturbance in males is not well tolerated by families at home and by the staff of day care centers.

Although severity of retardation, gender, and the presence of disabilities may each contribute to the placement of mentally retarded young people in day or residential care, another important factor is the families from which they come. The ability of the parents to care for and manage a young mentally retarded person depends on the characteristics of the parents, the other stresses and problems they experience, the extent to which they receive informal help and support from their extended families and friends, and the extent to which there are formal services available to which they can turn for help.

In a previous paper (Richardson et al., in press) the combined prevalence of young adults in long-term day and residential care was shown to be 5 per 1,000. This may provide an estimate for other communities of those who will need services after leaving school. However, there may be considerable variation in the proportions of those in long-term services who are in day or residential care. The findings of the present study of a ratio of two persons in day care for every one in residential care is for a stable community without undue poverty or widespread family breakdown and with good community services. Under conditions of poverty, family disruption, and poor support services, it would be more difficult for families to keep their children at home and more likely that residential placement would be needed. There may also be variation from one community to another in the proportions of mentally retarded people who have associated disabilities. Such variation might be related to differences in the prevalence of conditions that place a child at risk of both mental retardation and other disabilities (e.g., spina bifida), and differences in community resources in such areas as physical medicine and speech therapy, which could help to lessen an impaired person's disabilities. Other research is needed to resolve these issues.

ACKNOWLEDGMENTS

The authors wish to thank R. Illsley and G. Horobin of the Medical Research Council for their help and support.

REFERENCES

Abramowicz, H. K., and Richardson, S. A. 1975. Epidemiology of severe mental retardation in children: Community studies. Am. J. Ment. Defic. 80:18–39.

Bernsen, A. H. 1981. Severe mental retardation among children in a Danish urban area. Assessment and etiology. In: P. Mittler (ed.), Frontiers of Knowledge in Mental Retardation. Vol. II: Biomedical Aspects, pp. 53–61. University Park Press, Baltimore.

Birch, H., Richardson, S. A., Baird, D., Horobin, C., and Illsley, R. 1970. Mental Subnormality in the Community: A Clinical and Epidemiological Study. The Williams & Wilkins Co., Baltimore.

Koller, H., Richardson, S. A., Katz, M., and McLaren, J. 1983. Behavior disturbance since childhood among a five-year birth cohort of all mentally retarded young adults in a city. Am. J. Ment. Defic. 87:386–395.

Kushlick, A., and Blunden, R. 1974. The epidemiology of mental subnormality. In: A. M. Clarke and A. D. B. Clarke (eds.), Mental Deficiency, The Changing Outlook, pp. 31–81. Methuen & Co., Ltd., London.

Richardson, S. A., Koller, H., Katz, M., and McLaren, J. 1981. A functional classification of seizures and its distribution in a mentally retarded population. Am. J. Ment. Defic. 85:457–466.

Richardson, S. A., Koller, H., Katz, M., and McLaren, J. Career paths through mental retardation services: An epidemiological perspective. Appl. Res. Ment. Retard. (in press)

World Health Organization. 1980. International Classification of Impairments, Disabilities and Handicaps: A Manual of Classification Relating to the Consequences of Disease. World Health Organization, Geneva.

PERSPECTIVES AND PROGRESS IN MENTAL RETARDATION
Volume II—Biomedical Aspects
Edited by J. M. Berg

EPIDEMIOLOGY OF DOWN'S SYNDROME IN WALLONIA (SOUTH BELGIUM) Recent Data (1979–1981)

L. Koulischer and Y. Gillerot

Institut de Morphologie Pathologique, Allée des Templiers 41,
6270 Loverval, Belgium

Recent (1979–1981) epidemiological findings on Down's syndrome in Wallonia (South Belgium) are presented. The effects of changing maternal age distribution in the general population are analyzed, and consideration is given to the role of prenatal diagnostic amniocentesis as a preventive measure. Fluctuations in the sex ratio of newborn children with Down's syndrome are noted.

In Wallonia (the South Belgium French-speaking region), until the end of 1974 more than half of all Down's syndrome (DS) births occurred to mothers over 35 years of age. Since 1975, the number of DS births in mothers over 35 dropped rather abruptly from 52% to 32% (Koulischer and Gillerot, 1980, 1981). These data are in keeping with observations in other developed countries that most (75–80%) trisomy 21 persons are now born to mothers younger than 35. This is linked with a remarkable decrease in the number of mothers over 35 in the general population.

A particular feature of our Wallonia data is that, in a large and densely populated area of the region (the city of Charleroi), the incidence of DS births to younger mothers tended to increase since 1975 in a statistically significant manner. This suggests that one or more new environmental factors could be operating on births from 1975 on. In this context, it seems noteworthy that from September 1973, for the first time since 1918, the advertisement of contraceptive devices and drugs became legal, with a presumed increase of contraceptive pill users.

Our last published observations concerning the epidemiology of DS included data up to December 1978 (Koulischer and Gillerot, 1980); the present paper provides more recent figures, from January 1, 1979 to December 31, 1981. Our aims in analyzing these data were to check if the trend toward a decrease in the number of DS children born to mothers over 35 was persisting, to note any change in DS incidence at birth in a given age group, and to ascertain the impact of prenatal diagnosis on the birth of DS children in this region. In addition, because an increased proportion of males has been reported recently in DS populations (Bernheim et al., 1979; Nielsen et al., 1981) and because this increase was correlated with the use of estrogen/progesterone contraceptive pills in the maternal age group 30 to 38 years (Lejeune and Prieur, 1979), we also studied the sex ratio in our trisomy 21 population since 1971.

MATERIAL AND METHODS

Our approach, described in detail elsewhere (Koulischer and Gillerot, 1980), had the following main characteristics. We surveyed two-thirds of all live births in Wallonia for the period 1971 to 1981. Chromosome studies (lymphocyte culture) were performed on every newborn child suspected of having Down's syndrome. We included in our series only those children showing trisomy 21 or de novo translocation Down's syndrome; those with a transmitted translocation were excluded. The age of the mother at birth was recorded, as well as the birth date and sex of the child.

Our results are presented here comparing three periods: 1971–74, 1975–78, and 1979–81. Official statistics (*Statistiques Démographiques*, Institut National de Statistiques, Ministère des Affaires Economiques) for 1973, 1976, and 1978 (the last available for mother's age in the general population) have been used to determine the DS incidence at birth for each period considered.

RESULTS

Wallonia, with an area of 16,848 km^2, has a population of 3.2 million, and had an average of 38,500 live births per year between 1971 and 1981. As previously mentioned, our survey involved two-thirds of all live births in the region (an average of 25,500 births per year surveyed). These births were widely distributed geographically, including densely populated and rural areas.

The number of DS births in relation to mother's age is given in Table 1. The decrease in the total number of DS births between the 2

Table 1. Number of DS births by maternal age in Wallonia, 1971–81

Period	<20	20–24	25–29	30–34	35–39	40+	Totals
1971–1974	2	21	25	22	28	48	146
1975–1978	3	25	35	19	23	17	122
1979–1981	6	21	30	12	7	11	87
Totals	11	67	90	53	58	76	355

4-year periods 1971–74 and 1975–78 is due to the overall decrease in total births in the general population; the still smaller figure for the third period, 1979–81, is of course due to the fact that it is shorter than the other periods (3 years instead of 4).

When incidence at birth is considered (Table 2), no dramatic overall change is observed. When the two periods 1975–78 and 1979–81 are compared, there is, in the latter period, an increase in DS incidence at birth in mothers below 20, relative stability from 20 to 29, a slight decrease from 30 to 34, a sharper decrease from 35 to 39, and relative stability for the age group over 40 years. Grossly, the risk from puberty to 34 is about 1/1,000, with an increase from 35 to 39 and a much more marked increase after 40 years.

The distribution of mother's age in the general population is shown in Table 3. Important changes have occurred in the relatively short period from 1973 to 1978. (Figures for 1966 have been included in the table for general interest.) In these 5 years there was an overall increase in mother's age in the general population, even though the total number of mothers over 35 declined. A decrease in the last 10 years in the percentages of DS babies born to mothers age 35 and over is apparent in Table 4. At present, in Wallonia, 80% of all DS babies are born to mothers below 35, compared to 48% less than a decade earlier. Hence, if prenatal diagnosis were limited to older mothers, the impact on the total number of DS births would now be rather small (Table 5). About 7 years ago, if prenatal diagnosis had been performed on all mothers age 40 and over, or age 35 and over, about one-third or more than half, respectively, of all DS cases would have been detected before birth. At present, the equivalent figures would be about 12% and 20%, respectively. To now achieve a detection percentage similar to that for mothers of 40 and over in 1974, prenatal diagnosis would have to be extended to mothers age 30 and over.

Finally, we have observed some fluctuation in the DS sex ratio in Wallonia in the past 10 years. An excess of males (56.41%) was present during 1971 to 1974, an opposite trend was noted from 1975 to 1978 (45.80% males), and from 1979 to 1981 the sex ratio for DS males

Table 2.   Incidence of DS per thousand live births by maternal age in Wallonia 1971–81

Period	Maternal age						
	<20	20–24	25–29	30–34	35–39	40+	Overall
1971–1974	0.17	0.37	0.77	1.56	3.97	20.65	1.27
1975–1978	0.28	0.65	0.99	1.50	4.90	13.41	1.23
1979–1981	0.95	0.74	1.08	1.06	2.49	14.28	1.13

Table 3.   Maternal age in the general population in Wallonia as a percentage of all live births

Year	Maternal age					
	<20	20–24	25–29	30–34	35–39	40+
1966	8.75	31.18	28.58	18.43	10.06	2.95
1973	10.27	38.73	30.48	12.32	6.14	2.03
1976	10.29	37.41	34.21	12.28	4.57	1.23
1978	8.19	36.79	35.77	14.60	3.64	1.02

Table 4.   Number of DS live births to mothers 35 and over in Wallonia, 1971–81

Period	Maternal age[a]		
	35 and over	38 and over	40 and over
1971–1974	76 (52%)	60 (41%)	48 (32.8%)
1975–1978	40 (32.8%)	28 (23%)	17 (13.9%)
1979–1981	18 (20.6%)	14 (16%)	11 (12.6%)

[a] Corresponding percentage of all DS births during the period are in parentheses.

Table 5.   Prenatally detectable percentages of DS cases in Wallonia (assuming testing of all pregnancies)

Maternal age	Period		
	1971–1974	1975–1978	1979–1981
20 and over	98.6%	97.5%	93.1%
25 and over	84.2%	77.0%	69.0%
30 and over	67.1%	48.3%	34.5%
35 and over	52.0%	32.8%	20.6%
38 and over	41.0%	23.0%	16.0%
40 and over	32.8%	13.9%	12.6%

(51.13%) approximated the ratio in the general population (51.57% males).

DISCUSSION

It is apparent from our Wallonia data and from similar reports elsewhere (see references in Koulischer and Gillerot, 1980; also Adams et al., 1981; Sadovnick and Baird, 1982) that DS births now occur mostly in mothers below 35 years of age. This is due to the fact that fewer women are now willing to be pregnant after 35. Also, the male/female sex ratio in Wallonia among DS newborns is similar to the newborn sex ratio in the general population, at least during the period 1979–81. We make the following additional comments related to these considerations.

Demographic Data and DS Incidence at Birth

The maternal childbearing age has changed in Belgium during the last 15 years; pregnancies after 35 are now less common. Our figures for Wallonia confirm this trend. In 1966, 13% of all mothers were 35 or older; only 12 years later, in 1978 (last official data), the figure dropped to 4.66%, and it was still lower in 1981 (unpublished personal observations). Also, the proportion of births to mothers ages 20 to 29 has increased during the same period, from 59.76% (1966) to 72.56% (1978). If only the 5-year interval from 1973 to 1978 is considered, an increase of pregnancies in women from 25 to 34 is apparent. The incidence of DS at birth has remained fairly constant between 1971 and 1981 for the 20–29-year age group; however, there was an increase before 20 years and a decrease after 30 years. In general, the risk from puberty to 34 is about 1/1,000; it increases thereafter, particularly at age 40 and over.

Impact of Prenatal Diagnosis on DS Prevalence

Prenatal diagnosis limited to mothers of 40 and over would now have a small effect on the total number of DS births, even if all mothers over 40 are tested and choose abortion if DS is diagnosed. In Wallonia, the number of affected children would be reduced by 12%; should prenatal diagnosis be extended to mothers over 38, the reduction would be 16%. In this region, to reduce the number of DS births by one-third in 1973 it would have been sufficient to limit amniocentesis to mothers of 40 and over; only 5 years later it would have been necessary to extend the procedure to all mothers of 30 and over to achieve the same result. This is not as unrealistic as it may appear at first glance. In 1966, the total number of live births to mothers of 35 and over in Wallonia was 6,994; in 1978; it was 7,046 for mothers over 30, and was probably lower still in 1981. Because of these demographic changes since 1966, the number of women now eligible for prenatal diagnosis on the basis of a maternal age of 30 years or more would not be higher than the number age 35 years or more only 10 years ago.

In Belgium, abortion is still illegal and prosecuted more or less severely in different jurisdictions. This is an unfavorable environment for extending prenatal diagnostic procedures with possible abortion as a consequence, even with a "general feeling" that there would be no prosecution if it were certain that the newborn would have been abnormal. Hence, the number of patients undergoing prenatal diagnosis in Belgium is still low, and amniocentesis for cytogenetic purposes in women over 40 is very unusual (only six during 1981 in our laboratory). This is reflected by a slight increase (from 13.41/1000 to 14.28/1000) in the incidence of DS to mothers above 40 during the last several years (Table 2). Belgium exemplifies that the introduction of a new diagnostic procedure may have little effect, especially if its consequences are illegal.

Sex Ratio and DS

An increased proportion of males in DS is a relatively old observation, and was also found recently in France (Bernheim et al., 1979) and Denmark (Nielsen et al., 1981). Lejeune and Prieur (1979) noted a significant decrease in the proportion of males among the DS progeny of women ages 30 to 38 who used estrogen/progesterone contraceptive pills. In our DS population, during the period 1971–74, the proportion of males was indeed higher than that of newborn infants in general. During 1975–78, the trend was reversed: the proportion of males was lower than in the general population, and this decrease coincided with a decrease of DS newborns to older mothers. A retrospective study concerning cases born in Charleroi, which showed an increased DS incidence in younger mothers, was inconclusive. Specifically, we could not demonstrate a possible link between hormonal contraceptives and trisomy 21. During 1979–81, the sex ratio of DS at birth was similar to the sex ratio at birth in the general population.

These fluctuations are difficult to explain, not the least because the sex of a child is male determined. In our series, conditions seemed the same in the two periods 1975–78 and 1979–81; nevertheless, the sex ratio changed. If environmental factors influence both chromosome 21 meiotic nondisjunction and sex ratio, our observations suggest that they did not alter effects in the last few years.

CONCLUSIONS

After analyzing our data concerning DS births from 1971 to 1981 in Wallonia, we have concluded that:

1. DS births now occur mostly in mothers below 35.
2. Limiting prenatal diagnosis to mothers of 40 and over will have only a small effect on the total number of DS births.
3. Prenatal diagnosis currently reaches only a very small proportion of women at risk in Belgium, where abortion is still illegal.
4. The DS male/female sex ratio has fluctuated, but from 1979 to 1981 it was identical to the sex ratio at birth in the general population.
5. In order to reduce the total number of DS births, new criteria for detecting young mothers at risk are necessary; otherwise the number of persons with DS in the population will alter little for many years.

REFERENCES

Adams, M. M., Erikson, S. D., Layde, P. M., and Oakley, G. P. 1981. Down's syndrome. Recent trends in the United States. JAMA 246:758–760.
Bernheim, A., Chastang, C., Heaulme, M., and de Grouchy, J. 1979. Excès de garçons dans la trisomie 21. Ann. Génét. 22:112–114.
Institut National de Statistiques. 1977. Statistiques Démographiques, 1973. Vol. 4, pp. 44–50. Ministère des Affaires Economiques, Bruxelles, Belgium.
Institut National de Statistiques. 1978. Statistiques Démographiques, 1976. Vol. 4, pp. 74–77. Ministère des Affaires Economiques, Bruxelles, Belgium.
Institut National de Statistiques. 1980. Statistiques Démographiques, 1978. Vol. 4, p. 45. Ministère des Affaires Economiques, Bruxelles, Belgium.
Koulischer, L., and Gillerot, Y. 1980. Down's syndrome in Wallonia (South Belgium), 1971–78. Cytogenetics and incidence. Hum. Genet. 54:243–250.
Koulischer, L., and Gillerot, Y. 1981. Age of mothers at births of Down's syndrome patients in Wallonia (South Belgium), 1971–78. In: P. Mittler (ed.), Frontiers of Knowledge in Mental Retardation, Vol. II, pp. 87–92. University Park Press, Baltimore.
Lejeune, J., and Prieur, M. 1979. Contraceptifs oraux et trisomie 21. Ann. Génét. 22:61–66.
Nielsen, J., Jacobsen, P., Mikkelsen, M., Niebuhr, E., and Sorensen, K. 1981. Sex ratio in Down's syndrome. Ann. Génét. 24:212–215.
Sadovnick, A. D., and Baird, P. A. 1982. Impact of prenatal chromosomal diagnosis in older women on population incidence of severe mental retardation. Am. J. Obstet. Gynecol. 143:486–487.

PERSPECTIVES AND PROGRESS IN MENTAL RETARDATION
Volume II—Biomedical Aspects
Edited by J. M. Berg
Copyright © 1984 by I.A.S.S.M.D.

COMPARATIVE MORBIDITY OF DOWN'S SYNDROME CHILDREN AND THEIR PARENTS

J. C. Murdoch

Department of General Practice, University of Otago, Dunedin, New Zealand

A prospective study of children with Down's syndrome, matched with nonretarded children of the same age, sex, sibship size, and social class, has been carried out through the observations of family doctors in Scotland in 1981. The Down's syndrome children had a highly significantly greater number of contacts with the family doctor, mainly with the problem of respiratory disease. Family doctor contacts of Down's syndrome children with congenital heart disease showed no significant difference from contacts of such children without congenital heart disease. The parents of Down's syndrome children had no increased family doctor contact rate, nor was there any evidence of a greater tendency to develop psychological problems after the birth of the affected child.

On two occasions in 1981, the International Year of the Disabled, the press in the United Kingdom contained articles about newborn children with Down's syndrome (DS). The burden of the controversy was whether allowing such children to live might impose intolerable pressures on their families, with resulting psychological breakdown. Amid the conflicting views, one fact became clear—the lack of scientific evidence on the topic under discussion.

It is the family doctor who, in Scotland, deals with the whole spectrum of physical, psychological, and social problems in the DS individual and his/her family. Yet, up to now, we have lacked a view of the DS person from family practice. This study, done from the per-

The Down's Family Project is supported by the Chief Scientist Organisation, Scottish Home and Health Department.

spective of family practice, is presented in the hope that some scientific comparisons might be made of the health of DS and nonretarded children and their respective parents that might help us in advising the parents of newborn DS children.

PATIENTS AND METHODS

From a survey of DS individuals living in Scotland (Murdoch, 1982), 136 children with Down's syndrome of ages 1 to 10 years, living at home with both parents, were selected. The child's general practitioner was then asked to select a child without DS of the same age, sex, social class, and sibship size (± 1) living at home with both parents. Both the children and their parents were then studied.

Data on the patients were collected in two ways. *Retrospective data* (full details of the children's and parents' past history) were obtained from the medical record, which is held by the general practitioner. It was found that 44 DS children had congenital heart disease (CHD), thus creating a subgroup of the DS sample. *Prospective data* were collected during 1981 regarding each contact of the physician with the patients, looking at whether this was a new or a repeat episode, whether it took place at home or in the office, what the problem was, whether a drug was prescribed, whether a referral was made to a specialist, and whether any subsequent operation was performed. This information was then returned and the health problems were coded according to the International Classification of Diseases (ICD) (World Health Organization, 1965).

RESULTS

The mean age of the mothers and fathers of the DS children was 36.4 years and 38.5 years, respectively; that of the control mothers and fathers was 32.3 years and 34.9 years, respectively.

Children

Table 1 shows the physician workload involving DS children with and without CHD and controls during 1981. The number of visits paid by the DS children to the doctor was significantly greater than that of the control children ($P < 0.01$) and this was true both for home and new visits. However, there were no significant differences between the DS children with and without CHD.

Table 2 shows the distribution of new problems presented by the two groups of children over the year. Respiratory conditions (ICD 460.0–519.9 and 783.3) accounted for a preponderance of the problems

Table 1. Contacts of DS children with and without congenital heart
disease (CHD) and of controls with family doctor, 1981

Group	Number observed	Any contact (%)	Mean contacts/patient[a]		
			Total	Home	New
DS with CHD	44	43 (98)	6.9	1.2	3.8
DS without CHD	92	84 (91)	5.1	0.9	3.6
Controls	136	102 (75)	2.6	0.4	2.0

[a] DS children versus controls highly significant ($P < 0.01$; t test). DS with CHD versus DS without CHD not significant (t test).

presented by the DS children. However, other infectious diseases (ICD 91–799) and eye and ear diseases occurred approximately equally in the DS and control children. Table 3 shows that DS children with CHD did not present any more frequently with new respiratory problems than did DS children without CHD.

Parents

Table 4 shows that the workload presented to the family doctor by the parents of DS children did not differ significantly from that of control parents.

From the retrospective and prospective data it was possible to ask the question: "Does parenting a DS child make mothers or fathers any more liable to psychological problems than parents of normal children?" Table 5 shows the prevalence of new psychological problems from the retrospective data (conception to 1981) and from the prospective data (during 1981). Twenty-five mothers of DS children (21%) and 30 mothers of controls (22.7%) who had no histories of psychological problems before conception had presented with psychological problems since conception. Thirteen fathers of DS children (9.8%) and seven fathers of controls (5.2%) had presented psychological problems to the doctor. In neither mothers nor fathers was this result statistically significant. It is notable that 19 DS children's mothers (13.8%), eight controls' mothers (5.8%), five DS children's fathers (3.6%), and four controls' fathers (2.9%) had histories of psychological illness before conception of the DS or control child. It is interesting to note also that 20 of these (55%) had histories subsequent to the conception of the child.

DISCUSSION

I believe that this is the first reported prospective study of the morbidity of DS children living at home compared with control children. Much valuable information concerning life expectancy has been published by

Table 2. Distribution of new diagnoses in DS children and controls (% of total)

Diagnosis	Down's syndrome	Controls
Respiratory disease	266 (48.5%)	107 (36.3%)
Infectious disease	51 (9.3%)	36 (12.2%)
Eye disease	41 (7.5%)	14 (4.7%)
Ear disease	27 (4.9%)	31 (10.5%)

Table 3. New respiratory problems in DS children with and without congenital heart disease (CHD) and in controls in 1981

Group	Number	New contacts/patient	Respiratory problems/patient
DS with CHD	44	3.6	2.1
DS without CHD	92	3.8	1.9
Controls	136	2.0	0.8

Table 4. Comparison of contacts of parents of DS children and controls' parents with family doctor, 1981

Group	Number observed	Any contact (%)	Mean contacts/patient		
			Total	Home	New
Mothers					
DS children	136	103 (75.7%)	3.9	0.5	2.1
Controls	136	112 (82.4%)	3.8	0.3	2.0
Fathers					
DS children	130	89 (68.5%)	2.1	0.1	1.2
Controls	130	75 (57.7%)	1.8	0.2	1.1

Table 5. Prevalence of psychological problems in parents of DS and of control children following conception of study child

Group	Number without history of psychological problem at conception	Psychological problem in retrospective data	Psychological problem in prospective data
Mothers			
DS children	119	17 (14.3%)	8 (6.7%)
Controls	132	16 (12.1%)	14 (10.6%)
Fathers			
DS children	133	6 (4.5%)	7 (5.3%)
Controls	136	4 (3.0%)	3 (2.2%)

Carter (1958), Collmann and Stoller (1963), Fabia and Drolette (1970), and Øster et al. (1975). The problem with these studies is that they are so retrospective as to be misleading by the time they come to be used in evidence. An illustration of this is Collmann and Stoller's statistic that only 50% of DS children were alive at the age of 5 years. However easily remembered the statistic, the fact that it relates to children born between 1948 and 1952 is easily forgotten.

This report provides a current picture of the day-to-day care of children and their parents by the family doctor. The first important message is that of contact. Virtually all the DS children saw the family doctor over the course of the year; indeed, one child with Down's syndrome and congenital heart disease saw the family doctor 42 times during 1981. Most control children and parents of DS children and of controls also saw the family doctor at least once during the year. In our approach to the care of the handicapped child we tend to ignore this contact and to spurn the opportunity given by it to enhance care in the community.

The results of this study indicate that DS children are vulnerable individuals with regard particularly to respiratory infection, a previously known fact. Many reasons have been given for this. Evidence has been sought for an immunological defect; other reasons might be a deficiency of respiratory tract ciliated cells in clearing mucus, or the presence of tenaceous mucus. The high prevalence of serous otitis media ("glue ear") reported by Balkany et al. (1979) may reinforce this hypothesis.

The proved susceptibility of Down's children to intercurrent illness points to two possible growth points in their management in the future. First, family doctors who look after such children must be aware of their vulnerability and its management. The primary care of those who are mentally handicapped is a much neglected field of endeavor, particularly in these days of a move to community care. Although various reports have indicated that more than 50% of DS children have significant hearing loss (Davies and Penniceard, 1980) involving mainly serous otitis media, our series of DS children had relatively few ear problems, indicating the importance of educational programs for family doctors based on current needs of DS individuals. Second, we must look for possible ways of reducing the DS child's vulnerability to infection. One way may be through the effect, if any, of megadose vitamin and mineral supplement therapy, although this is not yet of proved benefit.

In this study, the presence of congenital heart disease did not increase vulnerability to respiratory problems, although it increased the tendency for the family doctor to visit the child more often at home and for review. This is of interest in view of a recent editorial in the *British Medical Journal* (1981) that suggested that such was the serious prognostic significance of CHD in Down's syndrome that infants so affected, and rejected by their parents, should be allowed to succumb to the effects of starvation. The present results indicate that outcome studies such as those produced by Fabia and Drolette (1970) require further validation before they are applied to prognostication on today's DS infants.

It is comforting to those of us who have often admired the courage and tenacity of parents of DS children that there is no evidence of their attending their family doctors more often than parents of controls, and that those without a previous history develop psychological illness after the birth of a DS child no more often than do controls' parents. Perhaps these findings will dispel the powerful stereotype of anxious DS mothers hooked on tranquilizers and of fathers turning to drink for consolation.

There are many views of the normal experience of DS individuals and their families, and this is only a preliminary look at the view from family practice. To those who look at the DS child through the keyhole of a specialty it may appear to be an optimistic view, but it is prospective information collected by a valid method from a significant number of families. It demonstrates the physical vulnerability of the DS child being managed within a family structure without a demonstrable increase in the prevalence of psychological disorder in the parents. It also demonstrates the potential opportunity of involving the family physician as the major coordinator in the achievement of full potential for the DS child and his family. We are currently looking at Down's syndrome adults over the age of 25 years for further information of the view at that end of the spectrum.

ACKNOWLEDGMENTS

I thank Simon Ogston and Roy Anderson for their statistical help, Teresa Stewart and Lorna McGoldrick for secretarial help, and the general practitioners of Scotland who provided the data so willingly.

REFERENCES

Balkany, T. J., Downs, M. P., Jafek, B. W., and Krajicek, M. J. 1979. Hearing loss in Down's syndrome—a treatable handicap more common than generally recognised. Clin. Paediatr. 18:116–118.
Carter, C. O. 1958. A life table for mongols with the causes of death. J. Ment. Defic. Res. 2:64–74.
Collmann, R. D., and Stoller, A. 1963. A life table for mongols in Victoria, Australia. J. Ment. Defic. Res. 7:53–59.

Davies, B., and Penniceard, R. M. 1980. Auditory function and receptive vocabulary in Down's syndrome children. In: I. G. Taylor and A. Markides (eds.), Disorders of Auditory Function, Vol. 3, pp. 51–58. Academic Press, London.

Editorial. 1981. The right to live and the right to die. Br. Med. J. 283:569–570.

Fabia, J., and Drolette, M. 1970. Life tables up to age 10 for mongols with and without congenital heart defect. J. Ment. Defic. Res. 14:235–241.

Murdoch, J. C. 1982. A survey of Down's syndrome under general practitioner care in Scotland. J. R. Coll. Gen. Pract. 32:410–418.

Øster, J., Mikkelson, M., and Nielson, A. 1975. Mortality and life-table in Down's syndrome. Acta Paediatr. Scand. 64:322–326.

World Health Organization. 1965. International Classification of Diseases. World Health Organization, Geneva.

PERSPECTIVES AND PROGRESS IN MENTAL RETARDATION
Volume II—Biomedical Aspects
Edited by J. M. Berg
Copyright © 1984 by I.A.S.S.M.D.

INCIDENCE OF MEMORY DETERIORATION IN AGING PERSONS WITH DOWN'S SYNDROME

A. J. Dalton[1] and D. R. Crapper McLachlan[2]
[1] *Behavior Research Program, Surrey Place Centre, Toronto, Ontario M5S 2C2, Canada*
[2] *Departments of Physiology and Medicine, University of Toronto, Toronto, Canada*

The prevalence of memory deterioration associated with early Alzheimer's disease in persons with Down's syndrome 40 years of age or older was found to be 24% in a series of prospective studies conducted over an 8-year period. The age of onset of the memory deterioration averaged 49.1 years with a range from 41.5 to 59.5 years. The rate of appearance of new cases of memory failure in those who were 40 years of age or older was 9% per year.

Alzheimer's disease is a lethal, progressive, degenerative disease of the brain. Neither the primary pathogenic events that initiate this condition nor the factors regulating the spread of the degenerative process through the brain are understood. Remarkably, there is an increased incidence of the histopathology of Alzheimer's disease in Down's syndrome. This well-documented association (Jervis, 1948; Malamud, 1972) is of importance to workers in the fields of both dementia and amentia.

The natural course of Alzheimer's disease has been described in adults without retardation (Wolstenholme and O'Connor, 1970; Katzman et al., 1978), but very little is known with certainty concerning the functional consequences of the brain pathology in persons with

This work was supported by Medical Research Council of Canada grant MA-5364, National Institute of Child Health and Human Development of the United States grant HD-08993, and Ontario Health Research grant PR-633.

55

Down's syndrome (Jervis, 1948; Haberland, 1969; Owens et al., 1971; Brun et al., 1978; Reid et al., 1978). Memory deficits suggestive of the early stages of Alzheimer's disease have been reported in patients with Down's syndrome over the age of 44 years (Dalton et al., 1974) and further memory deterioration has been observed in follow-up examinations (Dalton and Crapper, 1977). Other indications of the disease, such as electroencephalographic changes, also have been observed (Crapper et al., 1975).

We undertook a series of prospective studies extending over an 8-year period to establish the prevalence and incidence rates of the clinical manifestations of Alzheimer's disease in Down's syndrome. The studies were based on the assumption that the hallmark of Alzheimer's disease is a progressive deterioration in memory and that a delayed matching–to–sample memory test measures memory functions rather than other phenomena.

PATIENTS AND METHODS

Patients

Selection of all participants was based on the following criteria: 1) a normal birth record, 2) no history of seizures, 3) no gross sensory or motor impairment, 4) no evidence of focal neurological signs at the start of the studies, and 5) successful performance on a visual matching-to-sample discrimination test to a preset criterion of mastery. Data were collected from 219 adults with a diagnosis of Down's syndrome based on karyotypes and/or clinical findings (Smith and Berg, 1976) and from 22 mentally retarded adults without Down's syndrome. Of the Down's syndrome adults, 127 were residents in five institutions for developmentally handicapped persons and the remaining 92 were living either at home or in community-based residential settings. Sixty-eight (54%) of the institutionalized adults and two adults (2%) residing in noninstitutional settings failed to meet one or more of the selection criteria; consequently their data are not included in the present report.

For the purposes of analysis the remaining 149 Down's syndrome subjects were divided into three subgroups. Group 1 consisted of 20 adults ranging in age from 19 to 58 years for whom data were collected repeatedly over an 8-year period. Group 2 consisted of 39 adults of comparable age who began their participation 4 years after Group 1. Group 3 consisted of 90 adults who were all working full-time in sheltered workshop settings, who lived at home or in community-based residences, and who began their participation 7 years after Group 1 and 3 years after Group 2. There were no statistically significant differences between Group 1 and Group 2 on IQ scores, which ranged from moderate to profound levels of retardation, and on length of institutionalization (average stay = 25.4 years; range = 3 to 44 years). IQ scores for Group 3 were not available.

Learning and Memory Test Procedures

Standardized tests of memory function and delayed response procedures were found unsatisfactory. Visual matching-to-sample discrimination and delayed matching–to-sample memory tests were therefore constructed. Patients were tested in a sound-attenuated mobile laboratory equipped with a special box that contained three rear-projection plastic keys (10 cm × 10 cm) mounted in a row on the front panel. Three carousel projectors mounted in the interior of the box were used to project training and test images (6–10 cm in diameter) on each of the plastic keys. The stimuli employed for the tests consisted of patterns such as a white circle and square, or colored stimuli depicting such objects as food items, vehicles, animals, and wearing apparel. Details of the training and test procedures are provided elsewhere (Dalton et al., 1974). The learning test required matching correctly a series of stimuli during 10 consecutive trials. Failure to meet this acquisition criterion led to termination of the test after 108 practice trials had been completed.

After achieving the acquisition criterion, each participant was presented with a delayed matching–to–sample memory test involving 48 trials that sampled retention capability at various memory retention intervals from 0 to 30 seconds (0 to 60 seconds in the original test with Group 1). The tests were conducted under similar conditions at 1.5-year intervals following the previous test.

Thirty-one of the participants with Down's syndrome were examined neurologically by one of us (Crapper McLachlan). The remainder received only routine annual physical examinations. Electrophysiological studies and brain scans of 13 cases were consistent with a clinical diagnosis of Alzheimer's disease. Postmortem tissue analysis in seven cases provided diagnostic confirmation. Global personality deterioration was ruled out because all of the patients for whom ratings on a 320-item checklist of daily behaviors (Cibiri and Jackson, 1976) were available (n = 20) obtained scores that were in the top 50% of the normative distribution of scores (Dalton et al., 1981).

RESULTS

Age of Onset of Memory Deterioration in Down's Syndrome

The delayed matching–to–sample retention test performances of the Down's syndrome patients over the age of 44 years were significantly inferior to the performances of younger persons with Down's syndrome and of mentally retarded adults of comparable age and IQ without Down's syndrome (Dalton et al., 1974). Several measures of memory performance were generated, including percentage of correct memory test trials and longest memory interval with 75% correct responses. The age at which a person first showed a drop in memory performance to a level at or below the 50% correct memory trials level was defined as the age of onset of memory impairment. This criterion measure was picked because it represents the level for a chance performance. Analysis of the data revealed that the average age of memory impairment onset was 49.1 years, with a range from 41.5 years to 59.5 years, for the 32 persons in Groups 1 and 2 who were 40 years of age or older at the start. The calculation of average age of onset is slightly on the high side because the decline in memory could have occurred at any time during the 1.5-year intervals between test sessions.

It is noteworthy that none of the age-matched mentally retarded control subjects (n = 14), none of the young mentally retarded control subjects (n = 8), and none of the young subjects with Down's syndrome (n = 18) showed any evidence of memory loss or deterioration during identical follow-up tests extending up to 8 years.

Prevalence of Memory Deterioration in Down's Syndrome

Persons with Down's syndrome age 40 years or more are considered here as being at risk of developing the memory impairment that is associated with the early stage of Alzheimer's disease. The prevalence ratio of memory loss for those at risk was computed from an analysis of the data obtained from 49 persons with Down's syndrome who were 40 years of age or older at the start of the study. Twelve persons (five women and seven men) in this at risk group showed signs of memory impairment on the above-mentioned measures. The remaining 37 persons showed no evidence of failing memory function. Thus, the prevalence of memory impairment was 24% in the total group at risk. This result is practically identical to a prevalence rate of 25% reported by Reid and Aungle (1974) in their study of 8 cases of Down's syndrome in persons over 45 years of age.

Incidence Rate of Memory Deterioration in Down's Syndrome

Incidence rate provides a measure over time and is thus an indicator of the likelihood of appearance of newly affected cases. It was computed using the formula:

$$\text{Incidence rate} = \frac{\text{number of newly affected persons/unit time}}{\text{number at risk}}$$

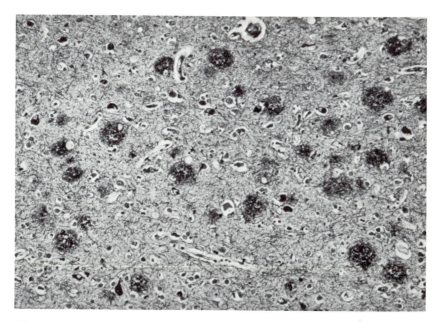

Figure 1.   A representative field of striate cortex from Bielschowsky-stained brain tissue of a patient with Down's syndrome who died at age 54 years. (×400)

This was applied to the persons age 40 years and older with Down's syndrome who met the matching–to–sample acquisition criteria at the start of the study ($n = 41$). The incidence rate was found to be 9% per year.

Histopathology

Ten patients have died, at an average age of 56.4 years (range = 47.2 to 62.6 years), since the start of this study. Brain histopathological examination was carried out in seven of them; each revealed the characteristic changes of Alzheimer's disease, including widespread neurofibrillary degeneration and senile plaques (Figure 1). These seven cases all showed impaired memory functions on the delayed matching–to–sample test prior to death. The course of the illness from onset of memory impairment to death ranged from 3.7 years to 6.1 years, with an average of 4.5 years duration.

DISCUSSION

The presence of memory deterioration in only 24% of our cases of Down's syndrome in persons age 40 years or more is contrary to expectation based on the long-established observation of 100% occurrence of neurofibrillary degeneration in this age group. The absence of measurable memory deterioration in 76% of our cases after repeated testing over periods extending up to 8 years suggests that many of them may be unaffected, or affected only at a clinically undetected level, by Alzheimer's disease. This suggests that, although persons with Down's syndrome may be biologically predisposed to develop Alzheimer's disease, there is no simple relationship (apparent by present techniques) between the occurrence of the disease and age.

There are alternative explanations for our data. However, it is unlikely that the memory test instrument itself was unreliable because the test-retest memory scores obtained by a subgroup of 39 patients younger than 40 years were statistically indistinguishable, and data obtained with different examiners testing the same subgroup of patients yielded a high degree of interexaminer reliability (Pearson $r = 0.90$). It is also unlikely that sampling biases accounted for the findings because the memory performances of a subgroup of 14 Down's syndrome patients from one institution were statistically indistinguishable from the memory performances of a second and comparable subgroup of 12 patients residing at a second institution. Thus, differences in residential conditions, including diet, education, recreational opportunities, specific training, and rehabilitation, cannot reasonably account for the findings.

Variations in the ability to attend to the test stimuli are also excluded as a plausible explanation because the test procedures were explicitly designed so that the visual gaze of each patient was fixated immediately in the vicinity of the stimuli during discrimination training and memory test presentations. Memory test performances could also be adversely affected by inadequate motivation and fatigue. To minimize these factors each correct test response was rewarded with soft drinks or money as part of an incentive system. All the patients appeared to appreciate and to enjoy this feature of the test procedure. Fatigue was minimized by restricting the length of the test sessions to less than 1 hour, a duration chosen after experimenting with various session lengths.

Finally, alternate explanations based on possible sensory deficits can also be ruled out because the preliminary screening procedures that were employed as part of the criteria for selection of participants excluded all candidates who had gross sensory or motor impairments, as well as those who were unable to acquire mastery of the visual matching–to–sample discrimination task. Medical causes for impaired memory function in all but four persons showing deterioration were excluded through the use of standardized clinical and laboratory diagnostic tests, including computerized tomography of the brain. None of the cases included in the study was receiving medication at the times of examination. One case was excluded because of neurological evidence compatible with a diagnosis of multi-infarct dementia, and another because of hypoxia.

Thus, we conclude that the delayed matching–to–sample performances constitute a valid and reliable monitor of memory functions rather than of other unidentified phenomena. Furthermore we conclude that the incidence rate for memory deterioration in Down's syndrome is a valid behavioral marker for estimating the incidence rate of Alzheimer's disease in these patients. Direct evidence in support of this latter conclusion was obtained from seven cases who showed memory impairment while alive and who revealed characteristic histopathological changes of Alzheimer's disease at autopsy. However, we recognize that data derived from autopsy series may be unrepresentative of the pattern of the disease in the general population. Furthermore, because no young person with Down's syndrome in our series has died yet we cannot ascertain precisely the relationship between memory performance and the absence of histopathological evidence of Alzheimer's disease.

ACKNOWLEDGMENTS

The assistance and cooperation of the staff and the generous participation of the residents and their families from the Huronia Regional Centre, Pine Ridge, Oxford Regional Centre, Rideau Regional Centre, and the Muskoka Centre, Ontario, are gratefully acknowledged, as well as the assistance of those involved with the Metro Toronto Association for the Mentally Retarded.

REFERENCES

Brun, A., Gustafson, L., and Risberg, J. 1978. The development of Alzheimer's encephalopathy and its clinical expressions. J. Neuropathol. Exp. Neurol. 37:595–601.
Cibiri, S. M., and Jackson, L. J. 1976. Training Developmentally Handicapped Persons Basic Life Skills: A Task Analysis Approach. Ministry of Community and Social Services, Toronto, Ontario, Canada. (Revised edition published in 1981.)
Crapper, D. R., Dalton, A. J., Skopitz, M., Scott, J. W., and Hachinski, V. C. 1975. Alzheimer degeneration in Down syndrome. Arch. Neurol. 33:618–623.
Dalton, A. J., Cibiri, S. M., Baker, J. G., Malik, H. S., and Wu, B. 1981. Basic Life Skills Scale: Manual of Norms and Standardization. Ministry of Community and Social Services, Toronto, Ontario, Canada.
Dalton, A. J., and Crapper, D. R. 1977. Down's syndrome and aging of the brain. In: P. Mittler (ed.). Research to Practice in Mental Retardation, Vol. 3, pp. 391–400. University Park Press, Baltimore.

Dalton, A. J., Crapper, D. R., and Schlotterer, G. R. 1974. Alzheimer's disease in Down's syndrome: Visual retention deficits. Cortex 10:366–377.

Haberland, C. 1969. Alzheimer's disease in Down syndrome. Acta Neurol. Belg. 69:369–380.

Jervis, G. A. 1948. Early senile dementia in mongoloid idiocy. Am. J. Psychiatry 105:102–106.

Katzman, R., Terry, R. D., and Bick, K. L. 1978. Alzheimer's Disease: Senile Dementia and Related Disorders. Raven Press, New York.

Malamud, N. 1972. Neuropathology of organic brain syndromes associated with aging. In: C. M. Gaitz (ed.), Aging and the Brain, 3rd ed., pp. 63–87. Plenum Publishing Corp., New York.

Owens, D., Dawson, J. C., and Losin, S. 1971. Alzheimer's disease in Down's syndrome. Am. J. Ment. Defic. 75:606–612.

Reid, A. H., and Aungle, P. G. 1974. Dementia in ageing mental defectives: A clinical psychiatric study. J. Ment. Defic. Res. 18:15–23.

Reid, A. H., Maloney, A. F. J., and Aungle, P. G. 1978. Dementia in ageing mental defectives: A clinical and neuropathological study. J. Ment. Defic. Res. 22:233–241.

Smith, G. F., and Berg, J. M. 1976. Down's Anomaly. Churchill Livingstone, Edinburgh.

Wolstenholme, G. E., and O'Connor, M. 1970. Alzheimer's Disease and Related Conditions. Churchill, London.

PERSPECTIVES AND PROGRESS IN MENTAL RETARDATION
Volume II—Biomedical Aspects
Edited by J. M. Berg
Copyright © 1984 by I.A.S.S.M.D.

NEUROFIBROMATOSIS
An Epidemiological, Clinical, and Genetic Study in Gothenburg, Sweden

B. Samuelsson and H. O. Åkesson
Psychiatric Department III, University of Gothenburg, Lillhagen Hospital, S-422 03 Hisings Backa 3, Sweden

The prevalence, psychiatric and somatic manifestations, and genetic aspects of neurofibromatosis were studied in a Swedish population. The 96 patients fulfilling the diagnostic criteria were extensively investigated. A genealogical analysis of their ancestry included about 3,000 individuals. About 200 relatives were examined. Borderline mental retardation was found in 45% of the adult patients, and mental illness in 33%. Organic brain syndrome and depression were the most common psychiatric conditions. No significant correlation was found between the severity of neurofibromatosis and mental retardation or mental illness. The mutation frequency of neurofibromatosis, calculated on the basis of the prevalence of sporadic cases, was extremely high. No common ancestor or gene source was revealed.

Over the centuries, the interest in neurofibromatosis has resulted in both scientific and literary descriptions of the disease. The most famous case of neurofibromatosis in medical history is probably that of John Merrick, described in great detail by the surgeon Sir Frederick Treves in 1885 (the case has also been the subject of a play and a movie entitled *The Elephant Man*). It also seems probable that the "Hunchback of Notre Dame" suffered from neurofibromatosis because the account of his appearance given by Victor Hugo included several of the manifestations commonly seen in this disease.

There is generally no doubt about the diagnosis of neurofibromatosis in its typical clinical form, with multiple café-au-lait (CAL) spots and neurofibromas (Figure 1), but there are cases with few and rare manifestations of the disease. The nature of the condition, with a

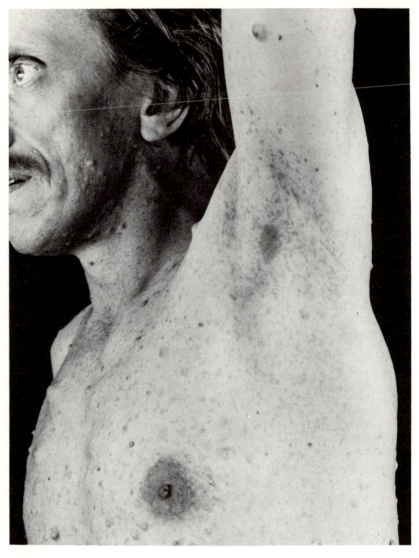

Figure 1. Neurofibromas, one café-au-lait spot in the axilla, and axillary freckling. (Photo by Bo Timback)

slow clinical evolution over decades, contributes to the diagnostic difficulties. Usually, the typical cutaneous neurofibromas do not develop before puberty and sometimes they are not seen until considerably later in life.

Neurofibromatosis is one of the most common dominantly inherited diseases, but opinions differ about its prevalence, penetrance, and mutation frequency. Little attention has been paid to the psychiatric aspects of neurofibromatosis; mental symptoms have been just incidentally noted in most case reports and few, if any, studies have been based on homogeneous populations. Therefore, the aims of the present study were:

To study the prevalence of neurofibromatosis in a Swedish population

To provide a description of the clinical, particularly psychiatric, aspects of the disease

To perform a genetic analysis of the condition, including both familial and genealogical investigations

MATERIAL AND METHODS

Inclusion in the study required findings in agreement with one of three alternative groups of diagnostic criteria (Samuelsson, 1981):

1. *Pigmentary disorders:* Adults—6 or more CAL spots, each with a widest diameter of at least 1.5 cm (Crowe et al., 1956); Children—5 or more CAL spots, each with a widest diameter of at least 0.5 cm (Whitehouse, 1966).

2. *Neurofibromas with a positive biopsy:* Ten or more neurofibromas with one positive biopsy showing plexiform neurofibroma, or 20 or more neurofibromas with one positive biopsy showing neurofibroma.

3. *Combined manifestations:* With no positive biopsy, 200 or more nodules with the appearance typical for neurofibromatosis in addition to CAL spots or axillary freckling.

In the search for cases of neurofibromatosis in the city of Gothenburg, Sweden, all doctors in the district were asked by letter to report patients with the disease. The archives of the Health Services and all hospitals in the area were also searched for cases. Patients satisfying the diagnostic criteria for neurofibromatosis who were living in Gothenburg on January 1, 1978 and had been registered by the Health Services of the city were included in the study. The patients received letters with information and invitations to participate.

During the investigation, which continued from 1978 to 1980, the patients were questioned about close relatives, with regard to illness and possible signs of neurofibromatosis in the family. Ancestors were traced with the aid of information from the parish archives, which in Sweden contain records of citizens as far back as the middle of the eighteenth century. The search for ancestry and place of origin could thus be made through several generations. About 200 relatives (parents, siblings, and children) of the patients with neurofibromatosis were interviewed and examined.

General physical examinations were made with particular attention to the nervous system. The body was examined for presence of pigmentary disorders, especially CAL spots and axillary freckling. The skin was inspected for nodules and palpated to detect subcutaneous ones. Data were also collected about birth, upbringing, school, vocational training, nervous trouble in childhood, drug abuse, mental or physical illness, in- or outpatient treatment and periods of sick certification. The subjective experiences of difficulties caused by neurofibromatosis were explored.

A general psychiatric interview about current mental problems was followed by a structured inquiry with the aid of the Comprehensive Psychopathological Rating Scale (CPRS) (Åsberg et al., 1978), which includes a wide range of both reported and observed psychiatric symptoms. In order to assess the level of intellectual performance, education authorities were contacted with requests for copies of school records and school leaving certificates stating whether normal, special, or remedial classes had been attended.

RESULTS

A total of 96 patients, 74 adults (20 years and older) and 22 children, were included in the study. The patients, 52 males and 44 females, ranged in age from 2 to 81 (mean 36.5) years. Of the adults, 28 were reported from dermatological departments, eight from psychiatric departments, eight from pathology departments, nine from internal medicine departments, 13 from surgical (most often plastic surgery) departments, and eight from other disciplines.

The prevalence of neurofibromatosis in Gothenburg was estimated to be 1/4,600 inhabitants. The age distribution of the patients with neurofibromatosis showed a significant reduction in number of older individuals (Samuelsson and Axelsson, 1981), indicating an excess mortality in the disease (Figure 2).

Only 69 of the 74 adults allowed physical and neurological examinations; information about the remaining five adults had to be col-

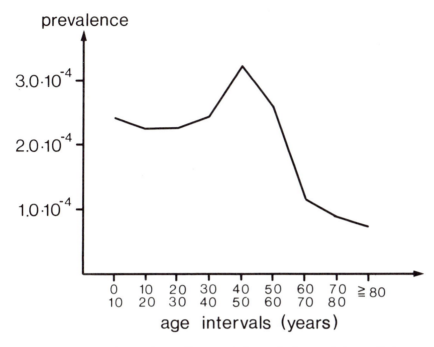

Figure 2.   Prevalence of neurofibromatosis by age in the population studied.

lected from medical records. Although all 22 children were examined, they were excluded from the following presentation of somatic, neurological, and psychiatric findings because the clinical differences between adults and children have been described elsewhere (Samuelsson and Axelsson, 1981).

Somatic Findings

Pigmentary Disorders   The majority of the 69 examined adults had six or more CAL spots with a widest diameter of at least 1.5 cm. Sixteen of the adults had 0–5 such spots, 23 had 6–10, 18 had 11–15, 10 had 16–20, and two had more than 20 spots. Older patients had significantly fewer CAL spots than younger ones ($P < 0.01$), probably because of bleaching of the spots with advancing age.

Neurofibromas   All 74 adults had neurofibromas. One of the 69 examined patients had less than 10, 21 had 10–99, 19 had 100–500, and 28 had more than 500 neurofibromas. The younger patients had significantly fewer neurofibromas than the older ones ($P < 0.01$). The cutaneous or subcutaneous nodules were generally scattered over the trunk and limbs. The greater the number of neurofibromas on the body, the more frequent also were nodules in the face and, in some cases, the soles and/or palms.

Osseous Dysplasias   Dysplasia of the tibia was found in three patients and of the orbital region in three. Two patients had severe scoliosis with respiratory insufficiency and five had moderate thoracic scoliosis.

Malignant Disease   Three out of seven patients with malignant disease were found to have sarcoma.

Pheochromocytoma   Operations for pheochromocytoma had been required in two patients. Increased blood pressure was noted in 12 patients.

Neurological Findings

In one-third of the patients, the neurological findings suggested central nervous system involvement by neurofibromatosis.

Hearing   The hearing was impaired in 12 patients, eight with bilateral and four with unilateral hearing loss. Ten of these patients had mental retardation of borderline character, combined with mental illness in seven.

Vision   Impaired vision was found in 10 patients, involving one eye only in nine and combined with strabismus in four. Four of these 10 patients had borderline mental retardation combined with mental illness.

Epilepsy   Two adults had epilepsy of the grand mal type. In a woman, the seizures had first occurred at the age of 20, and in a man at the age of 29 years.

Psychiatric Findings

Three grades were used in the global rating of mental illness, according to the CPRS scale: grade 1 indicated minimal illness, grade 2 moderate and definite illness, and grade 3 severe or incapacitating illness. One-third of the examined adults (23 out of 69) were diagnosed as mentally ill. The psychiatric diagnoses and rated severity of the disorders are given in Table 1. Fifteen of the patients had previously received psychiatric inpatient treatment, most commonly with the diagnoses of mental retardation, organic brain disease, chronic alcoholism, and depressive neurosis. Most of the patients suffered from nervous symptoms. The majority reported hostile feelings (52%) and autonomic disturbances (51%). Other frequent items from the CPRS scale were inner tension (33%), aches and pains (33%), worry over trifles (32%), fatiguability (32%), and reduced sleep (29%).

Intelligence Level

The intelligence level was estimated with the aid of data on school performance, educational and vocational careers, previous tests results

Table 1. Psychiatric findings in 69 patients with neurofibromatosis

Main psychiatric diagnosis	Number of patients	Global assessment of mental illness		
		Grade 1	Grade 2	Grade 3
Depressive syndrome	7	1	4	2
Anxiety states (+vegetative dysfunction)	6	5	1	
Organic brain syndrome	5	2	1	2
(Pre-)senile dementia	3		1	2
Chronic alcoholism	1			1
Mental defect (after chronic psychosis)	1			1
Total	23	8	7	8

when available, and a global assessment. Because of lack of information, three of the 74 adult patients could not be assessed. Normal intelligence was indicated in 39 patients, borderline mental retardation (requiring remedial education) in 30, and slight mental retardation (requiring special education) in two. None of the patients was severely mentally retarded.

There is reason to suspect that neurofibromatosis itself leads to some impairment of intellectual development in all patients, because the intellectual achievements of those whose intelligence was judged to be within the normal range appeared to fall short of the average. None of the patients with normal intelligence had passed any academic examination and many showed achievements inferior to those of their healthy relatives. In certain families, the disease appeared more often to be associated with mild mental retardation than in others. It was not possible to make any systematic investigation of this. Patients with mild mental retardation did not show any significantly increased proportion with severe somatic disease.

Severity of Neurofibromatosis

Classification of the patients according to severity of the manifestations of neurofibromatosis showed a mild grade in 18 patients, a moderately severe grade in 43, and a severe grade in 13. Mild neurofibromatosis involved mainly cosmetic problems. Patients with more than 100 nodules scattered over the body but without pronounced disability were considered to have moderately severe neurofibromatosis. The severe cases included patients with neurofibrosarcoma, extensive plexiform neurofibromas, severe scoliosis, or dysplasia of the tibia. The classification was used for descriptive purposes and to determine whether

Table 2.   *P*-values for correlations between clinical findings[a]

	Mental retardation	Positive neurological findings	Grade of neurofibromatosis
Mental illness	0.0003	0.0003	n.s. (0.06)
Mental retardation	—	n.s. (0.07)	n.s.
Positive neurological findings	—	—	n.s. (0.07)
Grade of neurofibromatosis	—	—	—

[a] Test for trend in contingency table; n.s. = nonsignificant.

frequency and degree of mental disorders varied with the severity of neurofibromatosis.

Correlations between Different Findings

The most important clinical findings and their intercorrelations are given in Table 2. Patients with mental illness, compared to those without, were significantly more often affected by slight mental retardation. Neurological findings indicating central nervous system involvement by neurofibromatosis were also significantly more common in these patients. There was a tendency toward a more severe grade of neurofibromatosis in patients with mental illness than in others, but the difference was not statistically significant. As expected, disability pension was often required by patients with multiple handicaps, severe grade of neurofibromatosis, and mental disorders.

Genetic Analysis

Determination of familial and sporadic cases was made for comparative purposes. Cases with reliable information showing that parents and siblings of the propositus were unaffected were considered to be sporadic, whereas cases with one affected parent were classed as familial. Among the 74 adult patients, there were 35 familial and 32 sporadic cases, with uncertainty in the remaining seven cases because of lack of information (Table 3). Men were in the majority among the familial cases, and most of the sporadic cases were women.

No clinical difference was found between the familial and sporadic cases, both of which showed a wide range of manifestations. The two groups did not differ with regard to degree of severity of the disease or in respect to psychiatric disorders. The distribution within sibships and the parental age at delivery among the sporadic cases did not differ from the expected random distribution. Two of the sporadic cases with segmental distribution of lesions were interpreted as representing new somatic mutations.

Table 3.   Familial and sporadic cases among 74 patients with
neurofibromatosis

	Men	Women	Both sexes
Familial cases	22	13	35
Sporadic cases	11	21	32
Undetermined	5	2	7
Total	38	36	74

The familial analysis confirmed the findings of other authors that
neurofibromatosis shows full penetrance and is inherited in an autosomal dominant way. The 74 adults in our study had a total of 69
children, and the fact that 36 of these children were affected and 33
healthy was in full accordance with the expectations of a dominantly
inherited disease. Furthermore, there was no sequence of diseased-
healthy-diseased in any of the 74 family trees examined.

Mutation Frequency   On the basis of the sporadic cases, the mutation frequency of neurofibromatosis was estimated with the aid of
the so-called direct method of calculation. The following, extremely
high, mutation frequency was obtained:

$$M = \tfrac{1}{2} \times \frac{29}{337979} = 4.3 \times 10^{-5}$$

Gene Sources   The genealogical investigation of possible gene
sources included particulars of about 3,000 ancestors of the patients
in Gothenburg with known neurofibromatosis. Although the families,
as a rule, were traced back to the middle of the eighteenth century, it
proved impossible to detect families with common ancestors or geo-
graphical origin. There was no tendency to clustering in any geograph-
ical area, and the ancestral origin showed random distribution.

Our negative findings were in accordance with the expected consequences of a disease with a high mutation frequency, low fertility,
and reduced life expectancy. Because no progressive increase of the
frequency of neurofibromatosis has been noticed in the population, new
mutants must be compensated by a relatively rapid elimination of the
gene from the population, which also reduces the possibility of a common origin.

REFERENCES

Åsberg, M., Perris, C., Schalling, D., and Sedvall, G. 1978. The Comprehensive Psychopathological Rating Scale: Development and application of a
psychiatric rating scale. Acta Psychiatr. Scand., Suppl. 271.

Crowe, F. W., Schull, W. J., and Neel, J. V. 1956. A Clinical, Pathological and Genetic Study of Multiple Neurofibromatosis. Charles C Thomas Publisher, Springfield, Illinois.

Samuelsson, B. 1981. Neurofibromatosis—A Clinical-Psychiatric and Genetic Study. Gotab. Kungälv, Göteborg, Sweden.

Samuelsson, B., and Axelsson, R. 1981. Neurofibromatosis. Acta Derm. Venereol. [Suppl.] (Stockh.) 95:67–71.

Treves, F. 1885. A case of congenital deformity. Trans. Pathol. Soc. 36:494–498.

Whitehouse, D. 1966. Diagnostic value of the café-au-lait spot in children. Arch. Dis. Child. 41:316–319.

PERSPECTIVES AND PROGRESS IN MENTAL RETARDATION
Volume II—Biomedical Aspects
Edited by J. M. Berg

SJÖGREN-LARSSON SYNDROME
Update of a Clinical, Genetic, and Epidemiological Study

S. Jagell,[1] **K.-H. Gustavson,**[2] **and G. Holmgren**[3]

[1] *Department of Pediatrics, University Hospital of Uppsala,
750 14 Uppsala, Sweden*
[2] *Department of Clinical Genetics, University Hospital of Uppsala,
750 14 Uppsala, Sweden*
[3] *Department of Clinical Genetics, University Hospital, 901 85 Umeå,
Sweden*

Sjögren-Larsson syndrome is a disorder with autosomal recessive inheritance, characterized by congenital ichthyosis, spastic di/tetraplegia, and mental retardation. The syndrome has been studied in a countrywide survey in Sweden on the basis of 59 identified patients in 42 families. Glistening dots in the fundus of the eye seem to be a fourth cardinal sign. Fatty acid patterns of plasma lipids indicate defects in metabolism of essential fatty acids.

The Sjögren-Larsson syndrome (SLS) is characterized by mental retardation, spastic diplegia or tetraplegia, and congenital ichthyosis, with an autosomal recessive mode of inheritance (Sjögren and Larsson, 1957) (Figure 1). The syndrome, which was originally described in Sweden, has been studied by us in a countrywide Swedish survey. A total of 59 SLS patients in 42 families were identified, 36 of them still alive in 1982. All the SLS patients developed the full syndrome.

FREQUENCY AND LOCATION

The mean incidences per 100,000 persons in the years 1901–81 were found to be 0.6 in the whole of Sweden, 10.2 in the county of Väster-

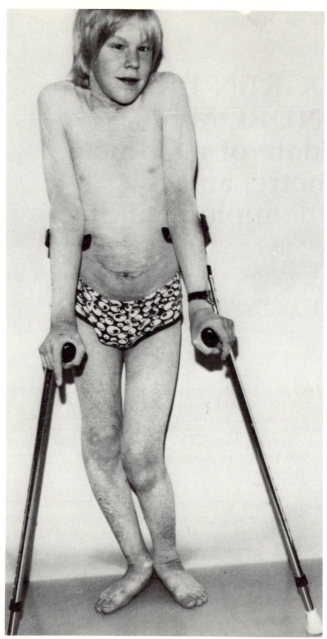

Figure 1.   Thirteen-year-old boy with spastic diplegia, mild mental retardation, and generalized ichthyosis (Sjögren-Larsson syndrome). Reprinted by permission from: Jagell, S., and Lidén, S. 1982. Ichthyosis in the Sjögren-Larsson syndrome. Clin. Genet. 21:243–252.

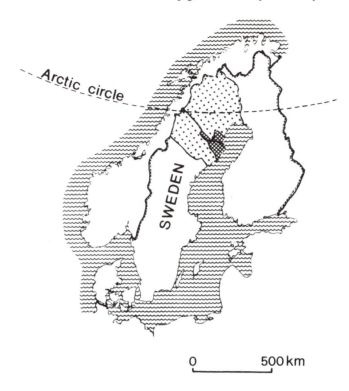

0 _____ 500 km

Figure 2.   Map of Sweden showing the counties of Norrbotten and Västerbotten (dotted) and the Sjögren-Larsson syndrome area (crosshatched). Reprinted by permission from: Jagell, S., Gustavson, K.-H., and Holmgren, G. 1981. Sjögren-Larsson syndrome in Sweden: A clinical, genetic and epidemiological study. Clin. Genet. 19:233–256.

botten, and 2.6 in the county of Norrbotten. The prevalence figures for SLS on December 31, 1981 were estimated to be 0.4, 8.7, and 2.6 per 100,000 persons, the frequencies of SLS gene carriers 0.5%, 2.0%, and 1.0%, and the gene frequencies 0.0002, 0.010, and 0.005, respectively.

Of the 59 identified Swedish SLS patients, 46 were born in a restricted area in the northeast of Sweden (Figure 2). Ancestors of most patients from this area were traced back to the late seventeenth century (as many as 10 generations often could be identified from church records) without a common ancestor being found (Figure 3). This is not surprising if the gene was well distributed in the population, which seems probable. Most SLS individuals were related to other patients with the syndrome. Parental consanguinity was noted in one-fourth of the SLS families, but the parents' relationship was usually distant.

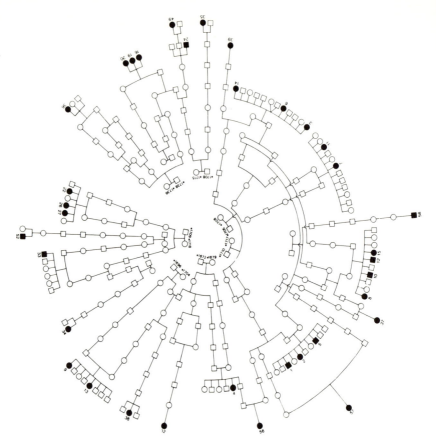

Figure 3.   Pedigrees of families from the Sjögren-Larsson syndrome area. Filled quadrants = affected males; filled circles = affected females; * = birth year.

Autosomal recessive inheritance was supported on the basis of a sex ratio (male/female) close to 1, healthy parents, and consanguinity in and blood relationships between many of the SLS families (Jagell et al., 1981a).

The mean yearly incidence of SLS in the county of Västerbotten (10/100,000) will probably remain at its relatively high level until further migration of people to and from this county lowers the SLS gene frequency. On the other hand, the very low incidence of SLS in southern and central Sweden (0.1/100,000) due to the low frequency of the SLS gene will remain low but show local variations influenced by chance.

In 1957 the mean life expectancy for persons with SLS was about half that of the general population (Sjögren and Larsson, 1957). Most deceased SLS individuals died from respiratory diseases at a young age. Another probable reason for the low mean life expectancy was poor living conditions. Nowadays, this group of patients are not more susceptible to infections than the general population and the rate of mortality due to infections is low. Both the life expectancy and the prevalence of SLS have increased considerably during the last two decades and will probably increase further.

CLINICAL FINDINGS

Congenital Ichthyosis

The ichthyosis in the SLS patients was always present at birth to a slight or, most often, moderate degree (Figure 4). The parents, who are heterozygotes for the SLS gene, had normal skin. The ichthyosis showed furfuraceous, lamellar, and, most frequently, nonscaly hyperkeratosis in various combinations in the same individual. It was generalized, with a predilection for flexures, the sides and back of the neck, and the lower abdomen (Figure 1). The hair and nails were clinically normal, as was, in most cases, the ability to sweat. The DNA synthesis in the epidermis was increased, as was the production of keratin. The ichthyosis in SLS belongs to the rather heterogeneous group of hyperkinetic ichthyoses named "lamellar ichthyosis," recessive congenital ichthyosis, or nonbullous ichthyosiform erythroderma (Jagell and Lidén, 1982). The histopathological picture of the skin was characterized by a thick stratum corneum with slight parakeratosis, a thickened stratum granulosum, acanthosis, and papillomatosis (Hofer and Jagell, 1982).

Dermatoglyphics

Variations in the frequencies of dermatoglyphic patterns in the SLS patients, compared with normal controls, indicate an early prenatal pathological influence on the formation of dermatoglyphics in the syndrome. However, the dermatoglyphic alterations were not sufficiently pronounced to be of diagnostic value in individual cases (Gustavson and Jagell, 1980).

Neurological, Neurophysiological, and other Somatic Investigations

About half of the 36 SLS patients alive in 1982 were born preterm with a normal weight and length for their gestational age. The prematurity did not have any prognostic importance (Jagell and Heijbel, 1982). The first observation of pathological reflexes, muscular hypertonia, and

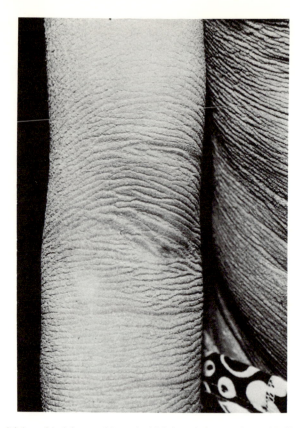

Figure 4.   Right cubital fossa with typical ichthyosis in a patient with Sjögren-Larsson syndrome. Reprinted by permission from: Jagell, S., and Lidén, S. 1982. Ichthyosis in the Sjögren-Larsson syndrome. Clin. Genet. 21:243–252.

paresis in the legs, as well as of mental retardation, was made between the ages of 4 and 30 months. Neurological symptoms were noticed earlier in those who later turned out to have severe motor handicaps. All patients were diagnosed as having spastic diplegia during childhood.

Most patients had several orthopedic operations to improve the function of the legs and feet. Height was reduced as a result of shortness of the legs, kyphosis, scoliosis, and contractures in hip and knee joints. Sensory and motor conduction velocity and EMG did not reveal any dysfunction of the sensory system or of the peripheral motor neurons. No specific morphological abnormalities or atrophic changes of the brain were found in five SLS patients examined by cranial computed tomography. Mental retardation was noted in all the SLS patients and was severe (IQ below 50) in two-thirds of them. There were no ob-

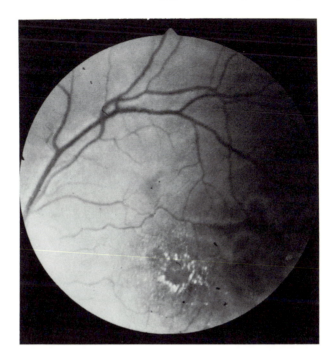

Figure 5.   Glistening dots in the fovea of the eye in a patient with Sjögren-Larsson syndrome. Reprinted by permission from: Jagell, S., Polland, W., and Sandgren, O. 1980. Specific changes in the fundus typical for the Sjögren-Larsson syndrome. An ophthalmological study of 35 patients. Acta Ophthalmol. 58:321–330.

servations of progression of the mental retardation. Disturbed mineralization of the permanent teeth was a common finding (unpublished data).

Ophthalmological Investigations

In the retina there were small white glistening dots located in the macular region and arranged in a circle (Figure 5). These dots, which were noted in all 30 SLS patients examined in this respect, are not known in other disorders and seem to be pathognomonic for SLS. The dots varied in number from about five to 50, with approximately the same number in each eye in any one person. It is not known at what age the dots first become visible, but in the present study the youngest patient found with these dots was only 12 months old. An increasing number or size of the dots with advancing age might be expected if the disease has a progressive course. We have not followed individual patients to see whether this number or size increases with age. In the whole group of SLS patients, no correlation was found between the number of dots and either age or the severity of spasticity, mental retardation, or ichthyosis (Jagell et al., 1980).

Biochemical Investigations

A metabolic study of urinary samples from 35 SLS patients was performed by means of a series of chemical tests and by analysis of amino acid pattern with high-voltage paper electrophoresis. Organic acids were analyzed by gas chromatography–mass spectrometry, and qualitative analyses for mono- and disaccharides were performed by thin-layer chromatography on cellulose. These analyses revealed no error in metabolism of amino acids, organic acids, or carbohydrates (Holmgren et al., 1981).

The fatty acid patterns of plasma phospholipids, cholesterol esters, triglycerides, and free fatty acids in SLS patients were examined. Mainly in plasma phospholipids, but to a lesser degree also in the cholesterol esters, triglycerides, and free fatty acids, the relative concentrations of metabolites derived from linoleic acid by Δ^6 desaturation were found to be significantly lower than in controls, suggesting a defect in polyunsaturated fatty acid (PUFA) metabolism in SLS. The defect appears to lie in the Δ^6 desaturation of PUFA metabolism, because the relative concentrations of plasma long-chain ω^6 acids derived from linoleic acid were lower than in controls (Hernell et al., 1982). Serum zinc and serum copper levels were examined in 18 of the individuals with SLS and no indications of disturbed zinc or copper metabolism were found (Jagell et al., 1981b).

DISCUSSION

Our genetic analyses strongly support an autosomal recessive mode of inheritance of SLS with full penetrance. The concentration of SLS patients to a restricted area in northeastern Sweden is probably the result of a founder effect—transmission of a SLS gene mutation from early immigrants to this area followed by little migration to or from the area. The founder effect hypothesis is supported by the observation that in only six of 42 families with SLS children were one or both parents born *outside* the two northern-most counties in Sweden. Ancestors of SLS patients are known to have been among the first immigrants to this area in the early fourteenth century.

Correct delineation and diagnosis of SLS is of fundamental importance for genetic and epidemiological investigations as well as for pathogenic studies and evaluation of the effects of treatment. SLS should be suspected in a child with slight or moderate ichthyosis present at birth. The ichthyosis never has a "collodion-membrane" appearance at birth. SLS is confirmed when signs of spastic diplegia and mental retardation develop; these findings were noted in the Swedish patients between 6 and 30 months of age.

Generalized, dry, slight or moderately hyperkeratotic skin, sometimes with erythema, is always present at birth in SLS patients, indicating a form of congenital ichthyosis. Autosomal recessive inheritance of congenital ichthyosis, also called "lamellar ichthyosis," must be suspected if the parents themselves do not have ichthyosis. Other rare syndromes with congenital ichthyosis are known, but SLS is the most common. The SLS diagnosis is supported by typical, but not pathognomonic, histopathological features (Hofer and Jagell, 1982).

SLS is characterized by disturbed function of the central nervous system causing mental retardation, and moderate or pronounced spastic paresis affecting the lower extremities more than the upper. Our neurological findings do not differ from those previously reported in SLS or in spastic di- or tetraplegia with mental retardation of other origins. The degree of motor handicap parallels the severity of the mental retardation. None of our clinical observations supported the concept of a progressive course of the disease. However, a slight progression of the motor handicap may be masked by beneficial effects of physiotherapy or of orthopedic corrective operations, or it may be too slight to be recognized with present examination techniques.

We have found that glistening dots in the fundus of the eye is an additional cardinal sign of SLS. The pathogenic significance of these dots is unknown. They occur in the area of the macula where the ganglion cells are numerous, and may be a sign of ganglion degeneration or fatty degeneration of microglial cells. This presumed degeneration may be the cause of reduced visual acuity found in many SLS patients. Similar changes might also be present in other parts of the central nervous system in SLS patients and be related to the motor handicap and the mental retardation.

Our results of analyses of the fatty acid pattern in plasma of SLS patients indicated a defect in the Δ^6 desaturation of PUFA metabolism. The decrease of plasma long-chain ω^6 acids derived metabolically from linoleic acid might affect the composition and function of cellular membranes, with a shift of microsomal, mitochondrial, and extracellular membranes in composition and perhaps also in function. It is tempting to speculate that an abnormal composition of PUFA in structural lipids such as phospholipids could be the underlying cause of SLS. Analysis of PUFA may have a diagnostic value in differentiating SLS from various conditions with congenital ichthyosis and mental retardation in which spasticity does not develop.

Compensation for some of the results of the metabolic defects in essential fatty acid metabolism may be afforded by diets rich in γ-linolenic acid ($18:3 \omega^6$), arachidonic acid ($20:4 \omega^6$), and long-chain ω^3 acids. Alternatively, the Δ^6 desaturase activity can perhaps be enhanced by zinc supplementation. However, zinc deficiency has not been found in SLS (Jagell et al., 1981b). In a dietary trial, γ-linolenic acid (Primrose oil) was given for 3 months to nine SLS patients ages 1 to 61 years. Blood samples for lipid analyses were collected before and after the institution of the treatment. No clinical effects on skin (ichthyosis) or neurological symptoms were seen. We also treated the ichthyosis of seven patients with SLS with an aromatic retinoid (etretinate) for 6 months. Very good results were registered, measured both as clinical improvement and as reduction in the quantity of emollients needed. No unexpected side effects were noted (Jagell and Lidén, 1983).

REFERENCES

Gustavson, K.-H., and Jagell, S. 1980. Dermatoglyphic patterns in the Sjögren-Larsson syndrome. Clin. Genet. 17:120–124.

Hernell, O., Holmgren, G., Jagell, S., Johnson, S., and Holman, R. T. 1982. Suspected faulty essential fatty acid metabolism in Sjögren-Larsson syndrome. Pediatr. Res. 16:45–49.

Hofer, P. A., and Jagell, S. 1982. Sjögren-Larsson syndrome. A dermato-histopathological study. J. Cutan. Pathol. 9:360–376.

Holmgren, G., Jagell, S., Seeman, H., and Steen, C. 1981. Urinary amino acids and organic acids in the Sjögren-Larsson syndrome. Clin. Genet. 20:64–66.

Jagell, S., Gustavson, K.-H., and Holmgren, G. 1981a. Sjögren-Larsson syndrome in Sweden. A clinical, genetic and epidemiological study. Clin. Genet. 19:233–256.

Jagell, S., Hallmans, G., and Gustavson, K.-H. 1981b. Zinc and copper concentration in serum of patients with congenital ichthyosis, spastic di- or tetraplegia and mental retardation (Sjögren-Larsson syndrome). Uppsala J. Med. Sci. 86:291–295.

Jagell, S., and Heijbel, J. 1982. Sjögren-Larsson syndrome. Physical and neurological features. A survey of 35 patients. Helv. Paediatr. Acta 37:519–530.

Jagell, S., and Lidén, S. 1982. Ichthyosis in the Sjögren-Larsson syndrome. Clin. Genet. 21:243–252.

Jagell, S., and Lidén, S. 1983. Treatment of the ichthyosis of the Sjögren-Larsson syndrome with etretinate (Tigason). Acta Derm. Venereol. (Stockh.). 63:89–92.

Jagell, S., Polland, W., and Sandgren, O. 1980. Specific changes in the fundus typical for the Sjögren-Larsson syndrome. An ophthalmological study of 35 patients. Acta Ophthalmol. 58:321–330.

Sjögren, T., and Larsson, T. 1957. Oligophrenia in combination with congenital ichthyosis and spastic disorders. Acta Psychiatr. Scand. 32(suppl. 113):1–113.

PERSPECTIVES AND PROGRESS IN MENTAL RETARDATION
Volume II—Biomedical Aspects
Edited by J. M. Berg

MATERNAL PHENYLKETONURIA IN THE REPUBLIC OF IRELAND

S. O'Connor[1] and M. Mulcahy[2]

[1] *Department of Sociology, University of Toronto, 563 Spadina Avenue, Toronto M5S 1A1, Canada*
[2] *The Medico-Social Research Board, 73 Lower Baggot Street, Dublin 2, Ireland*

A research project aimed at the identification and assessment of maternal phenylketonuria in the Republic of Ireland is described. Problems concerned with follow-up and diet are illustrated. The pregnancy outcome in five cases is reported.

A study on the prevalence of phenylketonuria (PKU) in the Republic of Ireland in 1974, conducted by the Medico-Social Research Board (Chadwick et al., 1977), highlighted the problem posed by the increasing number of fertile women with PKU. Since Dent (1957) reported the birth of nonPKU mentally handicapped offspring to a PKU mother there has been increasing evidence that persistent maternal hyperphenylalaninemia during pregnancy is harmful to the fetus in most cases (Lenke and Levy, 1980). In view of this it was decided, in 1978, to establish a register of females of childbearing age with PKU, and a renewed effort was made to determine the exact prevalence of PKU.

This effort consisted chiefly of following up persons for whom diagnostic confirmation was not available at the initial enquiry. Personal contacts were made with pediatricians and other doctors involved and, as a result, a further 39 adult cases were added to the 1974 figure of 211. In addition, between November 1, 1974 and December 31, 1979, 91 children with PKU were born. Thus, the total number of cases known on January 31, 1978 was 341. Twelve cases of hyperphenylalaninemia had also been identified up to that date, and are included in the age and sex breakdown in Table 1. Although hyperphenylalani-

Table 1. Phenylketonuria in the Republic of Ireland by age and sex—January 1, 1980

Age group	All cases			Cases outside residential centers		
	Male	Female	Total	Male	Female	Total
0–4	31	35	66	31	35	66
5–9	32	32	64	32	32	64
10–14	33	37	70	33	35	68
15–19	25	22	47	20	14	34
20–24	14	20	34	8	12	20
25–29	14	8	22	3	5	8
30–34	7	10	17	1	1	2
35–39	4	3	7	1	1	2
40 and over	13	10	23	2	2	4
Age unknown	1	2	3			
Total	174	179	353	131	137	268[a]

[a] The 85 additional persons identified as having PKU are in residential centers.

nemia differs from PKU in its biochemical manifestations, it is equally dangerous in terms of fetal outcome.

It is notable that there is a marked decrease in the numbers of cases of known PKU in the age group 15–19 and over (Table 1). Two possible reasons can be suggested for this. First, because screening was not initiated until 1966, those born prior to 1966 only came to attention either because of mental handicap or because of the detection of PKU in siblings; consequently not all those with PKU may have been identified. Second, there may be a higher than average mortality among persons with untreated PKU.

MATERNAL PKU REGISTER

The initial entrants onto the register of females of childbearing age with PKU were those females born prior to the introduction of the National Screening Programme in 1966. Thirty-five such females presently living in the community were identified. Nine of this group are either severely or profoundly mentally handicapped. Thus, the remaining 26 are taken as the population at risk. Given the aim of establishing procedures for ensuring appropriate treatment in the event of pregnancy, it was decided to make personal contact with the females at risk. At the request of the treating pediatrician six of the 26 were not contacted. For the 20 females contacted the procedures adopted were as follows:

1. The relevant Director of Community Care (Community Physician) was informed about the project. In seven cases the girl concerned

Table 2.   Dietary status at time of contact related to intellectual functioning

Dietary status	Intellectual functioning			
	Average/dull normal	Mild mental handicap	Moderate mental handicap	Total
On diet	4	3	—	7
Previously on diet	—	4	1	5
Never on diet	2	4	2	8
Total	6	11	3	20

was not known to the Director as having PKU. The name of the family doctor was obtained from the Director of Community Care.

2. Permission of the family doctor was sought to contact the patient and her family. Agreement was received in all cases.

3. At the first visit the dietary status was established (Table 2) and the complications associated with pregnancy in the case of females with PKU were explained to the parents. Thirteen of the families were not aware of these complications; in the cases of those who were aware, the girls were still on diet in six cases and in the other had recently come off diet. In two families, siblings had not been tested for PKU. These tests were arranged.

The cases fell into three groups as far as dietary status was concerned:

1. Seven were on diet at the time of contact.

2. Five had been on diet in the past, two up to the age of 18 and the other three up to the age of 5 or 6.

3. Eight had never been on diet.

PROCEDURE

The objective that evolved following consultation with the main treatment center (the Metabolic Unit at Temple Street Hospital, Dublin) was to try to continue or reintroduce full dietary control in every case. In view of the complication of mental handicap and other problems this objective was to prove only partly realizable. However, regular contact was established and maintained with all the females at risk. Contact was more frequent with those who had never been on or had not gone back on diet (13 cases). In these cases the importance of commencing the diet prior to pregnancy was stressed. In the event of this not taking place it was strongly urged that as soon as a pregnancy was suspected the family doctor and the hospital should be notified with a view to immediate introduction of the diet. The regular contacts for this purpose revealed the difficulties experienced particularly by those women with mental handicap. These related chiefly to training and employment opportunities and the absence of social outlets. Referrals to appropriate service agencies were made where possible.

By September 1980 diet had been successfully introduced in three cases and refused in seven cases (see "Discussion" below). In the remaining three cases it was still under discussion. The following case histories illustrate the types of situation encountered.

Never on Diet—Diet Successfully Introduced

Case A (born 1966) is the only female and youngest child in a family of six. One brother has also been identified as having PKU. He was never on diet and is working in open employment. PKU was detected in this girl at the age of 6 following referral to a pediatrician because of underfunctioning at school. She has been found to be functioning within the mild mental handicap range and is attending a special school. This family was not aware of the implications of maternal PKU and had had no contact with a treatment service. Introduction of the diet had not been previously suggested and the mother reacted positively at once. The girl, who was 13 when the diet was introduced, has accepted it well and manages it adequately herself.

Previously on Diet—Successful Reintroduction

Case C (born 1959) was identified as having PKU at 11 months and was on diet up to the age of 6. The diet was discontinued by her mother, who felt that she might be undernourished because she was starting school. In addition, at this time the mother was caring for a severely mentally handicapped son who was 11 years older than C and also had PKU; this boy has since died.

Although not aware of the exact implications of maternal PKU, this woman's mother had been concerned that there might be complications in pregnancy; thus she was very willing to cooperate in the reintroduction of the diet. The diet was reintroduced at the age of 20 and has not presented any major problems since. C was identified as mildly mentally handicapped and spent 8 years in a residential special school. On leaving school she worked as a kitchen helper. She has since transferred to a community workshop for training as a machinist; she is making good progress and is expected to be ready for open employment within a year. She is engaged to be married and intends to marry in 2 years time. A female sibling age 23 had not been tested for PKU; test results showed that she did not have it.

Previously on Diet—Failed Reintroduction

Case F (born 1958), was detected at the age of 2 and this woman remained on diet up to age 18. She was identified as mildly mentally handicapped at the age of 7 and attended a special school on a 5-day residential basis until the age of 18. Apparently, very great difficulties were experienced with the diet both at school and at home. The mother reported that the child had to be forced to take the diet at school, and at home the rest of the family and the mother in particular partook of a restricted diet in an effort to get the child to adhere to her diet.

This woman is now working in open employment and is leading a normal social life. Her mother refuses to discuss the implications of PKU in pregnancy with her at present because she feels it would cause a serious emotional upset to her daughter. The mother feels at this stage that the most appropriate time to inform her daughter of these facts will be if and when she decides to marry. The local public health nurse is aware of the situation and keeps in contact with the family.

Never on Diet—Failed Introduction

Case I (born 1958) is the second eldest in a family of five. She has never been on diet. She was identified as having PKU at the age of 10 when a brother was detected under the National Screening Programme. One other brother who was then age 6 was also found to have PKU. Neither of the two older children was put on diet. Both had at this stage been identified as mildly mentally handicapped and were attending special schools. Case I went to a residential workshop after she had finished school and is now engaged in domestic-type employment. This family was not aware of the implications of maternal PKU. The feasibility of introducing the diet was discussed; however, the mother does not regard the diet as feasible at present and feels that her daughter is unlikely to marry or have children. Regular contact is maintained with the family.

DISCUSSION

The females with PKU described in this paper are unusual in that they were born prior to the introduction of the National Screening Programme in 1966 and, with the exception of one girl, PKU was not detected within the first 2 weeks of life. In contrast, the majority of females coming onto the register in future will have been on diet consistently since soon after birth and will probably be functioning within the range of average intelligence. It is likely that they will remain on diet, so that the question of resumption of diet will not arise, and it can be expected that they will be able to assume greater responsibility for their dietary control than many of the present population. However, it is notable that eight children with PKU born after 1966 were identified in the Census of the Mentally Handicapped in 1974. Six of these are

Table 3. Pregnancy outcome in maternal PKU, 1979–81

Case	Dietary treatment	Child's birth weight	Neonatal problems
F.M.	Preconception	3300	Normal
M.C.	Preconception	3200	Normal
M.G.	Uncontrolled	3490 ⎫	Microcephaly, severely
Y.C.	None	2460 ⎭	mentally handicapped
A.D.	None before 36 weeks	3490	Still-birth, microcephaly

female and are living in the community. Thus, it is possible that at least some future entrants onto the register will be similar in many respects to the present study population.

It is notable also that three of the girls who had been previously on diet did not resume it. All three families had perceived their experience with the diet in a very negative way. Two of the other females who did not take up the diet come from families where there were problems with siblings in adhering to it. Thus, familiarity with the diet is no guarantee of adherence in adulthood, and it is possible that some females born after the introduction of the National Screening Programme may not adhere to the diet and/or be prepared to attend clinics on a regular basis, particularly in adulthood. This points to the crucial importance of continuous contact with such families by professional personnel familiar with the implications of maternal PKU.

FOLLOW-UP

Subsequent to the demonstration by the Medico-Social Research Board that maternal PKU was a major problem in Ireland, a decision was made to transfer the register to the Metabolic Unit at Temple Street Children's Hospital from where further surveillance was to be directed. Since the transfer in 1980, five known pregnancies to PKU mothers have been reported. Their outcome is detailed in Table 3. Of the five infants involved, two are progressing normally. Two are both microcephalic and mentally handicapped; one was stillborn with associated microcephaly. Failure to achieve dietary control in the three affected cases has been ascribed to the following:

Case MG—Noncooperation with the treatment center to a major degree. A complicating factor was that both parents joined a religious sect that they claimed was against artificial diets.

Case YC—Had not been on diet since age 14. Was not contacted by us during setting up of register because of objection by treating pediatrician. This woman was 20 and single when her child was born. She had attended a school for the mildly mentally handicapped up to the age of 18.

Case AD—Contacted during the setting up of the register. At age 17 then, she had never been on diet, although two male siblings had and one was still; this family was one of those that experienced difficulty with the diet. Introduction of diet was discussed but not considered feasible by the family. On attendance at the treatment center, diet was again refused but she was persuaded to start at 36 weeks of pregnancy when she first presented for antenatal care.

COMPARISON WITH UNITED KINGDOM

The most recent figures from the United Kingdom register (Smith and Wolff, 1982) are interesting in that some untreated cases have apparently had successful outcomes. Of 26 pregnancies reported, 11 were terminated, one ended in spontaneous abortion, and there were 14 live births. Of the live births, two died in the neonatal period from heart defects, six were normal, five had head circumferences at the lower limit of normal, and only one had both reduced head circumference and definite mental retardation. Although there was a definite association between dietary status and suspected or real pathology in two cases, normal infants also were reported to mothers not on diet. Smith and Wolff concluded that the prognosis in the untreated case may not be altogether as bad as originally feared.

CONCLUSIONS

The treatment of PKU started in 1966, and the treated females are now entering the fertile period of life. Thus, the number of fertile women with PKU can be expected to increase annually for the next 30 years, i.e., until the first cohort reaches approximately age 45. At that stage the number of new entrants or treated females will be balanced by those no longer capable of reproducing. It is essential that registers of children with PKU be continued to include all adult cases. Various methods will be employed in different situations to prevent the complication of microcephaly and other harmful effects in maternal phenylketonuria. Among the options available in Ireland are genetic counseling, whereby pregnancies can be planned to coincide with the reintroduction of diet, maintaining all affected females on the phenylalanine-free diet throughout their reproductive lives, or advising against a pregnancy in all cases. However, a prerequisite for inter-

vention is that contact with a treatment center be maintained throughout the affected females' reproductive lives.

ACKNOWLEDGMENTS

We wish to thank Dr. D. Murphy and Dr. S. Cahalane of the Children's Hospital, Temple Street, Dublin for their help and cooperation, and the United
Kingdom Medical Research Council Steering Committee for permission to pub-
lish their data.

REFERENCES

Chadwick, G., Cahalane, S., and Mulcahy, M. 1977. Phenylketonuria in the
    Republic of Ireland, 1974. Irish Med. J. 70:612–614.
Dent, C. E. 1957. Discussion of Armstrong, M. D.: Relation of biochemical
    abnormality to development of mental defect in phenylketonuria. Etiologic
    factors in mental retardation. Report of twenty-third Ross Pediatric Research
    Conference, November 1956, p. 32. Ross Laboratories, Columbus, Ohio.
Lenke, R. R., and Levy, H. K. 1980. Maternal phenylketonuria and hyper-
    phenylalaninemia: An international survey of the outcome of untreated and
    treated pregnancies. N. Engl. J. Med. 303:1202–1208.
Smith, I., and Wolff, O. H. 1982. Phenylketonuria Register Newsletter, No.
    8. Medical Research Council/Department of Health and Social Security,
    London.

PERSPECTIVES AND PROGRESS IN MENTAL RETARDATION
Volume II—Biomedical Aspects
Edited by J. M. Berg

A STUDY OF MYOTONIC DYSTROPHY IN JAPAN

K. Takeshita, K. Tanaka, K. Ohno, and I. Eda
*Division of Child Neurology, Institute of Neurological Sciences,
Tottori University Medical School, Yonago 683, Japan*

An epidemiological, genetic, and biochemical analysis of early-onset myotonic dystrophy in the San-in district of Japan is reported. The prevalence of this early-onset form in patients under 30 years was 1.50×10^{-5}.
All patients showed definite mental retardation or borderline mentality.
Analysis of the pregnancies in which one parent had myotonic dystrophy
suggested that some maternal intrauterine factor could effect the early
onset of the disease in a genetically predisposed individual. It is also
suggested that a raised maternal serum deoxycholic acid level could cause
acid to cross the placenta and affect the fetus, resulting perhaps in abortion, stillbirth, or delayed development.

Myotonic dystrophy is an autosomal dominant disease with clinical
manifestations in many organ systems. Myotonia, muscular weakness,
cataract, frontal alopecia, involvement of the endocrine glands, cardiac
abnormalities, and mental disorders are common in this disease. Its
expression varies markedly, depending on the age at onset. Early-onset
myotonic dystrophy has also been called neonatal, congenital, and infantile myotonic dystrophy. In the neonatal form, facial muscle weakness, poor sucking and swallowing, respiratory difficulty, arthrogry-
posis, and various skeletal anomalies have been described. These
problems often improve within weeks to months after birth, but many
features of the adult form of the disease then appear at an unusually
early age. In the infantile form, hypotonia, talipes, muscle weakness,
and delayed motor and intellectual development can occur.

Mental retardation is arguably the most important feature of early-
onset myotonic dystrophy in terms of its effects on the child's development, even though it is not of diagnostic help in infancy and may be
difficult to assess accurately even at a later stage. In the authors' series,

This work was supported by funds from the Ministry of Health and Welfare, Japan.

nine out of 11 patients showed definite mental retardation and the remaining two had a borderline mental level. The IQ was between 40 and 90 with a mean of 63 ± 16. It has been reported (Watters and Williams, 1967; Harper, 1975) that almost all patients with early-onset myotonic dystrophy have an affected parent and over 90% of patients with the neonatal form have an affected mother.

The recognition of the clinical syndrome of early-onset myotonic dystrophy has raised a number of questions concerning its pathogenesis, inheritance, and other possible etiological factors. The following is a review of our epidemiological, genetic, and biochemical studies of the relationship between the early-onset form and the adult form, including consideration of the problem of maternal transmission.

EPIDEMIOLOGY

To collect myotonic dystrophy patients, records from all pediatric and neurological departments of public hospitals and prefectural institutions for the handicapped in the San-in district of Japan were surveyed. In addition, we obtained information from population surveys on myopathies, performed annually from 1973 to 1979. Suspected myotonic dystrophy cases were also collected, irrespective of age. All patients were reexamined neurologically and electromyographically and their serum creatine phosphokinase levels were determined. Selection was on the basis of clinical criteria and characteristic findings of electromyography for myotonic dystrophy.

Our investigation detected 49 confirmed myotonic dystrophy patients; 30 (61%) were males and 19 (39%) were females, all belonging to 20 families. In June 1980, 38 of these patients, ranging in age from 1 to 65 years, were alive, resulting in a prevalence in the San-in district of the disease in all forms of 2.73×10^{-5}, or 1 in 36,630 inhabitants (Takeshita et al., 1981). Of the 38 living patients, 11 had the early-onset form of the disease. The syndrome in these early-onset patients was characterized by generalized hypotonia, mental retardation or borderline mentality, delayed motor development, and striking facial muscle weakness. Our criterion for early onset was onset of the disease before 3 years of age. The prevalence, as of June 1980, of the early-onset form of the disease in the population under 30 years was 1.50×10^{-5} (1 in 66,667) (Takeshita et al., 1981) (Table 1).

GENETICS

As much information as possible was collected on all relatives of the patients, living and deceased, as well as on stillbirths and spontaneous

Table 1. Patients with myotonic dystrophy in the San-in district as of June, 1980

Age	Adult form			Early-onset form			Total	Population
	Male	Female	Subtotal	Male	Female	Subtotal		
0– 9	0	0	0	1	2	3	3	192,601
10–19	1	0	1	1	2	3	4	230,023 ⎱ 5,999,085
20–29	1	0	1	2	1	3	4	176,461 ⎰
30–39	3	5	8	2	0	2	10	195,684
40–49	5	2	7	0	0	0	7	201,387
50–59	4	3	7	0	0	0	7	165,083
60–	3	0	3	0	0	0	3	233,315
Total	17	10	27	6	5	11	38	1,394,554

Reprinted by permission from: Takeshita, K., et al. 1981. Survey of patients with early-onset myotonic dystrophy in the San-in district, Japan, Jpn. J. Hum. Genet. 26:295–300.

95

abortions in the extended family. Particular efforts were made to examine the siblings, parents, and grand-parents of affected individuals, irrespective of whether they were affected or not.

Analysis of 60 pregnancies in which one parent had myotonic dystrophy revealed that the rate of conception was similar irrespective of the sex of the affected parent (Table 2). However, the rate of healthy offspring, and of offspring developing the adult form of myotonic dystrophy, was approximately twofold higher when the father was affected. By contrast, in pregnancies in which the mother had the disease, the rate of offspring with neonatal onset of myotonic dystrophy was approximately seven times higher and the rate of spontaneous abortions also was significantly ($P < 0.05$) increased (Takeshita et al., 1981). These data suggest that a maternal intrauterine factor may affect fetal development in these cases, resulting in severe neonatal hypotonia or spontaneous abortion. The tendency for the mother to be the affected parent in patients with the neonatal form of myotonic dystrophy has been noted in previous reports (Watters and Williams, 1967; Harper, 1975).

BIOCHEMISTRY

A relationship between myotonic dystrophy and cholesterol metabolism has been demonstrated in human and animal experiments involving administration of a cholesterol synthesis inhibitor (Winer et al., 1965). Cholesterol metabolism is regulated by bile acids (Hofmann, 1977). In patients with myotonic dystrophy gallstones are a common complication (Kuhn, 1966), and such patients sometimes have a high level of serum γ-glutamyltranspeptidase activity, which may be a pointer to cholestasis (Alevizos et al., 1976). For these reasons we measured serum bile acids in five women ages 29 to 55 who were mothers of patients with early-onset myotonic dystrophy.

Bile acid in serum was extracted through a column of Amberlite XAD-2 (Ikawa et al., 1977). The extract was fractionated into sulfate-conjugated and nonsulfate-conjugated fractions through a column of Sephadex LH-20 (Makino et al., 1974) and treated by alkaline hydrolysis. After methylation and acetylation, samples of bile acids were analyzed by gas-liquid chromatography. Mass spectra of bile acids were obtained on a Hitachi M-80 gas chromatograph–mass spectrometer.

Analysis of serum bile acids in five female patients who had an affected child of early-onset form, two male patients with the adult type of the disease, and five controls is shown in Table 3. Total serum bile acids were normal in all of them, but the mothers of children with

Table 2.   Analysis of 60 pregnancies in which the father or mother (n = 24) had myotonic dystrophy

		Affected offspring							
		Healthy offspring (male:female)	Adult onset (male:female)	Infantile onset (male:female)	Neonatal onset (male:female)	Died at young age (male:female)	Stillbirths (male:female)	Spontaneous abortions	Total pregnancies
Affected husband / Healthy wife n = 14	No	15 (8:7)	9 (6:3)	3 (2:1)	1 (1:0)	1 (1:0)	3 (2:1)	0	32
	%	46.9	28.1	9.4	3.1	3.1	9.4	0.0	100.0
Healthy husband / Affected wife n = 10	No	7 (5:2)	3 (1:2)	1 (1:0)	6 (2:4)	2 (1:1)	1 (0:1)	8	28
	%	25.0	10.7	3.6	21.4	7.1	3.6	28.6 (p < 0.05)	100.0

Reprinted by permission from: Takeshita, K., et al. 1981. Survey of patients with early-onset myotonic dystrophy in the San-in district, Japan. Jpn. J. Hum. Genet. 26:295–300.

97

Table 3.   Analysis of serum bile acids in patients with the adult form of myotonic dystrophy (the identity of each component was confirmed by gas chromatography–mass spectrometry in comparison with authentic reference compounds)

	Female patients having affected child of early-onset form (N = 5)	Male patients (N = 2)	Controls (N = 5)
Non–sulfate-conjugated acids (μmol/L)			
Deoxycholic acid	2.14 ± 0.52	1.61 ± 0.02	0.65 ± 0.04
Chenodeoxycholic acid	1.79 ± 0.55	2.21 ± 0.79	2.30 ± 0.15
Cholic acid	0.39 ± 0.30	0.59 ± 0.23	1.47 ± 0.17
Ursodeoxycholic acid	0.50 ± 0.21	0.60 ± 0.04	1.07 ± 0.08
Hyocholic acid	0.89 ± 0.41	1.25 ± 0.07	0.94 ± 0.13
β-muricholic acid	1.04 ± 0.43	1.09 ± 0.05	trace
Sulfate-conjugated acids (μmol/L)			
Lithocholic acid	0.18 ± 0.12	0.26 ± 0.06	0.16 ± 0.04
Deoxycholic acid	0.11 ± 0.06	0.22 ± 0.20	not detected
Ursodeoxycholic acid	not detected	not detected	0.13 ± 0.01
Total	7.04 ± 1.06	7.83 ± 1.21	6.72 ± 0.36

the early-onset form differed strikingly from the controls with respect to deoxycholic acid. Their mean ($\pm$ SD) serum deoxycholic acid level was 2.14 ($\pm$ 0.52) μmol/L, three times that of controls (Tanaka et al., 1982). Ursodeoxycholic acid was hardly detectable in either the male or the female patients. This may be associated with accumulation of deoxycholic acid in serum. Maternal serum deoxycholic acid crosses the placenta (Sharp et al., 1971), is toxic to cells, and affects the breakdown and resynthesis of phosphatidylinositol in response to acetylcholine at nerve endings (Lapetina and Hawthorne, 1971). Thus an abnormal concentration of deoxycholic acid in maternal serum throughout pregnancy could affect the development of the embryo, resulting perhaps in abortion or neonatal hypotonia and delayed motor and mental development.

ACKNOWLEDGMENTS

We are grateful to the *Japanese Journal of Human Genetics* for permission to use Tables 1 and 2.

REFERENCES

Alevizos, B., Spengos, M., Vassilopoulos, D., and Stefanis, C. 1976. γ-Glutamyl transpeptidase, elevated activity in myotonic dystrophy. J. Neurol. Sci. 28:225–231.
Harper, P. S. 1975. Congenital myotonic dystrophy in Britain. 2. Genetic basis. Arch. Dis. Child. 50:514–521.
Hofmann, A. F. 1977. The enterohepatic circulation of bile acids in man. Clin. Gastroenterol. 6:3–24.
Ikawa, S., Yamamoto, T., Takita, M., Ogura, M., and Kishimoto, Y. 1977. Isolation of bile acids from biological fluids using Amberlite XAD-2. Yonago Acta Med. 21:76–82.
Kuhn, E., 1966. Myotonia congenita und Dystrophia congenita. In: P. S. Harper and E. Kuhn (eds.), Progressive Muskeldystrophie Myotonie: Myasthenie, p. 237. Springer, Berlin.
Lapetina, E. G., and Hawthorne, J. N. 1971. The diglyceride kinase of rat cerebral cortex. Biochem. J. 122:171–179.
Makino, I., Shinozaki, K., Nakagawa, S., and Mashimo, K. 1974. Measurement of sulfated and non-sulfated bile acids in human serum and urine. J. Lipid Res. 15:132–138.
Sharp, H. L., Peller, J., Carey, J. B., Jr., and Krivit, W. 1971. Primary and secondary bile acids in meconium. Pediatr. Res. 5:274–279.
Takeshita, K., Tanaka, K., Nakashima, T., and Kasagi, S. 1981. Survey of patients with early-onset myotonic dystrophy in the San-in district, Japan. Jpn. J. Hum. Genet. 26:295–300.
Tanaka, K., Takeshita, K., and Takita, M. 1982. The abnormalities of bile acids in serum and bile from patients with myotonic dystrophy. Clin. Sci. 62:627–642.

Watters, G. V., and Williams, T. W. 1967. Early onset myotonic dystrophy. Clinical and laboratory findings in five families and a review of the literature. Arch. Neurol. 17:137–152.

Winer, N., Maritt, J. M., Somers, J. E., Wolcott, L., Dale, H. E., and Burns, T. W. 1965. Induced myotonia in man and goat. J. Lab. Clin. Med. 66:758–769.

PERSPECTIVES AND PROGRESS IN MENTAL RETARDATION
Volume II—Biomedical Aspects
Edited by J. M. Berg
Copyright © 1984 by I.A.S.S.M.D.

SPECIFIC DISORDERS LEADING TO MENTAL RETARDATION IN FINLAND

M. V. Iivanainen

*Department of Neurology, University of Helsinki, Haartmaninkatu 4,
00290 Helsinki 29, Finland*

Recent studies in Finland have disclosed some specific and even new disorders in mentally retarded subjects, including aspartylglucosaminuria, mannosidosis, infantile neuronal ceroid-lipofuscinosis, atelencephaly, muscle-eye-brain disease, Salla disease, juvenile metachromatic leukodystrophy, fetal alcohol syndrome, moyamoya disease, and marker X–linked mental retardation. These studies show that investigation of the causes of mental retardation is fruitful and that the proportion of etiologically undefined cases can be considerably reduced. Early and precise diagnosis of mental retardation and its causes is important for optimum management of patients, appropriate support of relatives and guardians, and prevention of mental retardation.

Mental retardation is a serious social, financial, and emotional burden. Currently, more than 250 causes of mental retardation are known, but the percentage of unknown causes is still very substantial. A recent study indicated that thorough biomedical examination, including the use of current developmental neurological techniques, often makes it possible to determine the etiology of mental retardation fairly accurately (Iivanainen, 1981, in press). Recent biomedical research conducted in collaboration between the Research Department at Rinnekoti Institution for the Mentally Retarded and various departments at the University of Helsinki has revealed some rare and even new disorders leading to mental retardation (Table 1). These conditions are reviewed here.

ASPARTYLGLUCOSAMINURIA

Aspartylglucosaminuria (AGU), which was first diagnosed in England (Jenner and Pollitt, 1967; Pollitt et al., 1968) and first reported under

102   Iivanainen

Table 1.   Some conditions recognized recently among mentally retarded
patients in Finland

Diagnosis	Reference
Aspartylglucosaminuria	Autio (1972)
Mannosidosis	Autio et al. (1973, 1982)
Infantile neuronal ceroid-lipofuscinosis	Santavuori et al. (1974)
Atelencephaly	Iivanainen et al. (1977)
Muscle-eye-brain disease	Santavuori et al. (1977)
Salla disease	Aula et al. (1979)
Juvenile metachromatic leukodystrophy	Haltia et al. (1979, 1980)
Fetal alcohol syndrome	Strömland (1981)
Moyamoya disease	Haltia et al. (1982)
Marker X–linked mental retardation	Kähkönen et al. (1983)

the term peptiduria in Finland (Palo, 1966, 1967), is the most common
lysosomal storage disease among the Finnish population (Autio, 1972);
by contrast, phenylketonuria is rare in Finnish children (Palo, 1967).
The incidence of AGU is at least 1 in 26,000 live-born children. AGU
can be diagnosed by demonstrating aspartylglucosamine in the urine
by chromatographic or electrophoretic methods. Recurrent infection,
attacks of diarrhea, and hernias are common in the early life of affected
children. Further clinical manifestations can be seen beginning at
school age, including mental retardation, coarse and typical facial appearance (Figure 1A), reduced elasticity of the skin, hypermobility of
joints, osteochondrotic vertebral changes, thin cortex of tubular bones,
thick skull, vacuolated lymphocytes (Figure 1B), and abnormalities of
the heart and digestive tract.

The disease is progressive and has an autosomal recessive mode
of inheritance. It is a generalized storage disease (Haltia et al., 1975),
caused by deficiency of the lysosomal enzyme aspartylglycosamine
amidohydrolase (AADGase), which is involved in the catabolism of
glycoproteins. There is no specific treatment. The determination of the
activity of enzyme AADGase in peripheral blood lymphocytes is used
clinically to detect carriers (Figure 1C), and the enzyme assay on cultured cells from amniotic fluid makes prenatal diagnosis of AGU possible (Aula et al., 1982).

MANNOSIDOSIS

Mannosidosis, another autosomal recessive lysosomal storage disorder, is caused by defective activity of α-D-mannosidase (Öckerman,
1970). The clinical characteristics include psychomotor retardation,
coarse facies, ataxia, impaired hearing, slightly Hurler-like skeletal
changes, and vacuolated lymphocytes in the peripheral blood and bone

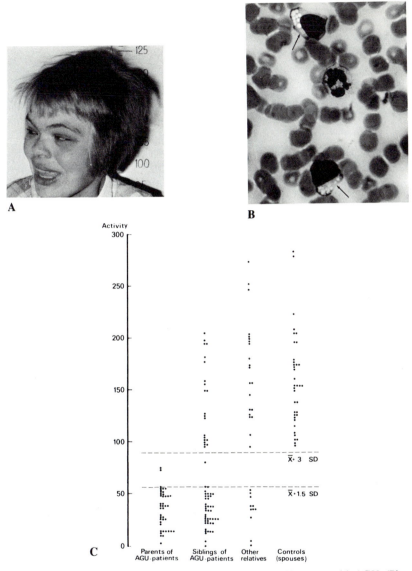

Figure 1A.   Typical coarse facial appearance in a 21-year-old woman with AGU. (Photo courtesy of Dr. Seppo Autio)
Figure 1B.   Cytoplasmic vacuoles (*arrow*) in peripheral blood lymphocytes with AGU. (Photo courtesy of Dr. Seppo Autio)
Figure 1C.   Carrier detection in AGU with assay of AADGase activity in peripheral blood lymphocytes. Values above the upper dotted line (showing the mean activity $+3$ SD of obligate heterozygotes) indicate normal genotype; values below mean heterozygote activity $+1.5$ SD indicate a carrier genotype. Enzyme activities between the two lines indicate "inconclusive" cases that need to be subjected to further studies. Reprinted by permission from: Aula, P., Autio, S., Raivio, K., and Rapola, J. 1982. Aspartylglucos-aminuria. In: P. Durand and T. S. O'Brien (eds.), Genetic Errors of Glycoprotein Metabolism, pp. 123–152. Edi-Ermes and Springer-Verlag, Milan and Heidelberg.

marrow (Kjellman et al., 1969; Autio et al., 1973, 1982). The age of onset varies from 6 months to 3 years. The first symptom is usually delayed development in speech or in motor or mental functioning, often accompanied by recurrent infections. The disease is progressive. Ataxia and sensorineural hearing loss can be absent during the first years of life but may appear later in childhood. Two clinical forms have been reported: a severe form with hepatomegaly, severe infections, and early death; and a milder form with mental retardation, hearing loss, less marked dysostosis, and survival into adulthood (Desnick et al., 1976; Bach et al., 1978). Stunted growth may be present in adult patients. More than 60 patients with mannosidosis have been reported so far. Seven out of eight Finnish cases had the milder form of the disease (Autio et al., 1982).

INFANTILE NEURONAL CEROID-LIPOFUSCINOSIS

Infantile neuronal ceroid-lipofuscinosis (INCL) is a progressive disease with a higher prevalence in the Finnish population than elsewhere (about 1 in 13,000 live-born infants). The disease is characterized by psychomotor retardation beginning between the ages of 8 and 18 months and accompanied by ataxia, muscular hypotonia, visual loss, myoclonic jerks, and microcephaly (Santavuori et al., 1974). Death occurs usually between 11 and 13 years of age. Before the appearance of clinical signs, a tapetoretinal degeneration, reflected by extinction of the electroretinogram when studied by corneal electrodes, is typical in INCL (Raitta and Santavuori, 1973). The constant evolution of the EEG toward final isoelectricity by the age of 3 years facilitates the differential diagnosis in older patients.

INCL leads to severe brain atrophy caused by loss of neurons (Figures 2A, 2B), with brain weight at the age of 10 years being of the order of 300 grams. The histological picture varies depending on the age of the patient and the duration of the disease (Haltia et al., 1973a). Abundant deposits of lipofuscinlike autofluorescent granules in neurons and other neuroectodermal cells is a constant finding (Figure 2C). These granules consist of membrane-bound conglomerations of spherical globules with a finely granular internal ultrastructure (Haltia et al., 1973b) (Figure 2D). The absence of any definite lamellar structures, except for occasional zebralike bodies, differentiates INCL from other neuronal ceroid-lipofuscinoses. Recent biochemical studies have shown increased amounts of dolichols in the isolated storage cytosomes (Palo et al., 1982). So far, these studies have not given any leads for specific treatment of INCL.

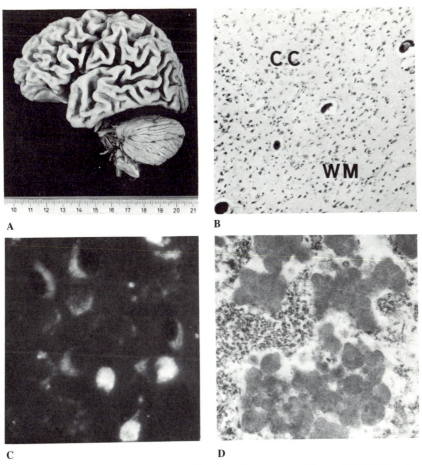

Figure 2A. Extreme diffuse atrophy of the brain in a 9-year-old boy with INCL (scale in cm). Reprinted by permission from: Haltia, M., Rapola, J., Santavuori, P., and Keranen, A. 1973. Infantile type of so-called neuronal ceroid-lipofuscinosis. Histological and electronmicroscopic studies. Acta Neuropathol. 26:157–170.

Figure 2B. Precentral cortex showing a few remaining Betz giant cells with storage material (*black*). All other neurons of the cerebral cortex (*CC*) are lost. There is a total loss of myelin in the white matter (*WM*). Both cerebral cortex and white matter show intense proliferation of hypertrophic astrocytes. (Paraffin section, PAS stain, × 200) (Photo courtesy of Dr. Matti Haltia)

Figure 2C. Autofluorescent granules within neuronal perikarya (semilunar structures with weaker autofluorescence) and phagocytes (more intense autofluorescence). (Unstained paraffin section, ultraviolet light, × 790) Reprinted by permission from: Haltia, M., Rapola, J., Santavuori, P., and Keranen, A. 1973. Infantile type of so-called neuronal ceroid-lipofuscinosis. Part 2: Morphological and biochemical studies. J. Neurol. Sci. 18:269–285.

Figure 2D. The storage granules in the cytoplasm of neurons are composed of aggregates of globules with a finely granular ultrastructure. (× 20,000) (Photo courtesy of Dr. Matti Haltia)

On the other hand, the peroxidation hypothesis on the pathogenesis of juvenile neuronal ceroid-lipofuscinosis, or Spielmeyer-Sjögren's disease, has prompted trials of antioxidative treatment, including sodium selenite, vitamin E, and vitamin B_6, for these patients. The preliminary experience is promising in many cases (Santavuori and Moren, 1977; Santavuori et al., 1981).

ATELENCEPHALY

A malformation syndrome with almost total absence of the telencephalon, associated with a small but otherwise intact cranial vault, was described independently in single cases in the United States (Garcia and Dundan, 1977) and in Finland (Iivanainen et al., 1977). Maldeveloped genitalia with undescended testes, a tendency to hypothermia, severely retarded psychomotor development, a negative perinatal history, normal amino acids and normal karyotypes were noted in both cases. One of the children died at the age of 2 months and another lived for more than a year. Whether this disorder is a primary disturbance of development or is related to a destructive event at approximately the time of prosencephalic development remains unclear.

MUSCLE-EYE-BRAIN DISEASE

Muscle-eye-brain (MEB) disease appears to be a new syndrome leading to mental retardation (Santavuori et al., 1977). Muscular symptoms include severe hypotonia during the early neonatal period. Motor development is severely retarded, most children being bedridden and unable to lift their heads or move about. Neonatal sucking difficulties and apathy are common. Spasticity may occur. Tendon reflexes may be normal at birth but weak or absent by 1 year of age. Eye symptoms and signs consist of severe visual failure, severe myopia, congenital glaucoma, hypoplastic choroids, optic atrophy, optic colobamata, and cataracts. Mental retardation, convulsions, and signs of increased intracranial pressure indicate brain involvement. Although these children may have increased head circumference, their heads are often microcephalic in adulthood. Ventricular enlargement is a constant neuroradiological finding. The EEG shows abnormal monotonic activity predominating in the central and temporal regions and high-voltage beta activity in the frontocentral regions.

The characteristic physical features include a large head with a high and prominent forehead and wide fontanelle, temporally narrow calvarium, narrow palate with prominent lateral ridges, flat midfacies with a short nose and philtrum, reduced muscle mass, abundant and soft subcutaneous tissue (edematous hands and dorsum of feet), small hands and feet, thin and atrophic skin and short, tapering fingers. Because of its familial aggregation, the disease seems likely to be autosomal recessive in nature. Clinically the disorder resembles a variant, with ocular abnormalities (Dambska et al., 1982), of Fukuyama congenital cerebromuscular dystrophy (Stevens, 1982), but the biochemical defect has not yet been determined.

SALLA DISEASE

Salla disease appears to be a new lysosomal storage disorder (Aula et al., 1979). Severe mental retardation, coarse facial features, clumsiness, and absence of speech are common. Electron microscopy of fresh skin biopsy specimens may show cytoplasmic inclusions in various cells. Vacuolated lymphocytes may be seen in peripheral blood. The disease is progressive. The eponym "Salla disease" refers to the geographically restricted area in northeastern Finland where the only described affected kinship resides.

JUVENILE METACHROMATIC LEUKODYSTROPHY

Metachromatic leukodystrophy (MLD) is an autosomal recessive, progressive neurological disease characterized by accumulation of sulfatides in various tissues, including brain and peripheral nerve. In most patients the accumulation is caused by reduced activity of arylsulfatase A (ASA; aryl sulfate sulfohydrolase, EC 3.1.6.1) (Austin et al., 1963), and the disorder manifests itself in the late infantile or, infrequently, in the adult age range. In Finland, nine patients with a juvenile form of MLD have been reported recently (Haltia et al., 1979, 1980). Age at onset varied from 1 to 18 years and duration from 3 to 17 years. Mental retardation was common and often associated with motor impairment, convulsions, and balance and speech disturbances. EEG abnormalities included slowed labile basal rhythm, often mixed with asymmetrical slow bursts. Electromyography showed lowered motor conduction velocity. Segmental demyelination, remyelination, onion bulb formation, and occasional perivascular macrophages containing metachromatic lipid were found in sural nerves studied after biopsy. The ASA activity in peripheral leukocytes of the heterozygotes appeared to be half the values in healthy controls, but was high compared with that in juvenile MLD patients (Haltia et al., 1980).

FETAL ALCOHOL SYNDROME

Fetal alcohol syndrome (FAS) is well documented in mentally retarded children born to mothers with a history of severe alcohol abuse during pregnancy (Jones et al., 1973; Iosub et al., 1981). Children with FAS have a characteristic appearance, with short eyelids, ptosis, epicanthus, hypertelorism, maxillary hypoplasia, and squint. In addition, a number of intraocular abnormalities have been found in affected Finnish and Swedish children, consisting of hypoplasia or atrophy of the optic discs and maldeveloped retinal vessels, including increased tortuosity and anomalous branching (Strömland, 1981). Because reports on FAS are relatively infrequent and ethanol consumption in the general population is increasing in many countries, it may be worth paying special attention to this condition.

MOYAMOYA DISEASE

Moyamoya disease is characterized angiographically by an occlusion of the circle of Willis, combined with typical collateral networks at the base of the brain and on the convexity (Iivanainen, 1974, Figure 24). The stenosing process starts in the region of the carotid siphon and spreads distally, reaching the anterior and middle cerebral arteries, the posterior communicating arteries, the posterior cerebral arteries, and sometimes even the basilar artery. Usually, the disease process starts unilaterally and later spreads into the contralateral side. Within a few years, the circle of Willis may become totally occluded.

So far, about 1,000 patients have been described, some 600 from Japan. The highest incidences have been registered in Japan and Finland, but the disease does not appear to be confined to any particular race. The most common clinical manifestations are alternating hemiparesis, other neurological manifestations of focal cerebral ischemia, and subarachnoid and/or other intracranial hemorrhage. The age of onset of the disease varies from infancy to middle age. About two-thirds of the patients have been children. In some cases, moyamoya disease has been found in association with a number of other conditions, including neurofibromatosis, tuberous sclerosis, Marfan's syndrome, Apert's syndrome, and neonatal anoxia. Many children remain retarded, with spasticity and convulsions, but others recover.

The essential pathological alterations are confined to the vascular system, particularly to the arteries of the brain, but also to those of other internal organs, including the heart. Parenchymatous lesions are secondary to the vascular damage. Vascular alterations consist essentially of reduction of the external caliber of the vessel, intimal thickening without any inflammatory cell infiltrations, and degeneration of the internal elastic lamina. Focal atrophy of the tunica media is also frequent and sometimes associated with aneurysmal dilatations. There may be a continuous spectrum of alterations from slight focal intimal thickening of an otherwise normal artery to complete obliteration of the lumen of a severely atrophic vessel. These pathological alterations, distinct from atherosclerosis, fibromuscular dysplasia, and the established types of arteritis, confirm that moyamoya disease is a separate clinicopathological entity (Haltia et al., 1982), as Kudo (1967) has previously suggested.

MARKER X–LINKED MENTAL RETARDATION

X-linked mental retardation was carefully described in a Canadian family in 1962 (Renpenning et al., 1962). These mentally retarded boys often have macro-orchidism and sometimes prominent forehead, prognathism, and large ears, but other typical external features are lacking. The chromosome abnormality in many is a fragile site in the end of the long arm of an X chromosome: fra X(q28). It appears as a narrow constriction with two small projections distal to the fragile site. Marker X–linked mental retardation is one of many X-linked forms of mental retardation; it may also be found in mentally retarded girls (Turner et al., 1980; Kähkönen et al., 1983). Hitherto, about 100 cases of this syndrome have been diagnosed in the Finnish population (Kähkönen, personal communication).

COMMENTS

The fact that several rare and even new disorders leading to mental retardation were diagnosed during a relatively short period of time confirms our previous experience that study of the causes of mental retardation is fruitful. In our work, cooperation with the families has been close, all investigations have been done with their permission, and they have been informed of the results. This information has been useful in many ways. It has helped many parents and other relatives to relate to the problems that arise because of their mentally retarded child. In this research activity, no negative feedback from any direction has ever been received.

Why some of the disorders described are more, and others less, common in Finland than elsewhere may be explained genetically. The fact that there still are a number of genetic isolates in the Finnish population accounts for the rather high incidence of some autosomal recessive disorders. Genes responsible for AGU, for instance, show a similar increased frequency in the Finnish population, as is the case with many other rare recessive diseases (Nevanlinna, 1972, 1980).

Of course, whenever possible, the results of our research have been used for the benefit of the patients themselves in the choice of optimum treatment and rehabilitation, and also for the purposes of prevention of mental retardation. It is hoped that the heterogeneous collection of rare disorders and syndromes described here would arouse interest among investigators elsewhere and open the doors for fruitful international cooperation in recognizing diseases and their causes leading to mental retardation and, in that way, result in reduction of preventable forms of mental retardation.

REFERENCES

Aula, P., Autio, S., Raivio, K., and Rapola, J. 1982. Aspartylglucosaminuria. In: P. Durand and J. S. O'Brien (eds.), Genetic Errors of Glycoprotein Metabolism, pp. 123–152. Edi-Ermes and Springer-Verlag, Milan and Heidelberg.

Aula, P., Autio, S., Raivio, K. O., Rapola, J., Thoden, C.-J., Koskela, S.-L., and Yamashina, I. 1979. "Salla disease"—a new lysosomal storage disorder. Arch. Neurol. 36:88–94.

Austin, J. H., Balasubramanian, A. S., Pattabiraman, T. N., Saraswathi, S., Basu, D. K., and Bachhawat, B. K. 1963. A controlled study of enzymic activities in three human disorders of glycolipid metabolism. J. Neurochem. 10:805–816.

Autio, S. 1972. Aspartylglucosaminuria. Analysis of thirty-four cases. Journal of Mental Deficiency Research Monograph Series No. 1. National Society for Mentally Handicapped Children, London.

Autio, S., Louhimo, T., and Helenius, M. 1982. The clinical course of mannosidosis. Ann. Clin. Res. 14:93–97.

Autio, S., Norden, N. E., Öckerman, P.-A., Riekkinen, P., Rapola, J., and Louhimo, T. 1973. Mannosidosis: Clinical fine-structural biochemical findings of three cases. Acta Paediatr. Scand. 62:555–565.

Bach, G., Kohn, G., Lasch, E., El Massri, M., Omoy, A., Sekeles, E., Legum, G., and Cohen, M. 1978. A new variant of mannosidosis with increased residual enzymatic activity and mild clinical manifestation. Pediatr. Res. 12:1010–1015.

Dambska, M., Wisniewski, K., Sher, J., and Solish, G. 1982. Cerebro-ocular-muscular syndrome: A variant of Fukuyama congenital cerebromuscular dystrophy. Clin. Neuropathol. 1:93–98.

Desnick, R. J., Sharp, H. L., Grabowski, G. A., Brunning, R. I., Quie, A. G., Sung, J. H., Görlin, R. J., and Ikonne, J. U. 1976. Mannosidosis: Clinical, morphologic, immunologic and biochemical studies. Pediatr. Res. 10:985–996.

Garcia, C. A., and Dundan, C. 1977. Atelencephalic microcephaly. Dev. Med. Child Neurol. 19:227–231.

Haltia, T., Icén, A., and Palo, J. 1979. Arylsulphatase A and B in juvenile metachromatic leukodystrophy. Clin. Chim. Acta 95:255–261.

Haltia, M., Iivanainen, M., Majuri, H., and Puranen, M. 1982. Spontaneous occlusion of the circle of Willis (moyamoya syndrome). Clin. Neuropathol. 1:11–22.

Haltia, M., Palo, J., and Autio, S. 1975. Aspartylglucosaminuria: A generalized storage disease. Morphological and histochemical studies. Acta Neuropathol. 31:243–255.

Haltia, T., Palo, J., Haltia, M., and Icén, A. 1980. Juvenile metachromatic leukodystrophy. Clinical, biochemical and neuropathologic studies in nine new cases. Arch. Neurol. 37:42–46.

Haltia, M., Rapola, J., Santavuori, P., and Keränen, A. 1973a. Infantile type of so-called neuronal ceroid-lipofuscinosis. Part 2: Morphological and biochemical studies. J. Neurol. Sci. 18:269–285.

Haltia, M., Rapola, J., Santavuori, P., and Keränen, A. 1973b. Infantile type of so-called neuronal ceroid-lipofuscinosis. Histological and electronmicroscopic studies. Acta Neuropathol. 26:157–170.

Iivanainen, M. 1974. A Study on the Origins of Mental Retardation. Clinics in Developmental Medicine No. 51. Spastics International Medical Publications, William Heinemann Medical Books, London, and J. B. Lippincott Company, Philadelphia.

Iivanainen, M. 1981. Neurological examination of the mentally retarded child: Evidence of central nervous system abnormality. In: B. Cooper (ed.), Assessing the Handicaps and Needs of Mentally Retarded Children, pp. 55–77. Academic Press, London.

Iivanainen, M. Manifestations and Causes of Brain Development Disorders Leading to Mental Retardation. Charles C Thomas Publisher, Springfield, Illinois. (in press)

Iivanainen, M., Haltia, M., and Lydecken, K. 1977. Atelencephaly. Dev. Med. Child Neurol. 19:663–668.

Iosub, S., Fuchs, M., Bingol, N., and Gromisch, D. S. 1981. Fetal alcohol syndrome revisited. Pediatrics 68:475–479.

Jenner, F. A., and Pollitt, R. J. 1967. Large quantities of 2-acetamido-1-(beta-L-aspartamido)-1,2-dideoxyglucose in the urine of mentally retarded siblings. Biochem. J. 103:48–49.

Jones, K. L., Smith, D. W., Ulleland, C. N., and Streissguth, A. P. 1973. Pattern of malformation in offspring of chronic alcoholic mothers. Lancet 1:1267–1271.

Kähkönen, M., Leisti, J., Wilska, M., and Varonen, S. 1983. Marker-X associated mental retardation. A study of 150 retarded males. Clin. Genet. 23:397–404.

Kjellman, B., Gamstorp, J., Brun, A., Öckerman, P. A., and Palmgren, B. 1969. Mannosidosis: A clinical and histopathologic study. J. Pediatr. 75:366–373.

Kudo, T. (ed.). 1967. A disease with abnormal intracranial vascular networks—Spontaneous occlusion of the circle of Willis. Proceedings of the Symposium of the 25th Congress of the Japanese Neurosurgical Society, 1966. Igaku Shoin, Tokyo.

Nevanlinna, H. 1972. The Finnish population structure: A genetic and genealogical study. Hereditas 71:195–236.

Nevanlinna, H. 1980. Rare hereditary diseases and markers in Finland: An introduction. In: A. W. Eriksson, H. R. Nevanlinna, P. L. Workman, and R. K. Norio (eds.), Population Structure and Genetic Disorders, pp. 569–576. Academic Press, London.

Öckerman, P. A. 1970. A generalized storage disorder resembling Hurler's syndrome. Lancet 2:239–241.

Palo, J. 1966. Eräiden aineenvaihduntahäiriöiden esiintyminen keskushermoston kehitysvauriotapauksissa. Tutkimus 2177 suomalaisesta henkilöstä. Thesis, University of Helsinki, Helsinki. (in Finnish)

Palo, J. 1967. Prevalence of phenylketonuria and some other metabolic disorders among mentally retarded patients in Finland. Acta Neurol. Scand. 43:573–579.

Palo, J., Elovaara, I., Haltia, M., Ng Ying Kin, N. M. K., and Wolfe, L. S. 1982. Infantile neuronal ceroid-lipofuscinosis: Isolation of storage material. Neurology 32:1035–1038.

Pollitt, R. J., Jenner, F. A., and Merskey, H. 1968. Aspartylglucosaminuria. An inborn error of metabolism associated with mental defect. Lancet 2:253–255.

Raitta, C., and Santavuori, P. 1973. Ophthalmological findings in so-called neuronal ceroid-lipofuscinosis. Acta Ophthalmol. 51:755–763.

Renpenning, H., Gerrard, J. W., Zaleski, W. A., and Tabata, T. 1962. Familial sex-linked mental retardation. Can. Med. Assoc. J. 87:954–956.

Santavuori, P., Haltia, M., and Rapola, J. 1974. Infantile type of so-called neuronal ceroid-lipofuscinosis. Dev. Med. Child Neurol. 16:644–653.

Santavuori, P., Leisti, J., Kruus, S., and Raitta, C. 1977. Muscle, eye and brain disease: A new syndrome. Doc. Ophthalmol. Proc. Ser. 17:393–396.

Santavuori, P., and Moren, R. 1977. Experience of antioxidant treatment in neuronal ceroid-lipofuscinosis of Spielmeyer-Sjögren type. Neuropädiatrie 8:333–344.

Santavuori, P., Westermarck, T., and Moren, R. 1981. Antioxidant therapy in Spielmeyer-Sjögren's disease. Neuropediatrics 12(suppl.):433–434.

Stevens, D. L. 1982. Muscular dystrophy, congenital with mental retardation and epilepsy (Fukuyama syndrome). In: P. J. Vinken and G. W. Bruyn (eds.), Handbook of Clinical Neurology. N. C. Myrianthopoulos (ed.), Neurogenetic Directory, Part II, pp. 91–92. North-Holland Publishing Co., Amsterdam.

Strömland, K. 1981. Eyeground malformations in the fetal alcohol syndrome. Neuropediatrics 12:97–98.

Turner, G., Brookwell, R., Daniel, A., and Selikowitz, M. 1980. Heterozygous expression of X-linked mental retardation and the marker X: fra (X) (q27). N. Engl. J. Med. 303:662–664.

SECTION II
Prenatal Environmental Hazards

PERSPECTIVES AND PROGRESS IN MENTAL RETARDATION
Volume II—Biomedical Aspects
Edited by J. M. Berg

ENVIRONMENTAL TOXINS AND MENTAL RETARDATION

J. H. French, R. K. Haddad, A. Rabe, R. M. Dumas, R. Rudelli, and B. Sinha

New York State Institute for Basic Research in Developmental Disabilities, 1050 Forest Hill Road, Staten Island, New York 10314

Exposure to environmental toxins during pregnancy and early postnatal development is a significant cause of developmental disabilities. A single large oral dose of alcohol (binge drinking) during pregnancy can result in severe brain malformations; chronic consumption of amounts insufficient to cause malformations can nevertheless produce lasting behavioral deficits. A single exposure to another naturally occurring neurotoxin, methylazoxymethanol, invariably results in brain malformations when it occurs at critical times during brain development. Excessive exposure to lead is a recognized hazard for developing organisms—our concern has been to delineate critical periods of susceptibility and the lowest levels of exposure resulting in functional deficits.

Food, drugs, and a contaminated ambient environment may be the source of a toxic substance exposure that can drastically alter the developing nervous system (Wilson, 1973). The presence of nervous system anomalies in the progeny of teratogen-exposed laboratory animals demonstrates the ability of toxic substances to alter gross development of the nervous system. Some neuroteratogens can cause persisting behavioral deficits even when there are no gross anomalies (Vorhees and Butcher, 1982).

Human nervous system malformations occur at a frequency of at least 2–3/1,000 births (live and stillborn) (Kurtze et al., 1973). Nervous system anomalies have been reported in 3–4% of persons with significant degrees of mental retardation (Cooke, 1979). The several imperatives that must be accomplished to prevent these disorders include identification of agents that can produce human nervous system anomalies and/or significant behavioral deficits, and elucidation of fundamental mechanism(s) whereby these agents alter normal nervous system development, as well as characterization of basic developmental processes of response that occur in the teratogen-exposed nervous system. This communication reports work in progress with three recognized neuroteratogens.

ALCOHOL (ETHANOL)

Maternal consumption of ethanol during pregnancy is clearly associated with a recognizable pattern of human anomalies (Nitkowsky, 1982). Criteria that have been recommended for establishing a diagnosis of fetal alcohol syndrome (FAS) are the presence of intrauterine and postnatal growth deficiency, central nervous system dysfunction, and a characteristic cluster of facial abnormalities. However, a spectrum of alcohol-related birth defects has been recognized.

We have found that a single large dose of ethanol given orally to pregnant C57Bl/6J mice on gestation day (GD) 8 or 9 (gastrulation or neurulation) results in externally observable malformations in approximately 25% of the near-term (GD 19) fetuses (Haddad and Dumas, 1982). This malformation rate is similar to that reported by Webster et al. (1980), who gave a single large dose of ethanol intraperitoneally. We have also given pregnant CBA/J mice an oral dose of ethanol comparable to that given the C57Bl/6J mice; the CBA/J mice did not show a significant incidence of malformations. In contrast, Chernoff (1980) compared C57Bl and CBA mice in a chronic alcohol administration paradigm, and found the CBA strain *more* susceptible. Thus, enhanced susceptibilities to acute or chronic ethanol teratogenicity appear to have different genetic bases.

One of the most severe neuroteratogenic effects of ethanol that we have found in viable specimens is alobar holoprosencephaly (Figure 1); this is a failure of the cerebrum to divide into two hemispheres. We have also observed a lesser expression, lobar holoprosencephaly, in which the cerebral hemispheres are incompletely divided. Some consider agenesis of the corpus callosum to be the least expression of a continuum of midline developmental deficits—the prosencephalies. This also was seen in a specimen that had a cerebral neuroglial heterotopia (Figure 2). Agenesis of the corpus callosum and cerebral neuroglial heterotopias have been reported in human FAS. Sulik and Johnston (1982) have proposed that FAS is a mild form of holoprosencephaly. Our experimental findings support their hypothesis. Currently, only the mildest of the prosencephalies have been reported clinically (Majewski and Goecke, 1982). However, neuropathological data are sparse.

If comparable effects of a single heavy intrauterine exposure to alcohol occur in man, the presently reported incidence of alcohol-re-

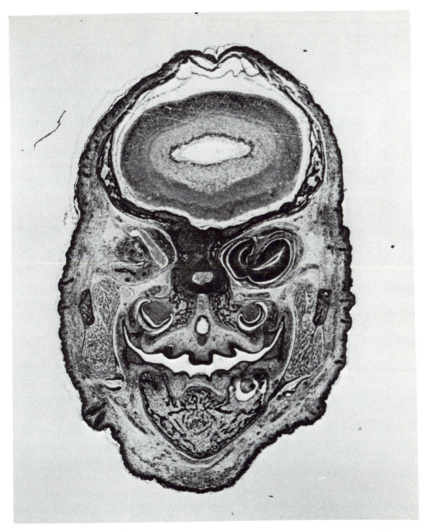

Figure 1.   Alobar holoprosencephaly in a GD 19 mouse fetus. The pregnant dam was given 5.8 g/kg of ethanol per os on GD 8. Coronal section through the frontal level of the monoventricle.

lated birth defects is an underestimate. The human gestational time equivalent to our mouse model is the third to fourth week; the mother's pregnancy may not be recognized this early. Maternal recollection of ethanol consumption prior to the moment of clinical knowledge of pregnancy may not exist at the time of the diagnosis of a possible alcohol-related birth defect in her child. Experimental studies conducted on

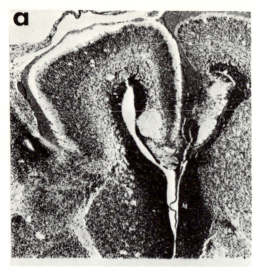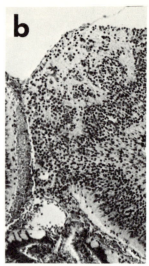

Figure 2.   A: Agenesis of corpus callosum in a GD 19 mouse fetus. Mother treated on GD 9 with 5.8 g/kg ethanol per os. Note the prominent noncrossing, longitudinal callosal fibers (Probst bundles). B: Leptomeningeal neuroglial heterotopia, parietal cortex (Same fetus as in A). Note thinning and disorganization of underlying cortical layers.

laboratory rodents have also shown that sustained consumption during pregnancy of ethanol volumes insufficient to produce gross malformations can nevertheless result in functional deficits in the progeny. Some of these effects are interpretable as a developmental lag (e.g., Lee et al., 1980), whereas other behavioral alterations persist into adulthood (e.g., Plonsky et al., 1982).

    Patterns of ethanol consumption include social drinking as well as binge drinking and sustained heavy drinking. The data reported above suggest significant interactions of patterns of maternal alcohol use with genetic factors. This may contribute to the variability in the reported frequency and severity of alcohol-related birth defects (Russell, 1982).

METHYLAZOXYMETHANOL (MAM)

MAM is a neuroteratogen found in cycad plants (Laqueur, 1977). Cycads have been used in folk medicine and as a staple or emergency food source (Whiting, 1963). Cycad starch, called Florida arrowroot, was sold in the United States and used as a constituent of infant food during the nineteenth century. Naturally occurring MAM conjugates and synthetic MAM acetate (Figure 3) are biochemically transformed to MAM (Laqueur, 1977; Fiala, 1981). Spontaneously occurring and

Cycasin

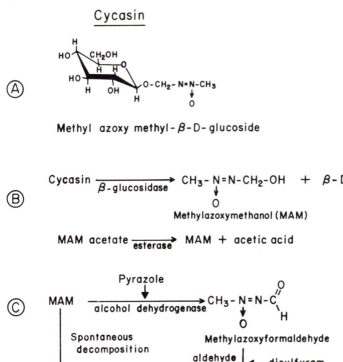

Methyl azoxy methyl-β-D-glucoside

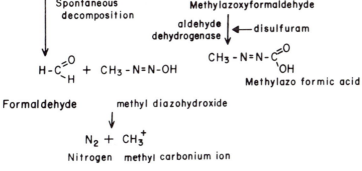

MAM acetate $\xrightarrow{\text{esterase}}$ MAM + acetic acid

Figure 3.   Pathways of metabolism of MAM. *A*: Structure of a naturally occurring MAM glycoside. *B*: Bioactivation of cycasin and MAM acetate. *C*: Pathways to biologically active MAM derivatives.

enzymatically catalyzed decomposition products of MAM chemically alter biological polymers. MAM has also been identified as a cytotoxin, mutagen, and carcinogen.

A single dose of MAM acetate given to pregnant ferrets on GD 32 (full term 42 days) consistently results in progeny with a smooth cerebrum (lissencephaly) (Haddad et al., 1975); normal ferrets are gyrencephalic (Figure 4). The affected brains also are hydrocephalic and invariably display defects of neuronal migration (Haddad and Rabe,

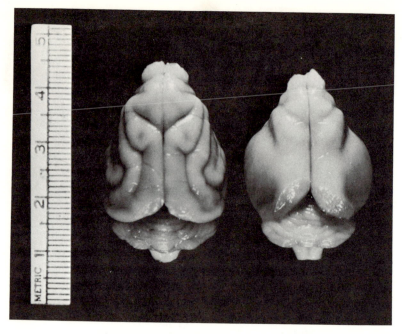

Figure 4.   Brains of adult ferrets. The lissencephalic brain on right is from a ferret whose mother received a single dose of MAM acetate on GD 32. A normal control brain is shown on the left.

1980; Wisniewski et al., 1977); cortical cytoarchitectonics are greatly distorted (Figure 5). The gross somatic appearance of these lissence-phalic ferrets does not readily distinguish them from normal controls.

Lissencephalic ferrets learn a simple task—to turn left or right for reward in a T maze—as readily as do normal ferrets (Figure 6). However, they are severely impaired when required to reverse their previously learned response. Although there is no impairment of initial learning of a simple T-maze task, initial learning of more complex tasks, e.g., a multiple T maze, is markedly impaired (Haddad et al., 1979a). These learning deficits, initially demonstrated in adult lissencephalic ferrets, also are found in juvenile and weanling ferrets (Haddad et al., 1980). Thus, their impaired learning is a persistent developmental deficit.

Human lissencephaly is a rare congenital anomaly invariably associated with severe mental retardation (Lemire et al., 1975; Wright, 1982). The etiology of individual cases of human lissencephaly is obscure, although familial occurrence is known. Many of the neuropathological and electrophysiological features of human lissencephaly are

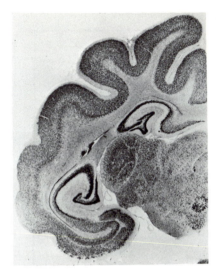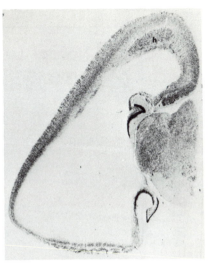

Figure 5.   Coronal sections of normal (*left*) and lissencephalic (*right*) ferret brains. Lissencephaly, hydrocephaly, a thin disarranged cortex, and heterotopic neurons (*h*) are present on the right. Reprinted by permission from: Haddad, R. K., Rabe, A., and Dumas, R. M. 1979. Neuroteratogenicity of methylazoxymethanol acetate: Behavioral deficits of ferrets with transplacentally induced lissencephaly. Neurotoxicology 1:171–189.

present in the ferret MAM model (Haddad and Rabe, 1980; Lee et al., 1981).

MAM has been more often utilized to produce a variety of nervous system anomalies in rodents than in carnivores (Jones et al., 1973). The most extensive use has been to produce micrencephaly in the rat. Micrencephalic rats have other neuropathological and behavioral abnormalities as well; recently they have also been found to have neurotransmitter changes (Johnston and Coyle, 1982). Congruent neurochemical findings are also present in the lissencephalic ferret (Johnston et al., 1982). The altered neurochemistry may be a substantial determinant of the anomalous behavior of micrencephalic rats and lissencephalic ferrets. The availability of these models permits objective tests of pharmacological agents that may be used to ameliorate anomalous behavior associated with such congenital cerebral defects.

LEAD

The industrial fabrication of lead results in biomass contamination. Approximately 200,000 tons of aerosol lead, a by-product of industrial activity, are emitted into the Northern Hemisphere annually (Settle

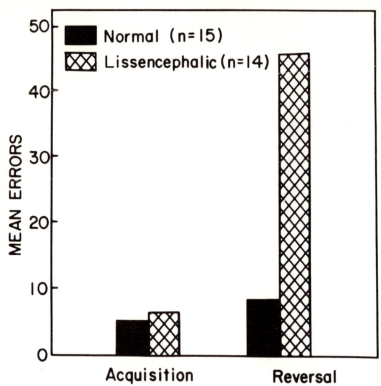

Figure 6.   Error scores for normal and lissencephalic ferrets for initial learning and subsequent reversal of a left-right discrimination in a T maze. Initial learning is not detectably impaired; the reversal performance is markedly impaired in the lissencephalic ferrets ($P < 0.001$, Mann-Whitney U test).

and Patterson, 1980). Lead encephalopathy in older infants and young children was recognized by late-nineteenth century physicians (Gibson et al., 1892). Chronic low-level lead exposure during the early postnatal years has recently been implicated as a cause of behavioral and cognitive impairment in school-age children (David et al., 1972; Needleman et al., 1979). Even though lead was recognized as a human teratogen during the nineteenth century (Rennert, 1881), few investigations have examined the effect of moderate levels of in utero lead exposure on subsequent behavioral and cognitive development.

   We have not yet been able to detect signs of impaired postnatal development in Long-Evans rats that were exposed in utero to lead via maternal ingestion of either 500 mg/L or 5000 mg/L of lead acetate–

Table 1. Consequences of exposure to lead acetate during gestation in the newborn rat

	Body weight (g)	Brain weight (g)	Lead in brain (μg/g dry tissue)	Lead in blood (μg/dl)
Controls	6.2	0.25	0.04	13.1
500 mg lead acetate in 1 liter water	5.9	0.25	0.22	40.6[a]
5000 mg lead acetate in 1 liter water	5.4[a]	0.25	0.72[a]	109.0[a]

[a] Values significantly different from controls. No significant effects could be detected by day 16 except for elevated brain lead (0.52 μg/g) in the 5000 mg/L group. The control group consists of both pair-fed and normal litters. All values in the table are based on 6 to 25 litters.

containing drinking water for a period commencing 2 weeks prior to mating and continuing to term. The offspring were tested for the onset of three developmental landmarks (eye opening, surface righting, and negative geotaxis), learning of a homing-motivated spatial left-right discrimination task starting on postnatal day (PD) 17, and its reversal, as well as exploratory behavior and activity level (spontaneous alternation in a T-maze on PD 25, ambulation, and head dipping in a hole board on PD 30). These behavioral measures have been proved in our laboratory and others to be sensitive in detecting developmental delays and other functional deficits of rat pups that were exposed to intrauterine ethanol (Riley et al., 1979; Lee et al., 1980), MAM acetate (Haddad et al., 1979b), or phenylacetate (Rabe, Loo, Fersko, and Wang, unpublished data). Controls included pups born of both pair-fed and free access–fed dams. All pups were transferred to normal surrogate mothers on PD 2.

No change was found in the birthweight of pups born of dams that received only 500 mg/L of lead in their drinking water (Table 1). A slight, but significant, reduction in birthweight was found in pups whose mothers had received the larger lead dose; this decrement disappeared prior to weaning. The blood lead concentration at birth was elevated in a dose-related fashion. Brain lead content was elevated significantly only in pups of mothers that had received the larger dose.

Our failure to find a developmental delay or other behavioral impairment in the progeny of rats given lead during pregnancy, notwithstanding the presence of elevated blood and brain lead concentrations, suggests that this species may require both pre- and postnatal lead exposure at the doses used in order to cause such deficits. Alternatively, a possible defect, if present, may be fragile and difficult to detect, or specific (e.g. involving visual function) rather than general, and

124   French et al.

therefore was not detected by the administered tests. However, this work does indicate that moderate prenatal lead exposure in the Long-Evans rat does elevate blood and brain lead content without producing a generalized behavior disturbance.

ACKNOWLEDGMENTS

We thank Regina Fersko for preparing animals, collecting tissue samples, and making behavioral measurements in the experiment on prenatal lead toxicity; Lawrence Black for bibliographic assistance; Peggy Clark for manuscript preparation; and Marilyn French for editorial assistance.

REFERENCES

Chernoff, G. F. 1980. The fetal alcohol syndrome in mice: Maternal variables. Teratology 22:2271–2275.
Cooke, R. E. 1979. Mental retardation—Can more be done? In: The Right to be Born Well: A Symposium on Prevention of Mental Retardation and Developmental Disabilities, Proceedings, pp. 2–18. New York Association for Retarded Children, Inc., New York.
David, O., Clark, J., and Voeller, K. 1972. Lead and hyperactivity. Lancet 2:900–903.
Fiala, E. S. 1981. Inhibition of carcinogen metabolism and action by disulfuram, pyrazole, and related compounds. In: M. S. Zedeck and M. Lipkin (eds.), Inhibition of Tumor Induction and Development, pp. 23–69. Plenum Publishing Corp., New York.
Gibson, J. L., Love, W., Hardine, D., Bancroft, P., and Turner, A. J. 1892. Note on lead poisoning as observed among children in Brisbane. Transactions of the 3rd Intercolonial Medical Congress, Volume 3, 1982, pp. 76–83. Charles Potter, Government Printer, Sydney.
Haddad, R., and Dumas, R. M. 1982. Teratogenicity of binge drinking: Comparative susceptibility of C57B1/6J and CBA/J mice to teratogenic effects of a single oral dose of ethanol. Alcoholism Clin. Exp. Res. 6:298, #65A.
Haddad, R. K., Lee, M. H., Rabe, A., Zatz, Y., Canlon, B., and Dumas, R. M. 1979b. Behavioral deficits in preweaning rats with transplacentally induced micrencephaly. Teratology 19:28A.
Haddad, R. K., and Rabe, A. 1980. Use of the ferret in experimental neuroteratology: Cerebral, cerebellar and retina dysplasias induced by methylazoxymethanol acetate. In: T. V. N. Persaud (ed.), Advances in the Study of Birth Defects, Neural and Behavioural Toxicology, Vol. 4, pp. 45–62. University Park Press, Baltimore.
Haddad, R. K., Rabe, A., and Dumas, R. M. 1975. CNS birth defects. Comp. Pathol. Bull. 7:1, 2, 4. Reprinted with revisions as model #55 in: Animal Models of Human Disease. Registry of Comparative Pathology, Armed Forces Institute of Pathology, Washington, D.C.
Haddad, R. K., Rabe, A., and Dumas, R. M. 1979a. Neuroteratogenicity of methylazoxymethanol acetate: Behavioral deficits of ferrets with transplacentally induced lissencephaly. Neurotoxicology 1:171–189.
Haddad, R. K., Rabe, A., Dumas, R. M., and Canlon, B. 1980. Maze learning deficit at the time of weaning in ferrets with transplacentally induced lis-

sencephaly. In: R. M. Gryder and V. H. Frankas (eds.), The Effects of Foods and Drugs on the Development and Function of the Nervous System: Methods for Predicting Toxicity, pp. 171–173. Office of Health Affairs, Food and Drug Administration, Washington, D.C.

Johnston, M. V., and Coyle, J. T. 1982. Cytotoxic lesions and the development of transmitter systems. Trends Neurosci. 5:153–156.

Johnston, M. V., Haddad, R. K., Carman-Young, A., and Coyle, J. T. 1982. Neurotransmitter chemistry of lissencephalic cortex induced in ferrets by fetal treatment with methylazoxymethanol acetate. Dev. Brain Res. 4:285–291.

Jones, M., Mickelsen, O. E., and Yang, M. 1973. Methylazoxymethanol neurotoxicity. In: H. M. Zimmerman (ed.), Progress in Neuropathology, Vol. II, pp. 91–114. Grune & Stratton, New York.

Kurtze, J. F., Goldberg, I. D., and Kurland, L. T. 1973. Congenital malformations of the nervous system. In: L. T. Kurland, J. F. Kurtze, and I. D. Goldberg (eds.), Epidemiology of Neurologic and Sense Organ Disorders, pp. 169–209. Harvard University Press, Cambridge, Massachusetts.

Laqueur, G. L. 1977. Oncogenicity of cycads and its implications. In: H. F. Kraybill and M. A. Mehlman (eds.), Environmental Cancer. Advances in Modern Toxicology Vol. 3, pp. 231–261. Hemisphere Publishing Corporation, Washington, D.C.

Lee, M. H., Haddad, R. K., and Rabe, A. 1980. Developmental impairments in the progeny of rats consuming ethanol during pregnancy. Neurobehav. Toxicol. 2:189–198.

Lee, M. H., Majkowski, J., and Haddad, R. K. 1981. EEG abnormalities in ferrets with transplacentally induced lissencephaly. Teratology 24:13A.

Lemire, R. J., Loser, J. D., Leech, R. W., and Alvord, E. (eds.). 1975. Normal and Abnormal Development of the Human Nervous System, pp. 239–241. Harper & Row Pubs., Inc., New York.

Majewski, F., and Goecke, T. 1982. Alcohol embryology. In: E. L. Abel (ed.), Fetal Alcohol Syndrome, Vol. 2, pp. 67–88. C.R.C. Press, Boca Raton, Florida.

Needleman, H. L., Gunnol., C., Leviton, A., Reed, R., Peresie, H., Maher, C., and Barrett, P. 1979. Deficits in psychologic and classroom performance of children with elevated dentine lead levels. N. Engl. J. Med. 300:689–695.

Nitkowsky, H. 1982. Fetal alcohol syndrome and alcohol-related birth defects. N.Y. State J. Med. 82:1214–1217.

Plonsky, M., Riley, E. P., and Rosellini, R. A. 1982. Acquisition of an unsignaled avoidance task in rats exposed to alcohol prenatally. Teratology 25:67A.

Rennert, O. 1881. Über eine hereditare Folge der chronischen Bleivergiftung. Arch. Gynaekol. 16:110–131.

Riley, E. P., Lochry, E. A., Shapiro, N. R., and Baldwin, J. 1979. Response perseveration in rats exposed to alcohol prenatally. Pharmacol. Biochem. Behav. 10:215–219.

Russell, M. 1982. The epidemiology of alcohol-related birth defects. In: E. L. Abel (ed.), Fetal Alcohol Syndrome, Vol. 2, pp. 89–126. C.R.C. Press, Boca Raton, Florida.

Settle, D. M. and Patterson, C. C. 1980. Lead in Albacore: Guide to lead pollution in Americans. Science 209:1167–1176.

Sulik, K. K., and Johnston, M. C. 1982. Embryonic origin of holoprosencephaly: Interrelationship of the developing brain and face. In: O. Johari and

R. M. Albrecht (eds.), Scanning Electron Microscopy, Part I, pp. 309–322. SEM Inc., AMF O'Hare, Chicago.

Vorhees, C. V., and Butcher, R. E. 1982. Behavioural teratogenicity. In: K. Snell (ed.), Developmental Toxicology, pp. 247–298. Croom Helm Press, London.

Webster, W. S., Walsh, D. A., Lipson, A. H., and McEwan, S. E. 1980. Teratogenesis after acute alcohol exposure in inbred and outbred mice. Neurobehav. Toxicol. 2:227–234.

Whiting, M. G. 1963. Toxicity of cycads. Econ. Bot. 17:271–302.

Wilson, J. G. 1973. Environment and Birth Defects. Academic Press, Inc., San Diego.

Wisniewski, K., Haddad, R., Rabe, A., Dumas, R., and Shek, J. 1977. Experimental lissencephaly in the ferret. J. Neuropathol. Exp. Neurol. 36:638.

Wright, F. S. 1982. Congenital structural defects. In: K. F. Swaiman and F. S. Wright (eds.), The Practice of Pediatric Neurology, 2nd ed., pp. 420–423. C. V. Mosby Company, St. Louis.

PERSPECTIVES AND PROGRESS IN MENTAL RETARDATION
Volume II—Biomedical Aspects
Edited by J. M. Berg
Copyright © 1984 by I.A.S.S.M.D.

ANIMAL MODELS FOR SMALL-FOR-GESTATIONAL-AGE NEONATES AND INFANTS AT RISK

O. Resnick and M. Miller

Worcester Foundation for Experimental Biology, 222 Maple Avenue, Shrewsbury, Massachusetts 01545

The weight changes seen in rat dams and pups as sequelae of either an overt or a hidden form of chronic protein deprivation have been examined. In the overt model, the 6%–casein diet pups showed the small-for-gestational-age weight deficits and metabolic imbalances at birth that are found in the severe forms of human in utero malnutrition. In contrast, the hidden form of prenatal deprivation did not cause weight deficits in the 8%–casein diet pups at birth, but their metabolic profiles, similar to those of small-for-gestational-age pups, categorizes them as infants at risk.

Although the deleterious effects of prenatal malnutrition on the developing central nervous system of humans have been known for a long time, relatively few studies have used the rat as a model for these brain deficits until fairly recently. By 1970, however, Winick showed that in utero malnourished rats displayed many of the same brain alterations as those found in the prenatally deprived small-for-gestational-age (SGA) human infant. Other investigators have extended his findings, but few of the studies have been entirely parallel to the human condition. Because most animal studies begin the dietary restrictions at conception, these depict an acute stage of deprivation rather than the chronic undernutrition (childhood and adulthood) typically found in women from low socioeconomic groups.

These studies were supported by Grant HD-06364 from the National Institute of Child Health and Human Development.

To more closely parallel the nutritional status of these women, our studies on brain development in the rat have initiated the dietary restrictions (use of an 8% casein diet) to the females well prior to conception (Stern et al., 1975). However, because the protein deficits of this diet are relatively mild and are compensated by the addition of excess carbohydrates, the 8% pups do not show the typical SGA weight losses at birth. This appearance of normalcy in these pups is nevertheless highly deceptive because many of their peripheral metabolic processes at birth show the same alterations (Miller et al., 1977) found in the SGA human neonate (Sinclair et al., 1974). Also, this hidden form of maternal deprivation causes the 8%-diet pups to display a reduced capacity to learn new tasks in adolescence (Resnick et al., 1979), which appears to be similar to some forms of minimal brain dysfunction (MBD) found in children. Because many "normal" birthweight children show signs of MBD (Singer et al., 1968), it is possible that part of their mental disabilities may be due to the same type of mild fetal deficits occurring in the 8%-diet rats. Thus, this apparent lack of overt symptoms in these pups (and probably many children) places them in a different category of malnutrition—infants at risk (IAR).

In this paper, we describe the weight changes that accompany this IAR syndrome in the rat to show how it remains hidden in the dams and offspring through parturition. To show that the 8% casein diet may represent the borderline whereby caloric compensation can maintain the appearance of dietary adequacies, we have devised a malnutritional paradigm in which the protein content of the maternal diet was reduced to a level (6% casein) where extra calories could not sustain the nutritional requirements of the dam. Placing female rats on this diet prior to pregnancy not only caused them to display the same nutritional status found in chronically undernourished women but also resulted in their offspring being SGA at birth. In depicting the differences in appearance between the overt and hidden form of maternal malnutrition, we have also described parallels from these animal models to the human condition in order to emphasize the potential consequences of either on the in utero growth and development of the human neonate.

METHOD

The diets and rearing procedures were the same as those previously described (Resnick et al., 1982). Briefly, virgin female Sprague-Dawley rats were fed isocaloric (4.3 kcal/g) diets containing either normal (25% casein), low (8% casein), or very low (6% casein) amounts of protein. This dietary paradigm was started 5 weeks prior to mating and continued through gestation and lactation. Body weights of the rats were

Table 1.   The effects of different levels of dietary protein on female weight gain before and during pregnancy

Time interval	Diet groups		
	6% Casein	8% Casein	25% Casein
Initial weights (g)[a]	193 ± 2	192 ± 2	190 ± 2
Pregravid period			
1 week	201 ± 3[b]	210 ± 3	219 ± 3
2 weeks	208 ± 3[b]	219 ± 3[c]	234 ± 4
3 weeks	214 ± 3[b]	227 ± 3[c]	242 ± 4
4 weeks	224 ± 3[b]	240 ± 3[d]	255 ± 6
5 weeks	233 ± 3[b]	252 ± 3[d]	267 ± 6
Pregnancy			
1 week	238 ± 5[b]	280 ± 5	287 ± 6
2 weeks	258 ± 6[b]	317 ± 6	321 ± 6
3 weeks	293 ± 8[b]	370 ± 7	379 ± 6

[a] Mean weight (g) ± SE.

[b] $P < 0.001$ for 6% or 8% casein diet females versus 25% casein diet females (2-tailed t test).

[c] $P < 0.01$ for 6% or 8% casein diet females versus 25% casein diet females (2-tailed t test).

[d] $P < 0.05$ for 6% or 8% casein diet females versus 25% casein diet females (2-tailed t test).

recorded once a week during the pregravid period and pregnancy. Following birth, the weights of the dams and their pups were recorded. Some pups from some 6%-diet or 8%-diet dams were also cross-fostered at birth to dams fed the 25% diet.

RESULTS

SGA Offspring

The relationship between the maternal nutritional status (Table 1) and the subsequent birthweights of the pups (Table 2) can clearly be seen for the 6%-diet dams. Although the diets are isocaloric, the inadequate protein content of this diet was responsible for the 48% decreases in pregnancy weight gains of these dams compared to those fed the 25% diet. Thus, this condition of maternal malnutrition was responsible for the SGA birthweights (20% less than normal) of their pups.

These data are typical findings from studies on protein and/or protein-calorie malnutrition in humans and rats (Rosso and Cramoy, 1979). In both species, prepartum weight gains that are about one-half of the normal pregnancy values are accompanied by an increased number of SGA births. This would be expected because fetal growth and development depends on access to maternal nutrients and on the amounts

Table 2.   Growth indices at birth for pups from dams fed different amounts of dietary protein

Pups at birth	Diet of dams		
	6% casein	8% casein	25% casein
Body weight (g)[a]	4.95 ± 0.2[c]	6.00 ± 0.2	6.20 ± 0.1
Brain weight (mg)[a]	241 ± 12[b]	280 ± 11	275 ± 10

[a] Mean ± SE.

[b] $P < 0.05$ for pups of 6% casein diet dams versus 8% or 25% casein diet dams (2-tailed t test).

[c] $P < 0.001$ for pups of 6% casein diet dams versus 8% or 25% casein diet dams (2-tailed t test).

of reserves amassed during early pregnancy that can be mobilized later to ensure fetal needs. Because the latter are determined by the maternal nutritional status, poorly nourished, low-pregnancy-weight-gain females like the 6%-diet dams will have inadequate reserves available to maintain normal fetal growth.

Another important, but often ignored, factor in fetal growth retardation is the pregravid nutritional status of the female. By starting the dietary restrictions at conception in most animal studies of malnutrition, the dams have pregravid stores available to support some degree of fetal development, which is usually not the case for chronically undernourished women. For such women, however, this factor makes an important contribution to the subsequent birthweights of their infants. For example, Eastman and Jackson (1968) showed that, among women with small pregnancy weight gains (5 kg), the incidence of SGA births was 1.5% for those with pregravid weights of 72 kg as compared to 10% for women with pregravid weights of 54 kg. Thus, high pregravid weights can furnish reserves to support a good birthweight even when the pregnancy weights are low, whereas the lack of the former (Table 1) in the 6%-diet dams (33% weight decreases), coupled with their small pregnancy weights, makes them more typical of the chronically undernourished woman.

Interestingly, in common with SGA humans, the 6%-diet pups also showed smaller deficits in brain weights compared to body weights at birth (Table 2). However, this brain "sparing" effect does not prevent the losses in cells and myelin and the impaired dendritic formation and development that occurs in the in utero–deprived offspring of either species (Rosso and Cramoy, 1979). Although all of these brain deficits can affect intelligence, it is perhaps the damage to dendritic development that has a greater impact on the learning potential of SGA progeny rather than the concurrent decreases in myelin or cell numbers (Shanklin and Hodin, 1979). Because the 6%-diet pups showed marked ab-

Table 3. Influence of maternal gestational and lactational diets on growth
of pups at weaning (day 21)

| Pups at weaning | Maternal gestational/lactational diets[a] | | |
	6/25	8/25	25/25
Body weight (g)	40.9 ± 0.5^b	65.0 ± 1.0	64.9 ± 0.3
Brain weight (mg)	1128 ± 26^b	1393 ± 32	1410 ± 50

[a] The slash mark separates the prenatal and postnatal nutritional status of the pups.
Values given are mean weight $\pm$ SE.
[b] $P < 0.001$ for 6/25 pups versus 8/25 or 25/25 pups (2-tailed t test).

errations in dendritic formation (unpublished observations), their learning abilities will probably reflect these impairments in later life.

Along with brain deficits, SGA offspring display alterations in peripheral metabolic pathways that can affect brain functioning. These
include hypoalbuminemia and a hyperlipolysis of adipose tissue to provide energy (Sinclair et al., 1974). In the 6%-diet pups, these metabolic
imbalances increase the availability of tryptophan to their brains and
cause them to have markedly higher than normal brain serotonin levels
(Miller et al., 1981). (Whether SGA humans would show the same
increases in brain serotonin values is not known, because no measurements of brain indoleamine levels have been made on children who
died from in utero malnutrition.)

Finally, like many SGA humans, the 6%-diet pups showed postnatal growth deficits (or stunting) as sequelae of in utero deprivation.
Although they received adequate lactational nutrition by being fostered
at birth to 25% dams they had markedly lower than normal brain and
body weights (20% and 37% decreases, respectively) at weaning (Table
3). For both species this "failure to thrive" syndrome seems to be
related to their poorer absorption of foods or needs for additional nutritional intake that is not attained from breastfeeding or from infant
formulas. Thus, the insults of severe in utero deprivation do not end
at birth but continue to display their ramifications throughout the infancy of SGA offspring.

IAR Progeny

In contrast to the weight changes seen for the 6%-diet animals, there
were no visible indicators of nutritional deficiencies in the 8%-diet dams
or pups until after the onset of lactation. Although the pregravid weights
of these rats (Table 1) were slightly lower (6–7%) than those of the
25%-diet rats, these may represent some metabolic readjustments to a
diet with a different composition from their usual food. Also, the caloric
compensation of this diet caused the 8%-diet dams to look like normal
dams during gestation, i.e., both their weekly and total prepartum

weight gains were the same as the 25%-diet rats (Table 1). Therefore, the energy recompense in the maternal diet of these dams caused their pups to have normal growth indices at birth (Table 2).

In spite of the appearance of both a normal pregnancy and normal neonates for the 8%-diet rats, the pups can be categorized as IAR at birth. Not only do they show many of the peripheral alterations seen in SGA humans and in the 6%-diet pups, they also have markedly higher than normal brain serotonin levels at this age (Miller et al., 1977). Moreover, this IAR syndrome can remain hidden in the 8%-diet pups if they receive adequate postnatal nutrition. Although the poor milk production of their dams caused the 8%-diet pups to have markedly lower than normal brain and body weights (13% and 60% decreases, respectively) at weaning (Resnick et al., 1982), fostering of these rats at birth to the 25%-diet dams assured their normal weaning growth indices. However, these postnatal adequacies were unable to effect rehabilitation of their in utero–determined SGA-like peripheral imbalances and impaired brain neurochemistry (Miller and Resnick, 1980).

DISCUSSION

These data show the fallacy of assessing the nutritional status of a female and its effect on her offspring by her pregravid weight, her pregnancy weight gain, or the birthweight of the neonate. Although there is a strong association between birthweights and pregravid weights, they are not necessarily a reliable indicator of good maternal health or the intake of essential nutrients. This is especially true among mildly overweight women from low socioeconomic groups in this country whose pregravid weights may reflect a type of caloric compensation as a replacement for much of their essential protein needs as a result of the escalating price of the latter. Also, a high pregnancy weight gain in women gives no assurance that the fetus is receiving the proper nutrients to ensure adequate growth and development. As in the non-gravid state, a high weight gain can result from a high-caloric diet that may be deficient in protein. For example, not only do these protein deficits cause pregnant women to show a rapid accumulation of fluid (up to 7 kg) in a short period of time, but they may also account for the high percentage (6–7%) of their children who show abnormal growth and neurological functioning at 1 year of age (Shanklin and Hodin, 1979).

Because fetal deficiencies can accompany a large maternal weight gain in women as in the 8%-diet dams, it becomes evident that normal birthweights may not be predictive of normal in utero development. Certainly, our findings of abnormal brain functioning in the 8%-diet pups as sequelae of mild maternal protein deficits may be applicable to many normal-birthweight infants. Also, human birthweights above 2.5 kg are defined as normal even though they are below the optimum of 3.5 kg. Because mild fetal deficits may afflict infants with birthweights between these values, this may account for the 6–13% of them who showed later signs of MBD or severe mental retardation (Singer et al., 1968). Thus, many children who are considered "normal" at birth because their birth weights are within the so-called normal range may, in reality, be better classified as IAR.

Finally, the lack of breastfeeding in this country may allow this IAR syndrome to remain hidden during infancy. Using our 8%-diet pups as a model, it was noted that: 1) this mild form of chronic protein lack only becomes noticeable during early lactation when the body weights of these pups become markedly lower than normal; and 2) if they were nursed by 25%-diet dams, the postnatal body weight gains of these pups were normal. Thus, the use of infant formulas rather than breastfeeding in our society would allow for the "normal" postnatal growth of the infant (case 2) and would miss any signs of low-level maternal protein lacks that could appear during early lactation if the mother nursed her baby (case 1). Because the normal weight gain (8%-diet mother, 25%-diet nurse) pups still showed the altered brain and peripheral functioning of IAR offspring at weaning, it becomes less surprising to find many "normal" birthweight children who have low IQs or show signs of MBD in the absence of perinatal brain damage.

REFERENCES

Eastman, N. J., and Jackson, E. 1968. Weight relationships in pregnancy. 1. The bearing of maternal weight gain and prepregnancy weight on birth weight in full term pregnancies. Obstet. Gynecol. Survey 23:1003–1025.

Miller, M., Leahey, J. P., Stern, W. C., Morgane, P. J., and Resnick, O. 1977. Tryptophan availability: Relation to elevated brain serotonin in developmentally protein-malnourished rats. Exp. Neurol. 57:142–157.

Miller, M., and Resnick, O. 1980. Tryptophan availability: The importance of prepartum and postpartum dietary protein on brain indoleamine metabolism in rats. Exp. Neurol. 67:298–314.

Miller, M., Hasson, R., and Resnick, O. 1981. Developmental protein malnutrition in rats: Adaptive changes in brain indoleamine metabolism in small-for-gestational-age offspring. Proceedings of the Society for Neurosciences (11th Annual Metting), Los Angeles, California, p. 72. (unpublished proceedings)

Resnick, O., Miller, M., Forbes, W., Hall, R., Kemper, T., Bronzino, J., and Morgane, P. J. 1979. Developmental protein malnutrition: Influences on the central nervous system of the rat. Neurosci. Biobehav. Rev. 3:233–246.

Resnick, O., Morgane, P. J., Hasson, R., and Miller, M. 1982. Overt and hidden forms of chronic malnutrition in the rat and their relevance to man. Neurosci. Biobehav. Rev. 6:55–75.

Rosso, P., and Cramoy, C. 1979. Nutrition and pregnancy. In: M. Winick (ed.), Nutrition and Pre- and Postnatal Development, pp. 133–228. Plenum Publishing Corp. New York.

Shanklin, D. R., and Hodin, J. 1979. Maternal Nutrition and Child Health. Charles C Thomas Publisher, Springfield, Illinois.

Sinclair, J. C., Saigal, S., and Yeung, C. Y. 1974. Early postnatal consequences of fetal malnutrition. In: M. Winick (ed.), Nutrition and Fetal Development, pp. 147–171. John Wiley & Sons, Inc., New York.

Singer, J. E., Westphal, M., and Niswander, K. 1968. Relationship of weight gain during pregnancy to birth weight and infant growth and development in the first year of life. Obstet. Gynecol. 31:417–423.

Stern, W. C., Miller, M., Forbes, W. B., Morgane, P. J., and Resnick, O. 1975. Ontogeny of the levels of biogenic amines in various parts of the brain and in peripheral tissues in normal and protein malnourished rats. Exp. Neurol. 49:314–326.

Winick, M. 1970. Nutrition and nerve cell growth. Fed. Proc. 29:1510–1515.

PERSPECTIVES AND PROGRESS IN MENTAL RETARDATION
Volume II—Biomedical Aspects
Edited by J. M. Berg

MATERNAL PHENYLKETONURIA
Basic Research and Clinical Problems

H. M. Wisniewski, Y. H. Loo, and K. Wisniewski
*New York State Institute for Basic Research in Developmental Disabilities,
1050 Forest Hill Road, Staten Island, New York 10314*

Associated with successful mass screening for phenylketonuria (PKU) and effective dietary therapy is the problem of maternal PKU. A recently diagnosed case of maternal PKU is presented, and our work on producing a simulation of clinical maternal PKU in pregnant rats is reported. Measures to effectively control tissue levels of both phenylalanine and phenylacetate and to counteract the neurotoxicity of phenylacetate are needed to protect against maternal PKU and its hazards to the fetus. Studies now in progress with our animal model are directed toward this goal.

Phenylketonuria (PKU) is an inborn error of metabolism characterized by the inability to convert phenylalanine to tyrosine (Jervis, 1947) because of a deficiency of the liver enzyme phenylalanine hydroxylase (Kaufman and Max, 1971), resulting in hyperphenylalaninemia and usually profound mental retardation (Fölling, 1934). Diagnostic tests for early detection (McCaman and Robins, 1962; Guthrie and Susi, 1963) and a dietary therapy (Bickel et al., 1954; Armstrong and Tyler, 1955; Woolf et al., 1955) have been developed. Severe mental retardation in PKU has been effectively prevented by early diagnosis and treatment with a low-phenylalanine diet from the first month of life until 5–7 years of age. Today, in at least 45 states in the U.S. and 19 other countries, mass screening of all newborn infants for PKU is required by law. In these regions, the number of PKU children institutionalized has been reduced to practically zero.

This investigation is supported by the New York State Office of Mental Retardation and Developmental Disabilities and Grant HD 16153 from the National Institutes of Health.

Table 1.   Abnormalities in offspring of untreated women with PKU or hyperphenylalaninemia

Abnormality	Percentage of non-PKU offspring affected when maternal blood phenylalanine level (mg/100 ml) is:[a]			Normal frequency
	>20	16–19	11–15	
Mental retardation (IQ or DQ below 75)	92 (172)	73 (37)	22 (23)	5.0
Microcephaly	73 (138)	68 (44)	35 (23)	4.8
Congenital heart disease	12 (225)	15 (46)	6 (33)	0.8
Low birthweight	40 (89)	52 (33)	56 (9)	9.6

[a] Figures in parentheses indicate sample size from which percentages were calculated

Those who have benefited from these programs, which were initiated in the 1960s, are leading a normal life in the community, and the females are approaching childbearing age. These women, although of normal intelligence, of course still bear the genetic defect, and on a normal diet they remain hyperphenylalaninemic. Consequently, the PKU female who is not on diet control during pregnancy exposes the non-PKU fetus to an abnormal intrauterine environment that causes brain damage. Thus, we are confronted with an emerging problem of maternal PKU.

A thorough world-wide survey of published and unpublished data on 524 pregnancies in 155 phenylketonuric and variant-hyperphenylalaninemic mothers not on diet control was recently made by Lenke and Levy (1980). A summary of some of their findings is shown in Table 1. Obviously, the most serious consequence of untreated maternal PKU is the mental deficit among the progeny, even though they do not have the metabolic defect; as the table shows, the likelihood of this occurring is related to the maternal blood phenylalanine level. Other abnormalities consistently observed include microcephaly, congenital heart disease, and low birthweight.

Attention must also be given to the small percentage (about 0.5–1.0%) of adult phenylketonurics who have nearly normal IQ scores and hence have escaped detection. Females among them have been reported to give birth to non-PKU children with varying degrees of intellectual deficit (Levy et al., 1970; Perry et al., 1973; Lenke and Levy, 1980). Recently at our Institute such a case of maternal PKU was diagnosed. To date this is the only one recorded in the State of New York, and is reported below.

CASE REPORTS

Margaret D. (Case 3), a 29-year-old housewife of dull normal intelligence, was seen in our diagnostic unit with her two children Lucien, age 3.5 years (Case 1) and Danielle, age 1.5 years (Case 2).

Case 1

Lucien is the product of his mother's second pregnancy. Maternal age at delivery was 25.5 years. Prenatal care was good. He was born by normal, spontaneous vaginal delivery in St. Vincent's Medical Center, New York, with a birthweight of 6 lb 8 oz. There were no perinatal or postnatal complications.

Developmental Milestones   He smiled at 1 month, sat without support at 8 months, walked unassisted and was toilet trained at 18 months, and started to say "mama" and "dada" at 2 years. At present he has some comprehension, but only about four or five words, and his speech is unintelligible.

Past Medical History   At birth the feet were rotated outward; he was put into braces for a few months and then received special shoes. There is a history since early childhood of behavior problems, hyperactivity, and short attention span.

Family History   This information was obtained from the PKU patient and her husband. On the maternal and paternal side of the family, there is no history of neurological or psychiatric disorders and no known consanguinity. The father had two brothers who died at birth of unknown causes. Four older sisters are married and have normal children.

The mother had a spontaneous abortion before Lucien's birth. After Lucien came Michael, who died a few days after birth. He had a small head and a cardiac defect. The youngest is Danielle (Case 2). The mother had two male siblings who died at birth of unknown causes. Her two younger unmarried siblings are reported to have had difficulty with learning at school.

General Examination   Height 36.5" (3rd percentile); weight 29 lb (10th percentile); head circumference 18.4" (below 3rd percentile). The child is ambidextrous but uses the right hand more than the left (the father and mother and their siblings are all right handed). Abnormalities found were a systolic murmur in the left sternocostal margin in the range of 4/6, growth retardation, microcephaly, and one café-au-lait spot on the left buttock measuring 1 × 0.5" in greater diameter.

Neurological Examination   The child is alert, has a short attention span, will point to body parts, and his speech is unintelligible. Only on two occasions did he say "da" and "ma." He is able to scribble and to follow simple commands. The cranial nerves from II to XII are grossly intact except that speech is delayed. The motor system shows normal muscle tone, strength, and deep tendon reflexes. He has difficulty in walking up and down stairs, and falls frequently. He has poor visual motor and fine motor coordination. He cannot catch or throw a ball, walk tandem, or stand or hop on one foot. Hearing is grossly intact. He reacts to painful stimuli. Other tests were not performed because of lack of cooperation.

Clinical Chemistry   Amino acid analyses of blood and urine specimens were normal.

Case 2

Danielle is the product of her mother's fourth pregnancy. Maternal age at delivery was 27.5 years. The mother was well throughout her pregnancy with the exception of a minor cold in the first trimester. The child was born at full term by normal spontaneous vaginal delivery with a birthweight of 6 lb 2 oz. Mother and child were discharged 5 days after delivery. There were presumably no perinatal complications. At birth, microcephaly and a cardiac defect were noted.

Developmental Milestones   She smiled at 1 month, sat without support at 8 months, walked unassisted at 17 months, and has babbled occasionally since 15 months. At present she still has no speech or comprehension.

Past Medical History   There have been no serious illnesses.

Family History   See Case 1.

General Examination   Height 19.2" (3rd percentile); weight 7 lb 9 oz (3rd percentile); head circumference 12.8" (below 3rd percentile). There is a systolic murmur in the left sternocostal margin in the range of 3/6. When she cries, she becomes blueish around the mouth. No other abnormalities were noted.

Neurological Examination   The child is alert, blinks to light, startles to noises, and occasionally babbles. Her pupils are 3 mm and react to light, and both discs are normal. The face and tongue are symmetrical. The corneal and gag reflexes are present. Muscle tone and reflexes are normal. Movement of all extremities is symmetrical. No focal or lateralizing abnormal signs were noted.

Clinical Chemistry   Amino acid analyses of blood and urine specimens were normal.

Cases 1 and 2: Summary and Conclusions

General and neurological examination of Cases 1 and 2 showed microcephaly, growth retardation, and mental retardation. In view of the

Table 2.   Biochemical evidence of maternal PKU: phenylalanine metabolism

Tissue	Metabolites derived from phenylalanine[a]						
	Phenyl-alanine	Unconj. PA	Conj. PA	Mandelic acid	O-HPA	Phenyl-lactic acid	Phenyl-pyruvic acid
Plasma (μmol/ml)	1.28	0.11	1.13	not detected	0.016	0.069	0.023
Urine (μmol/mg of creatinine)	0.99	0.48	5.36	0.31	1.67	3.06	4.48

[a] Unconj. PA = phenylacetate + phenylacetyl-CoA; Conj. PA = phenylacetylglutamine; O-HPA = ortho-hydroxyphenylacetic acid

history of similar symptomatology in the mother's siblings (microcephaly, cardiac defect, and growth retardation), intrauterine toxic encephalopathy, or a less likely chromosomal abnormality, was suspected.

Case 3—Mother

She is married and lives independently in the community. General and neurological examination was normal with the exception of borderline retardation, emotional instability, and poor fine motor coordination. A psychological evaluation in April 1982 (Wechsler Adult Intelligence Scale) showed a Verbal IQ of 67, a Performance IQ of 60, and a Full Scale IQ of 62, with subtest scores indicative of possible psychoeducational disadvantage (similarities = 8; other subtest scores below normal).

These clinical observations are similar to published descriptions of maternal PKU, and we have obtained biochemical evidence in support of this diagnosis (Table 2). The elevated plasma and urinary phenylalanine concentrations of the mother, as well as the pattern of metabolites derived from phenylalanine in plasma and urine, are typical of PKU (Loo et al., 1978a). Of special interest are the high phenylacetylglutamine concentration in the plasma and the excessive amount of phenylacetate plus phenylacetyl-CoA (unconjugated phenylacetate) excreted. The large amount of phenylalanine metabolized by the transamination pathway (urinary phenylpyruvic plus phenyllactic and o-hydroxyphenylacetic acids) is also noteworthy (specimens of urine and blood were collected approximately 4 hours after a light breakfast of coffee with evaporated milk). Disposition of phenylalanine predominantly by conversion to phenylpyruvic acid was again observed when the subject was fed 7 g of L-phenylalanine after an overnight fast. Plasma levels of phenylalanine were sustained between 2.1 and 3.2

μmol/ml, whereas tyrosine concentrations remained at 0.05–0.06 μmol/ml, over a period of 6 hours. During this experimental period, the major metabolite derived from phenylalanine in the plasma was phenyllactic acid (0.11–0.30 μmol/ml).

Neopterin and biopterin assays of three different urine samples (courtesy of Seymour Kaufman, Ph.D., National Institutes of Health) indicated that the subject is not deficient in dihydropteridine reductase or in biopterin synthesis.

DISCUSSION

A troublesome increase in the number of mentally handicapped children as a consequence of diet-uncontrolled maternal PKU poses a major problem, when the following statistics and the autosomal recessive mode of transmission of the disease are considered together. It is estimated that by 1984 about 40 million infants in the United States will have been screened for PKU and about 4,000 will have been treated for the disease and will consequently be able to lead a normal life. About 300 new cases are detected in the U.S. each year (Scriver and Clow, 1980). At present the number of carriers is at least 2% of the population (Fenichel, 1980) and will continue to increase as PKU females bear children (Figure 1). The genetic defect will thus be perpetuated, because the chances of two carriers marrying are 1 in 4,000 (Fenichel, 1980). The need to treat maternal PKU as a preventative measure is clear and urgent.

Diet control of maternal PKU appears to be an overwhelming problem. The adult with PKU who has grown accustomed to normal food finds it extremely difficult to return to the very restricted, unpalatable diet for PKU. Some do not tolerate the dietary therapy and become nauseous. In some cases, good diet control during pregnancy prevented fetal brain damage but not congenital heart disease; it appears that diet control must be initiated before conception (Zaleski et al., 1979). There is clearly a need to improve the present dietary measures for the control of maternal PKU.

With this in mind, we are at present focusing attention on the nature of biochemical abnormalities and behavioral deficits induced in animals exposed to maternal PKU. Results of human (Menkes and Aeberhard, 1969; Lenke and Levy, 1980) and animal (Kerr et al, 1968) studies indicate that fetal brain damage is related to prenatal maternal exposure to high concentrations of phenylalanine and/or phenylalanine metabolites. In earlier investigations we have clearly and consistently demonstrated that phenylacetate, which is produced in excessive amounts during sustained hyperphenylalaninemia, is primarily respon-

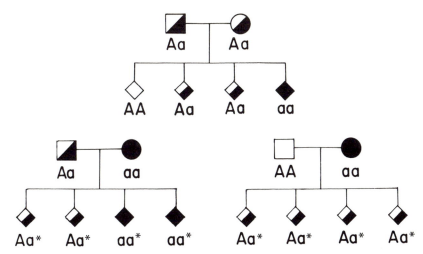

Figure 1. Mode of transmission of autosomal recessive PKU gene. Key: A = normal gene; a = PKU gene; *square* = male parent; *circle* = female parent; *diamond* = offspring; AA = normal; Aa = heterozygous carrier, normal mental development; aa = homozygous PKU, postnatal brain damage if untreated; * = fetus exposed to maternal PKU (both heterozygous and homozygous offspring of a PKU mother will be exposed to this hazard if the mother is not treated).

sible for postnatal brain damage in experimental PKU (Loo et al., 1978b, 1980; Fulton et al., 1980; Wen et al., 1980; Robain et al., 1981). Accordingly, we are examining two animal models of maternal PKU: the hyperphenylalaninemic pregnant rat and the pregnant rat exposed to phenylacetate.

Plasma phenylalanine levels sustained over 24 hr at 1.5–3.0 μmol/ml, with tyrosine concentrations remaining normal at 0.15–0.25 μmol/ml, are produced in pregnant rats by continuous subcutaneous infusion of p-chloro-phenylalanine (p-CPA) and L-phenylalanine. Because p-CPA is a potent inhibitor not only of phenylalanine hydroxylase but of tryptophan hydroxylase as well, we have included L-5-hydroxytryptophan (L-5HTP) in the infusion fluid. Synaptosomal serotonin levels may be increased by intraperitoneal injections of L-5HTP (Loo, 1974).

A second group of pregnant rats are similarly infused to maintain plasma levels of total phenylacetate (unconjugated + conjugated) at 0.30–0.60 μmol/ml over 24 hr. Control rats are infused with saline. Infusion is started on the ninth day of gestation, when the fetal neural tube first appears. To ensure normal delivery and good care of the offspring, the infusion is terminated on the twentieth day of gestation, 2 days prior to parturition. In order to study cerebral development in the rat during a period corresponding to that of the human fetal brain, treatment of the neonates is continued from the second to the seventh postnatal day. The behavior of the animals is tested at varying ages up to 75–85 days.

To date, we have observed the following manifestations of clinical maternal PKU in both animal models: low birthweight, microcephaly, greater than normal mortality among neonates, and lasting behavioral deficits. Measures devised for the prevention of fetal brain damage may be tested in our animal models as we gain more information from our ongoing studies on biochemical changes induced by hyperphenylalaninemia and phenylacetate.

Information on other maternal inborn errors of metabolism is scant. However, it is conceivable that fetal brain damage resulting from an abnormal intrauterine environment may occur in mothers afflicted with maple syrup urine disease, nonketotic hyperglycinemia, defects in metabolism of the urea cycle amino acids, histidinemia, methylmalonic aciduria, propionic aciduria, and galactosemia.

ACKNOWLEDGMENTS

We thank Dr. J. Heininger and his assistants for some of the amino acid analyses and Dr. C. M. Miezejeski for psychological evaluation of the subject.

REFERENCES

Armstrong, M. D., and Tyler, F. H. 1955. Studies on phenylketonuria. I. Restricted phenylalanine intake in phenylketonuria. J. Clin. Invest. 34:565–580.

Bickel, H., Gerrard, J., and Hickmans, E. M. 1954. The influence of phenylalanine intake on the chemistry and behavior of a phenylketonuric child. Acta Paediatr. 43:64–77.

Fenichel, G. M. 1980. Neonatal Neurology 2, p. 169. Churchill-Livingstone, New York.

Fölling, A. 1934. Über ausscheidung von Phenylbrenztraubensäure in den Harn als Stoffwechselanomalie in Verbindung mit Imbezzillitat. Z. Physiol. Chem. 256:1–14.

Fulton, T. R., Triano, T., Rabe, A., and Loo, Y. H. 1980. Phenylacetate and the enduring behavioral deficit in experimental phenylketonuria. Life Sci. 27:1271–1281.

Guthrie, R., and Susi, A. 1963. A simple phenylalanine method for detecting phenylketonuria in large population of newborn infants. Pediatrics 32:338–343.

Jervis, G. A. 1947. Studies on phenylpyruvic oligophrenia: The position of the metabolic error. J. Biol. Chem. 169:651–656.

Kaufman, S., and Max, E. E. 1971. Studies on the phenylalanine hydroxylating systems in human liver and their relationship to pathogenesis of phenylketonuria and hyperphenylalaninemia. In: H. Bickel, F. P. Hudson, and L.

I. Woolf (eds.), Phenylketonuria and Some Other Inborn Errors of Amino Acid Metabolism, pp. 13–19. Georg Thieme Verlag, Stuttgart.

Kerr, G. R., Chamove, A. S., Harlow, H. F., and Waisman, H. A. 1968. Fetal PKU: The effect of maternal hyperphenylalaninemia during pregnancy in the Rhesus monkey (*Macaca mulatta*). Pediatrics 42:27–36.

Lenke, R. R., and Levy, H. L. 1980. Maternal phenylketonuria and hyperphenylalaninemia. N. Engl. J. Med. 303:1202–1208.

Levy, H. L., Karolkewicz, V., Houghton, S. A., and MacCready, R. A. 1970. Screening the "normal" population in Massachusetts for phenylketonuria. N. Engl. J. Med. 282:1455–1458.

Loo, Y. H. 1974. Serotonin deficiency in experimental hyperphenylalaninemia. J. Neurochem. 23:139–147.

Loo, Y. H., Fulton, T. R., Miller, K. A., and Wisniewski, H. M. 1980. Phenylacetate and brain dysfunction in experimental phenylketonuria: Synaptic development. Life Sci. 27:1283–1290.

Loo, Y. H., Jervis, G. A., and Horning, M. E. 1978a. Possible role of phenylethylamine in the pathology of the central nervous system. In: A. N. Mosnaim and M. E. Wolf (eds.), Phenylethylamine: Biological Mechanisms and Clinical Aspects, pp. 419–445. Marcel Dekker, New York.

Loo, Y. H., Scotto, J., and Wisniewski, H. M. 1978b. Myelin deficiency in experimental phenylketonuria: Contribution of the aromatic acid metabolites of phenylalanine. In: J. Palo (ed.), Myelination and Demyelination, pp. 453–469. Plenum Publishing Corp., New York.

McCaman, M. W., and Robins, E. 1962. Fluorimetric method for determination of phenylalanine in serum. J. Lab. Clin. Med. 59:885–890.

Menkes, J. H., and Aeberhard, E. 1969. Maternal phenylketonuria: The composition of cerebral lipids in an affected offspring. J. Pediatr. 74:924–931.

Perry, T. L., Hansen, S., Tischler, B., Richards, F. M., and Sokol, M. 1973. Unrecognized adult phenylketonuria. N. Engl. J. Med. 289:395–398.

Robain, O., Wen, G. Y., Wisniewski, H. M., Shek, J. W., and Loo, Y. H. 1981. Purkinje cell dendritic development in experimental phenylketonuria: A quantitative analysis. Acta Neuropathol. 53:107–112.

Scriver, C. R., and Clow, C. J. 1980. Phenylketonuria and other phenylalanine hydroxylation mutants in man. Annu. Rev. Genet. 14:179–202.

Wen, G. Y., Wisniewski, H. M., Shek, J. W., Loo, Y. H., and Fulton, T. R. 1980. Neuropathology of phenylacetate poisoning in rats: An experimental model of phenylketonuria. Ann. Neurol. 7:557–566.

Woolf, L. I., Griffiths, R., and Moncrieff, A. 1955. Treatment of phenylketonuria with a diet low in phenylalanine. Br. J. Med. 1:57–64.

Zaleski, L. A., Casey, R. E., and Zaleski, W. 1979. Maternal PKU: Dietary treatment during pregnancy. Can. Med. Assoc. J. 121:1591–1596.

SECTION III
Chromosomal Aberrations

PERSPECTIVES AND PROGRESS IN MENTAL RETARDATION
Volume II—Biomedical Aspects
Edited by J. M. Berg
Copyright © 1984 by I.A.S.S.M.D.

CYTOGENETIC PERSPECTIVES IN MENTAL RETARDATION

W. H. Finley

Laboratory of Medical Genetics, University of Alabama in Birmingham, University Station, Birmingham, Alabama 35294

Advances in cytogenetics have permitted the recognition of many new mental retardation syndromes. In severely retarded groups up to one-third have chromosomal aberrations, including trisomies, partial trisomies, insertions, deletions, and translocations. The role of chromosome heteromorphisms in normal and abnormal cell growth and in subsequent clinical manifestations is now a major concern in basic and clinical research. High-resolution cytogenetics will continue to provide information on basic mechanisms and to give information for use in genetic counseling.

Cytogenetic studies permit the categorization of an increasing number of mental retardation syndromes that were previously unclassifiable. The large majority of patients with a chromosomal aberration have multiple congenital malformations, with mental retardation being a consistent clinical feature if an autosome is involved. Aberrations include both redundancy and deficiency of genetic material in the form of trisomies, insertions, deletions, and translocations. These aberrations cause an imbalance in gene function during embryogenesis, disturbance in synchrony of normal processes, and ultimately manifestations of a multiple-system disease.

Studies of interactions during fetal development of the products of extra genetic material or the results of its loss are major research fields. Awareness of the complexity of the development mechanisms affected leads to the conclusion that discovery of approaches to prevent chromosomal disorders through basic research would likely be more productive than reestablishing the balance of gene function after embryogenesis is underway. The discovery of biochemical and physiological events leading to abnormal gametogenesis, chromosomal rearrangements, or abnormal cell division will undoubtedly result in procedures to reduce the frequency of occurrence of abnormal conceptuses. Until these basic questions can be answered, the correlations of abnormal chromosomal findings with abnormal clinical features can be helpful in understanding the contribution of specific chromosomal aberrations to abnormal development. Increasing knowledge about cell division, cell cycle events, and cellular metabolism will in time result in more approaches to reduce fetal wastage and to improve the quality of life.

Currently much attention is given to the nosology of the chromosomal aberration syndromes and their clinical manifestations. Chromosome studies make possible accurate risk predictions and the utilization of results for diagnosis, patient management, and prenatal evaluation. Expectations are that these techniques, together with breakthroughs in other areas, will allow definition of basic mechanisms of growth and development. An individual with redundant or deficient chromosome material will most likely have mental retardation as a manifestation along with other abnormal clinical findings. However, slight variations in chromosome structure may not result in abnormal clinical findings in the first generation but may lead to abnormalities in the next generation.

The newer cytogenetic techniques have made it possible to learn more about chromosome structure and to make an increasing number of correlations of laboratory results with clinical findings. One area of interest includes the study of heteromorphisms, which are being described regularly. These slight variations seen in chromosomes are by definition those findings seen in the population more frequently than can be explained by new mutational events. Heteromorphisms are revealed through use of fluorescent studies, G-banding, C-banding, silver staining, and other cytological techniques. They include fragile sites; enlargement of heterochromatic areas; variations in satellite size, stalk length, and nucleolar organizing regions; and variation in size of fluorescent regions of selected chromosomes. Although phenotype associations or predispositions have not been attributed to most heteromorphisms, there is an association of mental retardation with the appearance of a fragile site on Xq. Heteromorphisms as linkage markers are proving valuable in prenatal evaluation of fetuses, assessing success of bone marrow transplants, and paternity testing.

The following discussion pertains to considerations of chromosomal aberrations as groupings of redundancy or deficiency of genetic material and chromosome heteromorphisms.

Table 1. Redundancy of chromosome material

Karyotype	Extra chromosome	Relative length[a]	Frequency in live births[b]
21-trisomy	21	1.88	1/800
18-trisomy	18	2.92	1/8,000
13-trisomy	13	3.75	1/20,000
22-trisomy	22	2.02	
8-trisomy	8	4.93	
Triple X	X	5.12	1/1,000 females
XYY	Y	2.16	1/1,000 males
XXY	X	5.12	1/1,000 males
1q+		2.30	
9p+		2.16	
Unbalanced rearrangements			1/2,000

[a] Data from Sutton (1980).
[b] Data from Hook and Hamerton (1977).

CHROMOSOME REDUNDANCY

Redundancy usually is seen either as one or more extra chromosomes or as a triplication of a part of a chromosome. Table 1 lists some of the better known trisomies and partial trisomies, the less common ones being represented by the 1q+ and 9p+ syndromes. Figures 1 and 2 show a patient and his partial karyotype with triplication of about one-fourth of chromosome 1 (Garrett et al., 1975). The effect of the comparatively common extra chromosome 21 seems to be quantitative rather than qualitative. Although there is a relationship between the amount of extra chromosome material and the severity of syndromes, there are exceptions. The extra sex chromosome in the XXX and XXY syndromes is not associated with such severe clinical manifestations even though there is a larger amount of genetic material involved than in some autosomal aberrations.

Aneuploidy, as represented in the trisomy syndromes in Table 1, is the result of meiotic nondisjunction, the cause of which is obscure. The increased risk with maternal age is well established, although trisomy occurs in offspring of mothers of all ages. As many as 30% of 21 trisomy cases have occurred as a result of nondisjunction in the father. The recurrence risk is increased in couples who have had a trisomy child; therefore it is assumed that there are genetic and/or environmental factors that predispose to meiotic nondisjunction events. It would seem important to develop laboratory techniques that could make possible identification of subgroups of parents at increased risk for trisomy.

Because the 21 trisomy and 13 trisomy aberrations involve acrocentric chromosomes, these particular chromosomes may have struc-

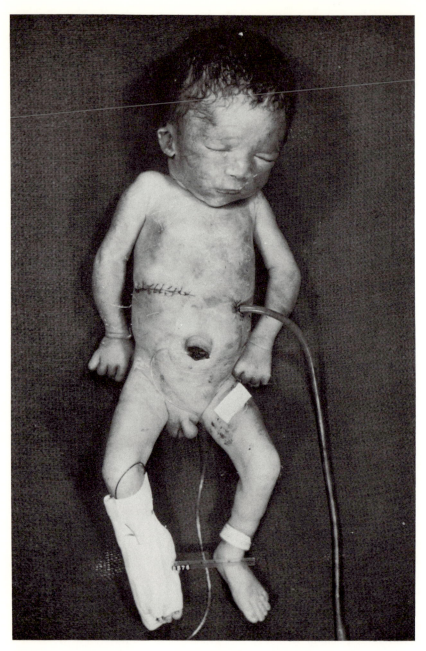

Figure 1. Patient with 1q+ (1q25 → 1qter). Reprinted by permission from: Garrett, J. H., Finley, S. C., and Finley, W. H. 1975. Fetal loss and familial chromosome 1 translocations. Clin. Genet. 8:341–348.

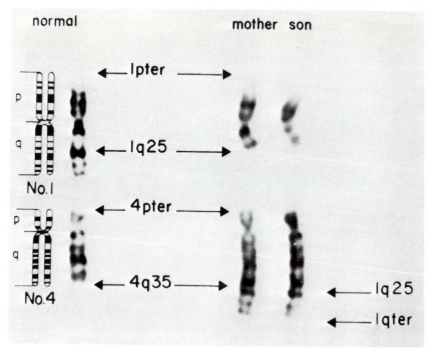

Figure 2.   Partial karyotype of mother [46,XX,t(1;4)(q25;q35)] and of her son with 1q + .

tures that facilitate nondisjunction events. The nucleolar organizing regions and satellites are two distinguishing features of chromosomes 13 and 21; however, 18 trisomy, which occurs more often than 13 trisomy, does not have these particular features. Smith et al.'s study (1982) of nucleolar organizing regions in young parents of 21-trisomic children showed an increase in G-G pairing in them, in comparison to controls. Chromosomes 14 and 15 have features similar to 13 but are not involved in nondisjunction as often. Alterations in normal physiological processes in gametogenesis may provide the clue to abnormal disjunctive events; hormonal imbalances are considerations. However, it is difficult to ascertain the status of influences during the first and second meiotic divisions.

The defects resulting from trisomy are multiple, with 21 trisomy patients being less severely affected than those with 18 trisomy, 13 trisomy, or 22 trisomy. It can be deduced, then, that the extra genetic material on chromosome 21, whether inhibitory or promotional during embryogenesis, causes a lesser problem quantitatively than those factors on other chromosomes. Because many trisomy cases do not reach term gestation, there must be genetic and/or environmental insults contributing to lethality.

Patients with chromosome redundancy also include those with mosaicism, partial triplication of a chromosome, and unbalanced karyotypes with translocations. Mosaic karyotypes are thought to arise during mitosis rather than meiosis, as is the case with full trisomy. The mitotic error may involve a mechanism similar to that at meiosis, but research has not yet yielded specific information. Chromosome rearrangements, such as translocations resulting from multiple breaks, may result in triplication of chromosome parts. This redundancy has allowed the study of clinical manifestations associated with partial triplication of a chromosome. Occasionally a part of a chromosome is not attached to another but occurs as a triplicate.

Mental retardation, the most frequently occurring handicap in children, is associated with chromosomal aberrations to a significant extent. Among 1-year-old children Gustavson et al. (1977) found chromosomal aberrations in 35% of cases with IQs less than 50 and in 8% of those with IQs between 50 and 70. The cause of retardation was unexplained in 20% of the children with IQs less than 50 and in 43% with IQs of 50 to 70 (Blomquist et al., 1981). In institutionalized retarded patients Sutherland et al. (1976) noted Down's syndrome in one-third of those with IQs less than 50. Various surveys indicate that 10–15% of institutionalized retarded persons (20 times the neonate rate) have chromosomal aberrations (Speed et al., 1976; Jacobs et al., 1978; Faed et al., 1979; Kondo et al., 1980). Studies done in institutions in Australia, England, Belgium, Scotland, Japan, and the United States (Kondo et al., 1980) all show that Down's syndrome accounts for the vast majority of chromosomal aberrations, with other trisomies constituting 1–2%, translocations less than 1%, and sex chromosomal aberrations about 1%. In newborn surveys, the frequency of chromosomal aberrations appears to be about 0.6% (Hook and Hamerton, 1977). Chromosomal aberration frequencies seem to occur approximately at the same rate worldwide (Kondo et al., 1980).

CHROMOSOME DEFICIENCY

A nondisjunctive event in gametogenesis can result in loss of an entire chromosome in the zygote or lead to mosaicism if a similar error occurs in somatic cell division. Monosomy of an autosome is very rare; in the few cases reported, only the small G chromosomes have been involved. Patients with a 45,XO karyotype constitute a most important group of monosomy patients. The vast majority of them, although not mentally retarded, are at increased risk for a number of health problems.

Table 2.   Deficiency of chromosome material

Clinical finding	Karyotype						
	4p −	4r	5p −	6r	13q −	18q −	18r
Mental retardation	+	+	+	+	+	+	+
High-pitched cry	—	—	+	—	—	—	—
Low birthweight	+	+	+	—	—	+	+
Microcephaly	+	+	+	+	+	+	+
Hypertelorism	+	+	+	+	+	+	+
Micrognathia	+	+	+	—	+	—	—
Retinoblastoma	—	—	—	—	+	—	—
Congenital heart disease	+	—	—	—	+	+	—

+, present; −, absent.

Before chromosome material is lost it becomes broken and disappears during gametogenesis or during cell division. Translocations, rings, and deletions can result after chromosome breaks. There are probably multiple causes for breakage but not all are known. Resulting deletions may be terminal or interstitial. A balanced translocation results from a breakage of two chromosomes and their subsequent fusion. Approximately 1 in 500 newborns have a balanced rearrangement. The carrier of a balanced rearrangement does not have abnormal clinical findings but is at increased risk for fetal wastage and children with chromosome abnormalities. In surveys of institutionalized retarded persons about 0.3% have deletions or ring chromosome formation (Jacobs et al., 1978).

The number of patients with chromosome deletions is not as great as that with trisomies. The amount of chromosome material lost varies among patients and is related to severity of clinical expression. Also, patients with the same breakpoints may have variation in expressivity. Table 2 illustrates the clinical findings in some of the deletion syndromes. In Figure 3 the ring 4 chromosome shows how the banding patterns permit recognition of breakpoints and determination of the amount of deleted material (Finley et al., 1981). As banding patterns with higher resolution become available, expectations are that contributions from specific chromosome areas become better defined.

CHROMOSOME HETEROMORPHISMS

Heteromorphisms are most often revealed by one of several staining procedures. Fluorescence studies using quinacrine, giemsa staining after various pretreatment techniques, and R-banding are the banding procedures most frequently used. The variation in number and size of nucleolar organizing regions as revealed by silver staining provides

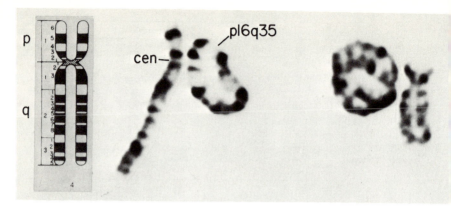

Figure 3.   Partial karyotype of patient with ring 4 chromosome. The ring is joined at
p16q35. Dicentric ring on right; *cen* = centromere. Reprinted by permission from Finley,
W. H., Finley, S. C., Chonmaitree, T., Koors, J. E., and Chandler, W. S. 1981. Ring
4 chromosome with terminal p and q deletions. Am. J. Dis. Child. 135:729–731. Copyright
1981, American Medical Association.

evidence of heteromorphisms (Figure 4). The use of folic acid–deficient
leukocyte culture medium to demonstrate the fragile site on the X chromosome is an approach to identification of a subgroup of mentally
retarded persons (see below). Although clinical significance has not
been attributed to most heteromorphic areas (Matsuura et al., 1979),
the potential for better understanding of genetic mechanisms is present
because the DNA constituents vary in these areas (Manuelidis, 1978).
Whether or not a heteromorphic site predisposes the individual to ab-

Table 3.   Some chromosomal polymorphisms

Chromosome number	Cytological description
1	Constitutive heterochromatin variation; secondary constriction
2	Prone to inversions; fragile site on 2q
3	Q-bright centric region
9	Constitutive heterochromatin variation; secondary constriction
12	Constitutive heterochromatin variation (slight)
13–15	Nucleolar organizing regions
16	Constitutive heterochromatin variation; secondary constriction
17	Constitutive heterochromatin variation (slight)
21–22	Nucleolar organizing regions
X	Fragile site at Xq2800
Y	Q-bright; length

CHROMOSOMES NOT IN ASSOCIATION

CHROMOSOMES IN ASSOCIATION

Figure 4.   Silver staining of metaphase plate for NORs (nucleolar organizing regions). (Photo courtesy of Dr. Janice Smith)

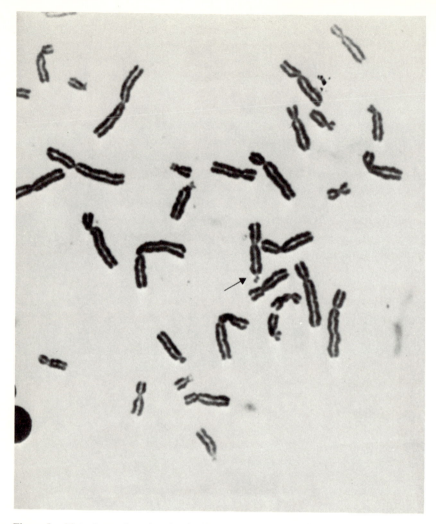

Figure 5.   Metaphase plate showing fragile X chromosome (*arrow*). (Photo courtesy of Dr. Andrew J. Carroll, III)

normal cell events is not known. Some of the chromosome variations referred to are shown in Table 3.

The fragile site on various chromosomes has been considered as heteromorphic (Sutherland, 1979). This marker area on the X chromosome (Figure 5) has been shown to be associated with mental retardation and macro-orchidism and follows an X-linked inheritance pattern. Blomquist et al. (1982) concluded that the fragile X syndrome accounted for about 6% of severely (IQ <50) retarded males, and that this syndrome appeared to be the second most common single type of severe mental retardation. The significance of the macro-orchidism is poorly understood (Howard-Peebles and Finley, 1982). It has become clear that chromosome studies using folic acid–deficient medium are mandatory in the diagnostic work up of retarded males (Turner and Opitz, 1980).

CONCLUSIONS

The classification of syndromes characterized by retardation in growth and development and associated with specific chromosomal aberrations will give additional clues to basic mechanisms. Preventive measures now include genetic counseling and prenatal evaluation. Improvement can be expected in the near future in the identification of subgroups at increased risk. As more is learned about the physiology of reproduction and the pattern of abnormal germ cell production, prevention measures can become better defined. It is important that research efforts be expanded to learn more about disorders of prenatal origin. Such research programs should continue to require emphasis on mechanisms involved in normal and abnormal cell growth.

REFERENCES

Blomquist, H. K., Gustavson, K.-H., and Holmgren, G. 1981. Mild mental retardation in children in a Northern Swedish County. J. Ment. Defic. Res. 25:169–186.
Blomquist, H. K., Gustavson, K.-H., Holmgren, G., Nordenson, I., and Sweins, A. 1982. Fragile site X chromosomes and X-linked mental retardation in severely retarded boys in a Northern Swedish County. A prevalence study. Clin. Genet. 21:209–214.
Faed, M. J. W., Robertson, J., Field, M. A. S., and Mellon, J. P. 1979. A chromosome survey of a hospital for the mental subnormal. Clin. Genet. 16:191–204.
Finley, W. H., Finley, S. C., Chonmaitree, T., Koors, J. E., and Chandler, W. S. 1981. Ring 4 chromosome with terminal p and q deletions. Am. J. Dis. Child. 135:729–731.
Garrett, J. H., Finley, S. C., and Finley, W. H. 1975. Fetal loss and familial chromosome 1 translocations. Clin. Genet. 8:341–348.
Gustavson, K.-H., Holmgren, G., Jonsell, R., and Blomquist, H. K. 1977. Severe mental retardation in children in a Northern Swedish County. J. Ment. Defic. Res. 21:161–180.
Hook, E. B., and Hamerton, J. L. 1977. The frequency of chromosome abnormalities detected in consecutive newborn studies—Differences between studies—Results by sex and by severity of phenotypic involvement. In: E. B. Hook and I. H. Porter (eds.), Population Cytogenetics. Studies in Humans, pp. 63–97. Academic Press, Inc., San Diego.

Howard-Peebles, P. N., and Finley, W. H. 1982. Macroorchidism and fragile X-linked mental retardation. Paper presented at the 1982 Birth Defects Conference, Birmingham, Alabama, June 14–16.

Jacobs, P. A., Matsuura, J. S., Mayer, M., and Newlands, I. M. 1978. A cytogenetic survey of an institution for the mentally retarded. I. Chromosome abnormalities. Clin. Genet. 13:37–60.

Kondo, I., Hamaguchi, H., Nakajima, S., and Haneda, T. 1980. A cytogenetic survey of 449 patients in a Japanese institution for the mentally retarded. Clin. Genet. 17:177–182.

Manuelidis, L. 1978. Chromosomal localization of complex and single repeated human DNAs. Chromosoma 66:23–30.

Matsuura, J. S., Mayer, M., and Jacobs, P. A. 1979. A cytogenetic survey of an institution for the mentally retarded. III. Q-band chromosome heteromorphisms. Hum. Genet. 52:203–210.

Smith, J., Finley, S., and Finley, W. 1982. Association of nucleolus organizer regions of human acrocentric chromosomes. Paper presented at the 1982 Birth Defects Conference, Birmingham, Alabama, June 14–16.

Speed, R. M., Johnston, A. W., and Evans, H. J. 1976. Chromosome survey of total population of mentally subnormal in North-East of Scotland. J. Med. Genet. 13:295–306.

Sutherland, G. R. 1979. Heritable fragile sites on human chromosomes II. Distribution, phenotypic effects, and cytogenetics. Am. J. Hum. Genet. 31:136–148.

Sutherland, G. R., Murch, A. R., Gardiner, A. J., Carter, R. F., and Wiseman, C. 1976. Cytogenetic survey of a hospital for the mentally retarded. Hum. Genet. 34:231–245.

Sutton, H. E. 1980. An Introduction to Human Genetics, 3rd ed., p. 66. W. B. Saunders Company, Philadelphia.

Turner, G., and Opitz, J. M. 1980. Editorial comment: X-linked mental retardation. Am. J. Med. Genet. 7:404–415.

PERSPECTIVES AND PROGRESS IN MENTAL RETARDATION
Volume II—Biomedical Aspects
Edited by J. M. Berg

RARE CHROMOSOMAL FINDINGS IN DOWN'S SYNDROME

H. C. Thuline

Genetics Program, State of Washington,
1704 N. E. 150th Street, Seattle, Washington 98155

Rare karyotypes reported in individuals with clinical Down's syndrome have a cumulative prevalence of about 1 in 250. These karyotypes include trisomy 21 associated with translocations; inversions or deletion involving other pairs; double aneuploidies; translocations of D;21 or G;21 other than the usual Robertsonian type; trisomy with del 21q or ring 21; isochromosome 21q; translocation or insertion of 21q to autosomes other than the acrocentrics; and mosaicism for structural rearrangements. The data are derived from review of the literature, the *Eighth Listing of the Repository of Chromosomal Variants and Anomalies in Man*, and our own case series since 1960.

Exemplifying the growth of human cytogenetics, the *Eighth Listing of the Repository of Chromosomal Variants and Anomalies in Man*, compiled by Borgaonkar et al. (1981), contains karyotype data for 269,478 individuals. Of these, 43,196 have various chromosomal abnormalities and variants. In that number, 22,636 are reports for Down's syndrome. This suggests that about one-half of abnormal karyotypes involve trisomy for all or part of the 21 chromosome. With so large a population for one clinical syndrome, rare chromosomal findings within the group might be expected. Reviews of the chromosomal types in Down's syndrome were made by Hamerton (1971) and by Smith and Berg (1976), who also gave an excellent review of case reports for double aneuploidy.

Three sources of data are used for this report: 1) published series for Down's syndrome; 2) personal communications to Borgaonkar et al.; and 3) the series in our laboratory since 1960. Each source has its limitations as to representing the whole population with Down's syndrome, but taken together they offer an approximation of pragmatic value. All three come under the rubric of "convenience samples" (Piper and Lippman-Hand, 1981).

As background, it is of interest to note that Polani (1981) estimated that 0.45% to 0.65% of all human conceptions may be trisomic for chromosome 21, and Stein et al. (1977) estimated that 70% of all recognized pregnancies with a trisomy 21 conceptus are spontaneously aborted. Polani cited the work of Creasy for a frequency of 0.9% for the double aneuploidy XXY + an autosome and 1.6% for double autosomal trisomy in abortuses. The combined frequency of 2.5% for double aneuploidy among aborted fetuses does not give a specific figure for double aneuploidies involving a 21.

As to frequency of Down's syndrome and double aneuploidies in live-born infants, a combined series of newborn males studied by buccal smears for XXY and clinically for Down's syndrome (Taylor and Moores, 1967) identified two individuals among 23,229 with XXY, +21 a frequency of 1 in 11,615 male births. Double aneuploidy in live-born infants with Down's syndrome appears to be more frequent than would be expected from the independent frequencies for each trisomy. Hecht et al. (1969) found a lower than expected prevalence of the 48,XXY, +21 karyotype among older males with Down's syndrome, and raised the question of increased mortality for those with double aneuploidy.

DISCUSSION OF UNUSUAL KARYOTYPES

An estimate of prevalence for the various karyotypes is made in Table 1. From these sources it appears that about 1 in 250 individuals with Down's syndrome has an unusual karyotype. To facilitate consideration of the chromosomal types found in Down's syndrome, they are presented in Table 2 in a format modified from Hamerton (1981).

Primary Errors in Meiosis or Mitosis

Category A-1 in Table 2 includes 95% of individuals with Down's syndrome. Trisomy 21 is known to result from nondisjunction in the father or mother, in first or second meiotic divisions, and, for mosaics, in postzygotic divisions. In category A-2 are mosaic karyotypes with a D;21 translocation in all cells but mosaicism for trisomy 21. We are aware of two cases. Our patient has a 14;21 translocation with mosaic trisomy for a complete 21. The most probable etiology is a somatic cell loss of the trisomic 21 from a 46,t(14;21) trisomy-21 zygote.

Under category A-3, translocations involving members of every pair except 7, 8, 10, and 11 have been seen, and inversions of 2, 5, 6 or X, 9, and Y have occurred, in addition to the trisomy 21 of Down's syndrome. The majority are case reports in the literature, reviewed by Smith and Berg (1976), or personal communications to Borgaonkar et

Table 1. Frequency of chromosomal types in Down's syndrome in various studies

	Gardner et al. (1973)	Giraud and Mattei (1975)	Dey (1977)	Casalone et al. (1979)	Thuline (1982)	Borgaonkar et al. (1981)	Total
Number of subjects	972	4760	485	729	883	22,636	30,465
Karyotypes (%)							
47,+21 including mosaicism	95.1	95.2	92.4	94.9	92.7	95.4	95.2
D;21 translocations	2.36	2.6	2.68	2.47	3.48 ⎫	4.3	4.55
G;21 translocations	1.3	1.96	2.68	2.19	1.9 ⎭		
Other (i.e., unusual)	1.1	0.24	0.41	0.44	1.93	0.34	0.40

Table 2.   Trisomy-21 karyotype classification[a]

A. Numerical: Primary errors in meiosis or mitosis
    1. 47,+21 and 46/47,+21
    2. D;21 translocation with mosaicism for +21
    3. +21 with translocation, inversion, or deletion in pairs other than 21
    4. +21 with double aneuploidy
    5. +del 21 or r 21

B. Structural: Rearrangements and malsegregation
    1. Secondary; 21,+(21q;21q)
       a. translocation; monocentric
       b. translocation; dicentric
       c. isochromosome 21q
       d. ring
    2. Tertiary; Translocations (de novo and familial)
       a. D;21, 21;22
          i. monocentric
          ii. dicentric
       b. Tandem
          i. monocentric
          ii. dicentric
       c. Reciprocal; autosome/21
       d. Insertion
       e. Mosaicism

[a] Adapted from Hamerton (1981).

al., but four are our patients (included in the 1.9% of karyotypes under "Other" in Table 1). These are a t(?4;?16) found in a proband with +21 Down's syndrome, his carrier mother, and carrier brother; a familial t(14;22)+21 Down's syndrome case with a carrier father; and pericentric inversions of a 5 and of a Y. Pericentric inversion of a 9 in association with Down's syndrome appears to be relatively common and has not been shown to be etiologically significant. Report of a structurally abnormal X in association with trisomy 21 appears to be limited to an Xq−. Those associations that include Turner's/Down's syndrome are discussed below. An apparent isolated instance in this category is our case with a fragile 16 and trisomy 21.

Table 3 lists the double aneuploidy karyotypes representing category A-4 in Table 2. It is noteworthy that many are mosaics with two, three, or even four cell lines. This variety of mosaicism has raised the possibility of an instability of the mitotic process with manifestation in such cases. Because extra X chromosomes are not associated with fetal loss, as are extra autosomes, the reported preponderance of gonosomal double aneuploidies is not unexpected. More surprising is the rare survival for study of fetuses and infants with double autosomal aneuploidy, as illustrated by those trisomic for an 8, a 13, an 18, a 22, or a fourth 21 in addition to trisomy 21, either in all cells or as mosaicism.

Table 3.   Karyotypes included in category A-4 of Table 2

a)   Trisomy-21 plus

X:	XXY;	48,XXY,+21;	47,XY,+21/48,XXY,+21
	XXX;	48,XXX,+21;	47,XX,+21/48,XXX,+21
Y:	XYY;	48,XYY,+21;	47,XY,+21/48,XYY,+21

8:   2 cases: 47,+21/48,+8,+21(severely affected)
46,XY/48,XY,+8,+21 in leucocytes, 46,XY in skin, of
female with gonadal dysgenesis

13:   46/47,+G/48,+D,+G;   47,+G/47,+D/48,+D,+G;
48,+D,+G;   47,+G/48,+D,+G

18:   48,+18,+21;   46/48,+18,+21;   47,+E/48,+E,+G;
46/47,+E/47,+G/48,+E/+G;   47,+G/48,+E,+G

21:   48,XY,+21,+21

22:   48,XY,+21,+22

b)   Monosomy-X (complete and mosaic)

c)   Mosaics and chimeras
47,+21/47,+9;   47,+21/47,+13;   47,+21/47,+16;   47,+21/
47,+18;   47,+21/47,+22;   47,+21/47,XXY;   45,X/47,XY,+21

Of interest are cases with complete or mosaic monosomy X in that a specific Turner's/Down's polysyndrome has been proposed by Villaverde and DaSilva (1975). Of 38 cases found in the literature (including our three), 10 were of the 45,X/47,XX,+21 type, 10 were of the 46,X,+21/47,XX,+21 type, four involved structurally abnormal X chromosomes, and the remainder were an array of varied mosaics except for one 46,X,+21.

In category c of Table 3 are instances, including abortuses, that may represent either chimerism or double nondisjunction mosaicism. It would be attractive to assume initial separate zygotes for the two cell lines, with fusion of the two making the resulting individual a chimera. However, no report has been published, to our knowledge, of experimental examination of this hypothesis. We attempted to establish the parental origin of nondisjunction using Q-band polymorphisms for our cases of 47,XY,+21/47,XY,+9 and 45,X/47,XX,+21. For the +21/+9 case the polymorphisms were compatible with both errors in maternal first meiotic division. The distinct polymorphisms required to make an unequivocal decision for or against chimerism in lymphocytes of the 45,X/47,XX,+21 case were not evident. Chimerism ceased to be a consideration when fibroblasts from skin culture showed a major cell line as 47,XX,+21 and minor cell lines of 46,XX; 45,X; and 46,X,+21. The last karyotype in the listing (45,X/47,XY,+21) is of clinical interest in that it was described in two males with Down's syndrome associated with genital anomalies and should be considered in those circumstances.

Category A-5 in Table 2, deletion of 21q with Down's syndrome, is very unusual. The one case we have seen was 47, +21 but with one of the 21 chromosomes showing an interstitial deletion of q11 → 21 and preservation of the 21q bands involved in the phenotype of Down's syndrome. Also in this category are the rare instances, including one of ours, with a ring 21 in the trisomy.

Rearrangements and Malsegregation

Part B of Table 2 includes the trisomies arising from two 21 long arms in a single chromosome. These may be true translocations, either monocentric or dicentric, or isochromosomes for 21q. Monocentric 21;21 translocations with juxtacentromeric breakpoints usually cannot be distinguished from an isochromosome of 21q, but occasionally it is possible to be confident of an isochromosome 21q. One of our patients has a karyotype of 46,XXX,21p−/46,XXX,i21q. The 21p− arose de novo because both parents had normal 21 chromosomes. An identical normal 21 was found in both patient cell lines, which indicates that the 21p− had become the i21q to give the mosaicism and the Down's syndrome. The second unusual feature in this patient is the XXX in all cells. The finding of mosaicism for 21p− and i21q has been reported twice before. Also, both 21 chromosomes of the normal cell line may show intact short arms and we have such a case. Thus, it appears that the i21q may arise in a postzygotic division from 1) a familial 21p−, 2) a postzygotic 21p− de novo to the patient, and 3) misdivision of the centromere in an apparently normal 21. A few instances, including one in our series, of ring formation in the 21q;21q translocation chromosome have been seen.

The Robertsonian translocations generally associated with Down's syndrome have been widely reported and studied. Tandem translocations are generally rare and are not limited to the 21;21 type, having been seen also as 13;21q, 14;21q, and 15;21q tandem rearrangements. More common are translocations of all or part of 21q to a nonacrocentric autosome. All autosomal pairs except 5, 9, 17, 18, and 20 have been reported involved in translocations with a 21q in Down's syndrome. Our own cases were both familial, a t(10;21q) and a t(16;21q). The t(10;21q) was associated with recurrence of Down's syndrome in siblings and sterility of a carrier male but not of the carrier mother. In the t(16;21q) only 21q22 → qter was attached to the end of 16p. The affected children in both families showed typical Down's syndrome. Perhaps the most rare rearrangement is insertion into another chromosome of the portion of 21q critical to Down's syndrome. Three siblings with Down's syndrome were born to a mother who carried an insertion of 21 (q21q22) into a 15 at 15q11. We also have a case of de novo insertion of 21(q22) into a long arm of a 6, at 6q21, in a child with Down's syndrome.

Mosaicism for structural rearrangements has been seen as mosaicism for a t(21;21) in one cell line and ring(21;21) in the other to give the karyotype 46,t(21q;21q)/46,rt(21q;21q). Other cases have been reported of 47, +21/46,t(D;21);45,t(15;21)/46,t(21;21) and 45,t(15;21)/46,i(21q). An explanation for these is that the t(15;21), in two cases, disassociated into a 15 and a 21p− that became the "t(21;21)" of one report and the "i(21q)" of the other. The same mechanism without i21q formation would explain the 47, +21/46,t(D;21) case.

CONCLUSIONS

From this review of rare cytogenetic findings in Down's syndrome it is apparent that the cytogenetic events associated with trisomy for the critical segment of 21q are multiple. These include nondisjunction of pairs in addition to number 21; metaphase lag; double fertilization; chromosome breakage and translocation or ring formation; stepwise breakage and isochromosome formation; translocation followed by ring formation; translocation followed by disassociation; and a parent with a translocation of 21q with malsegregation in meiosis. There is also the possibility that the risk of nondisjunction is increased by the presence of a structural rearrangement in a parent. Such considerations are relevant for specific rare karyotypes encountered in individuals with Down's syndrome.

REFERENCES

Borgaonkar, D. S., Shaffer, R., Reed, W. C., and Jackson, L. (eds.). 1981. Eighth Listing of the Repository of Chromosomal Variants and Anomalies in Man—An International Registry of Abnormal Karyotypes (1981). Wilmington Medical Center, Wilmington, Delaware.

Casalone, R., Fraccaro, M., Francesconi, D., Pasquali, F., Poloni, L., Zuffardi, O., Bellomi, A., Crosti, N., Lo Monaco, G. B., Patriarca, P. L., and Serventi, M. 1979. Five unusual karyotypes in Down syndrome. Ann. Genet. 22:17–20.

Dey, J. 1977. Clinical profiles of atypical chromosome-G anomalies. In: P. Mittler (ed.), Research to Practice in Mental Retardation, Vol. III, Biomedical Aspects, pp. 71–79. University Park Press, Baltimore.

Gardner, R. J. M., Veale, A. M. O., Parslow, M. I., Becroft, D. M. O., Shaw, R. L., Fitzgerald, P. H., Hutchings, H. E., McCreanor, H. R., Wong, J., Eiby, J. R., Howarth, D. A., and Whyte, J. E. 1973. A survey of 972 cytogenetically examined cases of Down's syndrome. N.Z. Med. J. 78:403–409.

Giraud, F., and Mattei, J. F. 1975. Aspects epidemiologies de la trisomy 21. J. Genet. Hum. 23:1–30.

Hamerton, J. L. 1971. Human Cytogenetics, Vol. II, pp. 196–261. Academic Press, Inc., New York.

Hamerton, J. L. 1981. Frequency of mosaicism, translocation and other variants of trisomy 21. In: F. F. de la Cruz and P. S. Gerald (eds.), Trisomy 21 (Down Syndrome): Research Perspectives, pp. 99–107. University Park Press, Baltimore.

Hecht, F., Neivaard, J. E., Duncanson, N., Miller, J. R., Higgins, J. V., Kimberling, W. J., Walker, F. A., Smith, G. S., Thuline, H. C., and Tischler, B. 1969. Double aneuploidy: The frequency of XXY in males with Down's syndrome. Am. J. Hum. Genet. 21:352–359.

Piper, M. C., and Lippman-Hand, A. 1981. The convenience sample as a source of data in the study of Down syndrome. J. Ment. Defic. Res. 25:217–223.

Polani, P. E. 1981. Chiasmata, Down syndrome and nondisjunction: An overview. In: F. F. de la Cruz and P. S. Gerald (eds.), Trisomy 21 (Down Syndrome): Research Perspectives, pp. 111–130. University Park Press, Baltimore.

Smith, G. F., and Berg, J. M. 1976. Down's Anomaly, pp. 169–233. Churchill Livingstone, New York.

Stein, Z. A., Susser, M., Kline, J., and Warburton, D. 1977. Amniocentesis and selective abortion for trisomy 21 in the light of the natural history of pregnancy and fetal survival. In: E. B. Hook and I. H. Porter (eds.), Population Cytogenetics: Studies in Humans, pp. 257–274. Academic Press, Inc., New York.

Taylor, A. I., and Moores, E. C. 1967. A sex chromatin survey of newborn children in two London hospitals. J. Med. Genet. 4:258–259.

Villaverde, M. M., and DaSilva, J. A. 1975. Turner-mongolism polysyndrome: Review of the first eight known cases. JAMA 234:844–847.

PERSPECTIVES AND PROGRESS IN MENTAL RETARDATION
Volume II—Biomedical Aspects
Edited by J. M. Berg

DOWN'S SYNDROME AND FAMILIAL ANEUPLOIDY

C. M. Tuck[1], J. W. Bennett[1], and M. Varela[2]

[1] *Department of Biology, Tulane University, New Orleans, Louisiana 70118*
[2] *Hayward Genetics Center, Tulane School of Medicine, New Orleans, Louisiana 70112*

Secondary (inevitable) nondisjunction and mosaicism are discussed in terms of familial aneuploidy. An extensive literature review, plus cases from our laboratory, revealed 31 examples of heteroaneuploidy in families. Such mixed aneuploidies may be due to chance, a genetic predisposition, environmental causes, or a combination of factors.

Aneuploidy originates through the gain and loss of chromosomes during mitosis or meiosis. The failure of two chromosomes or chromatids to separate properly and pass to opposite poles during division is termed *nondisjunction*. Several of the most important human cytogenetic aberrations are forms of aneuploidy (e.g., Down's, Turner's, and Klinefelter's syndromes); hence looking for the cause of these conditions is in effect looking for the cause of nondisjunction. Because the literature on Down's syndrome (DS) is more extensive than that on any other human aneuploid condition, much of this paper deals with trisomy 21; however, other aneuploidies are discussed where relevant.

Familial Down's syndrome has been recognized since the turn of the century and the older medical literature was reviewed by Brousseau (1928) and Penrose (1963). The incidence of affected sibs is about one for every 100 single cases collected at random. The origin of an aneuploid condition is clear when there is direct transmission from an affected or mosaic parent. Some familial cases of DS are due to translocation rather than trisomy and can be transmitted through balanced carriers. However, when more than one kind of aneuploidy occurs in a family (heteroaneuploidy) or when more than one form of aneuploidy

C. M. Tuck's research has been supported by a National Science Foundation Science Faculty Professional Development Award. Support is also acknowledged from a Biomedical Science Support Grant (Tulane University, #537826).

coexists in an individual (double aneuploidy), neither translocation nor mosaicism is an adequate explanation. Familial and individual clustering of aneuploidy may be coincidental, but genetic control is also a possibility. Specific genes causing nondisjunction are known in some nonhuman species.

In this paper we review the literature on familial Down's syndrome, with particular emphasis on multiple forms of aneuploidy within a single family. Environmental influences that could produce familial clustering are also described. Familial DS resulting from inherited translocations has been reviewed thoroughly elsewhere (Lilienfeld and Benesch, 1969; Smith and Berg, 1976).

DOWN'S SYNDROME AND SECONDARY NONDISJUNCTION

Secondary or "inevitable" nondisjunction refers to cases in which the parental gonad is already aneuploid. During meiosis both normal and aneuploid gametes are produced with equal frequency and the theoretical likelihood of transmission of the aneuploid condition is 50%. Fertile trisomics and mosaics with trisomic ovaries or testes have a high probability of passing on the extra chromosomes to their children.

Direct Transmission

There are no reports of DS males fathering children, probably because of a combination of social and biological factors. Women with DS have occasionally become mothers. Bovicelli et al. (1982) comprehensively reviewed reports of 30 pregnancies in 26 women between 1917 and 1982. Chromosome analysis had been performed in 19 of these women; all were 47,XX, +21. Theoretically such women should produce 23,X and 24,X, +21 gametes with equal frequency so that half their offspring should be normal and half trisomic. In actuality the outcome of the pregnancies was 10 DS babies, 17 non-DS babies, and three abortions or stillbirths. Six of the 17 non-DS babies had mental or physical retardation or nonspecific congenital malformations. Thus, only 35% of the 30 offspring were normal. The genetically imbalanced maternal "environment" could explain the low frequency of normal offspring, but paternal factors are also important. In the 15 cases of known or supposed paternity, eight fathers were themselves retarded and the remaining seven were close relatives of the DS women (Bovicelli et al., 1982). There is an additional case from Finland, not reviewed by Bovicelli et al., of a normal son born to a DS mother and a 63-year-old father (Kivimäki and Lagus, 1981).

These data are important because increasing interest in civil rights for the mentally retarded has extended to the right to bear children. A

National Committee of Mental Retardation in the United States reviewed existing eugenic sterilization laws, and their report states:

Compulsory sterilization laws are vulnerable. Unless there is unusually strong proof that the kind of retardation an individual has is inheritable, it is unlikely that he can be lawfully sterilized against his will. Even in inheritance retardation cases, there is a strong legal and moral question about the right to sterilize. Imagine the opposition to a law requiring all high-risk parents of children with cystic fibrosis, hemophilia, or cerebral palsy to undergo sterilization. . . . No parent should be allowed to "volunteer" his child for such an operation. Too often the parent seeks sterilization out of anxiety about legal responsibility for unwanted grandchildren, or even as a condition for getting a child into an institution. (Wald, 1976, pp. 12–13)

The apparent low fertility of DS adults may circumvent many of the potential moral and legal quandaries, but the high likelihood of abnormal offspring being born to DS women remains a matter for concern.

Mosaicism

Mosaic individuals (sometimes called "mixoploids" in the older literature), depending on the percentage of somatic cells with the extra chromosome, may or may not show characteristic phenotypic features. If the germinal tissue is aneuploid, whatever the extent of phenotypic expression, the theoretical risk of secondary nondisjunction is the same as it would be for a fully affected individual (50%).

About 1–2% of patients with a confidently diagnosed clinical profile of DS are mosaics (Lilienfeld and Benesch, 1969; Hamerton, 1971), but the frequency of undetected mosaicism in individuals with no clinical signs is unknown. Most cytogenetic surveys of newborns do not count enough cells to generate accurate estimates of prevalence, so that the contribution of occult parental mosaicism to the overall frequency of DS remains speculative. Penrose initiated the use of aberrant dermatoglyphic patterns for generating estimates of mosaicism among parents of trisomy 21 children and concluded that 10% of mothers and 1% of fathers were mosaics (Penrose, 1965; Penrose and Smith, 1966). Using a similar approach, Priest et al. (1973) came up with an even higher estimated frequency: 11% of mothers and 8% of fathers of DS children. The calculated frequency from actual cytogenetic surveys is much lower. Among 442 parents of trisomy 21 children screened, only seven mosaics (1.6%) were detected (Harris et al., 1982).

Mosaicism is presumed to arise through mitotic nondisjunction in early development. In a chromosomally normal conceptus, the nondisjunctional event creates both trisomic and monosomic cell lines. The monosomic cells are eliminated; the trisomic cell line and the normal diploid tissues not involved in nondisjunction both survive. Alternatively, if the zygote is trisomic, loss of the extra chromosomes at one of the early divisions would lead to a mixture of diploid and trisomic tissue. The second model postulates two chromosomal errors: the first during gametogenesis in the parent of the mosaic before conception, and the second after conception in one of the early mitoses of the trisomic zygote. Given the well-documented maternal age correlation with trisomy 21, if the second model were in operation a high frequency of advanced age in parents of mosaics would be predicted. Some studies have found evidence of elevated age among grandparents of DS children (Greenberg, 1963; Richards, 1970; Papp et al., 1977) whereas others have not (Stoller and Collmann, 1965; Forssman and Åkesson, 1967).

In a compilation of published studies on 26 known mosaics who gave birth to DS offspring, the average age of the mothers of mosaics was 30.7 years and the average age of the fathers was 32.6 years. These grandparents of trisomics were significantly older than average, suggesting an age-dependent factor in the genesis of mosaicism (Harris et al. 1982).

In summary, although neither the incidence nor the etiology of mosaicism for trisomy 21 is known, maternal or paternal mosaicism is a valid postulate whenever more than one case of DS occurs in a sibship. However, there are reports of families in which consecutive children with DS were born and no mosaicism could be detected in either parent (Dhadial and Pfeiffer, 1972; Frolich et al., 1979). Although germinal mosaicism without somatic mosaicism cannot be ruled out, other mechanisms may be operative.

HETEROANEUPLOIDY

Double aneuploidy is the condition where two aneuploidies occur simultaneously in one individual. The most frequently reported type is 48,XXY, +21. An extensive list of published examples was compiled by Hamerton (1971). Heteroaneuploidy refers to multiple types of aneuploidy within a family; for example, siblings with Down's syndrome and Turner's syndrome, respectively. Published cases of heteroaneuploidy are listed in Table 1. Of these 28 cases, 22 involved siblings. The remaining six were an aunt, an uncle, a cousin, a daughter, and two mothers of the proband. No sex chromosome–sex chromosome heteroaneuploidies were reported in this series; there were 18 sex chromosome–autosome heteroaneuploidies and ten autosome-autosome heteroaneuploidies. The single most common combination was trisomy 21 with trisomy 18. Of the 37 maternal ages available, 18 were 35 or older.

In addition, we have reviewed the records of the Hayward Genetics Center, Tulane School of Medicine, for the 20-year period between 1960 and 1980 for cases of familial aneuploidy. During this time, 2,785 cases were karyotyped of which 421 were aneuploid. More than one case of aneuploidy was found in nine families; in six of these families the multiple cases were all Down's syndrome. In three families, heteroaneuploidy occurred. These consisted of one family in which siblings with trisomy 21 and Turner's syndrome were found, as well as two additional families in which the birth of a trisomy 21 child was followed by amniocentesis in the subsequent pregnancies. In one family amniocentesis revealed a 47,XXX karyotype; in the other a 45,X/46,XX mosaic was demonstrated. Maternal age was under 30 in all six of these pregnancies (Tuck, Varela, and Bennett, unpublished data).

What mechanism gives rise to more than one child affected with aneuploidy in a family? Neither translocation nor gonadal mosaicism is an adequate explanation. Is heteroaneuploidy due to random associations of nondisjunctional errors with some families, or to genetic predisposition? Some researchers think chance is unlikely: "It is virtually certain that the co-occurrence in a sibship of two conditions as rare as XO gonadal dysgenesis and the D syndrome is no mere coincidence. An environmental causation is conceivable but does not fit too well with the circumstance that the two patients were born thirteen years apart" (Therman et al., 1961). Others are less certain: "Such families are interesting but they do not prove much. The population base from which the family comes is not known. The fact that both types of aneuploidy, such as trisomy 13 and XXX, are clearly dependent on maternal age, is ignored. The bias of ascertainment is frequently not stated. . . . In sum, such families are largely of anecdotal interest" (Hecht, 1977).

What is the evidence for the genetic control of nondisjunction in humans?

GENETIC TENDENCIES TOWARD NONDISJUNCTION

The first meiotic mutant was discovered by Gowen and Gowen (1922) in *Drosophila melanogaster*. Since then meiotic mutants have been characterized in numerous species; many of these mutant genes cause nondisjunction. [For an extensive review see Baker et al. (1976).]

There are no proved examples of meiotic mutants in humans, but several classes of data are suggestive. Baker et al. (1976) felt that the weakest evidence for meiotic mutants effecting nondisjunction is the nonrandom clustering of heteroaneuploidy. They described several genetic conditions that affect chromosome stability in mitosis, such as

Table 1. Published examples of mixed aneuploidies in families

Reference	Karyotype or diagnosis		Relationship of case 2 to proband	Mother's age at birth of	
	Proband	Case 2		Proband	Case 2
Miller et al. (1961)	49, XXXXY	47, XX + 21[a]	aunt	23	34
Therman et al. (1961)	45, X	47, XX + D	sibling	22	35
Zellweger and Mikamo (1961)	47, XX + 21	45, XO	sibling	39	
Benirschke et al. (1962)	47, XXY	46, XX + G/G	half-sibling[b]	24	30
Breg et al. (1962)	47, XXX	47, XX × 21	cousin		25
	47, XXX	Down's syndrome	sibling		19
	47, XYY		daughter		
Hauschka et al. (1962)	47, XX + 21	45, X	sibling	25	28
Johnston and Petrakis (1963)	47, XXY	47, XY + 21[c]	sibling	25	42
Wright et al. (1963)	47, XY + 21	47, XXY/46, XY	half-sibling[b]	16	26
	47, XX + 21	47, XY + small metacentric	sibling	25	28
Gustavson et al. (1964)	47, XX	Down's syndrome	sibling		
Hecht et al. (1964)	47, XY + 18	Down's syndrome	uncle		
	47, XX + 18	Down's syndrome	sibling		

172

Reference					
Turner et al. (1964)	47, XY + 18	47, XY + 21	sibling	38	36
Atkins et al. (1968)	47, XX + 18	47, XY + 21	sibling	36	39
Casteels-van Daele et al. (1970)	46, XY + 21[d]	49, XXXXY	sibling	36	38
Holmgren and Ånséhn (1971)	47, XY + 21	46, XXqi	sibling	34	37
Girardet et al. (1972)	47, XY + 21	47, XX + 18[c]	sibling	40	42
Singer et al. (1972)	47, XX + 21	47, XX + 18	sibling	29	
Iinuma et al. (1973)	trisomy 21	47, XXX	mother		
Crandall and Ebbin (1973)	47, XY + 21	47, XXY	sibling	42	42
Broustet et al. (1975)	47, XX + 21	47, XX + 18	sibling	27	41
David and Jones (1975)	45, X	47, XX + 21	half-sibling[b]	20	30
Leroy and Dumon (1980)	47, XY + 21	47, XX + 18	sibling	37	41
Hecht (1982)	47, XY + 21	47, XXY	sibling		38
	trisomy 21	46, XX/47, XXX	mother		
	trisomy 21	45, X	sibling		

[a] In addition, a first cousin was 47, XX + 21.

[b] Same mother.

[c] One of a set of fraternal twins.

[d] An inherited D/D translocation is also present.

Bloom's syndrome, Fanconi's anemia, and Louis-Bar syndrome. The existence of genes that cause mitotic nondisjunction, may, by analogy, constitute evidence for possible genes causing meiotic disturbances. In addition Baker et al. reviewed the evidence for meiotic drive in humans, as well as cases of meiotic anomalies in sterile men with possible evidence of segregation in families, as constituting putative support for meiotic mutants in humans. Hecht (1977) also reviewed the literature on nonrandom chromosome abnormalities.

The hypothesis that recessive genes that lead to nondisjunction would be most frequently expressed in inbred populations or among the offspring of consanguineous marriages has been investigated. In an early study, Penrose (1961) noted that among the relatives of 600 DS cases in England there were three sets of parents and 15 sets of grandparents who were cousins, a significantly higher frequency of consanguinity than in the general population. Subsequently, no evidence for an elevated frequency of consanguineous marriages could be found in a large population from Sweden (Forssman and Åkesson, 1967) or Japan (Matsunaga, 1966), nor could an increased frequency of DS be detected in two inbred Amish populations in the United States (Kwiterovich et al., 1966; Juberg and Davis, 1970). However, a significantly higher risk of DS among consanguineous marriages was recently reported from Kuwait (Alfi et al., 1980). Using a theoretical mathematical model, Yokoyama et al. (1981) challenged the data from Kuwait, demonstrating that consanguinity would increase the likelihood of expression for genes for mitotic but not meiotic nondisjunction.

These studies share a common pitfall. If genes for nondisjunction occur in human populations there is no reason to expect that they should be equally distributed. For example, it would be foolish to conclude that Tay-Sachs disease and sickle cell anemia have no genetic basis if a study of an inbred Amish population revealed little or no incidence of these diseases. Similarly, assuming that only some subset of aneuploidy is due to genes for nondisjunction, an increased incidence of consanguinity among the families of affected offspring would only be expected in populations where the gene occurs. Such hypothetical genes might be less rare in Kuwait than in Sweden or Japan.

ENVIRONMENT

As with all conditions involving sporadic familial incidence, it is difficult to distinguish between possible genetic and environmental etiology. A number of studies indicate that biological, physical, or chemical agents may contribute to the incidence of DS. In virtually every case data have been conflicting, with some studies supporting environmental etiology and others not.

Both temporal and geographic clustering have been reported for DS, with viruses suggested as possible causative agents (Pleydell, 1957; Collmann and Stoller, 1962; Robinson et al., 1969; Goad et al., 1976). Therapeutic X rays to mothers (Sigler et al., 1965; Uchida et al., 1968) and high levels of background radiation (Kochupillai et al., 1976) have also been implicated. Chemicals have caused sperm abnormalities (Wyrobek and Bruce, 1975); increases in Y chromosome nondisjunction among human males have been associated with the pesticide dibromochloropropane (Kapp et al., 1979), and Lejeune and Prier (1979) noted a correlation between oral contraceptives, Down's syndrome, and the sex ratio. On the other hand, there are publications that show no evidence for temporal clustering (Stark and Fraumeni, 1966), radiation effects (Schull and Neel, 1962; Stevenson et al., 1970; Cohen et al., 1977), or effects of birth control pill use (Carr, 1970). Differences in sample size, data collection, geography, and ascertainment make comparisons difficult.

If environmental agents do contribute to aneuploidy, this could account for some cases of familial aggregation. Members of a family are more likely to be exposed to the same environmental insult than non-members, and successive children within a marriage reflect both the genetic and environmental background of the parents. Temporal clustering implies that agents such as viruses might have transitory teratogenic effects, whereas radiation exposure may set up a continuing tendency toward nondisjunction. The interaction of environmental agents with genetic predispositions is another real possibility. Because the incidence of familial aneuploidy is so low, this hypothesis is particularly difficult to test.

Parental aging can be classified as a form of environmental influence. Maternal aging is the strongest variable correlated with DS and the maternal age effect has been documented repeatedly (Lilienfeld and Benesch, 1969; Smith and Berg, 1976). More recently, paternal age has also been accepted as an important variable (Stene et al., 1981). Endogenous factors (e.g., hormones, autoimmunity, genes) as well as exogenous factors (e.g., radiation, chemical pollutants, viruses) may all be involved, but despite numerous studies the mechanism by which age leads to increased nondisjunction remains unknown. Strain-specific differences in nondisjunction rates in aging female mice have been demonstrated (Martin et al., 1976; Fabricant and Schneider, 1978). Differential susceptibilities to endogenous and exogenous effects of aging are also likely in other species, including *Homo sapiens*.

CONCLUSIONS

Familial aneuploidy is easily explained in cases of secondary (inevitable) nondisjunction in affected individuals or mosaics, but most of the time this explanation does not suffice. Nonrandom clustering of trisomy 21 in certain families is often dismissed as the result of hidden gonadal mosaicism in a parent, but heteroaneuploidy requires another interpretation. Some families may harbor genes that increase the likelihood of nondisjunction. Theoreticians have not accepted that mixed familial aneuploidies represent anything more than tantalizing anecdotes. The possibility of biased ascertainment plagues the statistician. Because of the rarity of these cases, accurate registries of mixed chromosomal anomalies are difficult to obtain and unlikely to be forthcoming. Moreover, because the recurrence risk of 1% is an established rule of thumb in genetic counseling (Oetting and Steele, 1982), cytogenetics laboratories will continue to recommend chromosomal analysis in subsequent pregnancies after the birth of an aneuploid child, thereby perpetuating the problem of biased ascertainment. Two of the cases of familial aneuploidy we uncovered in our own laboratory were from amniotic fluids of women who had previously borne trisomy-21 children.

Given the widespread occurrence of meiotic mutants in nonhuman species, as well as the repeatedly proved complexity of "nature-nurture" interactions in gene expression, the existence of Mendelian genes for nondisjunction seems a reasonable hypothesis for some cases of familial aneuploidy. However, it would be naive to assume that there is only one cause for nondisjunction, or that there is only one gene that can cause nondisjunction. A participant in the symposium on Down's syndrome sponsored by the New York Academy of Sciences over 10 years ago wrote:

> It is evident to all students of the reduction divisions that aneuploid gametes may derive from alterations at a number of sites and times during meiosis. There may, for example, be failure of conjunction of homologues (asynapsis), premature disjunction (desynapsis), premature terminalization, and failure of chiasma formation, as well as classical nondisjunction of the conjoined homologues (first division) or chromatids (second division). Hence, the search for a gene conditioning the phenomena we lump under the notion 'nondisjunction' is unrealistic. (Young, 1970, p. 392)

As our ability to study human chromosomes becomes more refined, we may find better ways of collecting evidence for genetic control of nondisjunction. Families that contain multiple aneuploidies will be obvious targets for novel approaches and the identification of such families remains a worthwhile research objective.

ACKNOWLEDGMENTS

We thank K. I. Abroms, H. Lang-Brown, and G. Smith for their support and encouragement.

REFERENCES

Alfi, O. S., Chang, R., and Azen, S. P. 1980. Evidence for genetic control of nondisjunction in man. Am. J. Hum. Genet. 32:477–483.
Atkins, L., Bartsocas, C. S., and Porter, P. J. 1968. Diverse chromosomal anomalies in a family. J. Med. Genet. 5:314–318.
Baker, B. S., Carpenter, A. T. C., Esposito, M. S., Esposito, R. E., and Sandler, L. 1976. The genetic control of meiosis. Annu. Rev. Genet. 10:53–134.
Benirschke, K., Brownhill, L., Hoefnagel, D., and Allen, F. H., Jr. 1962. Langdon Down anomaly (mongolism) with 21/21 translocation and Klinefelter's syndrome in the same sibship. Cytogenetics 1:75–89.
Bovicelli, L., Orsini, L. F., Rizzo, N., Montacuti, V., and Bachetta, M. 1982. Reproduction in Down syndrome. Obstet. Gynecol. 59:13S–17S.
Breg, W. R., Cornwell, J. G., and Miller, O. J. 1962. The association of the triple-X syndrome and mongolism in two families. Am. J. Dis. Child. 104:134–135.
Brousseau, K. 1928. Mongolism. A Study of the Physical and Mental Characteristics of Mongolian Imbeciles. Williams & Wilkins Company, Baltimore.
Broustet, A., Serville, F., Roger, P., and Gachet, M. 1975. X monosomy and 21 trisomy in a sibship. Hum. Genet. 27:333–337.
Carr, D. H. 1970. Chromosomal studies in selected spontaneous abortions: Conception after oral contraceptives. Can. Med. Assoc. J. 103:343–348.
Casteels-Van Daele, M., Proesmans, W., Van den Berghe, H., and Verresen, H. 1970. Down's anomaly (21 trisomy) and Turner's syndrome (46,XXqi) in the same sibship. Helv. Paediatr. Acta 25:412–420.
Cohen, B. H., Lilienfeld, A. M., Kramer, S., and Hyman, L. C. 1977. Parental factors in Down's syndrome: Results of the Baltimore case-control study. In: E. B. Hook and I. H. Porter (eds), Population Cytogenetics, pp. 301–352. Academic Press, Inc., New York.
Collmann, R. D., and Stoller, A. 1962. A survey of mongoloid births in Victoria, Australia, 1942–1957. Am. J. Publ. Health 52:813–829.
Crandall, B. F., and Ebbin, A. J. 1973. Trisomy 18 and 21 in two siblings. Clin. Genet. 4:517–519.
David, T. J., and Jones, A. J. 1975. Trisomy 21 a..d trisomy 18 in half-siblings. Hum. Genet. 27:351–352.
Dhadial, R., and Pfeiffer, R. A. 1972. Cytogenetic studies in families with two 47,+21 siblings. J. Genet. Hum. 20:297–322.
Fabricant, J. D., and Schneider, E. L. 1978. Studies of the genetic and immunologic components of the maternal age effect. Dev. Biol. 66:337–343.
Forssman, H., and Åkesson, H. O. 1967. Consanguineous marriages and mongolism. In: G. E. W. Wolstenholme and R. Porter (eds.), Ciba Foundation Study Group No. 25: Mongolism, pp. 23–34. Little, Brown & Company, Boston.
Frolich, C. S., Schonhaut, A. G., and Tortora, J. M. 1979. Trisomy 21 Down syndrome in three siblings. N.Y. State J. Med. 79:929–930.

Girardet, P., Grosset, L., and Juillard, E. 1972. Trisomie 21 et trisomie 18 dans une même fratrie. Helv. Paediatr. Acta 27:583–589.
Goad, W. B., Robinson, A., and Puck, T. T. 1976. Incidences of aneuploidy in human populations. Am. J. Hum. Genet. 28:62–68.
Gowen, M. S., and Gowen, J. W. 1922. Complete linkage in *Drosophila melanogaster*. Am. Nat. 56:268–288.
Greenberg, R. C. 1963. Two factors influencing the births of mongols to younger mothers. Med. Offr. 109:62–64.
Gustavson, K. H., Atkins, L., and Patricks, I. 1964. Diverse chromosomal anomalies in two siblings. Acta Paediatr. 53:371–387.
Hamerton, J. L. 1971. Human Cytogenetics. Vol. II. Clinical Cytogenetics. Academic Press, Inc., New York.
Harris, D. J., Begleiter, M. L., Chamberlin, J., Hankins, L., and Magenis, R. E. 1982. Parental trisomy 21 mosaicism. Am. J. Hum. Genet. 34:125–133.
Hauschka, T. S., Hasson, J. E., Goldstein, M. N., Kopf, G. F., and Sandberg, A. A. 1962. An XYY man with progeny indicating familial tendency to nondisjunction. Am. J. Hum. Genet. 14:22–30.
Hecht, F. 1977. The nonrandomness of human chromosome abnormalities. In: E. B. Hook and I. H. Porter (eds.), Population Cytogenetics. Studies in Humans, pp. 237–250. Academic Press, Inc., New York.
Hecht, F. 1982. Editorial. Unexpected encounters in cytogenetics: Repeated abortions and parental sex chromosome mosaicism may indicate risk of nondisjunction. Am. J. Hum. Genet. 34:514–516.
Hecht, F., Bryant, J. S., Gruber, D., and Townes, P. L. 1964. The non-randomness of chromosomal abnormalities. N. Engl. J. Med. 271:1081–1086.
Holmgren, G., and Ånséhn, S. 1971. The trisomy 21 and the trisomy 17–18 syndromes in siblings. Hum. Hered. 21:577–579.
Iinuma, K., Nakagome, Y., and Matsui, I. 1973. 21 trisomy and prenatally diagnosed XXY in two consecutive pregnancies. Hum. Hered. 23:467–469.
Johnston, A. W., and Petrakis, J. K. 1963. Mongolism and Turner's syndrome in the same sibship. Ann. Hum. Genet. 26:407–413.
Juberg, R. C., and Davis, L. M. 1970. Etiology of nondisjunction: Lack of evidence for genetic control. Cytogenetics 9:284–293.
Kapp, R. W. Jr., Picciano, D. J., and Jacobson, C. B. 1979. Y-chromosomal nondisjunction in dibromochloropropane exposed workmen. Mut. Res. 64:47–51.
Kivimäki, T. J., and Lagus, T. E. J. 1981. A mother with Down's syndrome and her unaffected child. In: P. Mittler (ed.), Frontiers of Knowledge in Mental Retardation, Volume II, pp. 167–169. University Park Press, Baltimore.
Kochupillai, N., Verma, I. C., Grewal, M. S., and Ramalingaswami, V. 1976. Down's syndrome and related abnormalities in an area of high background radiation in coastal Kerala. Nature 262:60–61.
Kwiterovich, P. O., Cross, H. E., and McKusick, V. A. 1966. Mongolism in an inbred population. Bull. Johns Hopkins Hosp. 119:268–275.
Lejeune, J., and Prieur, M. 1979. Oral contraceptive and trisomy 21. Ann. Genet. 22:61–69.
Leroy, J. G., and Dumon, J. E. 1980. Prenatal diagnosis of an XXY-karyotype following the previous birth of a 21-trisomic sibling. Clin. Genet. 17:75–76.
Lilienfeld, A. M., and Benesch, C. H. 1969. Epidemiology of Mongolism. The Johns Hopkins Press, Baltimore.

Martin, R. H., Dill, F. J., and Miller, J. R. 1976. Nondisjunction in aging female mice. Cytogenet. Cell Genet. 17:150–160.

Matsunaga, E. 1966. Down's syndrome and maternal inbreeding. Acta Genet. Med. Gemell. 15:224–229.

Miller, O. J., Breg, W. R., Schmickel, R. D., and Tretter, W. 1961. A family with an XXXY male, a leukaemic male, and two 21-trisomic mongoloid females. Lancet 2:78–79.

Oetting, L. A., and Steele, M. W. 1982. A controlled retrospective follow-up study of the impact of genetic counseling on parental reproduction following the birth of a Down syndrome child. Clin. Genet. 21:7–13.

Papp, Z., Varadi, E., and Szabo, Z. 1977. Grandmaternal age at birth of parents of children with trisomy 21. Hum. Genet. 39:221–224.

Penrose, L. S. 1961. Mongolism. Br. Med. Bull. 17:184–189.

Penrose, L. S. 1963. The Biology of Mental Defect. Sidgwick and Jackson, Ltd., London.

Penrose, L. S. 1965. Dermatoglyphics in mosaic mongolism and allied conditions. In: S. J. Greets (ed.), Genetics Today, pp. 973–980. Pergamon Press, Oxford.

Penrose, L. S., and Smith, G. F. 1966. Down's Anomaly. Little, Brown & Company, Boston.

Pleydell, M. J. 1957. Mongolism and other congenital abnormalities. Lancet 1:1314–1319.

Priest, J. H., Verhulst, C., and Sirkin, S. 1973. Parental dermatoglyphics in Down's syndrome. A ten year study. J. Med. Genet. 10:328–332.

Richards, B. W. 1970. Observations on mosaic parents of mongol propositi. J. Ment. Defic. Res. 14:342–346.

Robinson, A., Goad, W. B., Puck, T. T., and Harris, J. S. 1969. Studies of chromosomal nondisjunction in man III. Am. J. Hum. Genet. 21:466–485.

Schull, W. J., and Neel, J. V. 1962. Maternal radiation and mongolism. Lancet 1:537–538.

Sigler, A. T., Lillienfeld, A. M., Cohen, B. H., and Westlake, J. E. 1965. Radiation exposure in parents of children with mongolism (Down's syndrome). Bull. Johns Hopkins Hosp. 117:374–399.

Singer, J., Sachdeva, S., Smith, G. F., and Hsia, D. Y. Y. 1972. Triple X female and a Down's syndrome offspring. J. Med. Genet. 9:238–239.

Smith, G. F., and Berg, J. M. 1976. Down's Anomaly, 2nd ed. Churchill Livingstone, Edinburgh.

Stark, C. R., and Fraumeni, J. F., Jr. 1966. Viral hepatitis and Down's syndrome. Lancet 1:1036–1037.

Stene, J., Stene, E., Stengel-Rutkowski, S., and Murken, J. D. 1981. Paternal age and Down's syndrome data from prenatal diagnosis (DFG). Hum. Genet. 59:119–124.

Stevenson, A. C., Mason, R., and Edwards, K. D. 1970. Maternal diagnostic X-irradiation before conception and the frequency of mongolism in children subsequently born. Lancet 2:1335–1337.

Stoller, A., and Collmann, R. D. 1965. Incidence of infectious hepatitis followed by Down's syndrome nine months later. Lancet 2:1221–1223.

Therman, E., Patau, K., Smith, D. W., and Demars, R. I. 1961. The D trisomy syndrome and XO gonadal dysgenesis in two sisters. Am. J. Hum. Genet. 13:193–204.

Turner, B., denDulk, G. M., and Watkins, G. 1964. The 17–18 trisomy and 21 trisomy in siblings. J. Pediatr. 64:601–604.

Uchida, I. A., Holunga, R., and Lawler, C. 1968. Maternal radiation and chromosomal aberrations. Lancet 2:1045–1049.

Wald, P. M. 1976. Basic personal and civil rights. In: M. Kindred, J. Coen, D. Penrod, and T. Shaffer (eds.), The Mentally Retarded Citizen and the Law, pp. 3–26. The Free Press, New York.

Wright, S. W., Day, R. W., Mosier, H. D., Koons, A., and Mueller, H. 1963. Klinefelter's syndrome, Down's syndrome (mongolism), and twinning in the same sibship. J. Pediatr. 62:217–224.

Wyrobek, A. J., and Bruce, W. R. 1975. Chemical induction of sperm abnormalities in mice. Proc. Natl. Acad. Sci. U.S.A. 72:4425–4429.

Yokoyama, S., Reich, T., and Morgan, K. 1981. Inbreeding and the genetic control of nondisjunction. Hum. Genet. 59:125–128.

Young, W. J. 1970. Genetic considerations in nondisjunction. Ann. N.Y. Acad. Sci. 171:391–395.

Zellweger, H., and Mikamo, K. 1961. Autosomal cytogenetics. Helv. Paediatr. Acta 16:670–690.

PERSPECTIVES AND PROGRESS IN MENTAL RETARDATION
Volume II—Biomedical Aspects
Edited by J. M. Berg
Copyright © 1984 by I.A.S.S.M.D.

SEASONALITY OF PREOVULATORY NONDISJUNCTION AND THE ETIOLOGY OF DOWN'S SYNDROME
A European Collaborative Study

P. H. Jongbloet,[1,2] A.-M. Mulder,[1] and A. J. Hamers[1]

[1] *Huize "Maria Roepaan," Siebengewaldseweg 15, 6595 NX Ottersum, The Netherlands*
[2] *Institute of Human Genetics, Free University, Van der Boechorststraat 7, 1081 BT Amsterdam, The Netherlands*

Six series of patients with Down's syndrome from different European countries (287 cases total), were differentiated into four categories according to parental origin of the additional chromosome 21 and the meiotic division in which the nondisjunction had occurred. The monthly birth or conception frequencies per category were analyzed graphically and compared with the total birth curve. The nondisjunctions during maternal meiosis I (63%), by far the largest category, occurred unexpectedly more frequently during the seasonal "restoration" and "inhibition" phase of the "ovulatory seasons" and less frequently when the ovulation rate is stabilized. The graph of the maternal meiosis II patients (17%) also seemed to conform to this phenomenon, although less obviously. In contrast, the paternal Down's syndrome graph (20%) was very divergent, although a seasonal cluster of nondisjunctions may also have occurred here. From these findings a seasonal disturbance of preovulatory ripening of the ovum emerged as a possible cause of first and second meiotic nondisjunctions. Seasonal periodicity of prolactin concentration in women and "transient hyperprolactinemia," shown to be allied with delayed ovulation, may be related with these seasonal Down's syndrome conception clusters.

This study was made possible by support from the Praeventiefonds, The Hague (No. 28,403,12). Reprinted by permission from *Human Genetics* 62:134–138 (1982).

It has been shown that children with Down's syndrome (DS) are not born evenly throughout the year (Harlap, 1974; Bennett and Abroms, 1979). DS conceptions appear to occur disproportionally more frequently during the seasonal transitions of increasing and decreasing ovulation rate and disproportionally less frequently during the seasons in which the ovulation rate is stable, as predicted by the Seasonal Preovulatory Overripeness Ovopathy (SPOO) hypothesis (Jongbloet, 1971a, 1975; Jongbloet et al., 1976, 1982).

This hypothesis is based on the existence in man of an evolutionary vestige of "ovulatory seasons" alternating with "anovulatory seasons," which is well known in nonhuman primates and other mammals. Such a seasonal alternation of the ovulatory pattern was proposed for humans by van Herwerden (1905) to explain the ubiquity of birth seasonality and has been confirmed by Timonen et al. (1964), at least in some women. This seasonality of ovulations diminishes in appropriately fed animals. Furthermore, human birth peaks and troughs appear to level out in industrialized societies, although they remain apparent (Cowgill, 1966).

The SPOO hypothesis presumes in humans two closely related phenomena. First, as in other mammals (Freedman et al., 1979; Snyder et al., 1979), ovulation is delayed during the transitions from anovulatory seasons to ovulatory seasons and vice versa. These transitions represent a "restoration phase" during which reproduction becomes functionally competent by inhibition of the pineal antigonadotrophic activity, and an "inhibition phase" during which reproduction decreases by resumption of this activity (Reiter, 1978). Second, as in amphibians (Mikamo, 1968) and other mammals (Butcher, 1981), preovulatory overripeness ovopathy caused by delayed ovulation leads to premature loss of tetrads and dyads from the maturation spindle in the oocyte, causing nondisjunction.

New developments in cytogenetics made it possible to divide DS populations into four categories: those resulting from a nondisjunctional event in paternal meiosis I (Pat M-I; 13%), in paternal meiosis II (Pat M-II; 7%), in maternal meiosis I (Mat M-I; 63%), and in maternal meiosis II (Mat M-II; 17%). In this paper the SPOO hypothesis is assessed for these four DS categories. This hypothesis applies particularly to nondisjunctions occurring before ovulation, i.e., Mat M-I, by far the largest category. It is known that nondisjunctions during Mat M-I can only occur before ovulation. In contrast, the nondisjunctions assigned to Pat M-I, Pat M-II, and Mat M-II take place either during spermatogenesis (i.e., about 6 weeks before conception) or after fertilization (i.e., postovulatory or intratubally). In this way, these three last categories are less expected to agree with the SPOO predictions.

STUDY POPULATION

A series of 115 DS patients and their parents were examined for polymorphisms of chromosome 21. Parental origin and the meiotic nondisjunction concerned were assigned in 83 cases. The source of the patients, the methods used, and the possible errors involved are described in detail elsewhere, as are the cytogenetic observations related to parental age and to α_1-antitrypsin phenotype (Jongbloet et al., 1981; Hamers et al., in press). In addition, data of all published DS patients examined in this manner were obtained from other European centers, as well as unpublished data from Lübeck and Göttingen (see Table 1).

METHODS

Frequence of Total Births and Conceptions per Month

From the Departments of Vital Statistics in the Netherlands, Denmark, France, and Austria, the monthly totals of live and stillbirths were obtained for the periods during which the DS patients were born. After correction for length of month (average = 30.44 days) these numbers were indexed (monthly average = 100). These indexed frequencies (ordinate) were graphed per month (abscissa). This resulted in a bimodal birth curve, apparently composed of two consecutive but uneven cycles: a major winter-spring peak and a minor trough in July/August, followed by a minor peak in September and a major autumn trough. In European countries this bimodal birth curve is generally identical (Huntington, 1938; Parkes, 1968) and is explained by the existence of alternating ovulatory and anovulatory seasons (van Herwerden, 1905), basic data for the SPOO hypothesis. Because the configurations of the curves in these countries coincide closely, we felt justified in compiling a "standard birth curve" from them by averaging the monthly indices (represented in Figures 1 to 4 by the shaded area). For the statistical analysis, these data can safely be taken as a single sample with a postulated H_o distribution corresponding to the average total monthly birth rates. The heterogeneity of the seasonal fluctuations of the total births is so small (relative to those in DS births) that they hardly influence the value of U_n^2 (see below).

Frequency of the DS Births or Conceptions per Month

Because the SPOO hypothesis is concerned with the moment of conception rather than that of birth, the monthly birth frequencies of DS children were first corrected for the shortened duration of DS pregnancies. For each subject, 11 days (Gustavson, 1964; Marmoll et al., 1969) were added to the day of birth (which meant that in about one-

Table 1. Number of DS patients per category and per period of birth

Source	Location	Period of birth	Paternal			Maternal			Total
			Pat M-I	Pat M-II	Pat M-I/ M-II?	Mat M-I	Mat M- II	Mat M-I/ M-II?	
Present series	Ottersum (NL)	1973–1979	7	8	2	40	16	10	83
Mikkelsen et al. (1980)	Copenhagen (DK)	1961–1977	10	2	1	49	12	5	79
Mattei et al. (1980)	Marseilles (F)	1969–1977	7	4	2	38	7	6	64
Rett et al. (1977)	Vienna (A)	1960–1974	6	3	3	13	5	4	34
Roberts and Callow (1980)	Newcastle-upon-Tyne (GB)	1964–1975	1	—	—	4	2	2	9
Unpublished data	Lübeck and Göttingen (D)	1974–1981	2	1	—	14	1	—	18
Totals			33 (13%)	18 (7%)	8	158 (63%)	43 (17%)	27	287

third of the cases the birth date shifted to the subsequent month). Second, as in the case of total births, the frequency was corrected for length of month and indexed. The DS birth frequencies from different countries can safely be taken as a single sample, because they are not significantly different (for category Mat M-I: $\chi^2 = 49.1$, $P > 0.10$).

In order to visualize (Figures 1 to 4) the fluctuations in the DS births or conceptions predicted by the SPOO hypothesis, and their relationship with the fluctuations of the total curve, the indexed frequencies (ordinate) were plotted per month (abscissa, indicating the month of birth at the bottom and of conception at the top). Agreement with the SPOO predictions are referred to as the "SPOO configurations," i.e., a disproportional increase in DS conceptions near the seasonal transitions from low to high (total) conception frequency (restoration phase) and vice versa (inhibition phase), and a disproportional decrease of DS conceptions during the seasons of stabilized conception frequency.

In order to test whether or not the DS birth frequencies deviated significantly from the expected frequencies, a Kolmogorov-Smirnov type statistic for cyclic trends (U_n^2), described by Watson (1961), was used. This statistical test is known to have high power with respect to an alternative hypothesis such as a sinusoidal pattern (Pearson and Hartley, 1972; Freedman, 1979); the discrete analogon (with 12 frequency classes) is defined as

$$U_n^2 = n \sum_{i=1}^{11} (f_n(i) - f(i) - \bar{v})^2$$

where n = the sample size, $f_n(i)$ = the observed cumulative distribution function, $f(i)$ = the cumulative distribution function under the null hypothesis, and $\bar{v}$ = the average value of $f_n(i) - f(i)$.

Unlike the classic Kolmogorov-Smirnov statistic, the value of U_n^2 is not influenced by the choice of the starting point ($i = 1$ is taken for January, but taking $i = 1$ for any other month will give the same result). This characteristic is obviously needed in a situation like the one under discussion (Freedman, 1979). Unfortunately, the sample distribution of U_n^2 is not known for an arbitrary postulated distribution f. Therefore, for each test the sample distribution has been estimated by Monte Carlo simulation (Freedman, 1979) of 20,000 sample values, using the corresponding total birth frequencies for f.

RESULTS

In order to analyze the SPOO configurations of the curve of DS births of paternal origin, their monthly birth curve was compared with the one for all DS subjects (Figure 1). In Figure 2 the curve for patients of maternal origin is given together with the one for all DS subjects. The SPOO configurations of patients of maternal origin thus appear more clearly profiled and the difference from the expected curve is statistically significant ($U_{287}^2 = 1.605$, $P < 0.20$; $U_{228}^2 = 2.71$, $P < 0.05$).

In Figure 3 the curve for subjects with nondisjunction during maternal meiosis II is given together with the one for all cases of maternal origin. In Figure 4, three curves are compared: one for the total DS subjects, the one for maternal origin patients, and one excluding Mat M-II cases. The last-mentioned group (Mat M-I') includes the Mat M-I ($n = 158$), together with the noninformative cases (Mat M-I/II?; $n = 27$). Theoretically, at most 5.8 Mat M-II cases are incorporated in the Mat M-I' category. Therefore, for a total of 185 cases, there is a negligibly small admixture of 3% Mat M-II cases. The SPOO configurations of the Mat M-I' curve once again show stronger profiles, and the statistical significance of these three curves with respect to the standard curve, or the expected frequencies, increases gradually ($U_{287}^2 = 1.605$, $P < 0.20$; $U_{228}^2 = 2.71$, $P < 0.05$; $U_{185}^2 = 3.225$, $P < 0.015$). In addition, a chi square test of independence revealed that the birth frequencies of Mat M-I' patients differed significantly from those of the other DS patients ($\chi_{11}^2 = 22.75$, $0.01 < P < 0.025$).

These graphical and statistical analyses were also applied separately for each country as well as for the various maternal age groups and secular time periods. The results all showed the same tendency and will be published elsewhere.

DISCUSSION

Total DS Birth or Conception Curve

The curve (solid line in Figures 1, 2, and 4), a constellation of four DS categories according to parental origin and meiotic nondisjunction, deviates, although not significantly, from the expected curve. The peaks and troughs appear at the expected places, the peaks corresponding with the restoration and inhibition phase of the ovulatory seasons and the troughs with the seasons in which the ovulation rate is stabilized. These are the SPOO configurations, in agreement with our previous findings (Jongbloet, 1975; Jongbloet et al., 1976, 1982) and with a general trend present in every published DS birth distribution known to us. In fact they are recognizable year after year and are independent of maternal age and standard of living (Harlap, 1974). Although this seasonal birth periodicity of the present DS curve is less clearly profiled

MONTH OF CONCEPTION

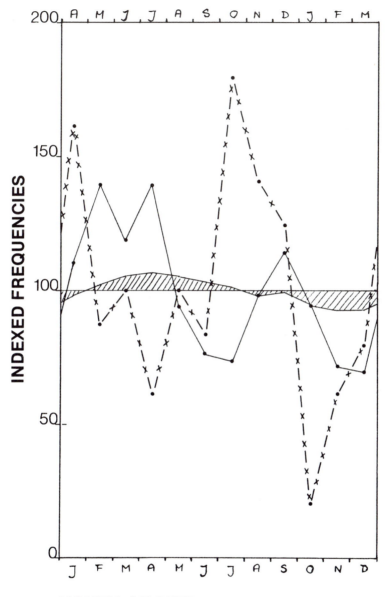

MONTH OF BIRTH

Figure 1.   Indexed (average = 100) monthly birth or conception frequencies of all DS subjects, of both paternal and maternal origin (——; $n = 287$), and of those of paternal origin (— × —; $n = 59$); limit of shaded area is the standard curve, or expected frequency.

MONTH OF CONCEPTION

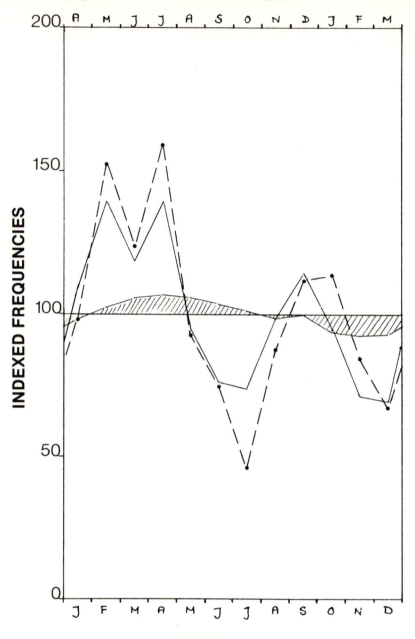

INDEXED FREQUENCIES

MONTH OF BIRTH

Figure 2.   Indexed (average = 100) monthly birth or conception frequencies of all DS subjects (——; n = 287) and of those of maternal origin ($---$; n = 228); limit of shaded area is the standard curve, or expected frequency.

MONTH OF CONCEPTION

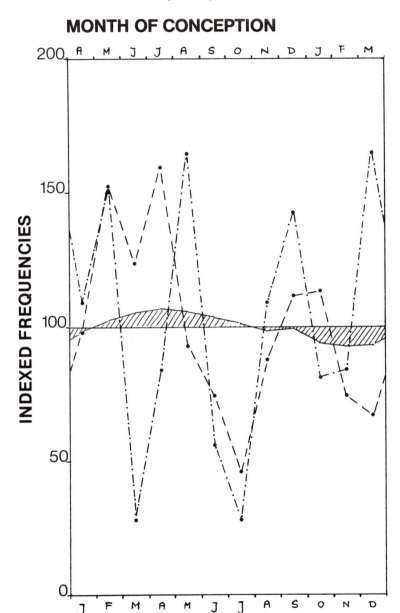

MONTH OF BIRTH

Figure 3.   Indexed (average = 100) monthly birth or conception frequencies of DS subjects of maternal origin (– – –; n = 228) and of those of Mat M-II nondisjunction (–·–; n = 43); limit of shaded area is the standard curve, or expected frequency.

MONTH OF CONCEPTION

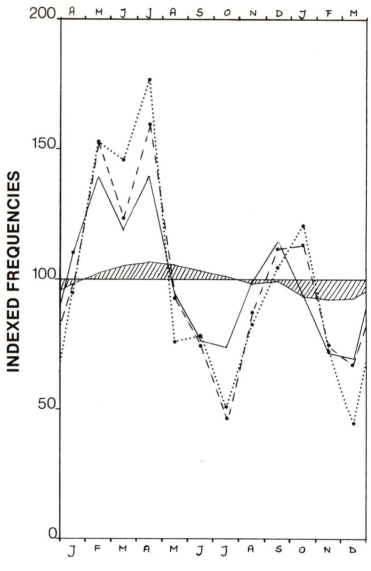

MONTH OF BIRTH

Figure 4.   Indexed (average = 100) monthly birth or conception frequencies of all DS subjects (——; $n = 287$) and of those of maternal origin including (– – –; $n = 228$) and excluding (······; $n = 185$) Mat M-II nondisjunction; limit of shaded area is the standard curve, or expected frequency.

than in total DS population studies [e.g., in Jerusalem (Harlap, 1974) and many other places (Bennett and Abroms, 1979)], it can hardly be explained as a bias in case collection from cytogenetic laboratories. Furthermore, case collecting as in the present study may introduce preferential loss of patients born in the peak months; perinatal and infant mortality, related with the same birth seasonality, cause sample depletion, and therefore even weaken the SPOO peaks and troughs (Jongbloet et al., 1976). There are arguments for claiming the same tendency in trisomy 21 abortuses, which also levels the original trisomy 21 conception peaks and troughs.

Paternal DS Birth or Conception Curve

The DS curve of paternal origin (Figure 1) differs from the SPOO configurations and thus militates against a paternal cause of seasonal fluctuations as advanced by Bennett and Abroms (1979). Nondisjunction in spermatocytes at the first and second meiotic division can be localized between 37 and 53 days prior to ejaculation and thus to conception (Heller and Clermont, 1963; Amelar, 1966). A backward shift of 6 weeks of the conception curve, in order to obtain a paternal nondisjunction distribution, does not result in coincidence of the fluctuations of nondisjunctions in spermatocytes and oocytes. The paternal DS curve seems to agree with seasonal fluctuations of sperm concentration, of necrospermia, and of teratospermia in healthy young men (Czyba et al., 1979; Pinatel et al., 1981).

Maternal Meiosis II DS Birth or Conception Curve

The DS curves of the Mat M-II and Mat M-I categories are partly synchronous and partly asynchronous. This might indicate a common epidemiology in line with the concept of deterioration of maturation spindles, as in experimentally delayed ovulation inducing nondisjunction during both meiosis I and II (Mikamo, 1968; Butcher, 1981). However, there are theoretical objections to considering the two maternal categories as one group. In fact, the effect of Mat M-I and M-II nondisjunctional events cannot be distinguished from that of mitotic nondisjunction either during embryonic life of the mother (leading to gonadal mosaicism and high recurrence risk) or in the early zygote (leading to somatic mosaicism). But, more importantly, nondisjunction during meiosis I can be caused exclusively before ovulation, whereas that during meiosis II is caused either before ovulation or after fertilization, i.e., either by delayed ovulation or delayed fertilization. Long intervals of sexual abstinence near the time of conception and unplanned conceptions have been related to the etiology of trisomy 21 (Milstein-Moscati and Beçak, 1981; Jongbloet, 1983).

Maternal Meiosis I DS Birth or Conception Curve

From graphical and statistical analysis it becomes evident that the seasonal birth curve of DS subjects is in essence molded by cases of maternal origin, particularly the Mat M-I category (by far the largest one at 63%). In that circumstance, nondisjunction occurs exclusively before ovulation. Admittedly, there are two phenomena that could have introduced incorrect assignment of the first meiotic error: crossing-over or "jumping" of the satellites, and mitotic nondisjunctions in the gonocytes during embryonic life before the start of the meiotic process. However, these two phenomena could hardly invalidate the results of this study, because crossing-over in the chromosomal regions involved occurs very rarely (Mikkelsen et al., 1980). On the other hand, premeiotic nondisjunctions in the gonocytes during embryonic life of the mother would lead to gonadal mosaicism and a high recurrence risk of DS. In addition, this phenomenon could hardly explain the presence of seasonal clusters of conceptions, unless by an intriguing seasonal selection of aneuploid oocytes during adult reproductive life. We conclude that the temporal birth clustering of Mat M-I DS conceptions supports our assertion that seasonal preovulatory overripeness ovopathy is an important cause of Down's syndrome.

These results may be a stimulus for examining in humans the above-mentioned biological basis and the two presumptions of the SPOO hypothesis. In fact, as in nonhuman primates, a circannual periodicity has been shown in women not only for anovulatory periods (Timonen et al., 1964), but also for the duration of menstrual intervals (Sundararaj et al., 1978) and for serum concentrations of prolactin (Tarquini et al., 1979) and melatonin (Arendt et al., 1979), two hormones with a definite antigonadotrophic activity. In this way, the seasonal periodicity of conceptions, and particularly of apparently pathological conceptions, found in this study can be interpreted in relation to "transient hyperprolactinemia" (Coutts et al., 1980). Hyperprolactinemia is characterized by inadequate follicle buildup and protraction of the preovulatory phase; in contrast, reduction of prolactin to normal levels is associated with midcycle ovulation (Tyson, 1977). This interfering action on preovulatory development of granulosa cells (McNeilly, 1980), and the subsequent delayed ovulation, may therefore offer the key for understanding the chronobiological cyclicity of Mat M-I and Mat M-II nondisjunctions and even their well-known increase in other high-risk groups characterized by hyperprolactinemia [e.g., adolescence in girls, premenopausal phase, long infertile periods, thyroid disturbances, (pre)diabetes (Jongbloet, 1971b)]. Hyperprolactinemia therefore may play the pivotal role in the etiology of delayed ovulation and chromosomal nondisjunction. The higher rates of aneuploidy after induction of ovulation in previously anovulatory animals or humans (Biggers, 1981), as well as after experimentally (Mikamo, 1968; Butcher, 1981) or physiologically delayed ovulation (Al Mufti and Bomsel-Helmreich, 1979) are quite well in line with this concept.

Our approach may be a stimulus to collect more data on the origin of the extra chromosome 21 in Down's syndrome. The duration of pregnancies should be ascertained and corrected per individual, because it may be that, for example, DS subjects of paternal and maternal origin differ in this respect. This is possibly true also for meiosis I and II. With sufficient data it would also be possible to construct 24-point curves instead of the present 12-point ones. In addition, the relationship of these seasonal factors with other parental phenomena that could induce Mat M-I nondisjunctions is of interest—e.g., an increased satellite association tendency (Hansson and Mikkelsen, 1978) and α_1-antitrypsin deficiency (Jongbloet et al., 1981).

ACKNOWLEDGMENTS

We thank Dr. Margareta Mikkelsen (Copenhagen), Dr. J. F. Mattei (Marseilles), Dr. D. F. Roberts (Newcastle-upon-Tyne), Dr. P. Wagenbichler (Vienna), Dr. E. Schwinger (Lübeck), and Dr. I. Hanssmann (Göttingen) for the information on birth dates of their patients, Dr. P. Stam and Dr. P. de Boer (Department of Genetics, Agricultural University of Wageningen) for the statistical analysis, Mrs. I. M. den Hartog-Adams for translation, Dr. J. Wind (Institute of Human Genetics, Free University, Amsterdam) for reviewing the manuscript, and Mrs. M. Peters-Derksen for its preparation.

REFERENCES

Al Mufti, W., and Bomsel-Helmreich, O. 1979. Etude expérimental de la surmaturité ovocytaire et ses conséquences chez les rongeurs. Contracept. Fertil. Sex. 7:845–847.

Amelar, R. D. 1966. Infertility in Man, p. 22. F. A. Davis Co., Philadelphia.

Arendt, J., Wirz-Justice, A., Bradtke, J., and Kornemark, M. 1979. Long-term studies on immunoreactive human melatonin. Ann. Clin. Biochem. 16:307–312.

Bennett, J. W., and Abroms, K. J. 1979. Gametogenesis and incidence of Down syndrome. Lancet 2:913.

Biggers, J. D. 1981. In vitro fertilization and embryo transfer in human beings. N. Engl. J. Med. 304:336–342.

Butcher, R. L. 1981. Experimentally induced gametopathies. In: L. Iffy and H. A. Kaminetzky (eds.), Principles and Practice of Obstetrics and Perinatology, pp. 323–338. John Wiley & Sons, Inc., New York.

Coutts, J. R. T., Fleming, R., Craig, A., Barlow, D., England, P., and MacNaughton, M. C. 1980. Role of transient hyperprolactinaemia in the short luteal phase. Prog. Reprod. Biol. 6:187–193.

194   Jongbloet et al.

Cowgill, U. M. 1966. Season of birth in man. Contemporary situation with special reference to Europe and the Southern Hemisphere. Ecology 47:614–623.

Czyba, J. C., Pinatal, M. C., and Souchier, C. 1979. Variations saisonnières dans la composition cellulaire du sperme humain. Sem. Hop. Paris 55:596–598.

Freedman, L. J., Garcia, M. C., and Ginther, O. J. 1979. Influence of photoperiod and ovaries on seasonal reproductive activity in mares. Biol. Reprod. 20:567–574.

Freedman, L. S. 1979. The use of a Kolmogorov-Smirnov type statistic in testing hypotheses about seasonal variation. J. Epidemiol. Community Health 33:223–228.

Gustavson, K. 1964. Down's Syndrome. A Clinical and Cytogenetical Investigation. Almqvist & Wiksells, Boktryckeri Aktiebolag, Uppsala, Sweden.

Hamers, A. J., Heijnen, G. C., and Jongbloet, P. H. 1983. De ouderlijke herkomst van het extra chromosoom 21 bij het Syndroom van Down en enige etiologische factoren. Tijdschr. Kindergeneesk. 51. (in press)

Hansson, A., and Mikkelsen, M. 1978. The origin of the extra chromosome 21 in Down's syndrome. Cytogenet. Cell. Genet. 20:194–203.

Harlap, S. 1974. A time series analysis of the incidence of Down's syndrome in West Jerusalem. Am. J. Epidemiol. 99:210–217.

Heller, C. G., and Clermont, Y. 1963. Spermatogenesis in man: An estimate of its duration. Science 140:184–185.

Huntington, E. 1938. Season of Birth. Its Relation to Human Abilities. John Wiley & Sons, Inc., New York.

Jongbloet, P. H. 1971a. Month of birth and gametopathy. An investigation into patients with Down's, Klinefelter's and Turner's syndrome. Clin. Genet. 2:313–330.

Jongbloet, P. H. 1971b. Diagnostic criteria for overripeness ovopathy. Maandschr. Kindergeneesk. 39:251–280.

Jongbloet, P. H. 1975. The effects of pre-ovulatory overripeness of human eggs on development. In: J. J. Blandau (ed.), Aging Gametes, pp. 300–329. Karger, Basel.

Jongbloet, P. H. 1953. "Natural" family planning. Aging of gametes and possible risk to offspring. In: International Symposium on Controversies, Risks and Advantages in the Pathophysiology of Human Reproduction in the Aula Magna (University of Milan October, 1981). Ric. Scient. Ed. Perm., Milan. 8/9:11–17.

Jongbloet, P. H., Bezemer, P. D., van Erkelens-Zwets, J. H. J., and Theune, J. A. 1982. Seasonality of anencephalic births and pre-ovulatory overripeness ovopathy. Chronobiologia 9:273–280.

Jongbloet, P. H., van Erkelens-Zwets, J. H. J., and Holleman-van der Woude, G. 1976. The significance of seasonality of birth in mental deficiency. Reap 2:243–263.

Jongbloet, P. H., Frants, R. R., and Hamers, A. J. 1981. Parental α_1-antitrypsin (PI) types and meiotic nondisjunction in the aetiology of Down syndrome. Clin. Genet. 20:304–309.

McNeilly, A. S. 1980. Paradoxical prolactin. Nature 284:212.

Marmoll, J. G., Scriggins, A. L., and Vollman, R. F. 1969. Mothers of mongoloid infants in the collaborative project. Am. J. Obstet. Gynecol. 104:533–543.

Mattei, J. F., Ayme, S., Mattei, M. G., and Giraud, F. 1980. Maternal age and origin of non-disjunction in trisomy 21. J. Med. Genet. 17:368–372.

Mikamo, K. 1968. Mechanism of non-disjunction of meiotic chromosomes and of degeneration of maturation spindles in eggs affected by intra-follicular overripeness. Experientia 24:75–78.

Mikkelsen, M., Poulsen, H., Grinsted, J., and Lange, A. 1980. Non-disjunction in trisomy 21: Study of chromosomal heteromorphisms in 110 families. Ann. Hum. Genet. 44:17–28.

Milstein-Moscati, I. and Beçak, W. 1981. Occurrence of Down syndrome and human sexual behavior. Am. J. Med. Genet. 9:211–217.

Parkes, A. S. 1968. Seasonal variation in human sexual activity. Eugen. Soc. Symp. 4:128–145.

Pearson, E. S., and Hartley, H. O. 1972. Biometrika Tables for Statisticians, Vol. 2. Biometrika Trust, London.

Pinatel, M. C., Souchier, C., Croze, J. P., and Czyba, J. C. 1981. Seasonal variation of necrospermia in man. J. Interdisciplinary Cycle Res. 12:225–235.

Reiter, R. J. 1978. Interaction of photoperiod, pineal and seasonal reproduction as exemplified by findings in the hamster. Prog. Reprod. Biol. 4:169–190.

Rett, A., Schnedl, W., and Wagenbichler, P. 1977. Im Haüfigkeit und Ätiologie des Down-Syndroms. Wien. Med. Wochenschr. 127:510–514.

Roberts, D. F., and Callow, M. H. 1980. Origin of the additional chromosome in Down's syndrome: A study of 20 families. J. Med. Genet. 17:363–367.

Snyder, D. A., Turner, D. D., Miller, K. F., Garcia, M. C., and Ginther, O. J. 1979. Follicular and gonadotrophic changes during transition from ovulatory to anovulatory seasons. J. Reprod. Fertil. Suppl. 27:95–101.

Sundararaj, J., Chern, M., Gatewood, L., Hickman, L., and McHugh, R. 1978. Seasonal behavior of human menstrual cycles: A biometric investigation. Hum. Biol. 50:15–31.

Tarquini, B., Gheri, R., Romano, S., Costa, A., Cagnoni, M., Keun Lee, F., and Halberg, F. 1979. Circadian mesor-hyperprolactinaemia in fibrocystic mastopathy. Am. J. Med. 66:229–237.

Timonen, S., Franzas, B., and Wichmann, K. 1964. Photosensibility of the human pituitary. Ann. Chir. Gynaecol. Fenn. 53:165–172.

Tyson, J. E. 1977. Nursing and prolactin secretion: Principal determinants in the mediation of puerperal infertility. In: P. G. Crosignani and C. Robyn (eds.), Prolactin and Human Reproduction, pp. 97–108. Academic Press, London.

van Herwerden, M. A. 1905. Bijdrage tot de kennis van menstrueelen cyclus en puerperium. Thesis, University of Utrecht, The Netherlands. (See also: Some remarks on the polyoestrus of primates. Anat. Rec. 30:221–223, 1925)

Watson, G. C. 1961. Goodness-of-fit tests on a circle. Biometrika 48:109–114.

SECTION IV
X-Linked Disorders

PERSPECTIVES AND PROGRESS IN MENTAL RETARDATION
Volume II—Biomedical Aspects
Edited by J. M. Berg

SIMPLE X-LINKED MENTAL RETARDATION
Clinical Diagnosis and Impact on the Family

M. W. Partington,[1] P. E. Hunter,[2] K. A. Lockhart,[2] B. Maidment,[3] and E. V. P. Sears[1]

[1] Division of Medical Genetics, Department of Paediatrics, Queen's University, Kingston, Ontario K7L 3N6, Canada
[2] Penrose Division, Ongwanada Hospital, Kingston, Ontario, Canada
[3] The Rideau Regional Centre, Smiths Falls, Ontario, Canada

The clinical diagnosis of "simple" X-linked mental retardation with and without the fragile X chromosome is reviewed in the light of personal experience with 31 families. Some of the practical, ethical, and genetic problems this disorder poses for the family are discussed.

There is now good evidence that "simple" mental retardation (i.e., without neurological, metabolic, or conspicuous dysmorphic features) can be transmitted by genes on the X chromosome (Turner and Opitz, 1980). Simple X-linked mental retardation is a heterogeneous group of disorders (Herbst and Miller, 1980), but it is now possible to identify one type because of its association with a fragile site on the X chromosome. This we refer to as the fragile X syndrome. There is no satisfactory name for the rest of the group except for the cumbersome term "X-linked mental retardation without the fragile X." Renpenning syndrome was a designation formerly used to describe the group as a whole (Turner et al., 1971), but it now seems preferable to restrict this name to that type of X-linked mental retardation without the fragile X described by Renpenning et al. (1962), which appears to be a distinct clinical and genetic entity (Fox et al., 1980).

X-linked mental retardation (XLMR) is common, to judge by epidemiological and clinical studies (Davison, 1973; Herbst et al., 1981; Blomquist et al., 1982) and our own experience. We have now studied

199

27 families with fragile X disease and four with XLMR without the fragile X; most of these were encountered in the past 4 years. This paper discusses the diagnosis of XLMR and some of the effects of the diagnosis on the family.

CASE MATERIAL

The families were found in genetics clinics, in long-stay institutions for the mentally retarded, in a community service organization for the retarded, and in an outreach program for the prevention of mental retardation. A total of 58 males with the fragile X syndrome and 16 males with XLMR without the fragile X were seen personally as well as 18 mothers and 15 sisters of the retarded males.

All chromosome studies were carried out in one laboratory by Dr. D. Soudek using methods to be described elsewhere (Soudek et al., in press).

DIAGNOSIS

Historically, XLMR was recognized by the X-linked pattern of inheritance in family pedigrees (Martin and Bell, 1943; Renpenning et al., 1962; Dunn et al., 1963). The association of XLMR and a fragile site on the X chromosome was clearly described in one family by Lubs in 1969 and again in 1976 by Giraud et al., but its diagnostic significance was not properly appreciated until 1977 when Harvey et al. reported four affected families in which all the retarded males and most of their mothers had the fragile X. Since then it has been possible to delineate the clinical picture of the fragile X syndrome more precisely (Jacobs et al., 1980; Turner et al., 1980a).

We have found the following clinical features to be of most value in the diagnosis of the fragile X syndrome in males:

1. *The facies:* The facies is distinctive and recognizable. The size and shape of the head is normal; the ears are large and often protrude from the side of the head, and the jaw is large and somewhat pointed with a long mandibular ramus (Figure 1). All the components of the facies can be seen separately and together in the normal population, so the facies is not diagnostic, but it is highly suggestive in the context of the other clinical features.
2. *Level of intelligence and personality:* The degree of mental retardation is usually severe (IQ range 26 to 39) but moderate retardation (IQ 40–54) is not uncommon. In general, these patients, although handicapped, are not incapacitated. They may carry on

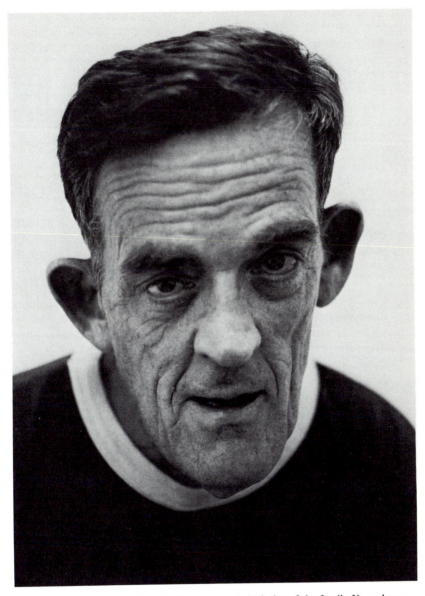

Figure 1.   A 55-year-old male with the characteristic facies of the fragile X syndrome. Note the large, protruding ears and long, pointed jaw.

a limited conversation, look after their personal hygiene, and do useful tasks under supervision. For the most part they are pleasant and cooperative and are well liked by their caretakers. Some develop distinctive personality traits and are known as "characters" in their community.

3. *Physique:* The birthweight, physical growth in childhood, and adult height and weight are within the normal range. Measurement shows that the head circumference is slightly above average. Normal physique is of particular diagnostic significance because so many other forms of mental retardation are associated with short stature or head sizes much above or below average.

4. *Macro-orchidism:* Macro-orchidism may be gross and obvious or it may be detected only by measurement. Measurement of testicular size in this group of patients is neither easy nor accurate but it is an essential part of the examination. In our experience, the best method is to use a short plastic ruler to measure length and width, from which testicular volume can be calculated using the formula $l \times w^2 \times \dfrac{\pi}{6}$ (Cantú et al., 1976).

5. *Family history:* A family history of one or more retarded brothers, maternal uncles, male maternal cousins, or other males connected to the proband through females is of great diagnostic help. However, the fragile X syndrome can now be confirmed by chromosome studies if the proband is the only retarded member of the family.

When four or five of these features are present a clinical diagnosis of the fragile X syndrome can be made with confidence. However, variation among patients is considerable and a firm clinical diagnosis is not always possible. The complete facies may be found in about two-thirds of patients, but several may only show either protruding ears or a big jaw. The facies may be obvious in childhood but it is not consistent within families. Most patients have moderate to severe mental retardation, but occasionally retardation is profound or only mild or borderline. It seems likely that rare males with the fragile X syndrome have intelligence within the normal range (Daker et al., 1981; Rhoads et al., 1982). A pleasant personality is the rule, but a few patients are withdrawn, autistic, anxious, or hyperactive. Some writers believe these traits are common (Mattei et al., 1981). A normal physique with no congenital anomalies is expected, but we have found a significant frequency of cleft palate, nystagmus, and kyphoscoliosis. Macro-orchidism (by measurement) is present in about two-thirds of affected adults; it may also be found in XLMR without the fragile X. In our families one-third of the pedigrees suggested X linkage; in another third there were two or more retarded males, and in the rest the proband was the only affected person in the family.

The clinical diagnosis is confirmed by demonstration of the fragile site on the X chromosome in lymphocytes. Up to 50% of cells may have the fragile X but the proportion is usually much less. We have found that the proportion of affected cells tends to be characteristic for the individual and his family (Soudek et al., in press). When this proportion is low (e.g., 1–4%), no fragile X may be found in some blood samples. Thus a single negative test does not rule out the diagnosis. Furthermore, the test itself is not easy; specific culture conditions are required and the assay is subject to unexplained variations. The test is not yet sufficiently reliable and standardized to be routine in all cytogenetic laboratories.

The fragile X syndrome is not confined to males (Turner et al., 1980b). Female heterozygotes may show some of the characteristic facial features. They may also be mentally retarded although the degree of retardation is usually less than that found in males.

XLMR without the Fragile X

The clinical features of the fragile X syndrome overlap with those of the group of disorders called XLMR without the fragile X. It could be that some families in the latter category have the fragile X syndrome but that this is not expressed in the chromosomes, or the frequency of affected lymphocytes is too low to be recognized by present techniques. In Renpenning syndrome the average height, weight, head circumference, and level of intelligence are all below those usually found in XLMR, suggesting that Renpenning syndrome is a discrete clinical entity (Fox et al., 1980). Other distinct types of XLMR may be recognized in the future (Herbst et al., 1981).

In general, the physique, level of intelligence, and personality in XLMR with and without the fragile X are similar. The characteristic facies of the fragile X syndrome and macro-orchidism may be found occasionally in patients where no fragile X is demonstrable. Retarded females are found in families with XLMR without the fragile X. Because there is no specific laboratory test, the diagnosis rests heavily on establishing an X-linked pattern of inheritance in the pedigree.

Unfortunately, evidence from pedigrees cannot prove X linkage, but only suggest it with increasing probability as more and more affected individuals are connected through females and instances of male-to-male transmission fail to occur. What is accepted as a convincing X-linked pedigree varies from one person to another. Figure 2 shows abbreviated pedigrees from nine of our families. Families 1 to 6 have

204   Partington et al.

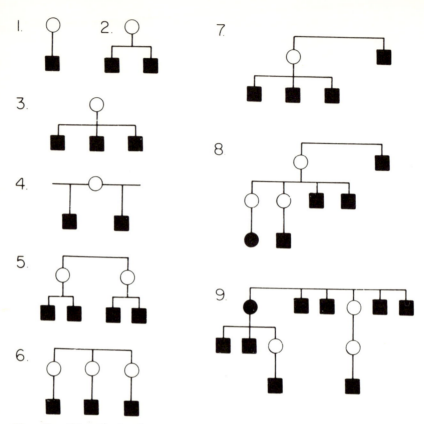

Figure 2.   Abbreviated pedigrees of nine families with X-linked mental retardation. Families 1 to 6 have the fragile X syndrome. Families 7 to 9 have XLMR without the fragile X.

the fragile X syndrome but only pedigrees 4 to 6 suggest X linkage to us. We have accepted pedigrees 7 to 9 as convincing evidence of X linkage but others might well debate this.

IMPACT ON THE FAMILY

When the diagnosis of XLMR is suspected in an individual patient an investigation of the family is necessary. If the patient has the fragile X syndrome the prime reason for a family investigation is to identify those females at high risk of having similarly retarded offspring and offer them genetic counseling. This also applies in XLMR without the fragile X, but before this is done it is crucial to establish X linkage in the pedigree.

The investigation of a family with XLMR has all the usual problems of any X-linked recessive disease that is essentially a genetic lethal in males (e.g., Duchenne muscular dystrophy). Because the gene is passed through females, the surnames of affected males often differ. The disease may appear to skip one or more generations. In Canada the population is comparatively mobile with a relatively high proportion of immigrants, so there may be difficulties in obtaining reliable medical evidence from other provinces and other countries. Frequently one needs information about previous generations and here XLMR has added problems. There are still social stigmata about mental retardation that are more evident the older the generation one is investigating.

Members of the older generations have usually accommodated to their retarded brothers, uncles, or sons. Such individuals may have been institutionalized for years and contact with the family may have been lost. The family may have its own explanation for the mental retardation (e.g., trauma or encephalitis) and may be unwilling or unable to consider a genetic interpretation. Next of kin may be inaccessible or unwilling to give permission for access to medical and psychiatric records. Investigation of the family is usually easier when one or more members have sought genetic counseling.

Ethical problems may arise. For example, is it justifiable to disregard the clearly expressed wishes of the mother of two boys with the fragile X syndrome and make contact with their sister? She is at 50% risk of being a heterozygote and may wish to know this before starting a family of her own. Is one justified in *not* giving her this information? What is the clinician's responsibility to more distant female relatives where the risk of the carrier state is less? Is prenatal sexing and abortion of all males an acceptable option for known female carriers and, if so, is it also acceptable for females at 50% risk or less of being carriers? There are no easy answers in this relatively new field of medical practice with few precedents and few guidelines. Three families are presented to illustrate some of these problems. The pedigrees are shown in Figure 3.

The T Family

The proband was a 34-year-old male who had lived in institutions for the retarded for 27 years. The fragile X syndrome was suspected because of his facies, normal physique, and macro-orchidism. His level of intelligence was lower than expected in this syndrome but this might have been explained by prematurity and a difficult delivery. The fragile X was found in 18% of his lymphocytes.

The family was Ashkenazi Jewish. The maternal grandparents had emigrated from Russia. The mother, age 72, had four normal brothers

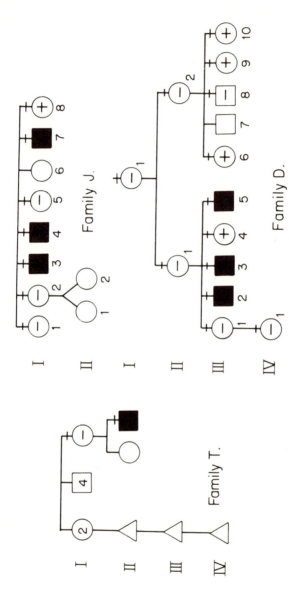

Figure 3.   Pedigrees of three families with the fragile X syndrome. Solid symbols mean an affected male; + means fragile X demonstrated; − means fragile X not demonstrated. Bar over symbol means that that individual was seen personally.

and two sisters. These latter were living in California; each had children, grandchildren, and great-grandchildren none of whom was mentally retarded. The proband's sister was an unmarried professional woman, age 42, who intended to have no children of her own and had had a tubal ligation.

Comment   Although the mother was interested to know that a cause had been found for her son's retardation, it is doubtful whether she understood the genetic explanation. No further investigation of the family is planned. It seems possible that, in this family, the fragile X syndrome represents a new mutation either in the mother or the maternal grandfather.

The J Family

In 1971 I-2 sought genetic advice because she had three retarded brothers. The clinician suggested XLMR because of their normal physique and lack of a specific diagnosis. However, the geneticist then, and again 3 years later, favored an autosomal interpretation. The same opinion was given independently by a second geneticist in 1978. I-2 married and had twin girls in February, 1979; tubal ligation followed. In August, 1979, the fragile X was demonstrated in all 3 brothers after which the clinician found marked macro-orchidism (missed by him 8 years earlier). One of the three brothers had the characteristic facies.

I-1, I-2, and I-5 have all had chromosome studies and no fragile X was found; this was found in I-8 who, by common consent, is the least bright intellectually of all the sisters. I-1, now age 35, intends to have a child; she will seek amniocentesis to avoid Down's syndrome but, if the karyotype is normal, she does not wish to know the sex of the fetus.

Comment   This history illustrates the evolution of present understanding of nonspecific mental retardation. Today, if only the information given in 1971 were available, XLMR would be the first diagnosis of clinician and geneticist alike. I-8 is now regarded as a heterozygote with a 1-in-4 risk of having a son with the fragile X syndrome; this risk is 1 in 2 if the sex of the child is known to be male. Prenatal sexing with abortion of all boys (half of whom would be normal) is an option open to her. It is expected that accurate prenatal diagnosis will be available soon (Shapiro et al., 1982). The other sisters have a prior 50% risk of being carriers with a consequent 1-in-8 risk of a boy with the fragile X syndrome (1 in 4 if the child is known to be male). Failure to find the fragile X lowers these risks. Theoretically, if 25% of heterozygotes fail to show the fragile X then the risk of the carrier state drops to 20% with a consequent 1-in-20 risk of an affected boy. Unfortunately, data on the proportion of heterozygotes without the fragile

X are not yet available; negative tests may increase with increasing age but the true situation is still far from clear.

The D Family

The mother (II-1) brought two of her sons (III-2 and III-5) to a Diagnostic and Assessment Clinic. Both boys were retarded and chromosome studies showed the fragile X. A history was then given of a third retarded son (III-3) who had been "given up for adoption" at 6 years of age. This boy was found to be a ward of the Children's Aid Society; he also had the fragile X syndrome. His existence was not mentioned in three subsequent family histories taken from the mother, the maternal aunt, and the maternal grandmother. It also emerged that a daughter (III-4) and a maternal cousin (III-9) were slow at school. III-4 was shown to have the fragile X but her older sister (III-1) and her daughter (IV-1) did not.

II-1 gave permission for these findings to be discussed with her sister. II-2 did not accept any connection between the problems in her own children and those of her sister. She did allow blood samples to be taken from her children. All 3 daughters had the fragile X; the one son tested did not. The father of this branch of the family was an alcoholic and separated from his wife. The oldest daughter had graduated from high school but had no job and was confused about relations with a boyfriend. She was upset further when informed that she had the fragile X; in counseling she would ask: "How can I tell my boyfriend? Will anyone want to marry me if they know?" Both sons in the family were probably of normal intelligence but they were both in penal institutions. III-9 (IQ 56) was having special education and III-10 (IQ 84) had had early school problems that had improved. Within 6 months both the mother and the eldest daughter refused further counseling and stated clearly that they did not want to discuss "it" (i.e., the fragile X) anymore.

Comment   This family had all but excluded one boy with the fragile X syndrome from its consciousness despite the fact that he lived in the same town, retained the family surname, and attended the same school as his older brother. We believe that, in at least two of the girls (III-4 and III-9), the gene for the fragile X syndrome is expressing itself as mental retardation (i.e., they are manifesting heterozygotes). If the second branch of the family had been ascertained independently it is likely that the mental retardation in III-9 would have been labeled cultural-familial. The discovery of the fragile X in this family opens up new perspectives on what the "familial" part of this unsatisfactory diagnostic label might mean. Our encounter with this family raised some of the problems of offering unsought genetic advice.

ENVOY

XLMR with and without the fragile X will likely prove to be one of the commonest forms of mental retardation. The magnitude of the problem and the extent of the genetic, medical, ethical, and social implications are only just beginning to emerge.

ACKNOWLEDGMENTS

We thank Dr. Bruce McCreary of the Ongwanada Hospital for continued support and encouragement and the many other physicians who referred patients to us. We also thank the patients and their families for their cooperation.

REFERENCES

Blomquist, H. K., Gustavson, K.-H., Holmgren, G., Nordenson, I., and Sweins, A. 1982. Fragile site X chromosomes and X-linked mental retardation in severely retarded boys in a northern Swedish county. A prevalence study. Clin. Genet. 21:209–214.

Cantú, J.-M., Scaglia, H. E., Medina. M., González-Diddi, M., Morato, T., Moreno, M. E., and Pérez-Palacios, G. 1976. Inherited congenital normofunctional testicular hyperplasia and mental deficiency. Hum. Genet. 33:23–33.

Daker, M. G., Chidiac, P., Fear, C. M., and Berry, A. C. 1981. Fragile X in a normal male: A cautionary tale. Lancet 1:780.

Davison, B. C. C. 1973. Genetic studies in mental subnormality. Br. J. Psychiatry Special Publication No. 8, pp. 1–60.

Dunn, J. G., Renpenning, H., Gerrard, J. W., Miller, J. R., Tabata, T., and Federoff, S. 1963. Mental retardation as a sex-linked defect. Am. J. Ment. Defic. 67:827–848.

Fox, P., Fox, D., and Gerrard, J. W. 1980. X-linked mental retardation: Renpenning revisited. Am. J. Med. Genet. 7:491–495.

Giraud, F., Ayme, S., and Mattei, J. F. 1976. Constitutional chromosomal breakage. Hum. Genet. 34:125–136.

Harvey, J., Judge, C., and Wiener, S. 1977. Familial X-linked mental retardation with an X chromosome abnormality. J. Med. Genet. 14:46–50.

Herbst, D. S., Dunn, H. G., Dill, F. J., Kalousek, D. K., and Krywaniuk, L. W. 1981. Further delineation of X-linked mental retardation. Hum. Genet. 59:366–372.

Herbst, D. S., and Miller, J. R. 1980. Non-specific X-linked mental retardation II: The frequency in British Columbia. Am. J. Med. Genet. 7:461–469.

Jacobs, P. A., Glover, T. W., Mayer, M., Fox, P., Gerrard, J. W., Dunn, H. G., and Herbst, D. S. 1980. X-linked mental retardation: A study of 7 families. Am. J. Med. Genet. 7:471–489.

Lubs, H. A. 1969. A marker X chromosome. Am. J. Hum. Genet. 21:231–244.

Martin, J. P., and Bell, J. 1943. A pedigree of mental defect showing sex-linkage. J. Neurol. Psychiatry 6:154–157.

Mattei, J. F., Mattei, M. G., Aumeras, C., Auger, M., and Giraud, F. 1981. X-linked mental retardation with the fragile X. A study of 15 families. Hum. Genet. 59:281–289.

Renpenning, H., Gerrard, J. W., Zaleski, W. A., and Tabata, T. 1962. Familial sex-linked mental retardation. Can. Med. Ass. J. 87:954–956.

Rhoads, F. A., Oglesby, A. C., Mayer, M., and Jacobs, P. A. 1982. Marker X syndrome in an oriental family with probable transmission by a normal male. Am. J. Med. Genet. 12:205–217.

Shapiro, L. R., Wilmot, P. L., Brenholz, P., Leff, A., Martino, M., Harris, G., Mahoney, M. J., and Hobbins, J. C. 1982. Prenatal diagnosis of fragile X chromosome. Lancet 1:101–102.

Soudek, D., Partington, M. W., and Lawson, J. S. The fragile X syndrome: I: Familial variation in the proportion of lymphocytes with the fragile site in males. Am. J. Med. Genet. (in press)

Turner, G., Brookwell, R., Daniel, A., Selikowitz, M., and Zilibowitz, M. 1980b. Heterozygous expression of X-linked mental retardation and X-chromosome marker fra(X) (q27). N. Engl. J. Med. 303:662–664.

Turner, G., Daniels, A., and Frost, M., 1980a. X-linked mental retardation, macro-orchidism, and the Xq27 fragile site. J. Pediatr. 96:837–841.

Turner, G., and Opitz, J. M. 1980. X-linked mental retardation. Am. J. Med. Genet. 7:407–415.

Turner, G., Turner, B., and Collins, E. 1971. X-linked mental retardation without physical abnormality: Renpenning's syndrome. Dev. Med. Child Neurol. 13:71–78.

PERSPECTIVES AND PROGRESS IN MENTAL RETARDATION
Volume II—Biomedical Aspects
Edited by J. M. Berg
Copyright © 1984 by I.A.S.S.M.D.

FRAGILE X SYNDROME

W. T. Brown and E. C. Jenkins
*New York State Institute for Basic Research in Developmental Disabilities,
Department of Human Genetics, 1050 Forest Hill Road, Staten Island,
New York 10314*

The fragile X syndrome is apparently very prevalent and some cases are
associated with autism. Our experience with a prenatal test indicates that
early detection is possible; thus it is now feasible to undertake primary
prevention. However, many dilemmas for genetic counseling of families
affected with fragile X syndrome remain. Who should be screened? Who
should be offered prenatal testing? What role does folic acid play in the
expression of the syndrome? Answers to these and other questions are
being intensively sought at our and other centers actively involved with
current investigations of the fragile X syndrome.

A fragile site on the long arm of the X chromosome (Xq27-28) has
recently been associated with a common form of X-linked mental retardation (Turner and Opitz, 1980). Males who possess this chromosome marker appear to have a distinct genetic condition, the fragile X
[fra(X)] syndrome. It is characterized by a fairly normal appearance
with the presence of some variable features, including enlarged head
circumference, long ears, thin midfacial diameter, high arched palate,
enlarged testicular volume, mild to severe retardation, repetitive
speech, poor fine motor coordination, and some autistic traits. It has
been estimated that the frequency of males in the general population
with this syndrome may be as high as 0.92/1000 (Herbst and Miller,
1980). This would make it second only to Down's syndrome in prevalence as a biomedical variety of mental retardation. From the stand-
point of counseling and prevention, the potential importance of this
syndrome may be greater because identified cases reveal families with
a high risk of recurrence. We are undertaking a comprehensive study
of many aspects of this condition. We summarize here information
regarding the fra(X) syndrome and our recent experience as it relates
to diagnosis, prenatal testing, and the finding of an association with
autism.

HISTORICAL BACKGROUND

Since the report of Penrose (1938) it has been generally recognized that
there is an excess of males who are mentally retarded and institution-

alized. This excess is usually 20–40%. It is thought that the excess could be explained by the presence of undiagnosed forms of X-linked mental retardation (Turner and Turner, 1974; Herbst and Miller, 1980).

In 1969, Lubs reported a family in which there was a marker X chromosome. The marker was described as "a small satellite separated from the main long arm of the chromosome by a constriction." Four male members of this family had the marker and were retarded, and the females, who were carriers with one normal X and one marker X chromosome, were normal. This association of a marker chromosome and mental retardation was not reported again until 1977 when Harvey et al. from Australia described 20 males in four families in which the retarded males had the marker chromosome. In retrospect, this long delay appears to have occurred because newer culture media with higher levels of folic acid were introduced in the early 1970s. Sutherland (1977a, b), in Australia, discovered that a cell culture medium deficient in folic acid, such as Lubs used, was necessary to detect the marker chromosome. He found that the "fragile site" on the marker X chromosome could be seen only in folate-deficient medium, a medium that was not in general use at the time. Following this discovery, many additional families have been identified. It appears that some 30–50% of families with apparent X-linked mental retardation possess the fra(X) chromosome (Herbst and Miller, 1980).

MACRO-ORCHIDISM

A distinctive feature of fra(X) males is macro-orchidism, i.e., enlarged testicular volume. Before the era of fra(X) testing, several families were identified that showed inheritance of X-linked mental retardation associated with macro-orchidism (Turner, et al., 1975; Cantú et al., 1976; Ruvalcaba et al., 1977; Bowen et al., 1978). When these families were later retested, they were found to have the fra(X) chromosome present (Turner et al., 1978). The normal male adult testicular volume is about 17 ml, with a 90th percentile of about 22 ml. Thus, any size greater than 25 ml may be suspect. By carefully measuring the length (l) and width (w) with calipers, the volume can be determined using the formula

$$V = l \times w^2 \times \frac{\pi}{6}$$

We screened for macro-orchidism in 15 severely mentally retarded males in a residential facility. Five had macro-orchidism; four of these showed fra(X) chromosomes (Brown et al., 1981). Others have found a somewhat lower positive frequency among the mentally retarded with macro-orchidism (Brondum-Nielsen et al., 1981; Howard-Peebles and Finley, 1981). However, no other medical syndrome is generally recognized as associated with macro-orchidism, with the possible exception of hypothyroidism (Laron et al., 1970). Therefore, the presence of macro-orchidism but absence of a fra(X) chromosome may be explained either by failure to detect the marker chromosome or by the existence of a different syndrome of mental retardation with macro-orchidism but without fra(X). Further testing of normal males and mentally retarded males is needed to assess the usefulness of macro-orchidism as a screen for individuals likely to be fra(X) positive. Our experience to date suggests that macro-orchidism is a sensitive initial criterion to detect males who should be chromosomally tested for fra(X).

LABORATORY IDENTIFICATION AND PRENATAL DIAGNOSIS

Heritable fragile sites on other chromosomes have also been reported, most with no associated abnormal phenotype (Sutherland, 1979). Fragile sites appear to be a general phenomenon. Only the X chromosome fragile site is regularly associated with mental retardation.

Following Sutherland's discovery that folic acid and thymidine concentrations need to be diminished in culture medium in order to induce the fra(X) marker, Glover (1981) reported that 5-fluorodeoxyuridine (FUdR), a specific inhibitor of thymidylate synthetase, was effective in allowing fragile site expression. Furthermore, FUdR could be used in the presence of enriched media containing folic acid and thymidine. Tommerup et al. (1981) reported that this method also can be used to successfully induce fra(X) expression in fibroblasts. Very little is known about the metabolic basis of fragile sites. It seems that the critical step necessary for fragile site induction is the inhibition of thymidine synthesis. If folate-deficient medium is employed, then a folic acid derivative that is a cofactor for thymidylate synthetase activity is removed from the medium and thymidine monophosphate cannot be synthesized. The same effect results by inhibiting thymidylate synthetase with FUdR, in the presence of folic acid. Finally, methotrexate interference of dihydrofolate reductase, an enzyme necessary for folic acid metabolism, also blocks thymidine synthesis. Thus, the induction of the fra(X) site is somehow dependent on thymidine availability.

With the development of the use of FUdR for fra(X) detection in fibroblasts (Glover, 1981; Jenkins et al., 1981; Tommerup et al., 1981), it became possible to attempt to detect the fra(X) site in amniocytes, which are similar to fibroblasts in growth properties. This would permit prenatal detection of the fra(X) chromosome. Using a modification of Glover's method, we showed for the first time (Jenkins et al., 1981) that it was feasible to detect the fra(X) chromosome in cultured amniotic fluid cells by exposing them to FUdR during the last 24 hours of culture. Using this approach, the first prospective prenatal diagnosis was subsequently carried out (Shapiro et al., 1982), and a positive male was verified by fetal blood sampling. We have now attempted seven additional prospective prenatal diagnoses (Jenkins et al., in press). One positive female was identified and carried to term. A second male was found and confirmed by cultured fetal skin. Both positive male fetuses showed macro-orchidism (Rudelli et al., 1983), indicating that the effects of the fra(X) chromosome are present during early development.

MENTAL EFFECTS

It appears that the heterozygous female who is a carrier of the fra(X) chromosome may be mildly affected in up to one-third of cases. Turner et al. (1980) found that six of 78 girls in a school for the mildly retarded in Australia, with IQs in the range of 55–75, possessed the fra(X) chromosome. Among 18 carrier relatives, six showed some mental impairment. Several families have now been reported with more severely affected females (Webb et al., 1982). We have also observed three females in three families with IQ levels less than 50. This appears to be consistent with expectations based on random inactivation of the X chromosome. Thus, a significant frequency of retardation among females also may be due to the fra(X) chromosome.

The spectrum of mental dysfunction among fra(X) males has yet to be clearly defined. However, we have identified five males with the fra(X) chromosome who had a previously well-established diagnosis of autism (Brown et al., 1982a, b). They were referred to us for clinical diagnostic evaluation for various reasons, and fra(X) testing was carried out. The first autistic male, age 17 years, had macro-orchidism and a family history of mental retardation. A brother and a male first cousin were fra(X) positive, but neither was thought to be autistic. The second autistic male, age 16, had no family history of mental retardation, but was noted to have enlarged testes. Two brothers, ages 6 and 12, autistic and retarded, were also found to carry the fra(X) chromosome. Another autistic fra(X) child, age 11, was tested because of the desire for possible prenatal testing by the mother. A sixth autistic male, age 16, was tested because of a family history of mental retardation.

Thus far, we have found that 19 of 24 fra(X)-positive families did not have affected males who were also autistic, whereas five families did. Autistic individuals usually have a male-to-female sex ratio of about 4:1 (Wing et al., 1971). Because the fra(X) syndrome is a common genetic syndrome associated with mental retardation in normal-appearing boys, we suggest it may show a significant frequency of association with autism. We have tested, with negative results, six other males referred to our facility for autism, and screening of 13 autistic males at a school for autistic children showed none with fra(X). Thus, in our experience to date, about one-fourth of autistic males tested have had the fra(X) syndrome. Meryash et al. (1982) reported one additional case of autism associated with fra(X) syndrome. Genetic causes for autism are suggested by the significant concordance for autism in identical twins (Folstein and Rutter, 1977). Although no primary genetic cause has yet been identified, some genetic syndromes (e.g., phenylketonuria) and neurological conditions (e.g., cerebral palsy) have been associated with autism (Knobloch and Pasamanick, 1975). We believe the fra(X) syndrome should be included among genetic syndromes that may be etiologically associated with autism.

MUTATION RATE

The new mutation rate appears to be high in fra(X) syndrome. Based on the genetics of a condition associated with greatly reduced male reproduction, it appears that new mutation should account for about one-third of cases (Vogel and Motulsky, 1979). Therefore, isolated cases with no family history are likely to be found, as has been our experience. This analysis suggests a mutation frequency equal to one-third of the estimated male frequency of the syndrome (0.92/1000), or about 3×10^{-4} per gamete. This frequency is one to two orders of magnitude higher than that of any other common genetic condition. This suggests that the nature of the mutation leading to the fra(X) marker chromosome must be unique.

REFERENCES

Bowen, P., Biederman, B., and Swallow, K. A. 1978. The X-linked syndrome of macroorchidism and mental retardation: Further observation. Am. J. Med. Genet. 2:409–414.

Brondum-Nielsen, K., Tommerup, N., Dyggve, H., and Schou, C. 1981. Macroorchidism, mental retardation and the fragile X. N. Engl. J. Med. 305:1348.

Brown, W. T., Friedman, E., Jenkins, E. C., Brooks, J., Wisniewski, K., Raguthu, S., and French, J. H. 1982a. Association of fragile X syndrome with autism. Lancet 1:99–100.

Brown, W. T., Jenkins, E. C., Friedman, E., Brooks, J., Wisniewski, K., Raguthu, S., and French, J. 1982b. Autism is associated with the fragile X syndrome. J Autism Dev. Disord. 12:303–308.

Brown, W. T., Mezzacappa, P. M., and Jenkins, E. C. 1981. Screening for fragile X syndrome by testicular size measurement. Lancet 2:1055.

Cantú, J.-M., Scaglia, H. E., Medina, M., González-Diddi, M., Morato, T., Moreno, M. E., and Pérez-Palacios, C. 1976. Inherited congenital normofunctional testicular hyperplasia and mental deficiency. Hum. Genet. 33:23–33.

Folstein, S., and Rutter, M. 1977. Infantile autism, a genetic study of 21 twin pairs. J. Child Psychol. Psychiatry 18:297–321.

Glover, T. W. 1981. FUdR induction of the X chromosome fragile site: Evidence for the mechanism of folic acid and thymidine inhibition. Am. J. Hum. Genet. 33:234–242.

Harvey, J., Judge, C., and Wiener, S. 1977. Familial X-linked mental retardation with an X chromosome abnormality. J. Med. Genet. 14:46–50.

Herbst, D. S., and Miller, J. R. 1980. Nonspecific X-linked mental retardation. II: The frequency in British Columbia. Am. J. Med. Genet. 7:461–469.

Howard-Peebles, P. M., and Finley, W. H. 1981. Testicular and cytogenetic screening of retarded males from the South for the fragile X-mental retardation syndrome. American Society of Human Genetics Annual Meeting, Dallas, Abstract 197A (302). (unpublished proceedings)

Jenkins, E. C., Brown, W. T., Brooks, J., Duncan, C., Rudelli, R. D., and Wisniewski, H. M. Experience with prenatal fragile X detection. Am. J. Med. Genet. (in press)

Jenkins, E. C., Brown, W. T., Duncan, C., Brooks, J., Ben-Yishay, M., Giordano, F. M., and Nitowsky, H. M. 1981. Feasibility of fragile X chromosome prenatal diagnosis demonstrated. Lancet 2:1292.

Knobloch, H., and Pasamanick, B., 1975. Some etiologic and prognostic factors in early infantile autism and psychosis. Pediatrics 55:182–191.

Laron, Z., Karp, M., and Dolberg, L. 1970. Juvenile hypothyroidism with testicular enlargement. Acta Paediatr. Scand. 59:317–322.

Lubs, H. A. 1969. A marker X chromosome. Am. J. Hum. Genet. 21:231–244.

Meryash, D. L., Szymanski, L. S., and Gerald, P. S. 1982. Infantile autism associated with the fragile-X syndrome. J. Autism Dev. Disord. 12:303–308.

Penrose, L. S. 1938. A clinical and genetic study of 1,280 cases of mental defect (Special Report Series no. 299). Medical Research Council, London.

Rudelli, R. D., Jenkins, E. C., Wisniewski, K., Moretz, R., Byrne, J., and Brown, W. T. 1983. Testicular size in fetal fragile X syndrome. Lancet 1:1221–1222.

Ruvalcaba, R. H. A., Myhre, S. A., Roosen-Runge, E. C., and Beckwith, J. B. 1977. X-linked mental deficiency megalotestes syndrome. JAMA 238:1646–1650.

Shapiro, L. R., Wilmot, P. L., Brenholz, P., Leff, A., Martino, M., Warris, G., Mahoney, M. J., and Hobbins, J. C. 1982. Prenatal diagnosis of the fragile X chromosome. Lancet 1:99–100.

Sutherland, G. R. 1977a. Marker X chromosomes and mental retardation. N. Engl. J. Med. 296:1415.

Sutherland, G. R., 1977b. Fragile sites on human chromosomes: Demonstration of their dependence on the type of tissue culture medium. Science 197:265–266.

Sutherland, G. R. 1979. Heritable fragile sites on human chromosomes. II. Distribution, phenotypic effects, and cytogenetics. Am. J. Hum. Genet. 31:136–148.

Tommerup, N., Poulsen, H., and Brondum-Nielsen, K. 1981. 5-fluoro-2'-deoxyuridine induction of the fragile site on X28 associated with X linked mental retardation. J. Med. Genet. 18:374–376.

Turner, G., Brookwell, R., Daniel, A., Selikowitz, M., and Zilibowitz, M. 1980. Heterozygous expression of X-linked mental retardation and X-chromosome marker fra(X) (q27). N. Engl. J. Med. 303:662–664.

Turner, G., Eastman, C., Casey, J., McLeay, A., Procopis, P., and Turner, B. 1975. X-linked mental retardation associated with macro-orchidism. J. Med. Genet. 12:367.

Turner, G., and Opitz, J. M. 1980. Editorial comment: X-linked mental retardation. Am. J. Med. Genet. 7:407–415.

Turner, G., Till, R., and Daniel, A. 1978. Marker X chromosomes, mental retardation and macroorchidism. N. Engl. J. Med. 299:1472.

Turner, G., and Turner, B. 1974. X-linked mental retardation. J. Med. Genet. 11:109–113.

Vogel, F., and Motulsky, A. G. 1979. Haldane's indirect method for mutation rate estimation. In: F. Vogel and A. G. Motulsky (eds.), Human Genetics: Problems and Approaches. Springer-Verlag, Berlin.

Webb, G. C., Halliday, J. L., Pitt, D. B., Judge, C. G., and Leversha, M. 1982. Fragile (X) (q27) sites in a pedigree with female carriers showing mild to severe mental retardation. J. Med. Genet. 19:44–48.

Wing, L., Yeates, S. B., Brierley, L. M., and Gould, J. 1971. The prevalence of early childhood autism: Comparison of administrative and epidemiological studies. Psychol. Med. 46:89–100.

PERSPECTIVES AND PROGRESS IN MENTAL RETARDATION
Volume II—Biomedical Aspects
Edited by J. M. Berg
Copyright © 1984 by I.A.S.S.M.D.

ADRENOLEUKO-DYSTROPHY
New Observations about the Phenotype, Genetic Counseling, and Prospects for Therapy

H. W. Moser, A. E. Moser, I. Singh, F. R. Brown III, and J. E. Trojak

John F. Kennedy Institute, 707 North Broadway, Baltimore, Maryland 21205

Adrenoleukodystrophy is a serious progressive disorder of the white matter of the nervous system and the adrenal cortex associated with the pathognomonic accumulation of saturated very long chain fatty acids. With the possible exception of the neonatal form, the illness is X linked, has a wider range of clinical manifestations, and occurs more commonly than had previously been appreciated. Diagnosis can be made by demonstrating abnormally high levels of saturated very long chain fatty acids in plasma, and the same approach can be used for carrier detection and prenatal diagnosis. Specific therapy is as yet unavailable, but several leads are being explored.

Adrenoleukodystrophy (ALD) is an X-linked disorder associated with progressive dysfunction of the nervous system white matter and the adrenal cortex. It was first described by Siemerling and Creutzfeld in 1923. In 1974, Powers and Schaumburg showed that ALD is a lipid storage disorder, and in 1976 the pathognomonic accumulation of saturated very long chain fatty acids was demonstrated in brain white matter and adrenal cortex by Igarashi et al. The phenotype of the childhood form was defined by Schaumburg et al. (1975), and in 1977 Griffin et al. described adrenomyeloneuropathy (AMN), an adult variant of ALD, which involves mainly the spinal cord.

Supported in part by Grants HD 10981 and NS 13513 from the United States Public Health Service.

Most of the advances in research about adrenoleukodystrophy and adrenomyeloneuropathy have resulted from the development of new diagnostic assays (Kawamura et al., 1978; Moser et al., 1980a, 1981, 1982a). Application of these assays has shown that the phenotype is more varied and that the disorder appears to be more common than had been realized. Because the phenotype is so varied, and because most forms appear to be variants of a single disease entity, we shall use the generic term adrenoleukodystrophy (ALD) for all forms of the disease. We summarize here recent advances about ALD and AMN, with emphasis on the phenotype, diagnosis, definition of the enzyme defect, genetic counseling, and prospects for therapy.

PHENOTYPE OF ADRENOLEUKODYSTROPHY

Table 1 lists seven forms of ALD and their relative frequency among the 113 patients studied at the John F. Kennedy Institute up to February 1982. In the childhood form cerebral dysfunction is the most common initial neurological sign whereas in the adult form spinal cord dysfunction is the most common initial manifestation. However, this distinction is not invariable. There are reports of cerebral dysfunction as the initial manifestation in a young adult (Case Records of Massachusetts General Hospital, 1979) and peripheral nerve involvement has also been reported in a teenager (Case Records of Massachusetts General Hospital, 1982).

Some women who are heterozygous for ALD may develop neurological symptoms. Most often these involve spastic paraparesis and resemble AMN (Moser et al., 1980b; O'Neill et al., 1982a), but cerebral dysfunction and demyelination have also been reported (Morariu et al., 1982). The incidence of neurological disability in the ALD heterozygote has not yet been defined. In one series signs of slight to moderate paraparesis were noted in 48% of the patients (O'Neill et al., 1982b). It is possible that symptomatic heterozygotes are clustered in certain kindreds (O'Neill et al., 1982a). In our experience, most women heterozygous for ALD do not have significant disability.

The frequency of the asymptomatic or presymptomatic forms of ALD has not yet been determined. Up to February 1982, we had identified 10 asymptomatic males who had the characteristic biochemical abnormalities of ALD and who were brothers of patients with ALD. Some of these young boys may later become symptomatic; in one of them this did occur 1 year after the demonstration of the biochemical abnormality. However, four of the asymptomatic males are older than their symptomatic brothers. Possibly these older boys will develop symptoms in adolescence or adulthood. It should be noted here that

Table 1.   Adrenoleukodystrophy-adrenomyeloneuropathy: Clinical forms and number of patients studied at John F. Kennedy Institute laboratory, 1979–February, 1982

Form[a]	Features	No. studied
1. Childhood ALD (Schaumburg et al., 1975)	Onset: 4–8 years Duration: 2–12 years Disturbed behavior, dementia, asymmetric paresis, ataxia, impaired vision and hearing, hyperpigmentation, impaired adrenal reserve	71
2. Adrenomyeloneuropathy (Griffin et al., 1977)	Onset: early adult Duration: decades Progressive paraparesis, mild neuropathy, intellect intact, adrenal insufficiency, may be misdiagnosed as multiple sclerosis.	20
3. Cerebral dysfunction in young adult	May be misdiagnosed as brain tumor or psychosis	2
4. Adrenal insufficiency only (O'Neill et al., 1982c)	Diagnosis suspected through family history	5
5. Symptomatic heterozygote	Resembles adrenomyeloneuropathy	—
6. Asymptomatic or presymptomatic	Male relatives of ALD patients who have biochemical abnormalities characteristic of ALD, but are asymptomatic	10
7. Neonatal ALD	Appears genetically distinct	5
		113

[a] Forms 1–6 have occurred in same kindred.

the childhood and adult form of ALD may occur in the same kindred and even in brothers (Davis et al., 1979). Possibly some men with the biochemical defect of ALD may never become ill. Systematic studies of this question are planned.

The connatal or neonatal form of ALD differs sharply from the other forms of ALD. Seizures, congenital anomalies, pigmentary degeneration of the retina, and polymicrogyria may be observed (Ulrich et al., 1978; Manz et al., 1980; Benke et al., 1981; Jaffe et al., 1982). Of the nine cases known to us, five have been male and four female, with the same severity of involvement in the two sexes. None of the cases of connatal or neonatal ALD has had relatives with the other forms of ALD.

X linkage has been established for ALD forms 1 through 6 (Table 1), on the basis of pedigree analysis and studies with fibroblast clones, and the ALD gene has been localized to the q28 segment of the X chromosome (Migeon et al., 1981). The location of the defective gene in neonatal-connatal ALD has not been established. The incomplete evidence available at this time suggests that it is autosomal.

BIOCHEMICAL DIAGNOSIS OF ALD

There are now several convenient assays that use cultured skin fibroblasts or plasma (Moser et al., 1982a, b) or red blood cells (Tsuji et al., 1981). In patients with ALD these assays demonstrate increased concentrations of hexacosanoic (C26:0) and/or tetracosanoic (C24:0) fatty acids. In contrast, the levels of dodecacosanoic acid (C22:0), or those with shorter chain length, are not increased. This results in abnormally high ratios of C26:0/C22:0 and of C24:0/C22:0 fatty acids. In our laboratory these tests have now been applied to samples from over 140 patients with ALD, and from more than 400 persons without known disease or with various other neurological, endocrinological, or metabolic diseases. Up to now, no false-positive or negative test results have been recognized. It should be noted that computer-assisted tomography is also a valuable diagnostic tool (Duda and Huttenlocher, 1976).

IDENTIFICATION OF ALD CARRIERS

In previous studies we found that most women who were obligate heterozygotes for ALD showed an elevated C26:0/C22:0 ratio in cultured skin fibroblasts (Moser et al., 1980a, b). Since then, we have studied plasma samples from 60 women who were ALD obligate heterozygotes, and compared them with 30 normal women of comparable age (Figure 1). In most instances the C26:0/C22:0 ratio for the obligate heterozygotes is clearly elevated, but, as shown in the figure, approximately 10 of the heterozygote samples overlap with controls. The discrimination is improved by the inclusion of two other parameters: the C24:0/C22:0 ratio and the level of C26:0 fatty acid (expressed as micrograms per milliliter of plasma).

Discriminant analysis of the data from 90 subjects (60 ALD obligate heterozygotes and 30 normal women) yielded the following classification function:

$$Y = -9.6129 + (-6.99856)(\ln\frac{C24}{C22}) + (-2.32689)(\ln\frac{C26}{C22})$$
$$+ (-1.93918)(\ln C26 \ \mu g/ml).$$

The decision point is 1.19237; any subject with a lower value is clas-

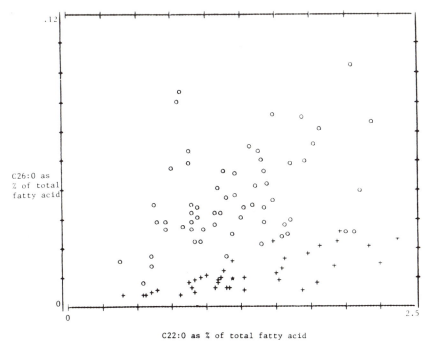

Figure 1.   C26:0 and C22:0 fatty acids in plasma of ALD obligate heterozygotes (O) and controls (+).

sified as normal and any subject with a greater value is classified as a carrier. Fifty-five of the 60 ALD obligate heterozygotes were correctly classified. There were no false-positive classifications. Studies are in progress to determine the extent to which heterozygote identification can be improved by addition of the fibroblast assay or by loading tests. Present data suggest that the plasma assay alone can identify approximately 90% of women who are heterozygous for ALD.

PRENATAL DIAGNOSIS OF ALD

The fatty acid patterns in cultured amniocytes resemble those in cultured skin fibroblasts. Table 2 summarizes our experience with prenatal studies. Cultured amniocytes of three male fetuses at risk for ALD were found to have a significantly elevated C26:0/C22:0 ratio. The pregnancies were interrupted, and in each instance the diagnosis was confirmed by study of fetal tissues. The fetal adrenal gland showed characteristic inclusions, and the very long chain fatty acid percentage in the adrenal cholesterol ester fraction was 1,000-fold higher than in controls (Moser et al., 1982b). So far, we have found normal C26:0

Table 2.   Prenatal studies of adrenoleukodystrophy at John F. Kennedy
Institute (up to February, 1982)

Case	Sex of fetus	C26/C22 cultured amniocytes	Outcome
1[a]	M	0.77	Abortion; fetus ALD
2	M	0.84	Abortion; fetus ALD
3	M	0.82	Abortion; fetus ALD
4[a]	M	0.20	Normal male child
5	F	1.50	Abortion (unrelated to ALD); heterozygote status confirmed
6	F	2.70	Female child—ALD heterozygote
7	F	0.17	Normal female child
8	F	0.06	Normal female child
9	F	0.09	Normal female child
10	F	0.17	Normal female child
11	F	1.30	Normal female child, ALD status not known
Controls (23)		0.17 ± 0.10	

[a] Cases 1 and 4 had the same parents.

levels in the cultured amniocytes of one male fetus at risk for ALD
(Case 4, Table 2). A normal boy was delivered, and plasma very long
chain fatty acid levels were normal at age 2 months. It is likely that
enzyme assays (see below) will also prove of aid for prenatal diagnosis.
Study of C26:0 levels in amniotic fluid has not been helpful.

GENETIC COUNSELING FOR ALD

The fear of bearing children with ALD has been a cause of concern
and anguish to female relatives of patients with ALD. The capacity to
identify approximately 90% of carriers by the plasma and/or fibroblast
assay and the ability to distinguish between normal and affected male
fetuses has been of aid in genetic counseling. Provided that this is
ethically acceptable to the family, we recommend prenatal monitoring
of pregnancies in women who have been identified to be heterozygous
for ALD. For at-risk women who have normal levels of very long chain
fatty acids in plasma and/or fibroblasts this decision requires individual
evaluation. In such instances, the risk can be estimated by applying
Bayesian principles of genetic counseling, which incorporate information on the family structure and conditional information from the
fatty acid analysis (Murphy and Chase, 1975).

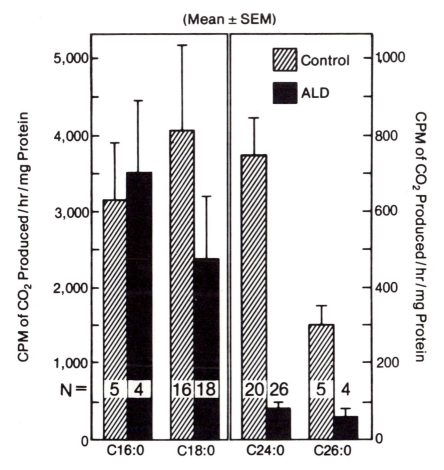

Figure 2. CO_2 evolution from $1-{}^{14}C$-fatty acids in homogenates of ALD and control cultured skin fibroblasts.

ENZYME DEFECT IN ALD

Singh et al. (1981) showed that homogenates of cultured skin fibroblasts of ALD patients have an impaired capacity to oxidize $C24:0$ and $C26:0$ fatty acids. These studies involved the incubation of homogenates with 1-${}^{14}C$-fatty acids and measurement of the liberated radioactive CO_2. Figures 2 and 3 show that the oxidation of C16 fatty acids is normal, whereas that of $C24:0$ and $C26:0$ fatty acids is reduced in both ALD-cultured skin fibroblasts and white blood cells. It is our current hypothesis that the oxidation of very long chain fatty acids involves an enzyme system distinct from that for C18 and shorter fatty acids, and

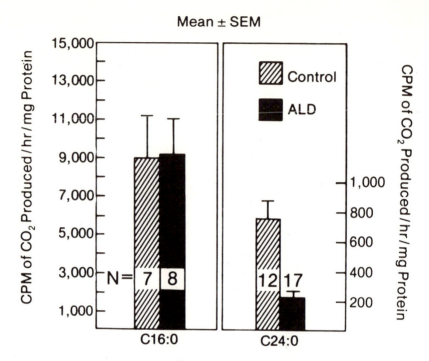

Figure 3. CO_2 evolution from $1-{}^{14}C$-fatty acids in homogenates of ALD and control white blood cells.

that this very long chain fatty acid oxidation system is deficient in ALD. CO_2 evolution from fatty acids is the end product of a large series of enzymatic reactions. Work is in progress to pinpoint the step that is deficient. The defect in CO_2 evolution from very long chain fatty acids appears to apply in the same way to samples from patients with childhood ALD, adrenomyeloneuropathy, or nenonatal ALD.

PROSPECTS FOR THERAPY

Replacement therapy for adrenal insufficiency is effective in relieving the adrenal dysfunction but does not alter the progression of the neurological disability. We have just completed a therapeutic trial of the dietary restriction of very long chain fatty acids in 16 patients with ALD (Moser et al., 1982a). The rationale for this diet was the demonstration, based upon studies with orally administered deuterium-labeled C26:0 fatty acid, that the very long chain fatty acids that accumulate in the brains of ALD patients are, at least in part, of dietary origin (Kishimoto et al., 1980). We devised a diet that reduces the daily intake of C26:0 fatty acid to less than 3 mg, compared to the 12–40 mg per day in the usual American diet. This diet was administered to 16 patients with various forms of ALD for periods from 6 months to 2 years. The diet did not alter the plasma levels of very long chain fatty acids, and did not appear to affect the clinical progression in children with ALD. Two patients with adrenomyeloneuropathy did report some clinical improvement, but it was difficult to determine whether or not this was related to the diet (Moser et al., 1982a). We concluded that the diet did not produce sufficient change to warrant its continuation. This differs sharply from results in another fatty acid storage disease, Refsum's disease, where dietary restriction of phytanic acid has brought about a lowering of plasma phytanic acid and clinical improvement (Refsum, 1981).

Other therapeutic approaches that have been tested with negative results are immunosuppression (Stumpf et al., 1981) and plasma exchange. A series of 14 plasma exchanges over a 6-week period brought about a slight lowering of very long chain fatty acids and a brief stabilization of the clinical course in one patient, but the possible benefits achieved were too slight to warrant continuation of the procedure (Murphy, 1982, personal communication).

Recently we have performed a bone marrow transplant in a 12-year-old boy with ALD, who had undoubted progressive neurological disability but had retained sufficient cognitive, sensory, and motor function to be capable of a meaningful existence if the neurological progression could be arrested. The rationale for the procedure was the above-mentioned demonstration that the oxidation of very long chain fatty acids is impaired in ALD white cells, coupled with the observation that ALD peripheral blood lymphocytes and macrophages do enter the central nervous system. At this time it is not yet possible to determine whether the transplant procedure was beneficial.

REFERENCES

Benke, P. J., Reyes, P. F., and Parker, J. C. J. 1981. New form of adrenoleukodystrophy. Hum. Genet. 58:204–208.
Case Records of the Massachusetts General Hospital. 1979. N. Engl. J. Med. 300:1037–1045.
Case Records of the Massachusetts General Hospital. 1982. N. Engl. J. Med. 306:286–293.
Davis, L. E., Snyder, R. D., Orth, D. N., Nicholson, W. E., Kornfeld, M., and Seelinger, D. F. 1979. Adrenoleukodystrophy and adrenomyeloneuropathy associated with partial adrenal insufficiency in three generations of a kindred. Am. J. Med. 66:342–347.
Duda, E. E., and Huttenlocher, P. R. 1976. Computed tomography in adrenoleukodystrophy: Correlation of radiological and histological findings. Radiology 120:349–350.

Griffin, J. W., Goren, E., Schaumburg, H., Engel, W. K.,and Loriaux, L. 1977. Adrenomyeloneuropathy: A probable variant of adrenoleukodystrophy. 1. Clinical and endocrinological aspects. Neurology 27:1107–1113.

Igarashi, M., Schaumburg, H. H., Powers, J., Kishimoto, Y., Kolodny, E., and Suzuki, K. 1976. Fatty acid abnormality in adrenoleukodystrophy. J. Neurochem. 26:851–860.

Jaffe, R., Crumrine, P., Hashida, Y., and Moser, H. W. 1982. Neonatal adrenoleukodystrophy. Clinical, pathological and biochemical delineation of a syndrome affecting both males and females. Am. J. Pathol. 108:100–111.

Kawamura, N., Moser, A. B., Moser, H. W., Ogino, T., Suzuki, K., Schaumburg, H., Milunsky, A. Murphy, J., and Kishimoto, Y. 1978. High concentration of hexacosanoate in cultured skin fibroblast lipids from adrenoleukodystrophy patients. Biochem. Biophys. Res. Commun. 82:114–120.

Kishimoto, Y., Moser, H. W., Kawamura, N., Platt, M., Pallante, S. L., and Fenselau, C. 1980. Adrenoleukodystrophy: Evidence that abnormal very long chain fatty acids of brain cholesterol esters are of exogenous origin. Biochem. Biophys. Res. Commun. 96:69–76.

Manz, H. J., Schuelein, M., McCullough, D. C., Kishimoto, Y., and Eiben, R. M. 1980. New phenotypic variant of adrenoleukodystrophy. Pathologic, ultrastructural and biochemical study in two brothers. J. Neurol. Sci. 45:245–260.

Migeon, B. R., Moser, H. W., Moser, A. B., Axelman, J., Sillence, D., and Norum, R. A. 1981. Adrenoleukodystrophy: Evidence for X-linkage, inactivation and selection favoring the mutant allele in heterozygous cells. Proc. Natl. Acad. Sci. 78:5066–5070.

Morariu, M. A., Chason, J. L., Norum, R. A., Moser, H. W., and Migeon, B. 1982. Adrenoleukodystrophy variant in a heterozygous female. Neurology 32:A81.

Moser, H. W., Moser, A. B., Frayer, K. K., Chen, W., Schulman, J. D., O'Neill, B. P., and Kishimoto, Y. 1981. Adrenoleukodystrophy: Increased plasma content of saturated very long chain fatty acids. Neurology 31:1241–1249.

Moser, H. W., Moser, A. B., Kawamura, N., Migeon, B., O'Neill, B. P., Fenselau, C., and Kishimoto, Y. 1980b. Adrenoleukodystrophy: Studies of the phenotype, genetics and biochemistry. Johns Hopkins Med. J. 147:217–224.

Moser, H. W., Moser, A. B., Kawamura, N., Murphy, J., Suzuki, K., Schaumburg, H., and Kishimoto, Y. 1980a. Adrenoleukodystrophy: Elevated C:26 fatty acid in cultured skin fibroblasts. Ann. Neurol. 7:542–549.

Moser, H. W., Moser, A. B., Powers, J. M., Nitowsky, H. M., Schaumburg, H. H., Norum, R. A., and Migeon, B. R. 1982b. The prenatal diagnosis of adrenoleukodystrophy. Demonstration of increased hexacosanoic acid levels in cultured amniocytes and fetal adrenal gland. Pediatr. Res. 16:172–175.

Moser, H. W., Schulman, J. D., Rizzo, W. B., Brown, F. R., III, Van Duyn, M. A., and Moser, A. B. 1982a. Dietary restriction of very-long chain fatty acids in adrenoleukodystrophy. Neurology 32:A81.

Murphy, E. A., and Chase, C. A. 1975. Principles of Genetic Counseling, pp. 202–211. Year Book Medical Publishers, Inc., Chicago, Illinois.

O'Neill, B. P., Moser, H. W., and Marmion, L. C. 1982a. Adrenoleukodystrophy: Elevated C26 fatty acid in cultured skin fibroblasts and correlation with disease expression in three generations of a kindred. Neurology 32:540–542.

O'Neill, B. P., Moser, H. W., and Saxena, K. M. 1982c. Familial X-linked Addison disease as an expression of adrenoleukodystrophy (ALD): Elevated C26 fatty acid in cultured skin fibroblasts. Neurology 32:543–547.

O'Neill, B. P., Moser, H. W., Saxena, K. M., and Marmion, L. C. 1982b. Adrenoleukodystrophy (ALD): Neurological disease in carriers and correlation with very long-chain fatty acids (VLCFA) concentrations in plasma and cultured skin fibroblasts. Neurology 32:A216.

Powers, J. M., and Schaumburg, H. H. 1974. Adrenoleukodystrophy. Similar ultrastructural changes in adrenal cortical and Schwann cells. Arch. Neurol. 30:406–408.

Refsum, S. 1981. Heredopathia atactica polyneuritiformis, Phytanic acid storage disease, Refsum's disease: A biochemically well-defined disease with a specific dietary treatment. Arch. Neurol. 38:605–606.

Schaumburg, H. H., Powers, H. M., Raine, C. S., Suzuki, K., and Richardson, E. P., Jr. 1975. Adrenoleukodystrophy. A clinical and pathological study of 17 cases. Arch. Neurol. 32:577–591.

Siemerling, E., and Creutzfeldt, H. G. 1923. Bronzekrankheit und sklerosierende Encephalomyelitis. Arch. Psychiatr. Nervenkr. 68:217–244.

Singh, I., Moser, H. W., Moser, A. B., and Kishimoto, Y. 1981. Adrenoleukodystrophy: Impaired oxidation of long chain fatty acids in cultured skin fibroblasts and adrenal cortex. Biochem. Biophys. Res. Commun. 102:1223–1229.

Stumpf, D. A., Hayward, A., Haas, R., Frost, M., and Schaumburg, H. H. 1981. Adrenoleukodystrophy. Failure of immunosuppression to prevent neurological progression. Arch. Neurol. 38:48–49.

Tsuji, S., Suzuki, M., Ariga, T., Sekina, M., Kurijama, M., and Miyatake, T. 1981. Abnormality of long-chain fatty acids in erythrocyte membrane sphingomyelin from patients with adrenoleukodystrophy. J. Neurochem. 36:1046–1049.

Ulrich, J., Herschkowitz, N., Heitz, P., Sigrist, T., and Baerlocher, P. 1978. Adrenoleukodystrophy. Preliminary report of a connatal case. Light and electron microscopical, immunohistochemical and biochemical findings. Acta Neuropathol. 43:77–83.

PERSPECTIVES AND PROGRESS IN MENTAL RETARDATION
Volume II—Biomedical Aspects
Edited by J. M. Berg
Copyright © 1984 by I.A.S.S.M.D.

NEUROLOGICAL FEATURES IN CHILDREN WITH ORNITHINE CARBAMOYLTRANS-FERASE DEFICIENCY
A Rare, Preventable Cause of Mental Retardation

S. Lingam,[1] J. Wilson,[2] and V. G. Oberholzer[1]

[1] Queen Elizabeth Hospital for Children, Hackney Road, London E2 8PS, England
[2] The Hospital for Sick Children, Great Ormond Street, London WC1N 3JH, England

Hyperammonemia due to ornithine carbamoyltransferase deficiency or other urea cycle disorders is reversible. With early management the prognosis may be improved, especially in girls. Hyperammonemia is a rare reversible cause of mental retardation.

Acute encephalopathy in childhood may be caused by hyperammonemia, and one group of disorders that may be responsible are inborn errors of the urea cycle. These are potentially treatable conditions of which the commonest is ornithine carbamoyltransferase deficiency (OCTD), which has an X-linked mode of inheritance. This condition was first described and reported from Queen Elizabeth Hospital for Children, London (Russell et al., 1962). The precise incidence is unknown but it is probably more common than has been recognized (Haan et al., 1979).

Most males with OCTD have little enzyme activity and are severely affected. They present with an overwhelming illness in the neonatal period and die even with the most vigorous treatment (Donn et

231

al., 1979; Wiegand et al., 1980). In girls, the severity of the illness is quite variable (even in the same kindred), depending on the percentage of enzyme activity. Those most severely affected present in the first year of life with persistent vomiting, lethargy, intermittent ataxia, failure to thrive, and developmental retardation.

The illness often has a fluctuating course and is exacerbated by intercurrent infections or any stress that precipitates protein catabolism. During exacerbations, neurological symptoms and signs, such as headache, irritability, ataxia, slurring of speech, alterations in consciousness, and fits may predominate (Shih, 1978). Some children have behavior problems with hyperactivity in the stable phase (Shih, 1978). Less severely affected girls [or rarely boys (Saudubray et al., 1975)] may have few symptoms but may still develop hyperammonemia unexpectedly and present with an acute encephalopathy. Even in these children, a previous history of intermittent vomiting, lethargy, failure to thrive, and mild developmental delay is often present.

Definitive diagnosis is by the measurement of enzyme activity in liver or small intestinal tissue because ornithine carbamoyltransferase is a mitochondrial enzyme found in adequate amounts only in those tissues. In practice, the diagnosis is usually established clinically and on biochemical grounds by demonstrating raised plasma ammonia, glutamine, and alanine levels and elevated urine orotic acid (Saudubray et al., 1975). The condition is amenable to prenatal diagnosis. Fetal sexing by examination of the external genitalia and in utero fetal liver biopsy (transcutaneous) for enzyme assay may be performed by fetoscopy in specialist centers (Rodeck et al., 1982). Early diagnosis is important; with long-term protein restriction, supplements of essential amino acids and arginine, and sodium benzoate therapy (Batshaw et al., 1982), as well as vigorous treatment of acute episodes, the clinical symptoms (including the mental retardation) may be ameliorated, especially in girls.

We document here seven patients with OCTD who presented with an undiagnosed encephalopathy and in whom we observed considerable variation in the neurological features. One case is described in detail and all are summarized clinically and biochemically in Table 1.

CASE PRESENTATION: CASE 1

This girl, whose two brothers died neonatally of "pulmonary hemorrhage," was born normally at term weighing 3.6 kg. There were no neonatal problems, but she was bottle fed and failed to thrive. At 9 months of age she had an episode of diarrhea, vomiting, and drowsiness that was thought to be caused by an encephalitis. She made a satisfactory

Table 1.   Clinical and biochemical findings and mother's carrier status in 7 OCTD patients

Case No.	Age at diagnosis	Sex	Neurological and other findings	Laboratory results[a]			Mother's carrier status[c]
				Initial plasma ammonia (μmol/L)	Urine orotic acid: creatinine ratio (μmol/mmol)	Liver enzymes (μmol/L per g wet weight)[b]	
1	2 yr 8 mo	F	9 mo: first attack—drowsiness, irritability, ataxia, "encephalopathy" × 4, mental retardation Alive	520	615	not done	+
2	7 yr	F	3 mo: first attack—vomiting, drowsiness, "encephalopathy"; bright child 7 yr: sudden deep coma with decerebrate rigidity and papilledema Dead	414	600	OCT 385 CPS 176	+
3	10–14 mo	F	9 mo: developmental delay (failure to thrive) 14 mo: vomiting, drowsiness, irritability; developmental delay with developmental arrest; hemiplegia Treated with low-protein diet with supplements of amino and keto acids; development normal and hemiplegia resolved (began to thrive)	236	103[d]	OCT 343 CPS 154	?

(continued)

233

Table 1. (Continued)

Case No.	Age at diagnosis	Sex	Neurological and other findings	Laboratory results[a]			
				Initial plasma ammonia (μmol/L)	Urine orotic acid: creatinine ratio (μmol/mmol)	Liver enzymes (μmol/L per g wet weight)[b]	Mother's carrier status[c]
4	10 wk	F	3 wk: drowsiness, twitching of lower limbs; 7 wk: grand mal seizures; diagnosis on this admission—"encephalitis" due to congenital infections Note: normal blood ammonia Repeat tests confirmed diagnosis 6 mo: no developmental progress Dead at 13 mo	36 275 (on repeat test)	13.9 23 (repeat test)	OCT 299 CPS 181	+
5	12 yr	M	3–4 yr, onward: several episodes of mild encephalopathy, vomiting, irritability, drowsiness Note: normal development 12 yr: admitted with sudden severe encephalopathy Dead	286	3.1 695 (repeat test)	OCT 209 CPS 271	not done

| 6 | 9 mo | M | 6 mo: vomiting, irritability, failure to thrive
12 yr: severe encephalopathy, coma, fits
Dead as a result of encephalopathy
[Full details in Levin et al. (1969)] | 182 | 2500 max.[d] | OCT 128.8
CPS 250 | ? |
| 7 | 12 mo | M | Neonatal period: preterm meningitis
8 mo: failure to thrive, irritability, developmental delay
12 mo: unconscious; left hemiplegia, brain edema
Dead as a result of tonsillar herniation | 700 | 462[d] | OCT 233
ASA lyase 199 | + |

[a] Reference values (Harris and Oberholzer, 1980):

Plasma ammonia: <40 µmol/L
Urine orotic acid:creatinine ratio (µmol/mmol):
2 weeks to 1 year   1.0–3.2
1–10 years   0.5–3.3
Over 10 years   0.4–1.2
Enzyme activities (µmol/g per hr)
OCT   >4000
CPS   70–550
ASA lyase   54–188

[b] OCT, ornithine carbamoyltransferase; CPS, carbamoylphosphate synthase; ASA lyase, argininosuccinate lyase.
[c] +, carrier status proved by protein load; ?, normal response to protein load—carrier status uncertain.
[d] Other pyrimidines, uridine, and uracil visible in chromatogram.

235

recovery, but subsequently had four further attacks, during which she became drowsy, irritable, and ataxic. Her developmental progress had been normal up to the time of the first attack, but thereafter her development slowed so that at the age of $2\frac{1}{2}$ years her performance was equivalent to that of a normal child of 18 months.

At 2 years 8 months, following a further episode of encephalopathy, she was admitted to hospital. She was small (height and weight below the third percentile) and mildly mentally retarded, but otherwise the general physical and neurological examinations were unremarkable. Plasma ammonia glutamine and alanine levels and urine orotic acid concentrations were elevated (Table 1); the ornithine carbamoyltransferase activity in the liver was not measured. Computerized tomography showed extensive, bilateral, symmetrical, well-defined low density of the white matter of the cerebral hemispheres, sparing the internal capsules because of cerebral edema. She was treated with a low-protein diet and supplements of arginine and has had no further episodes of encephalopathy with hyperammonemia. Repeat computerized tomography 1 month after the previous scan showed less extensive white matter of low density, suggesting resolution of the cerebral edema.

Her mother and a mentally retarded aunt had hyperammonemia and excess orotic acid in the urine following a standard protein load. The patient's mother also had a brother who died neonatally and a mentally retarded niece who died at 2 years of age; in both, OCTD was not diagnosed or considered. The mother of our patient became pregnant again and at 16 weeks of gestation fetoscopy was performed; a male fetus was visualized. A fetal liver sample was obtained and enzymes were analyzed. This analysis showed low levels of ornithine carbamoyltransferase but normal levels of carbamoylphosphate synthase. The pregnancy was terminated and subsequent analysis of the fetal liver confirmed the diagnosis.

DISCUSSION

Failure to thrive, mental retardation, and vomiting with acute exacerbations are typical of OCTD and the biochemical findings in all seven cases are diagnostic (Table 1). The computerized tomographic appearances of the brain in Case 1, although not specific, are consistent with a metabolic disorder (Kingsley and Kendall, 1981). The history of episodic encephalopathy in this case, combined with her tolerance to marked hyperammonemia, suggests that the latter was long-standing and was responsible for the scan appearances.

Acute encephalopathy in childhood has many causes, including infections, vascular disorders, cerebral tumors, drug intoxication, and poisoning, as well as many metabolic disorders. Hyperammonemia is just one cause, but it is still underdiagnosed. We emphasize the importance of measuring the plasma ammonia level in all children with an acute encephalopathy. Plasma ammonia levels in affected cases are variable, depending on the age of the patient, the protein intake, and the residual enzyme activity. In those with mild disease, the plasma ammonia concentration may be normal. During severe encephalopathy the concentration usually exceeds 300 μmol/L.

In OCTD there are no diagnostic abnormalities of the plasma amino acids, but, in common with other urea cycle disorders, the concentrations of glutamine and often of alanine are raised. As a result of the metabolic block, there is an increased synthesis of pyrimidines and their precursors, including orotic acid; the measurement of these compounds in the urine is a useful screening test for OCTD (Bachmann and Colombo, 1980). Final confirmation of the diagnosis is made by measuring the ornithine carbamoyltransferase activity in liver or jejunal biopsy material (Hoogenraad et al., 1980). The most satisfactory currently available method for the detection of carriers is to measure orotic acid excretion in the urine after a standard protein load (Batshaw et al., 1980; Harris and Oberholzer, 1980). The differential diagnosis of OCTD includes not only other disorders of the urea cycle but also Reye's syndrome (Krieger et al., 1979), inborn errors of amino acid metabolism and of organic acid and carnitine metabolism (Ware et al., 1978; Leonard et al., 1979), sodium valproate therapy (Coulter and Allen, 1981), and urinary tract infections (Samtoy and De Beukelaer, 1980).

Tripp et al. (1981) stressed the importance of considering inborn errors of metabolism such as OCTD in patients who are unduly susceptible to the effects of drugs. This was highlighted in a child who had fits and who was taking sodium valproate. This child was thought to be suffering from valproate hepatotoxicity when he developed coma. However, when investigated he was shown to have OCTD. Other reported cases of valproate hepatotoxicity may have had inborn errors of urea cycle metabolism, or neurometabolic conditions with hepatic and cerebral degeneration such as Huttenlocher disease (Huttenlocher et al., 1976).

Acute hyperammonemia, whether due to OCTD or other disorders, should be treated regardless of the severity of symptoms, because they are reversible; long-standing improvement can be maintained on a low-protein diet with supplements of amino acids and ketoacids. Therefore, it is important to diagnose this condition early and institute immediate treatment. Hyperammonemia, albeit rare, is a preventable cause of mental retardation.

REFERENCES

Bachmann, C., and Colombo, J. P., 1980. Diagnostic value of orotic acid excretion in heritable disorders of the urea cycle and in hyperammonaemia due to organic acidurias. Eur. J. Pediatr. 134:109–113.

Batshaw, M. L., Roan, Y., Jung, A. L., Rosenberg, L. A., and Brusilow, S. W., 1980. Cerebral dysfunction in asymptomatic carriers of ornithine transcarbamylase deficiency. N. Engl. J. Med. 302:482–485.

Batshaw, M. L., Brusilow, S., Waber, L., Blom, W., Brubank, A. M., Burton, B. K., Cann, H. M., Kerr, D., Mamunes, P., Matalon, R., Myerberg, D., and Schafer, I. A. 1982. Treatment of inborn errors of urea synthesis. Activation of alternative pathways of waste nitrogen synthesis and excretion. N. Engl. J. Med. 306:1387–1392.

Coulter, D. L., and Allen, R. J. 1981. Hyperammonaemia with valproic acid therapy. J. Pediatr. 99:317–319.

Donn, S. M., Swartz, R. D., and Thoene, J. G. 1979. Comparison of exchange transfusion, peritoneal dialysis and haemodialysis for the treatment of hyperammonaemia in an anuric new born infant. J. Pediatr. 95:67–70.

Haan, E. A., Danks, D. M., Hoogenraad, N. J., and Rogers, J. G., 1979. Hereditary hyperammonaemic syndromes—a six year experience. Aust. Paediatr. J. 15:142–146.

Harris, M. L., and Oberholzer, V. G. 1980. Conditions affecting the colorimetry of orotic acid and orotidine in urine. Clin. Chem. 26:473–479.

Hoogenraad, N. J., Mitchell, J. D., Don, N. A., Sutherland, T. M., and McLeay, A. C. 1980. Detection of carbamylphosphate synthetase deficiency using duodenal biopsy samples. Arch. Dis. Child. 55:292–295.

Huttenlocher, P. R., Solitare, G. B., and Adams, G. 1976. Infantile diffuse cerebral degeneration with hepatic cirrhosis. Arch. Neurol. 33:186–192.

Kingsley, D. P. E., and Kendall, B. E. 1981. Demyelinating and neurodegenerative disease in childhood. J. Neuroradiol. 8:243–255.

Krieger, I., Snodgrass, P. J., and Roskamp, J. 1979. Atypical clinical course of ornithine transcarbamylase deficiency due to a new mutant (comparison with Reye's disease). J. Clin. Endocr. Metab. 48:388–392.

Leonard, J. V., Seakins, J. W. T., and Griffin, N. K. 1979. β-Hydroxy β-methylglutaric aciduria presenting as Reye's syndrome. Lancet 1:680.

Levin, B., Dobbs, R. H., Burgess, E. A., and Palmer, T. 1969. Hyperammonaemia—A variant type of deficiency of liver ornithine transcarbamylase. Arch. Dis. Child. 44:162–169.

Rodeck, C. H., Patrick, A. D., Pembrey, M. E., Tzannatos, C., and Whitfield, A. E. 1982. Fetal liver biopsy for the prenatal diagnosis of ornithine carbamyl transferase deficiency. Lancet 2:297–299.

Russell, A., Levin, B., Oberholzer, V. G., and Sinclair, L. 1962. Hyperammonaemia, a new instance of an inborn enzymatic defect of the biosynthesis of urea. Lancet 2:699–700.

Samtoy, B., and De Beukelaer, M. M. 1980. Ammonia encephalopathy secondary to urinary tract infection with *Proteus mirabilis*. Pediatrics 65:294–297.

Saudubray, J. M., Cathelineau, L., Laugier, J. M., Charpentier, C., Le Jeune, J. S., and Mozziconacci, P. 1975. Hereditary ornithine transcarbamylase deficiency. Acta Paediatr. Scand. 64:464–472.

Shih, V. E. 1978. Urea cycle disorders and other congenital hyperammonaemic syndromes. In: J. B. Stanbury, J. B. Wyngaarden, and D. B. Fredrickson (eds.), The Metabolic Basis of Inherited Disease, pp. 362–386. McGraw-Hill Book Company, New York.

Tripp, J. H., Hargreaves, T., Anthony, P. P., Searle, J. F., Miller, P., Leonard, J. V., Patrick, A. D., and Oberholzer, V. G. 1981. Sodium valproate and ornithine carbamoyl transferase deficiency. Lancet 1:1165–1166.

Ware, A. J., Burton, W. C., McGarry, J. D., Marks, J. F., and Weinberg, A. G. 1978. Systemic carnitine deficiency. Report of a fatal case with multisystem manifestations. J. Pediatr. 93:959–964.

Wiegand, C., Thompson, T., Bock, G. H., Mathis, R. K., Kjellstrand, C. M., and Mauer, S. M. 1980. The management of life-threatening hyperammonaemia: A comparison of several therapeutic modalities. J. Pediatr. 96:142–144.

SECTION V
Biochemical and Electrophysiological Studies

PERSPECTIVES AND PROGRESS IN MENTAL RETARDATION
Volume II—Biomedical Aspects
Edited by J. M. Berg

THYROID FUNCTION STUDIES IN CHILDREN AND ADOLESCENTS WITH DOWN'S SYNDROME

F. Ziai, D. Rhone, P. Justice, and G. F. Smith

*University of Illinois at the Medical Center, Chicago,
and Illinois Masonic Medical Center, Chicago, 836 Wellington Avenue,
Chicago, Illinois 60657*

To investigate the incidence of thyroid function disorders in children and adolescents with Down's syndrome, 62 noninstitutionalized children ranging in age from 5 to 16 years, with a 35%/65% female-to-male ratio, were screened. Antithyroid antibodies were present in 30%; only 3% were hypothyroid and required treatment. Females had a higher incidence of antibodies and manifestations of symptomatic hypothyroidism. Antibodies are known to develop in early childhood that may lead to hypothyroidism later in life. Periodic screening of Down's syndrome cases measuring serum thyroxine, thyroid-stimulating hormone, and antithyroid antibodies, starting in early childhood, is recommended.

The association of thyroid disorders with Down's syndrome is well known. Either hypothyroidism or hyperthyroidism may be present. Infants, children, and adults may be affected, and there seems to be a predilection for females. Several studies have suggested the possible role of autoimmunity in the pathogenesis of thyroid disorders in Down's syndrome by demonstrating the presence of thyroid autoantibodies in symptomatic and asymptomatic patients. To investigate this theory a group of children and adolescents with Down's syndrome were evaluated for their thyroid function.

MATERIALS AND METHOD

Sixty-two children with Down's syndrome, living at home, were evaluated. Their ages ranged from 5 years 10 months to 16 years 6 months,

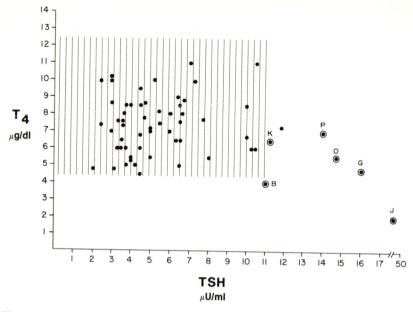

Figure 1. Concentration of serum TSH and T4 in children with Down's syndrome (letters indicate case as in Table 1). Hatched area represents normal range.

with a 35%/65% female-to-male ratio. One 12-year-old female had been previously diagnosed as having hypothyroidism and was on replacement thyroxine therapy. The remainder of the group were asymptomatic and none had a goiter. Thyroid function was studied in each individual by measuring thyroid-stimulating hormone (TSH) and thyroxine (T4) levels (Gamma Dab & Autopak Kits, Travenol Lab. & Rohm, Hass Co.). Detection of antithyroid antibodies was accomplished by measurements of antithyroglobulin and antimicrosomal antibody titers, using the tanned red cell hemagglutination technique (Thymune-T and Thymune-M kits by Wellcome Company). Patients with high TSH but with low or normal T4 were reexamined for clinical evidence of thyroid disease and given repeat laboratory studies.

RESULTS

Serum TSH was elevated in seven (11%) of the cases, and associated in three of these with a low T4 level (see Figure 1). However, clinical hypothyroidism was evident in only one female patient (Case 2-G) with high TSH and low T4. In another female (Case 3-J) who had the highest TSH and lowest T4 levels there were no clinical signs or symptoms of hypothyroidism (see Table 1). These two cases received thyroxine

Table 1. Down's syndrome patients with thyroid abnormalities

Case	Age	Sex	TSH[a]	T4[b]	Antithyroid antibodies		Clinical	R[c]
					Thyroglobulin	Microsome		
1-B	14 yr 6 mo	M	11	3.9	Neg	1:16	Hypothyroid	Yes
2-G	14 yr 5 mo	F	16.2	4.8	Neg	1:4096	Euthyroid	Yes
3-J	14 yr 7 mo	F	>50	2.3	Neg	Neg	Euthyroid	No
4-P	8 yr 11 mo	M	12.9	7.5	Neg	Neg	Euthyroid	No
5-K	9 yr 2 mo	F	11	6.5	Neg	1:16,364	Euthyroid	
6-O	11 yr	F	14.8	5.7	1:32	1:16,364	?	
1-K[d]	12 yr	F	2.4	10.6	Neg	1:4096	Euthyroid	Yes

[a] Normal values <10 mU/ml.
[b] Normal values 4.5–12 µg/dl.
[c] Thyroxine treatment.
[d] Previously diagnosed.

245

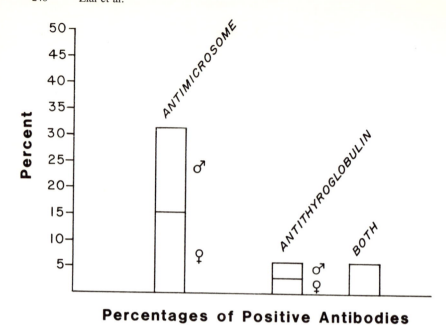

Figure 2.   Percentage of positive antimicrosomes and antithyroglobulin.

treatment, which corrected their abnormal TSH and T4 levels and in Case 2-G eliminated clinical findings of hypothyroidism. Microsomal antibodies were present in 30% of all cases and ranged in titers from 1:4 to 1:16,384. However, antithyroglobulin antibodies were present in only 6% of the cases, ranging in titers from 1:16 to 1:32. All cases with antithyroid antibodies were also positive for microsomal antibodies (see Figure 2).

The youngest child with positive microsomal antibodies was a 5 year–5 month–old boy with a titer of 1:4,096. Although antibodies were present in 50% of the females, they were detectable in only 25% of the males (see Figure 3). In four patients, all of whom were female, the concentrations of serum antibodies increased fourfold within a 6-month period even though none of these individuals showed biochemical or clinical evidence of hypothyroidism. The one patient with severe chemical hypothyroidism (Case 3-J) had undetectable thyroid antibodies on repeated tests. Four of the six individuals with evidence of abnormal biochemical findings were positive for microsomal antibodies and one was positive for antithyroglobulin antibodies (see Table 1).

DISCUSSION

Evaluation of the thyroid function in Down's syndrome has a history that predates Down's (1866) description of the condition. Previously

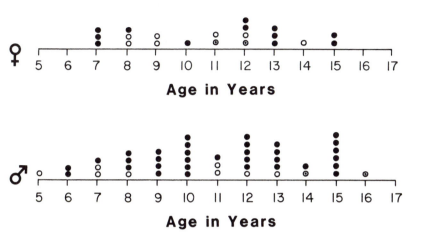

● = without antibodies
o = with Microsomal antibodies
⊙ = with Microsomal and Thyroglobulin antibodies

Figure 3.   Age and sex distribution of cases of Down's syndrome with and without antithyroid antibodies.

these children were usually classified as having a variation of cretinism. Prior to 1866 even Down considered these children as "cretins" and referred to them as "strumous cretins" (Shuttleworth, 1909). The scientific literature is replete with studies on the thyroid gland in Down's syndrome (Smith and Berg, 1976). In general, the impression has been that the thyroid gland is in the low normal range and that individuals with clinical hypothyroidism should be treated. It has also been shown that the routine use of thyroid hormone in individuals without established hypothyroidism has no beneficial effect.

The present study indicates that about 10% of children and adolescents with Down's syndrome have biochemical evidence of reduced thyroid function without clinical evidence of hypothyroidism. Of the six individuals in our study with biochemical evidence suggesting hypothyroidism, two were started on replacement thyroid therapy. The other four are being closely followed. The one individual who was treated without clinical evidence of hypothyroidism (Case 3-J) had very abnormal biochemical findings (TSH of 50, T4 of 2.3). On therapy, her biochemical findings returned to normal. It is not yet well established at what level biochemical evidence of reduced thyroid function without overt evidence of clinical hypothyroidism interferes with an individual's intellectual abilities.

The high incidence of 30% positive microsomal antibodies in our series is similar to the observation of Lobo et al. (1980). The incidence of thyroid antibodies in Down's syndrome has varied considerably. This has probably been due to the techniques used and the types of antibodies measured. In a study of 125 normal children with thyroid disorders, Hapwood et al. (1978) showed by radioimmunoassay that 85% of the cases had antithyroid antibodies. However, antibodies were positive in only 24% and 7% of the same cases when hemagglutination technique was used for antithyroglobulin and antimicrosomes, respectively. In a survey of over 5,000 normal schoolchildren, thyroiditis was present in 1.2% of the children (Rallison et al., 1975). Of the affected cases with thyroiditis, 93% had antibodies (using radioimmunoassay). This incidence was reduced to 75% when the tanned red cell hemagglutination test was used. To our knowledge, use of the radioimmunoassay technique has not been reported for the detection of antithyroid antibodies in children with Down's syndrome. It is quite possible that a higher incidence of thyroiditis could be detected using this more sensitive antibody test. Loeb et al. (1972) have suggested that in children lower concentrations of antithyroglobulin antibodies should be considered significant when compared with adults, as was shown in their group of children with biopsy-proved thyroiditis. Their findings led us to believe that a titer of greater than 1:4 of antithyroglobulin antibodies was positive. The detection of two cases of hypothyroidism in our study, out of 62 cases screened (3%), is a much higher incidence than that found in normal schoolchildren (4 per 10,000) and is in agreement with other surveys in children with Down's syndrome.

Aldenhoff et al. (1977), using a thyrotropin-releasing hormone (TRH) stimulation test in 122 patients with Down's syndrome, were able to detect 15 cases of "latent" hypothyroidism (12%), of which only three were positive for microsomal antibodies. All of these cases were found to be euthyroid. The youngest child in our series was a 5-year-old boy who was also positive for microsomal antibodies. Saxena and Pryles (1965) demonstrated the presence of antibodies in children with Down's syndrome as young as 2–3 years of age. Interestingly, in the Saxena and Pryles study, none of their 53 subjects was found to be hypothyroid using protein-bound iodine and ^{131}I thyroidal uptake. Autoimmunity is considered as a possible cause of thyroiditis in Down's syndrome, as evidenced by the presence of thyroid antibodies in the majority of cases, and its association with other autoimmune disorders such as vitiligo and diabetes mellitus. A 14-year-old female (Case 3-J) in our series with profound chemical hypothyroidism had undetectable thyroid antibodies on repeated tests using the hemagglutination technique. Aldenhoff et al. (1977) also reported the presence of antibodies in only 20% of their "latent hypothyroid cases." The absence of antibodies in the minority of cases therefore suggests that other thyroid defects such as dysgenesis or dyshormonogenesis may represent less frequent causes of hypothyroidism in Down's syndrome.

Hyperthyroidism has also been found with increased frequency in association with Down's syndrome. Ruvalcaba et al. (1969), in screening 307 institutionalized patients with Down's syndrome, found two adolescents with goiter and hyperthyroidism (6 per 1,000) both of whom had positive antibodies. Neither in our series of children nor in that of Lobo et al. (1980) was hyperthyroidism discovered during screening.

Murdoch et al. (1977), in a study of a large number of adults with Down's syndrome, demonstrated a higher incidence of hypothyroidism (16%) associated with increased antibodies. However, a correlation of antibody levels with increasing age was lacking. In our group of children, the affected subjects were all adolescents but, because of the small number of cases, correlations could not be done. Increasing concentration of antibodies in four of our cases, within a short period of time, is of interest. These cases are under observation for possible development of clinical hypothyroidism.

CONCLUSIONS

In view of our findings, we recommend that hypothyroidism diligently be watched for in children with Down's syndrome, because it can be masked by the syndrome. Laboratory investigation, including serum T4, TSH, antithyroglobulin, and antimicrosomal antibody tests, should be conducted regularly (probably annually, and more frequently if an abnormality is detected). Early intervention with thyroxine replacement will alleviate the physical and mental symptoms of hypothyroidism.

REFERENCES

Aldenhoff, P., Waldenmaier, C., Zabransky, S., and Helge, H. 1977. TRH stimulation test in children and adults with Down's syndrome. Monatsschr. Kinderheilkd. 125:544–545.

Down, J. L. H. 1866. Observations on an ethnic classification of idiots. Clin. Lect. Rep. Lond. Hosp. 3:259.

Hapwood, N. J., Rabin, B. S., Foley, T. P., Jr., and Peake, R. L. 1978. Thyroid antibodies in children and adolescents with thyroid disorder. J. Pediatr. 93:57–61.

Lobo, E. De. H., Khan, M., and Tew, J. 1980. Community study of hypothyroidism in Down's syndrome. Br. Med. J. 280:1253.

Loeb, P. B., Drash, A. L., and Kenny, F. M. 1972. Prevalence of low-titer and "negative" antithyroglobulin antibodies in biopsy-proved juvenile Hashimoto's thyroiditis. J. Pediatr. 82:17–21.

Murdoch, J. C., Ratcliffe, W. A., McLarty, D. G., Rodger, J. C., and Ratcliffe, J. G. 1977. Thyroid function in adults with Down's syndrome. J. Clin. Endocr. Metab. 44:453–458.

Rallison, M. L., Brown, M. D., Keating, F. R., Rall, J. E., and Tyler, F. H. 1975. Occurrence and natural history of chronic lymphocytic thyroiditis in childhood. J. Pediatr. 86:675–682.

Ruvalcaba, R. H. A., Ferrier, P. E., and Thuline, H. C. 1969. Incidence of goiter in patients with Down's syndrome. Am. J. Dis. Child. 118:451–453.

Saxena, K. M., and Pryles, C. V. 1965. Thyroid function in mongolism. J. Pediatr. 67:363–370.

Shuttleworth, G. E. 1909. Mongolian imbecility. Br. Med. J. 2:661–665.

Smith, G. F., and Berg, J. M. 1976. Down's Anomaly. Churchill Livingstone, London.

PERSPECTIVES AND PROGRESS IN MENTAL RETARDATION
Volume II—Biomedical Aspects
Edited by J. M. Berg

EARLY DIAGNOSIS OF MUCOPOLY- SACCHARIDOSES

A. E. Lorincz,[1] R. E. Hurst,[2] and E. H. Kolodny[3]

[1] Department of Pediatrics, University of Alabama in Birmingham,
Biomedical Science Building, Room 124, Birmingham, Alabama 35294
[2] School of Public Health, University of Alabama in Birmingham,
Biomedical Science Building, Room 102, Birmingham, Alabama 35294
[3] Eunice Kennedy Shriver Center for Mental Retardation,
200 Trapelo Road, Waltham, Massachusetts 02154

The needs and methods for the early laboratory diagnosis of the muco-polysaccharidoses are discussed. A comparison of simple laboratory diagnostic urine screening techniques is presented, as are the appropriate laboratory tests needed for follow-up of positive screens. The application of biophysical cytochemistry techniques to the study of uncultured, unfixed amniotic cells for earlier prenatal diagnosis is also presented.

The clinical diagnosis of the mucopolysaccharidoses, a heterogeneous group of inborn errors of glycosaminoglycan (mucopolysaccharide) metabolism, is not difficult in fully expressed severe forms with classical dysmorphic facies, organomegaly, and progressive mental and developmental retardation, e.g., in Hurler's syndrome (Type I/H mucopolysaccharidosis). However, certain clinical types are not associated with mental retardation, and other types have late or adult-onset symptomatology (Kolodny and Cable, 1982). Moreover, at birth nearly all affected individuals appear phenotypically normal, even though the metabolic defect is already present and can be detected by a clinical laboratory if appropriate studies are performed. In fact the diagnosis of mucopolysaccharidosis in utero has been achieved or considered possible for all of the present known mucopolysaccharidosis types.

The incidence and prevalence of the aggregate of these clinical disorders is probably much larger than previously believed, because many are never correctly diagnosed. Hopwood et al. (1982) diagnosed 96 cases in a 5-year period throughout Australia and New Zealand. Cited by these authors is Van der Kamp's study of 1979 in which the estimated incidence in Holland of Type III (Sanfilippo) syndrome alone was as high as 1 in 25,000. In the Lysosomal Storage Disease Laboratory directed by one of us (EHK) 20 new cases were definitively diagnosed in the past 2 years. Without a systematic screening program or an intensive search, over 80 living affected individuals with mucopolysaccharidosis were readily identified in the New England area during this same period (Kolodny and Lorincz, 1982, unpublished observations).

EARLY DIAGNOSIS

The early and accurate diagnosis of these lysosomal storage disorders remains a significant problem for the clinical laboratory. For a definitive diagnosis to be established, not only is the demonstration of a quantitative as well as qualitative abnormality of glycosaminoglycan excretion needed, but the laboratory assessment of a deficiency of a specific enzymatic activity must also be demonstrated. The activities of most lysosomal enzymes can be determined using artificial chromogenic or fluorogenic substrates or radioactively labeled natural substrates. Readily accessible body fluids and tissues such as plasma, leukocytes, hair follicles, and cultured fibroblasts or amniotic fluid cells can be used as enzyme sources. There are only a limited number of qualified laboratories throughout the world that have the technical skills, quality control, facilities, and access to specialized substrates to perform the majority of the 11 different enzymatic assays that have been identified with the mucopolysaccharidoses. Fortunately, it is not usually necessary to perform all of these assays for any given patient, because clinical symptomatology coupled with knowledge of the qualitative and quantitative nature of the glycosaminoglycans excreted permits a selective approach as to which enzymatic assays need to be performed.

As in all disease states, whether treatable, curable, or not, there are general needs of early diagnosis to assist the family and affected individual in adapting and coping. When accurate diagnosis and prognosis is known, medical treatment and management, such as orthopedic correction of flexion contractures, provision of hearing amplification aids, shunting for hydrocephalus, and replacement of calcified deformed cardiac valves, can be appropriately anticipated and instituted. Another reason for early diagnosis is that it is the keystone for prevention of recurrent cases in the same family. Through genetic counseling, in utero diagnosis via amniocentesis, and family planning, additional cases of these devastating developmentally disabling conditions may be prevented. With the recent report of Hobbs et al.

(1981) that clinical features in Hurler's disease can be reversed by treatment with bone marrow transplantation, as well as the portent of genetic engineering as a means for correcting specific enzymatic deficiencies, the need for early accurate definitive diagnosis, before irreversible mental or physical changes have occurred, becomes even more pressing.

METHODS OF LABORATORY DIAGNOSIS

The laboratory diagnosis of mucopolysaccharidosis can be ascertained even before clinical symptomatology becomes manifest. The demonstration of abnormal glycosaminoglycanuria is a cornerstone of laboratory diagnosis. The commonly used urinary screening tests are not adequate alone to establish altered glycosaminoglycanuria. Follow-up laboratory procedures to confirm increased excretion of dermatan sulfate and/or heparan sulfate, or in some instances keratan sulfate, is necessary (Lorincz, 1982). Other diagnostic modalities or approaches may all play a role in establishing the early diagnosis of the mucopolysaccharidoses. These include X rays, CAT scans, light and electron microscopic study of circulating cells, skin, and conjunctivae, or similar studies of other tissues such as liver, spleen, brain, nerves, bone marrow, and cartilage. Reported here are our findings in the systematic comparison of the ability of three common glycosaminoglycanuria screening procedures to detect the mucopolysaccharides; these procedures should be readily available to most clinical laboratory settings. Follow-up detailed laboratory analysis of glycosaminoglycans and information regarding the use of biophysical cytochemistry in the diagnosis of mucopolysaccharidoses is also presented.

Screening Procedures

The first test studied was the spot test reported by Berry and Spinager (1960). This test is dependent on the metachromasia that results from the organization of cationic dye molecules (toluidine blue) along a regular polyanionic matrix as is present in glycosaminoglycans. Despite its lack of specificity, it is simple and inexpensive. It requires only microliter quantities of urine, filter paper, 0.04% toluidine blue buffered solution, and an ethanol rinse. It can be performed in a few minutes.

The second test, the Ames MPS Paper spot test reported by Berman et al. (1971), is also a metachromatic test. It utilizes commercially available paper impregnated with azure A dye. The cost is a bit higher, and the test takes approximately 15 minutes to perform.

The third screening procedure studied, the gross acid albumin turbidity procedure described by Carter et al. (1968), was a reaction in which excess glycosaminoglycans interact with acidified albumin solutions to produce turbidity. This test requires 1 ml of acidified clear supernatant urine to which 2 ml of acidified bovine serum albumin reagent is added. In 10 minutes the resulting turbidity is graded on a scale of 0 to 4 + .

These three tests were run on random urine samples obtained from 35 definitively diagnosed, well-characterized cases of mucopolysaccharidosis representing nine different mucopolysaccharidosis types. To avoid problems of excessive urine dilution, we arbitrarily limited our studies to urine samples with a specific gravity greater than 1.005. Only a few random urine samples from normal subjects, as well as from selected individuals with other non-mucopolysaccharidosis genetic diseases, were tested in the same manner. By design this study focused upon sensitivity (false-negatives) and did not attempt to address the significant and complex epidemiological problem for determining specificity of these screening procedures.

All 35 mucopolysaccharidosis cases had positive Berry spot screening tests with the 10-μl and 25-μl urine applications. However, seven of 20 positives at 10 μl and 15 of 20 positives at 25 μl were found in a small population of presumed normal or non-mucopolysaccharidosis affected genetic disorders. This test has high sensitivity; however, because of its low specificity, it is imperative that it be used in conjunction with additional urinary glycosaminoglycan analyses. Thirty-two of the 35 mucopolysaccharidosis cases gave a positive test with the Ames MPS Paper test. The two Type IV and the one mild form of Type VI tested negatively. These three cases also had a negative gross albumin turbidity test. Only one of the clinically affected non-mucopolysaccharidosis group tested faintly positive with the Ames Spot test.

Only 27 of the 35 mucopolysaccharidosis cases had a positive gross acid albumin turbidity test. Of the eight negative mucopolysaccharidoses, five were Type III (Sanfilippo), two were Type IV (Morquio), and one was a mild form of Type VI (Maroteaux-Lamy). None of the 20 non-mucopolysaccharidosis group tested positive with this screening procedure. None of these three tests is completely specific for glycosaminoglycans, so that a certain number of false-positives results, which many investigators have previously reported, are to be expected.

Glycosaminoglycan Specification Procedures

There remains a large gap between the application of these urinary screening methods for glycosaminoglycans and the laboratory assessment of specific enzymatic activity deficiency evaluations. From the observations reported here, it can be concluded that if a positive screening test is obtained with the Berry spot test, and/or subsequently confirmed to be positive with the Ames MPS Paper test, it is then necessary to undertake a more detailed laboratory isolation and characterization of urinary glycosaminoglycan(s) excreted.

The method of Hurst et al. (1976) has been used for this purpose in our laboratories. Gel filtration is used to isolate the macromolecular fraction of urine. This fraction contains all the high molecular weight (> 4000) substances, but not the smaller substances. Colorimetric assessment of sulfaminohexose and uronate, in the macromolecular fraction, together with electrophoretic analyses, can assess the qualitative as well as quantitative nature of the glycosaminoglycans excreted. This information along with knowledge of clinical manifestations should permit the appropriate selection of the enzymatic hydrolase assays needed to establish the definitive diagnosis.

Diagnosis with Biophysical Cytochemistry

A fairly new approach to early diagnosis, through the application of biophysical cytochemistry to the study of unfixed cells (West and Lorincz, 1973; West, 1982) has been initiated by one of us (AEL), and promises an innovative approach to the early in utero diagnosis of the mucopolysaccharidoses. Amniotic fluid cells obtained at the time of amniocentesis from a pregnancy at risk for Type I Hurler/Scheie compound were vitally stained with buffered acridine orange at a concentration of about 10^{-5}M. Inspection under blue-light fluorescence microscopy revealed numerous bright orange-red cytoplasmic inclusions in many cells. Such inclusions have not been observed in amniotic fluid cells obtained from presumed normal pregnancies. Subsequent culture of amniotic cells and enzymatic assay for iduronidase activity several weeks later confirmed that this fetus indeed was affected.

The appearance of the cells filled with the orange-red fluorescent inclusions resembles those seen in cultured skin fibroblasts from known mucopolysaccharidosis-affected individuals. Whether the direct examination of uncultured, unfixed amniotic cells can rapidly establish the diagnosis of mucopolysaccharidosis where the fetus is affected remains to be validated through a detailed study of a large number of pregnancies at risk for these disorders.

CONCLUSIONS

At present, to achieve early diagnosis of the mucopolysaccharidoses, there needs to be a major increased effort to do simple laboratory screening (e.g., with the Berry Spot test and the Ames MPS Paper test) for glycosaminoglycanuria, particularly in those populations consid-

ered at risk. This population includes all severely or profoundly retarded persons in whom the cause of the retardation is unknown, as
well as all retarded individuals who have dysmorphic features, organomegaly, or evidence of plateauing or diminishing developmental progress. All positive screens require follow-up with specialized laboratory
studies for characterization of glycosaminoglycanuria as well as subsequent appropriate lysosomal enzyme assays. The need also exists
for establishing simpler methods for earlier diagnosis of the mucopolysaccharidoses in utero.

REFERENCES

Berman, E. R., Vered, J., and Bach, G. 1971. A reliable spot test for muco-
polysaccharidoses. Clin. Chem. 17:886–890.
Berry, H. K., and Spinager, J. 1960. A paper spot test useful in the study of
Hurler's syndrome. J. Lab. Clin. Med. 55:136–138.
Carter, C. H., Wan, A. T., and Carpenter, D. G. 1968. Commonly used tests
in the detection of Hurler's syndrome. J. Pediatr. 73:217–221.
Hobbs, J. R., Barrett, A. J., Chambers, D., James, D. C. O., High-Jones, K.,
Byrom, N., Henry, K., Lucas, C. F., Benson, P. F., Tansley, L. R., Patrick,
A. D., Mossman, J., and Young, E. P. 1981. Reversal of clinical features
of Hurler's disease and biochemical improvement after treatment by bone-
marrow transplantation. Lancet 2:709–712.
Hopwood, J. J., Muller, V., Harrison, J. R., Carey, W. F., Elliott, H., Rob-
ertson, E. F., and Pollard, A. C. 1982. Enzymatic diagnosis of the muco-
polysaccharidoses. Experience of 96 cases diagnosed in a five-year period.
Med. J. Aust. 1:257–260.
Hurst, R. E., Settine, J. M., and Lorincz, A. E. 1976. A method for the quantitative determination of urinary glycosaminoglycans. Clin. Chim. Acta
70:427–432.
Kolodny, E. H., and Cable, W. J. L. 1982. Inborn errors of metabolism. Ann.
Neurol. 11:221–232.
Lorincz, A. E. 1982. Glycosaminoglycans in heritable and developmental disorders of bone. In: R. S. Varma and R. Varma (eds.), Glycosaminoglycans
and Proteoglycans in Physiological and Pathological Processes of Body Systems, pp. 264–275. Karger, Basel.
West, S. S. 1982. Introduction to fluorescence diagnosis. In: J. G. Regan and
J. Parrish (eds.), The Science of Photomedicine, pp. 69–89. Plenum Publishing Corp., New York.
West, S. S., and Lorincz, A. E. 1973. Fluorescence molecular probes in fluorescence microspectrophotometry and microspectropolarimetry. In: A. A.
Thaer and M. Sernetz (eds.), Fluorescence Techniques in Cell Biology, pp.
395–407. Springer-Verlag, Berlin.

PERSPECTIVES AND PROGRESS IN MENTAL RETARDATION
Volume II—Biomedical Aspects
Edited by J. M. Berg

GROWTH FACTORS AND FIBROBLAST GROWTH FACTOR RECEPTORS IN CEREBRAL GIGANTISM

A. V. Plioplys,[1] C. L. Childs,[2] R. G. Rosenfeld,[3] H. L. Moses,[2] and G. B. Stickler[4]

[1] 79 Indian Grove, Toronto, Ontario, M6R 2Y5, Canada
[2] Department of Cell Biology, Mayo Clinic, Rochester, Minnesota 55901
[3] Department of Pediatrics, Stanford University Medical Center, Stanford, California 94305
[4] Department of Pediatrics, Mayo Clinic, Rochester, Minnesota 55901

In two children with cerebral gigantism serum growth hormone, somatomedin C, nerve growth factor, and epidermal growth factor levels were unremarkable. Skin biopsy–derived fibroblasts from one child, when grown in confluent monolayer culture, demonstrated epidermal growth factor and somatomedin C receptor concentrations that did not differ from controls. Qualitative growth kinetics of these fibroblasts were also unremarkable.

Serum and plasma protein dialysate from one child significantly stimulated the growth of AKR-2B mouse fibroblasts in tissue culture when compared to controls. This effect was reproducible.

These results indicate that currently assayable growth factors and fibroblast receptors for epidermal growth factor and somatomedin C are unremarkable in cerebral gigantism. The serum and plasma protein stimulation of AKR-2B mouse fibroblast growth in one child may be a demonstration of a novel growth factor in this condition.

Cerebral gigantism as described by Sotos et al. (1964) is a syndrome of macrocephaly, macrosomia, and mental retardation. It is an unusual affliction, in that mental retardation is associated with overgrowth, as contrasted to the more usual microcephaly and poor growth of retarded individuals. This syndrome offers a rare opportunity for investigating biological factors that may account both for abnormal growth and abnormal mentation in these individuals and, by extrapolation, in the retarded population more generally.

Previous investigators, including Saenger et al. (1976), have been unable to demonstrate abnormalities of serum growth hormone and somatomedin concentrations in patients with cerebral gigantism. The purposes of this study were to investigate serum- and plasma-derived growth factors using both conventional and novel methodologies, as well as to study the growth kinetics and surface growth factor receptors in skin biopsy–derived fibroblasts from individuals with the syndrome. We were able to demonstrate unusual serum and plasma protein growth-enhancing properties in one child, raising the possibility of a novel growth factor in this condition.

METHODS

Two children with cerebral gigantism were evaluated. Patient 1 was a 19-month-old male. By the age of 4 months his height, weight, and head circumference were just above the 95th percentile, rankings that he continued to maintain. He was slow in his developmental parameters; he spoke his first words at the age of 1 year, and at the time of examination was unable to sit or walk unsupported. During the examination he was noted to have a dolicocephalic skull with proportionately large hands and feet. Psychometric testing revealed his general development to be at the 11-month level, with gross motor abilities at a 5-month level.

Patient 2 was a 10-month-old male. At the time of birth and subsequently, his height, weight, and head circumference were just above the 95th percentile. His subsequent developmental milestones were slightly delayed and at the time of examination were estimated to be at a 7- to 8-month level. His hands and feet were noted to be proportionately large. In neither patient was there a family history of neurological abnormality.

Routine investigations were performed on both children in the clinical chemistry and hematology laboratories of the Mayo Clinic using standard procedures. These investigations consisted of serum sodium, potassium, calcium, phosphate, total protein, glucose, bilirubin, uric acid, creatinine, alkaline phosphatase, glutamicoxalacetic acid transaminase, total thyroxine, urine screen for inborn errors of metabolism, and cerebrospinal fluid analysis (cell count, glucose, and protein). All results on these tests were normal. Opthalmological examination and skull X-rays in patient 1 and electroencephalogram in patient 2 were normal. In both patients cranial computerized tomography revealed an enlarged brain with mildly enlarged ventricles and subarachnoid spaces. In all of the subsequent investigations, the control and patient blood samples and skin biopsies were obtained with informed consent.

RESULTS

In patient 1 fasting serum growth hormone was 16.5 ng/ml, with suppression 2 hours after an oral glucose challenge (8.8 ng/ml); both blood samples were obtained with difficulty while the patient was crying vigorously. Fasting serum somatomedin C (SM-C) concentration, as measured by radioimmunoassay at the Nichols Institute, Los Angeles, California, was 0.23 U/ml, which was within normal limits for the patient's age. Fasting serum nerve growth factor (NGF) was assayed by a qualitative, in vivo bioassay performed by Dr. David Wells in which chick dorsal root ganglia were incubated in the presence of the patient's serum. The rate and extent ot neurite outgrowth with the patient's serum was indistinguishable from that of serum from normal adults. Fasting serum epidermal growth factor (EGF) concentration was determined by radioreceptor assay and found to be identical to that of normal adults.

In patient 1, fibroblast tissue cultures were established from a skin biopsy obtained, under local xylocaine anesthesia, from the right upper thigh. With the cells grown to a confluent monolayer in McCoy's 5A modified medium, supplemented with 10% fetal bovine serum (FBS), EGF receptor assay did not differ significantly from control fibroblasts.

With the cells grown to a confluent monolayer in Dulbecco's modified Eagle's medium (MEM) with 20% FBS, penicillin (100 U/ml), and streptomycin (100 mg/ml), an assay of cellular binding of ^{125}I-SM-C was performed by the methodology described by Rosenfeld and Dollar (in press). The percent specific binding per 10^6 cells in two separate experiments was 16.58% and 8.21%, which was within the normal range for foreskin fibroblasts. Binding percentages in fibroblasts from adult controls run concurrently were 5.81%, 10.57%, 14.82%, 18.35%), and 15.72%, again demonstrating that SM-C binding in the fibroblasts of patient 1 was normal. Furthermore, the binding characteristics of SM-C to the patient's fibroblasts were normal, indicating that there was a normal SM-C receptor concentration and affinity.

The fibroblasts were plated and grown in Dulbecco's MEM, as described above, in multiple 60-mm tissue culture dishes. The plates were trypsinized at intervals ranging in time from 2 to 13 days and counted in a Coulter counter. There was no qualitative difference of the fibroblast growth curve in this patient when compared to those of three normal adults and three patients with Turner's syndrome (Figure 1).

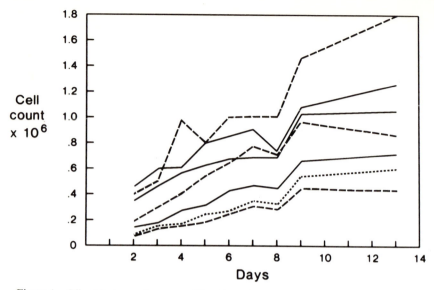

Figure 1.   Fibroblast growth curves. Fibroblasts from patient 1 (*dotted line*), three normal adults (*dashed lines*), and three patients with Turner's syndrome (*solid lines*) were plated on day 0 in multiple tissue culture dishes. The plates were trypsinized at intervals ranging in time from 2 to 13 days and the cells were counted by Coulter counter.

Serum and plasma protein dialysates were prepared from both patients. The ammonium sulfate precipitation used was that of Pederson (1947). Serum or plasma was diluted with an equal volume of 0.2 M sodium chloride, followed by addition of ammonium sulfate until a concentration of 45% $(NH_4)_2SO_4$ was obtained. The precipitate was centrifuged at 17,700 × g for 45 minutes, after which the supernatant was decanted. The pellet was washed twice by resuspension in 2.0 M ammonium sulfate and recovered by centrifugation as described above. The pellet was dissolved in 1 M acetic acid and dialyzed against 1% acetic acid in Spectropor 3 dialysis (molecular weight cutoff approximately 3,500; Spectrum Medical Industries No. 132720). Agar plates were prepared in 35-mm petri dishes by first applying a 1-ml base layer of 0.8% purified agarose in McCoy's 5A medium containing 10% FBS. After solidification, an additional 1 ml of 0.4% agarose in the same medium, but also containing the desired protein concentration of serum or plasma and 7,500 AKR-2B mouse fibroblasts, or the same number of normal rat kidney (NRK) fibroblasts, was applied to the upper layer. The dishes were incubated at 37°C in 5% CO_2 for 7 to 14 days, at which time the number of colonies per dish were counted by a computerized image analysis system.

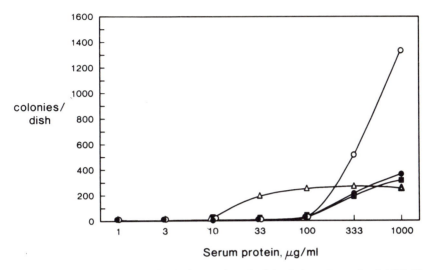

Figure 2.   AKR-2B growth stimulation (patient 1). Stimulation of growth of AKR-2B mouse fibroblasts at various serum protein concentrations is illustrated for patient 1 (*open triangles*), a 19-month-old age- and sex-matched control (*open circles*), and one adult control assayed twice (*closed circles and squares*).

The serum protein from patient 1, in the concentration range of 10 to 100 µg/ml, significantly stimulated the growth of AKR-2B mouse fibroblasts as compared to a 19-month-old age- and sex-matched control and to one adult control assayed twice (Figure 2). The enhancement of growth at higher protein concentrations (333 and 1,000 µg/ml) was below that of the age-matched control, and comparable to the adult control.

To see if these results were reproducible, the same experiments were repeated for patient 1 using both serum and plasma protein dialysates. When compared to the same age- and sex-matched control, the same results, although more evident, were obtained (Figure 3). When serum and protein dialysates from patient 2 were assayed in a similar manner, the results did not differ from those of a 10-month-old age- and sex-matched control (Figure 4).When NRK fibroblasts were substituted from the AKR-2B cells, the results were irreproducible.

DISCUSSION

In our study of two patients with cerebral gigantism, we were able to confirm the results of previous investigators that the serum levels of growth hormone and SM-C are unremarkable. NGF and EGF serum

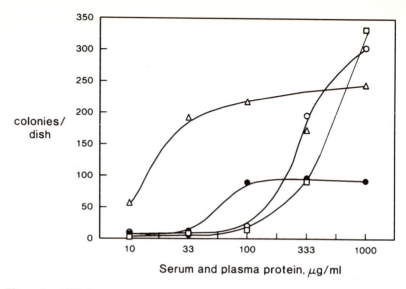

Figure 3. AKR-2B growth stimulation (patient 1). Stimulation of growth of AKR-2B mouse fibroblasts at various serum and plasma protein concentrations is illustrated for patient 1 (serum, *open triangles*; plasma, *closed circles*) and for a 19-month-old age- and sex-matched control (serum, *open circles*; plasma, *open squares*).

levels in patients with this syndrome had not been previously investigated, and were found to be comparable to those of normal adults.

In order to investigate the possibility of enhanced tissue growth responsiveness as reflected in surface growth factor receptor concentrations, a skin biopsy was obtained from patient 1 and fibroblast cultures established. When grown in confluent monolayer culture, the fibroblasts displayed EGF and SM-C binding that did not differ significantly from the controls. Furthermore, qualitative growth kinetics of these fibroblasts were not distinguishable from those of normal adults and patients with Turner's syndrome (Figure 1). These fibroblast culture experiments had not been previously performed in patients with cerebral gigantism.

In patient 1, serum and plasma protein dialysate, in the concentration range of 10 to 100 µg/ml, significantly stimulated the growth of AKR-2B mouse fibroblasts in tissue culture when compared to adult and age-and sex-matched controls (Figure 2). These results were reproducible for both patients as well as for the age-and sex-matched and adult controls, as illustrated in Figures 2, 3, and 4. This technique, although used to assay transforming growth factors as described by Moses et al. (1981), has not been previously applied to the study of

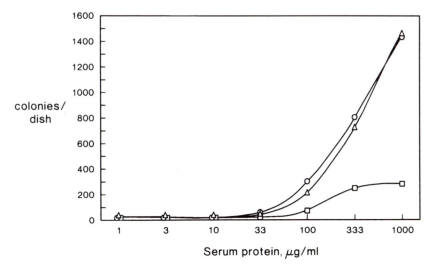

Figure 4. AKR-2B growth stimulation (patient 2). Stimulation of growth of AKR-2B mouse fibroblasts at various serum protein concentrations is illustrated for patient 2 (*open triangles*), a 10-month-old age- and sex-matched control (*open circles*), and an adult control (*open squares*).

patients with cerebral gigantism, nor to any other disorders of growth and mentation.

The serum and plasma protein stimulation of AKR-2B mouse fibroblast growth in one child may be a demonstration of a novel growth factor in cerebral gigantism. The reason why one patient demonstrated such a serum and plasma property and the other did not may be due to an age-related effect (patient 1 was 19 months old and patient 2 was 10 months). Alternatively, cerebral gigantism may be a heterogeneous disease with different causes. This syndrome has been associated with a variety of disease processes including thyroid abnormalities, cerebral dysgenesis, macular degeneration, autonomic insufficiency, peripheral dysostosis, and intestinal polyposis. Recently, Plioplys and Gomez (in preparation) noted markedly variable cranial computed tomography findings in patients with cerebral gigantism, as well as increased spinal fluid pressure in two children with this condition. All of these diverse associations argue that this syndrome may arise from various causes, one of which may be related to this demonstrable growth effect.

Further investigations using the AKR-2B mouse fibroblast assay technique are warranted in cerebral gigantism and may have applicability to the study of the possible causes of abnormal growth and mentation in other syndromes.

REFERENCES

Moses, H. L., Branum, E. L., Proper, J. A., and Robinson, R. A. 1981. Transforming growth factor production by chemically transformed cells. Cancer Res. 41:2842–2848.

Pederson, K. O. 1947. Ultracentrifugation and electrophoretic studies on fetuin. J. Phys. Colloid Chem. 51:164–171.

Plioplys, A. V., and Gomez, M. R. CSF pressure and CT scan findings in cerebral gigantism. (in preparation)

Rosenfeld, R. G., and Dollar, L. A. Characterization of the somatomedin-C/insulin-like growth factor 1 (SM-C/IGF-1) receptor on cultured human fibroblast monolayers: Regulation of receptor concentrations by SM-C/IGF-1 and insulin. (in press)

Saenger, P., Levine, L. S., Wiedemann, E., Schwartz, E., and New, M. I. 1976. Somatomedin in cerebral gigantism. J Pediatr. 88:155–156.

Sotos, J. F., Dodge, P. R., Muirhead, D., Crawford, J. D., and Talbot, N. B. 1964. Cerebral gigantism in childhood. N. Engl. J. Med. 271:109–116.

PERSPECTIVES AND PROGRESS IN MENTAL RETARDATION
Volume II—Biomedical Aspects
Edited by J. M. Berg
Copyright © 1984 by I.A.S.S.M.D.

BIOCHEMICAL STUDIES OF SYNAPTIC PLASTICITY IN THE ADULT MAMMALIAN BRAIN

M. D. Browning

*Pharmacology Department, Yale University School of Medicine,
333 Cedar St., P.O. Box 3333, New Haven, Connecticut 06510*

Little is known about whether organic defects underlie many of the less severe forms of mental retardation. This may be due in part to the fact that until recently little was known about the organic bases of learning and memory. Recent work has shown that the strength of nerve circuits (synapses) changes with experience. This phenomenon, which is known as long-term synaptic plasticity, is widely thought to be a neural base for learning and memory. In this paper work is described that examines the biochemical basis of long-term synaptic plasticity.

Mental retardation as defined by the American Association on Mental Deficiency refers to "significantly subaverage intellectual functioning existing concurrently with deficits in adaptive functioning" (Grossman, 1973). Among those described as mentally retarded, a minority are known to have some demonstrable form of organic deficit that is thought to be a significant factor in their intellectual impairment. Typically, the mentally retarded in whom organic deficits have been identified are also those suffering from the most severe forms of intellectual impairment. A majority of those classified as retarded have no detectable organic defects, and some workers have argued against any organic involvement in the relatively mild retardation found in this group. Others argue that organic defects may be detectable mainly among the severely retarded because of limitations in our understanding of the biological underpinnings of cognitive processes. These limitations may have precluded detection of any organic defects that underlie subtle cognitive deficits. According to this view, the possibility of organic involvement in all forms of mental retardation should remain an open issue. In support of this position, work by neuroscientists within the last decade has provided insights into the repertoire of neural behaviors that have dramatically altered our view of the adaptability or plasticity of the central nervous system.

An incontrovertible body of evidence now exists that demonstrates that neural growth is indeed found in the adult mammalian brain (Raisman and Field, 1973; Lynch et al., 1977; Lund, 1978). Such growth was widely thought to be impossible less than 10 years ago. The last decade has also witnessed the discovery of long-term synaptic plasticity, a form of synaptic adaptability that is thought by many to be an important component of cognitive processes. This paper focuses on recent studies of this long-term synaptic plasticity.

LONG-TERM SYNAPTIC PLASTICITY (LTP)

For biochemists, electrophysiologists, and cell biologists who are interested in studying the brain, an issue of paramount importance has been the identification of the neural processes that could form the substrates or building blocks of cognitive abilities such as learning and memory. In the late 1940s, Hebb suggested, in his still influential model, that the most likely locus of the cellular substrate of memory would be a synaptic circuit that changed in strength after a brief period of use (Hebb, 1949). There has been a tremendous amount of research devoted to the search for such synaptic systems. However, none had been identified until 1973 when Bliss and Lomo demonstrated that such plastic or modifiable synaptic systems could be found in the hippocampus.

Bliss and Lomo (1973) demonstrated that a brief (1-sec) burst of high-frequency electrical stimulation would produce an increase in the strength of the stimulated synapses, lasting for hours or even days. An example of such long-term synaptic plasticity is shown in Figure 1. A stimulating electrode is placed where it will activate one of the major axon bundles in the hippocampus, the Schaffer collateral-commissural axons. A recording electrode is placed in the region where these axons make synaptic contact with cells known as the CA-1 pyramidal nerves. A single test stimulus is then delivered via the stimulating electrode and an evoked potential is detected by the recording electrode. This evoked potential reflects the magnitude of the synaptic current generated by the test stimulus. Once a stable baseline evoked response is obtained and held for 30 minutes, a brief (1-sec) burst of high frequency (100 pulses/sec) is delivered and then single test pulses are resumed. A short-lasting increase in the magnitude of the evoked potential can

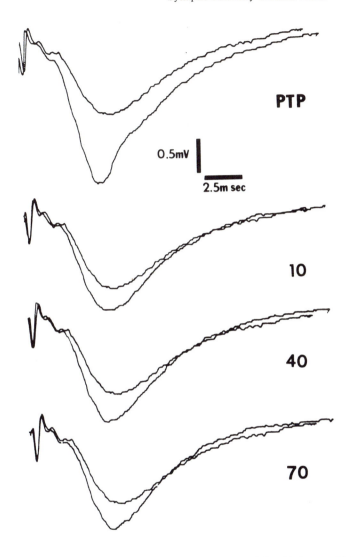

Figure 1.   Postsynaptic responses recorded in the region of the CA-1 pyramidal cells following stimulation of the Schaffer collateral-commissural projection to that region. Two responses are superimposed for each of the four conditions described: one is the control response that was obtained during a stable baseline period prior to the delivery of repetitive stimulation (100 pulses/sec for 1 sec), and the other is the potentiated response obtained at various times following repetitive stimulation. Note the increase in both the slope and the amplitude of the potentiated response. The numbers adjacent to each pair of traces represent the time (minutes) between the repetitive stimulation and the collection of the second response (*PTP* = post-tetanic potentiation, second response taken within seconds of cessation of the repetitive stimulation). Note that the marked potentiation present immediately after the repetitive stimulation (PTP) shows a marked decay with time; however, the long-term plasticity (LTP) that is present at 10 minutes persists essentially without decrement for at least 70 minutes.

be detected immediately. This increase in the strength of the synaptic circuit decays rapidly. However, the evoked response to the test stimulus does not return to control levels. Rather, by 10 minutes after the high-frequency conditioning stimulus, the evoked response has stabilized at a level that is 50–150% greater than the control response. Thus, 25 years after Hebb argued that a synaptic circuit that changed in strength after a brief period of use was an ideal cellular substrate for memory, Bliss and Lomo demonstrated that synapses in the hippocampus possess this remarkable capability. This finding dramatically increased our knowledge of the repertoire of neural behaviors and provided important new insights into the mechanisms whereby the nerves of the brain could effect cognition.

Having identified such plastic or adaptive synapses in the hippocampus (such synapses have now been found in cerebral cortex as well—Lee, 1981), two major approaches have characterized subsequent studies of what is now known as long-term synaptic plasticity (LTP). One approach has focused specifically on an examination of the relationship of LTP to cognitive abilities such as learning and memory. Recognizing that a connection between LTP and learning and memory, although intuitively reasonable, is at this point still hypothetical, many investigators have attempted to determine whether acquisition and/or extinction of specific learned behaviors is accompanied or preceded by changes in the strength of specific synaptic circuits. A second approach has focused on studies of the biochemical bases of LTP. Such an approach has the advantage of providing insight into the molecular mechanism of LTP while providing the potential for the development of pharmacological probes that could be used in specific neuronal pathways during learning. It is this biochemical approach that the present author has followed and that constitutes the focus of the remainder of this report.

BIOCHEMICAL STUDIES OF LTP

Studies of the biochemical bases of brain functions, particularly such discrete phenomena as changes in synaptic strength, face one major obstacle: assays can usually only be conducted in brain tissue that has been obtained from animals killed by decapitation. Decapitation produces massive seizures in the brain. It is unlikely that any subtle biochemical changes accompanying LTP would be detectable against the background of biochemical "noise" produced by the seizures. Therefore we were particularly interested in the demonstration by Yamamoto and McIlwain (1966) that it was possible to study isolated portions of the adult mammalian brain in vitro in specially designed chambers that permitted careful regulation of temperature, oxygen content, and essential nutrients. After incubation in such chambers, many of the effects of decapitation are reversed. Further work by Yamamoto (1972), by the present author and others in the laboratory of Dr. Gary Lynch (Lynch et al., 1975), and by many others (Schwartzkroin and Wester, 1975; Alger and Tyler, 1976; Andersen et al., 1977) demonstrated that in vitro brain slices maintained by this method exhibited many of the electrophysiological and biochemical properties seen in vivo. Because LTP could be reliably elicited in hippocampal brain slices, and because after 1 hour in vitro many of the side effects of decapitation have been reversed, we chose to use the in vitro hippocampal slice for our studies of the biochemical bases of LTP.

In studies of the biochemistry of brain functions, particularly as they relate to cognitive abilities such as learning and memory, considerable attention has been given to protein synthesis. However, because LTP can be elicited in brain slices where protein synthesis has been temporarily blocked, and because the time course of protein synthesis is considerably slower than that for the induction of LTP (minutes versus seconds or fractions of seconds), we decided not to focus on protein synthesis.

We felt it appropriate, in studying the biochemical bases of LTP, to consider first what properties this mechanism(s) must have. The time course of LTP requires a mechanism that can be activated almost instantaneously and, once initiated, it must persist or trigger changes that persist for hours. Also, the mechanisms must depend in some way on calcium because this ion must be present to produce LTP (Dunwiddie and Lynch, 1979). Finally, the mechanism must be shown to operate in synaptic regions. Protein phosphorylation is one process that fulfills these requirements. A protein is phosphorylated when an enzyme transfers phosphate from adenosine triphosphate (ATP) to the protein. Generally the addition of a charged phosphate group to the protein produces a change in the structure of the protein and hence a change in its activity. It is now thought that protein phosphorylation is one of the primary means of biological control of storage and breakdown of glucose, contraction of smooth muscle, synthesis of neurotransmitters, and a wide variety of other metabolic processes (for pertinent reviews see Krebs, 1972; Rubin and Rosen, 1975; Greengard, 1978, 1981). Moreover, there is good reason to believe that protein phosphorylation is particularly important for synaptic function. A series of papers from the laboratory of Paul Greengard has shown that phosphoproteins, as well as the enzymes that catalyze the phosphorylation process, are all present in high concentrations in synaptic regions (Johnson et al., 1971; Maeno et al., 1971; Maeno and Greengard,

1972). Our group therefore chose to attempt to determine in one particular instance—the induction of LTP—whether there was any effect on the phosphorylation of specific proteins.

We first prepared hippocampal brain slices and produced LTP by stimulating a specific synaptic region of the hippocampal slice. We then isolated the synaptic regions from the stimulated and control (or unstimulated) tissue and incubated these synaptic regions in the presence of radioactive ATP. Thus, when a protein became phosphorylated, it also became radioactively labeled. We next separated the proteins from each other on acrylamide gels and exposed these gels to X-ray film. The radioactive proteins exposed the X-ray film and we were thus able to determine which proteins were phosphorylated. We then compared the pattern of phosphorylation in a stimulated fraction with that seen in the control. As shown in Figure 2, stimulation produced effects on the phosphorylation of a number of proteins, with the most consistent effect being an alteration in the phosphorylation of a 40,000-dalton protein (see also Table 1). This finding suggested to us that the phosphorylation of this protein might in some way be involved in the effect produced by this high-frequency stimulation, i.e., in the increase in the strength of the synaptic circuit.

To further explore this possibility, we performed two sets of controls. First, we delivered the same number of electrical pulses as before, but at a lower frequency. This low-frequency stimulation did not produce LTP and it had no effect on the phosphorylation of the 40,000-dalton protein. In the second group of experiments, we delivered high-frequency stimulation, but under conditions that do not produce LTP (i.e., when calcium was not available). This high-frequency stimulation also failed to produce LTP and had no effect on the 40,000-dalton protein.

Given the possibility that this protein might be involved in altering the strength of synaptic circuits, we were particularly interested in trying to identify the protein. We examined the subcellular distribution of the protein and found that it was present in high concentrations in the mitochondria that are known to be densely packed in synaptic regions. The only known prominent mitochondrial phosphoprotein with a molecular weight of 40,000 is pyruvate dehydrogenase (PDH). Therefore, we compared the 40,000-dalton brain protein with highly purified PDH (Linn et al., 1972), which was a gracious gift of Dr. Tracy Linn (Figure 3).The two proteins were found to be identical based on comparisons of their pharmacological and physical properties. The 40,000-dalton brain protein was then shown to produce a tryptic fingerprint that was identical to PDH, thus conclusively demonstrating the identity of the two proteins (Browning et al., 1981). In light of this result, we

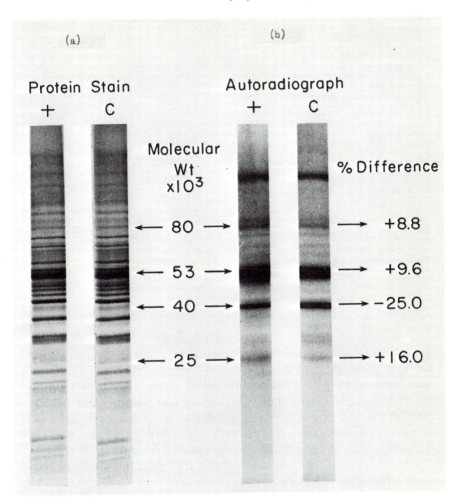

Figure 2. Polyacrylamide gel depicting the effects of repetitive stimulation on phosphorylation of specific synaptic plasma membrane components. +, Stimulated sample; C, control sample. *Left*: the protein staining pattern obtained with Coomassie blue in the 7.5% to 20% gel. *Right*: autoradiograph showing the bands that incorporated label. The molecular weight estimations were based on comparisons with the mobilities of standards of known molecular weight. Molecular weight values shown indicate bands in which significant stimulation-dependent changes in phosphorylation were observed (see Table 1) (Browning et al., 1979).

Table 1. Stimulation-dependent alterations in phosphorylation of specific synaptic plasma membrane components[a]

Molecular weight (daltons)	% change X	N^b +	N^b −	P^c
112,000	+3.6	10	4	
85,000	−1.8	6	6	
80,000	+7.9	12	5	
68,000	+3.4	11	9	
62,000	−0.9	5	8	
53,000	+8.6	16	4	0.012
50,000	−0.7	10	10	
45,000	−3.2	4	7	
40,000	−25.9	1	19	0.001
33,000	+3.7	6	6	
27,000	+16.0	15	2	0.002

Reprinted by permission from: Browning et al. 1979. Science 203:60–62.

[a] These data summarize the effects of 100/sec stimulation for 1 sec in 20 experiments. The bands listed include only those that demonstrated detectable incorporation of label in 10 or more of the 20 experiments.

[b] N = number of instances in which the stimulated value was greater (+) or less (−) than the control value.

[c] Two-tailed probability of rejecting the null hypothesis based on paired t test.

were naturally interested in determining what effect the phosphorylation of pyruvate dehydrogenase could have on the strength of synaptic circuits. Blass and Gibson (1978) had demonstrated that the level of PDH in brain is only minimally sufficient to support pyruvate flux through the oxidative pathway. This observation, coupled with the fact that brain metabolism is almost totally dependent on glucose, suggests that alterations in the phosphorylation of PDH could significantly influence mitochondrial functions such as ATP production and calcium sequestration. It is widely recognized that calcium plays a pivotal role in the release of neurotransmitters at the synapse, so this proposal is particularly attractive.

DISCUSSION

An important question concerns the significance of these results for mental retardation. The work described above is certainly only an initial stage in the attempt to probe the biology of cognition. Nevertheless, progress is being made. Specific synaptic systems in the hippocampus and cerebral cortex do have the ability to change their operating characteristics as a consequence of usage of these systems, and biochemical correlates of this synaptic potentiation have been identified.

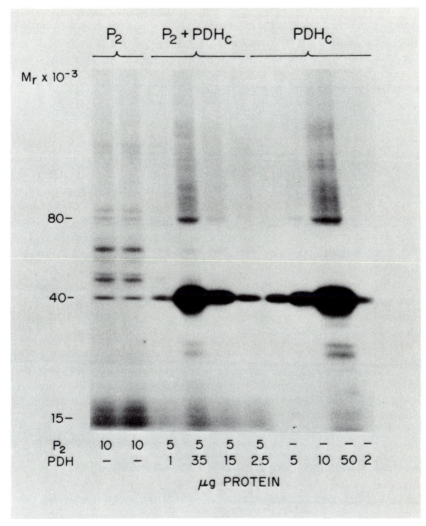

Figure 3.   Autoradiographic comparison of ^{32}P-labeled polypeptides from a brain synaptosomal fraction and the bovine kidney pyruvate dehydrogenase complex (*PDHc*). The synaptosomal fraction (P_2) and the complex were phosphorylated with endogenous kinases and γ-^{32}P ATP, solubilized in sodium dodecyl sulfate (SDS), and electrophoresed in an SDS-polyacrylamide gel. The two wells at the left contain the synaptosomal fraction alone, and the next four wells contain various amounts of the PDHc mixed with the P_2 fraction. Various amounts of the pyruvate dehydrogenase complex were electrophoresed alone in the four wells at the right of the figure (Browning et al., 1981).

In general terms, these results have significance for mental retardation because they typify the progress being made in our understanding of the brain. Our concept of the repertoire of neural behaviors that could subserve cognitive behaviors has increased enormously. Consequently, it is imperative that the issue of organic involvement in retardation be reevaluated frequently in light of the growing understanding of what properties of the nervous system are required for normal cognitive function.

In more specific terms, the data in this report may be directly pertinent to mental retardation. Enormous strides must still be taken to determine whether this alteration in synaptic strength (LTP) is indeed related to learning, and, furthermore, whether changes in pyruvate dehydrogenase are causally related to changes in synaptic strength. However, a recent report by Morgan and Routtenberg (1981) has shown a correlation between changes in the phosphorylation of pyruvate dehydrogenase and training in a passive avoidance paradigm. Furthermore, we are not the first to suggest the possibility of a relationship between pyruvate dehydrogenase and mental retardation. Blass et al. (1978) reported neurological impairment and mental retardation in 35 patients with severe deficiencies in pyruvate dehydrogenase. We suggest that even subtle changes in pyruvate dehydrogenase or in the enzyme system that controls the phosphorylation of pyruvate dehydrogenase could significantly affect neural function. We therefore echo the call of Blass and Gibson (1978) for a reevaluation with modern techniques of the possible role of pyruvate dehydrogenase in mental retardation.

REFERENCES

Alger, B., and Tyler, T. 1976. Long-term and short-term plasticity in the CA-1, CA-2 and dentate regions of the hippocampal slice. Brain Res. 110:463–480.

Andersen, P., Sandberg, S., Sveen, O., and Wigstrom, H. 1977. Specific long-lasting potentiation of synaptic transmission in the hippocampal slice. Nature 226:736–737.

Blass, J., Cederbaum, S., Kark, R., and Rodriguez-Budelli, M. 1978. Pyruvate dehydrogenase deficiency in 35 patients. Monogr. Hum. Genet. 9:12–15.

Blass, J., and Gibson, G. 1978. Studies of the pathophysiology of pyruvate dehydrogenase deficiency. Adv. Neurol. 21:181–194.

Bliss, T. V. P., and Lomo, T. 1973. Long-lasting potentiation of synaptic transmission in the dentate area of the anesthetized rabbit following stimulation of the perforant path. J. Physiol. (Lond.) 232:331–356.

Browning, M., Bennett, W., Kelly, P., and Lynch, G. 1981. Evidence that the 40,000 M_r phosphoprotein influenced by high frequency stimulation is the alpha subunit of pyruvate dehydrogenase. Brain Res. 218:255–266.

Browning, M., Dunwiddie, T., Bennett, W., Gispen, W., and Lynch, G. 1979. Synaptic phosphoproteins: Specific changes after repetitive stimulation of the hippocampal slice. Science 203:60–62.

Dunwiddie, T., and Lynch, G. 1979. The relationship between extracellular calcium concentrations and the induction of long-term potentiation. Brain Res. 169:103–110.

Greengard, P. 1978. Phosphorylated proteins as physiological effectors. Science 199:146–152.

Greengard, P. 1981. Intracellular signals in the brain. Harvey Lect. 75:277–331.

Grossman, H. D. (ed.). 1973. Manual on Terminology and Classification in Mental Retardation, rev. ed. American Association on Mental Deficiency, Washington, D.C.

Hebb, D. O. 1949. The Organization of Behavior. John Wiley & Sons, Inc., New York.

Johnson, E., Maeno, H., and Greengard, P. 1971. Phosphorylation of endogenous protein of rat brain by cyclic adenosine 3′, 5′-monophosphate dependent protein kinase. J. Biol. Chem. 246:7731–7735.

Krebs, E. 1972. Protein kinases. Curr. Top. Cell. Regul. 5:99–133.

Lee, K. S. 1981. Sustained facilitation of evoked potentials in the cerebral cortex following short trains of high frequency stimulation. Neurosci. Abstr. 7:627.

Linn, T., Pelley, J., Pettit, F., Hucho, F., Randall, D., and Reed, L. 1972. α-keto acid dehydrogenase complexes. XV. Purification and properties of the component enzymes of the pyruvate dehydrogenase complexes from bovine kidney and heart. Arch. Biochem. Biophys. 148:327–342.

Lund, R. D. 1978. Development and Plasticity of the Brain. Oxford University Press, New York.

Lynch, G., Gall, C., and Cotman, C. 1977. Temporal parameters of axonal sprouting in the brain of the adult rat. Exp. Neurol. 54:179–183.

Lynch, G., Smith, R., Browning, M., and Deadwyler, S. 1975. Evidence for bidirectional transport of horseradish peroxidase. Adv. Neurol. 12:297–314.

Maeno, H., and Greengard, P. 1972. Phosphoprotein phosphatases from rat cerebral cortex: Subcellular distribution and characterization. J. Biol. Chem. 247:3269–3273.

Maeno, H., Johnson, E., and Greengard, P. 1971. Subcellular distribution of adenosine 3′, 5′-monophosphate dependent protein kinase in rat brain. J. Biol. Chem. 246:134–140.

Morgan, D., and Routtenberg, A. 1981. Brain pyruvate dehydrogenase: Phosphorylation and enzyme activity altered by a training experience. Science 214:470–471.

Raisman, G., and Field, P. 1973. A quantitative investigation of the development of collateral reinnervation after partial deafferentation of the septal nuclei. Brain Res. 50:241–264.

Rubin, C., and Rosen, O. 1975. Protein phosphorylation. Annu. Rev. Biochem. 44:831–887.

Schwartzkroin, P., and Wester, K. 1975. Long-lasting facilitation of a synaptic potential following tetanization in the in vitro hippocampal slice. Brain Res. 89:107–119.

Yamamoto, C. 1972. Activation of hippocampal neurons by mossy fiber stimulation in thin brain sections in vitro. Exp. Brain Res. 14:423–435.

Yamamoto, C., and McIlwain, H. 1966. Potentials evoked in vitro in preparations from the mammalian brain. Nature 210:1055–1056.

PERSPECTIVES AND PROGRESS IN MENTAL RETARDATION
Volume II—Biomedical Aspects
Edited by J. M. Berg
Copyright © 1984 by I.A.S.S.M.D.

BRAINSTEM AUDITORY EVOKED RESPONSES IN CHILDREN WITH DOWN'S SYNDROME

G. L. Gigli,[1, 2] **R. Ferri,**[2] **S. A. Musumeci,**[2] **P. Tomassetti,**[1] **and P. Bergonzi**[1]

[1] *Istituto di Neurologia, Università Cattolica, Largo A. Gemelli 8, Rome, Italy*
[2] *Centro Studi e Ricerche, Oasi Maria SS., Via Conte Ruggero 73, Troina (EN), Italy*

Brainstem auditory evoked responses (BAERs) were recorded in 15 subjects with Down's syndrome and in 13 nonretarded controls. Significant reduction of the I–V wave interval was observed in Down's syndrome subjects as a result of a shortening of the I–III and of the III–V intervals. No significant correlation between the brainstem conduction time (I–V wave interval) and the inion–CVII distance was found. The possibility of an impaired inhibitory activity in the brainstem in Down's syndrome is suggested.

In 1967, Barnet and Lodge reported a significant increase of the amplitudes in the late components of the auditory evoked responses recorded during sleep in subjects with Down's syndrome (DS); they found no significant difference for latencies. Barnet et al. (1971) observed that the amplitude decrement usually recorded after repetitive stimulation in normal subjects was not evident in DS subjects. Straumanis et al. (1973a) obtained similar results and inferred, in agreement with Barnet et al., a difficulty of DS subjects in adaptation and moderation of their responses to repetitive stimuli. They suggested a hypothetical deficit of the inhibitory mechanisms in the central nervous system of DS subjects.

More recently, the same hypothesis was suggested by Dustman and Callner (1979) and by Yellin et al. (1980) and was used to explain the results of the evoked responses obtained by visual and somatosensory stimuli (Shagass, 1968; Bigum et al., 1970; Straumanis et al., 1973b; Callaway, 1975; Gliddon et al., 1975a, b; Dustman et al., 1976; Callner et al., 1978). This inhibitory deficit, by lowering the neural excitatory threshold, should lead to increased amplitudes and to lack of adaptation to repetitive or high-intensity stimulation.

Having in mind the possible contribution of specific sensory defects to behavior disturbance in mental retardation, Gliddon et al. (1976), instead of studying the late components of the evoked potentials (exploring the cortical, associative capacities), were the first to focus their attention on the early components of the auditory evoked responses (exploring the specific, sensory, subcortical, brainstem capacities). They recorded the brainstem auditory evoked responses (BAERs) in four DS subjects and, in comparison with four nonretarded controls, found shorter latencies for all the five major BAERs waves, with statistical significance for the II and IV waves. They found also lower amplitudes, with significance for the II, IV, and V waves.

Gliddon et al. (1976) tried to explain the shortened latencies by the shorter anatomical brainstem pathways of the DS subjects. In order to account for the reduced amplitudes, they indicated the greater variability in the different BAER sweeps recorded from DS subjects. This variability would lead to broadening and lowering of the waves in the process of summation and averaging. However, the small number and the related high variability of responses did not allow Gliddon et al. to verify their hypotheses. In fact, they suggested also an alternative hypothesis based on the same inhibitory deficit proposed for the late components of the evoked responses.

The aim of the present study was to increase the sample size in order to test the possibility of replicating the data of Gliddon et al. (1976) and of verifying their two hypotheses.

MATERIAL AND METHODS

BAERs were recorded in two groups of subjects. The first group consisted of 15 subjects with DS (diagnosis confirmed by karyotyping). In this group there were nine males and six females (mean age 11.1 years, SD 4.3, range 7–21). Two of these subjects had mental retardation of mild degree (IQ 55–69), 10 of moderate degree (IQ 40–54), and three of severe degree (IQ 25–39). The second group was composed of 13 nonretarded subjects, eight males and five females, between 6 and 19 years of age (mean 11 years, SD 4.1). The mean ages of the two groups were not significantly different (paired t test).

In all the subjects, the inion–VIIth cervical vertebra distance (inion–CVII) was measured. Before undergoing BAER recordings, all the subjects were examined by an ear, nose, and throat specialist and by a neurologist to exclude auditory and neurological disease. None of the subjects reported on here showed such disease.

BAERs were recorded by means of an Amplaid MK6 system, using the following parameters: analysis time, 10 msec; number of sweeps, 2048; sensitivity, ±20 uV; low-pass filter, 2,000 Hz; high-pass filter, 100 Hz. Clicks of positive polarity, at a rate of 15/sec and with an intensity hearing level of about 85 dB (decibels above normal threshold), were used as stimuli.

Silver-cup electrodes were placed with gauze and collodion, accepting impedances below 5 kohms and using the following positions: positive reference electrode on the auricular lobe ipsilateral to the stimulation; negative exploring electrode on the vertex; ground electrode on the forehead (FpZ). Seven DS subjects and five controls also had recordings with the reference electrode on the auricular lobe contralateral to the stimulation, in order to achieve a better identification of the V wave.

BAER traces were measured for latencies and amplitudes of the I, III, and V waves, as defined by Jewett and Williston (1971), and for interval I–III, III–V, and I–V waves. Traces (i.e., means and superimpositions of traces and statistical analysis) were also stored on floppy disk for further evaluations. Data obtained from the group with DS were compared with those of the control group by means of the paired *t* test. For both groups the inion–CVII distance was correlated with the V wave latency and with the I–V interval. These correlations were performed by calculating the least squares regression lines and Pearson *r* correlation coefficients.

RESULTS

Results are shown in the tables and figures. Table 1 gives the findings on wave latencies (I, III, and V), on interpeak intervals (I–III, III–V, and I–V) and on the interaural difference of the V wave latency. Findings for I, III, and V wave amplitudes and for I/V wave amplitude ratios are provided in Table 2.

V wave latency and all the intervals are significantly shorter in the DS subjects than in the nonretarded controls, III wave latency is not significantly different, and I wave is significantly retarded in the DS group. The nonsignificant interaural difference of the V wave latency indicates little intragroup variability and justifies the pooling of the left and right ear data in the statistical analysis. With regard to amplitudes, there were no significant differences between the DS and control groups.

Table 1.   Means and standard deviations of latencies and interpeak intervals in BAERs of Down's syndrome subjects and nonretarded controls

	Down's (n = 15)		Controls (n = 13)		
	Mean	SD	Mean	SD	P<
I wave latency	1.74	0.11	1.66	0.11	0.01
III wave latency	3.79	0.18	3.82	0.16	n.s.
V wave latency (ipsilateral)	5.41	0.22	5.63	0.23	0.001
V wave latency (contralateral)	5.63	0.15	5.78	0.20	0.02
I–III interval	2.02	0.18	2.16	0.12	0.001
III–V interval	1.62	0.17	1.80	0.16	0.001
I–V interval	3.67	0.22	3.95	0.18	0.001
V wave latency interaural difference	0.10	0.06	0.10	0.13	n.s.

Figure 1 shows the shape of the mean BAER traces in the two groups with the same values as indicated in Table 1. Figure 2 indicates that the shortening of the I–V interval in the DS group is due to reduction of both I–III and III–V intervals. Figure 3 shows the correlation between the V wave latency and the inion–CVII distance in the two groups. The same is shown in Figure 4 for the I–V wave interval. For each line, calculated with the least squares method, the Pearson r values have been computed:

	Controls	Down's
V wave latency	0.262 (n.s.)	0.286 (n.s.)
I–V wave interval	0.153 (n.s.)	0.217 (n.s.)

No significant correlations were found between the inion–CVII distance and the indicators of brainstem conduction time.

In Table 3 the sex distribution of the I–V interval data are presented. There was no statistically significant difference between the nonretarded males and females, whereas such a difference was found

Table 2.   Means and standard deviations of amplitudes and I/V amplitude ratio in BAERs of Down's syndrome subjects and nonretarded controls

	Down's (n = 15)		Controls (n = 13)		
	Mean	SD	Mean	SD	P
I wave amplitude	334	115	358	140	n.s.
III wave amplitude	228	95	200	106	n.s.
V wave amplitude	484	219	520	148	n.s.
I/V amplitude ratio	0.84	0.48	0.77	0.42	n.s.

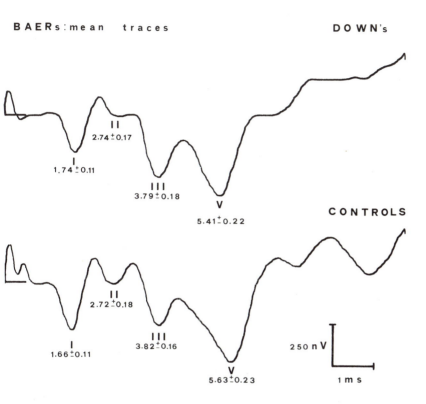

Figure 1.   BAER mean traces of Down's syndrome subjects and nonretarded controls. Latencies and SD indicated under each wave.

between the DS males and females. Significant differences also were present between the two male groups and between the two female groups, particularly the latter.

DISCUSSION

In comparison with the data of Gliddon et al. (1976), our sample (which was larger, had more adequate controls, and used newer technology for recordings) showed the same shortening of latencies except for the I wave, which was significantly retarded in the DS subjects.

This finding is consistent with the possibility of subtle transmissive changes in the hearing modalities of these subjects, because I wave latency represents the peripheral conduction time. The narrowing of the I–V wave interval (brainstem conduction time) is indicative of a

BAERs: mean traces

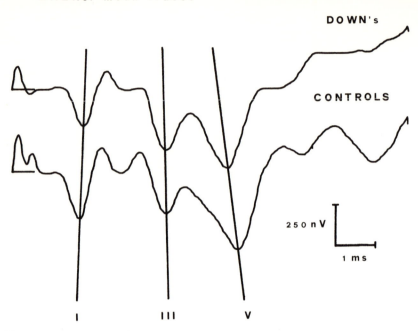

Figure 2.   BAER mean traces, indicating the narrowing of I–III, III–V, and I–V intervals in Down's syndrome subjects.

faster conduction along the auditory pathways. This faster conduction is determined both by the pontine and the mesencephalic part of the brainstem, because the I–V interval is shortened both in the I–III part and in the III–V part.

Regarding amplitudes, we did not find significant differences between the DS and control groups, in contrast with Gliddon et al. (1976). This could be because we observed no latency variability within the individual responses of each subject. Gliddon et al. explained the enlargement and lowering of the waves in their DS group by variability of latencies in each response.

In order to test the hypothesis of a reduced brainstem conduction time because of the shortened length of the brainstem, we correlated the inion–CVII distance with the V wave latency and with the I–V wave interval. Even though the regression lines tend to show a positive correlation, this trend is not statistically significant and does not explain the parallelism between the regression lines of the two groups; this parallelism is significantly different on the t test and thus requires another explanation.

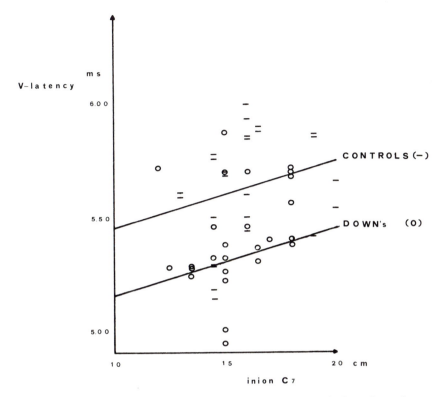

Figure 3. V wave latency and inion–CVII distance correlation in Down's syndrome subjects and nonretarded controls.

We think that the hypothesis of deficient inhibitory mechanisms suggested for associative responses (Barnet and Lodge, 1967; Shagass, 1968; Straumanis et al., 1973a, b; Gliddon et al., 1975b; Dustman et al., 1976; Dustman and Callner, 1979; Yellin et al., 1980) would also explain the reduced conduction time in the brainstem. In this regard, both sexes seem to behave in the same way, although a greater short-ening of the I–V interval was seen in our female DS subgroup. Possibly this is related to the fact that the female DS subjects were more mentally retarded than the males (see Table 3).

CONCLUSIONS

In conclusion, we think that our data on the early components of the auditory evoked responses suggest an inhibitory deficiency in the specific conduction pathways of the auditory system. In order further to test our hypothesis of an impaired inhibitory activity on the brainstem

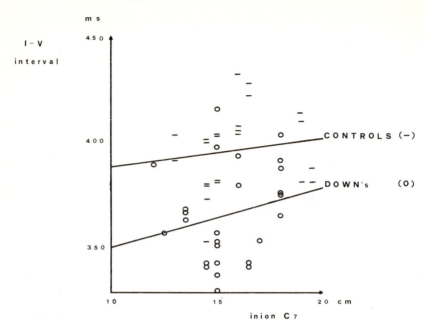

Figure 4.   I–V interval and inion–CVII distance correlation in Down's syndrome subjects and nonretarded controls.

Table 3.   Sex comparisons of I–V interval in Down's syndrome subjects and controls

	I–V interval length (±SD)	t test	P<
Down's syndrome subjects			
Male[a]	3.75 ± 0.21		
Female[b]	3.56 ± 0.19		
Male versus female		2.40	0.02
Controls			
Male	3.97 ± 0.21		
Female	3.92 ± 0.11		
Male versus female		0.78	n.s.
Males: DS versus control		2.91	0.001
Females: DS versus control		5.29	0.0005

[a] Nine cases: one mildly retarded, 8 moderately retarded.
[b] Six cases: one mildly retarded, 2 moderately retarded, 3 severely retarded.

nerve conduction of DS subjects, we intend to continue this research by: 1) controlling the BAERs obtained with different intensities and rates of stimulation; 2) correlating the responses of larger groups, homogeneous for the level of mental retardation; and 3) observing the inhibitory pattern, by means of the binaural interaction. At present, the possible role played by a generalized lack of inhibition in the central nervous system of DS subjects is speculative.

After this experimental work was conceived and its results discussed, we had an opportunity to look at two papers of Squires et al. (1980, 1982). These papers (the second one was based on the first) presented interesting results concerned with the BAERs in Down's syndrome that are partially in agreement with our data, especially for the shortening of the central conduction time (I–V wave interval). The major differences between the two samples are that the Squires et al. group was formed by adults with more severe mental retardation (mean IQ 28) and was not selected to exclude hearing problems.

REFERENCES

Barnet, A. B., and Lodge, A. 1967. Click evoked EEG responses in normal and developmentally retarded infants. Nature 214:252–255.

Barnet, A. B., Ohlrich, E. S., and Shanks, B. L. 1971. EEG evoked responses to repetitive auditory stimulation in normal and Down's syndrome infants. Dev. Med. Child Neurol. 13:321–329.

Bigum, H. B., Dustman, R. E., and Beck, E. C. 1970. Visual and somatosensory evoked responses from mongoloid and normal children. EEG Clin. Neurophysiol. 28:576–585.

Callaway, E. 1975. Brain Electrical Potentials and Individual Psychological Differences. Grune & Stratton, New York.

Callner, D. A., Dustman, R. E., Madsen, J. A., Schenkenberg, T., and Beck, E. C. 1978. Life span changes in the averaged evoked responses of Down's syndrome and normal subjects. Am. J. Ment. Defic. 82:398–405.

Dustman, R. E., and Callner, D. A. 1979. Cortical evoked responses and response decrement in nonretarded and Down's syndrome individuals. Am. J. Ment. Defic. 83:391–397.

Dustman, R. E., Schenkenberg, T., and Beck, E. C. 1976. The development of the evoked response as a diagnostic and evaluative procedure. In: R. Karrer (ed.), Developmental Psychophysiology of Mental Retardation. Charles C Thomas Publisher, Springfield, Illinois.

Gliddon, J. B., Busk, J., and Galbraith, G. C. 1975b. Visual evoked responses as a function of light intensity in Down's syndrome and nonretarded subjects. Psychophysiology 12:416–422.

Gliddon, J. B., Galbraith, G. C., and Busk, J. 1975a. Effect of preconditioning visual stimulus duration on visual-evoked responses to a subsequent test flash in Down's syndrome and nonretarded individuals. Am. J. Ment. Defic. 80:186–190.

Gliddon, J. B., Galbraith, G. C., and Kuester, D. 1976. Effects of stimulation rate on short latency far-field responses in the mentally retarded. Paper presented at the Meeting of the American Association on Mental Deficiency, Chicago.

Jewett, D. L., and Williston, J. S. 1971. Auditory evoked far fields averaged from the scalp of humans. Brain 94:681–696.

Shagass, C. 1968. Averaged somatosensory evoked responses in various psychiatric disorders. Rec. Adv. Biol. Psychiatry 10:205–219.

Squires, N., Aine, C., Buchwald, J., Norman, R., and Galbraith, G. 1980. Brain stem response abnormalities in severely and profoundly retarded adults. EEG Clin. Neurophysiol. 50:172–185.

Squires, N., Buchwald, J., Liley, F., and Strecker, J. 1982. Brainstem auditory evoked potential abnormalities in retarded adults. Adv. Neurol. 32:233–240.

Straumanis, J. J., Shagass, C., and Overton, D. A. 1973a. Auditory evoked responses in young adults with Down's syndrome and idiopathic mental retardation. Biol. Psychiatry 6:75–79.

Straumanis, J. J., Shagass, C., and Overton, D. A. 1973b. Somatosensory evoked responses in Down's syndrome. Arch. Gen. Psychiatry 29:544–549.

Yellin, A. M., Lodwig, A. K., and Jerison, H. J. 1980. Auditory evoked brain potentials as a function of interstimulus interval in adults with Down's syndrome. Audiology 19:255–262.

SECTION VI
Emotional and Behavioral Disturbance

PERSPECTIVES AND PROGRESS IN MENTAL RETARDATION
Volume II—Biomedical Aspects
Edited by J. M. Berg
Copyright © 1984 by I.A.S.S.M.D.

BEHAVIOR PROBLEMS OF YOUNG RETARDED CHILDREN

R. K. Kaminer, E. Jedrysek, and B. Soles

Children's Evaluation and Rehabilitation Center, Rose F. Kennedy Center, Albert Einstein College of Medicine, 1410 Pelham Parkway South, Bronx, New York 10461

This study describes the emotional and behavior status of 167 mentally retarded children ages 2 to 6 years who were evaluated by a multidisciplinary developmental evaluation clinic in a 1-year period. Seventy-five percent of the group had emotional or behavior problems. The type of problems noted varied with the intelligence, age, and sex of the children. The presence of speech and language problems correlated with specific behavioral manifestations.

The current literature stresses the importance of acceptable behavior and social skills as a prerequisite for the community adjustment and acceptance of retarded individuals. Emotional adjustment and social skills are areas in which early intervention can be effective. It is therefore important to identify the emotional problems of retarded children early and to intervene promptly.

The literature on emotional problems of young retarded children indicates that the prevalence is high. For instance, Chess and Hassibi (1970) found that 31 out of 52 (60%) retarded middle class children ages 5 to 12 years who were living at home had emotional problems; Webster (1963) noted problems in the emotional development of all 159 3- to 6-year-old retarded children he studied, with 66% showing moderate to severe disturbance.

These findings need to be compared to data on the general population. Richman et al. (1975) used a behavioral screening questionnaire administered to the parent and found a prevalence of 7% moderate to severe behavior problems and 15% mild problems in 705 children living in a London borough. Earls (1980) replicated the study with 100 children in a United States rural area and found a 24% prevalence of problems using the same criteria, and 11% prevalence using slightly stricter criteria.

METHOD

We report here a study on the emotional and behavioral status of a series of retarded children. The study was conducted in a multidisciplinary developmental evaluation unit of an urban medical school. The majority of referrals came from medical sources, and many were initiated following the children's failure on a developmental screening test. Data on all 198 children ages 2 to 6 years whose evaluation was completed in 1 year were reviewed. The 31 children who tested in the normal range were excluded and data on the remaining 167 were analyzed.

Previous analysis of demographic data for patients seen in this unit revealed that 42% were Hispanic, 39% black, and 19% white, which closely matches the ethnic distribution in the local public schools. Fifty-three percent of the children reside with both parents, 39% with one natural parent, and 8% are in foster care. Payment for evaluation was through Medicaid for 54% (the families received public assistance); 46% were self-paying (Kaminer et al., 1981).

The minimum workup for each child consisted of a screening appointment with a professional, a pediatric neurodevelopmental evaluation, and psychological testing. Most children had additional evaluations, such as audiology, speech and language, ophthalmology, and social service. Children known to be hearing impaired or physically handicapped are not evaluated by this unit. The team diagnostic formulations always included a statement on each of four areas: intellectual level, language skills in relation to performance, emotional status, and relevant medical diagnoses.

Information on the child's emotional status was based on all professional observations in the clinic, parental reports, and preschool reports when available. Emotional and behavior problems were defined as abnormalities in mood, interaction, or level of activity in relation to mental age, as observed during evaluation in the clinic. The observations had to be confirmed by the parent as reflecting the child's usual behavior. When behavior problems were reported by the parent but not observed by any team member, the category "management problem reported" was used. When behavior ranged from appropriate on some visits to abnormal on others, the designation "variable" was used. In all other cases there was professional agreement concerning behavior. A child was considered to have no problem if he was compliant to adult requests, interacted with appropriate affect, had no deviant behaviors noted or reported, and showed a level of attentiveness and activity appropriate for his mental age when given tasks at his mental age level and the parent did not report management problems.

DSM III (American Psychiatric Association, 1980) diagnostic categories were used whenever the findings fulfilled the stated criteria. However, many children had problems that did not precisely fit available categories, and these were described by their most salient features and tabulated by behavioral clusters. The children classified as "oppositional" had most or all of the features of Oppositional Disorder, but we used the designation even for children below 3 years of age. The category "anxious/inhibited" included children with many of the features of Overanxious Disorder. Children with autistic features fulfilled the DSM III criteria for Infantile Autism except that many of them showed some responsiveness to a parent. Attentional Deficit Disorder with Hyperactivity (ADDH) was defined by DSM III criteria.

Because psychiatric evaluation time was limited, only children whose behavior presented diagnostic or management problems to this experienced team were seen by the psychiatrist, and his diagnosis was used. The children diagnosed by the psychiatrist fall into two categories: "psychotic–not autistic" and "other." The "other" category included two children with Borderline Personality Disorder and one each with Gender Identity Disorder, Elective Mutism, and Adjustment Reaction of Childhood.

RESULTS

Of the 167 children evaluated, 125 (75%) were found to have behavior and emotional problems. The type of problems observed varied with the intelligence, age, and sex of the child. The presence of speech and language problems correlated with certain behavioral manifestations.

Intelligence

The 167 children included 61 (36.5%) with borderline intelligence and 66 (39.5%), 29 (17%), and 11 (7%) who were mildly, moderately, and severely retarded, respectively. The percentage of each IQ category was the same in children with and without behavior problems. We included children with borderline intelligence even though the American Association on Mental Deficiency classification no longer categorizes this group as retarded. However, young children referred for developmental delay, language delay, and/or behavior problems who test within the borderline range are at risk for mental retardation, because at an older age more cognitive aspects of development are tested.

They are also a group for whom early identification of problems and intervention may contribute to a more favorable outcome.

The relationship between intelligence level and type of emotional and behavior problems is shown in Figure 1. The 40 children whose level of retardation was moderate and severe represented 24% of our cohort. The prevalence of problems in these 40 children was 73% (29 children), which is similar to that of our total sample (75%). Autistic features were the most commonly observed problem in the moderately and severely retarded groups and were noted in 17 (59%) of the 29 children with problems. Another 10 children (35%) had attentional deficits. These two categories accounted for all but two of the children with problems.

Seventy-six percent of the 96 borderline and mildly retarded children had difficulties and all categories of emotional and behavior problems were represented. Only six of them had autistic features. An additional 10 children were diagnosed as psychotic, nine as having Atypical Pervasive Developmental Disorder, and one as having Schizophrenia; they all manifested difficulties in relating to people. When these autistic and psychotic categories are combined, the prevalence of unrelated behaviors among the intellectually higher functioning children is 16%, compared to 59% for the more retarded youngsters.

Sex

Boys are overrepresented in our clinic's population and even more markedly among the children with behavior problems (Table 1). Girls accounted for 28% of the total cohort, and only 22% of the children with problems. This 4 : 1 male-to-female ratio generally persisted across behavior clusters with two exceptions. Only one of 13 children with oppositional behavior was a girl and only one of 10 children diagnosed as psychotic was a girl.

Age

Several trends associated with age are evident from the data (Table 1). Our study included more young children than did previous studies, with 2-year-olds comprising 19% of the sample. The proportion of children with problems increased with age: two-thirds of the 2- and 3-year-olds, three-fourths of the 4-year-olds, and all but one of the 5-year-olds had problems. The categories of attention deficit disorders, psychotic, and "other psychiatric diagnoses" were seen increasingly with age. The prevalence of autistic behaviors dropped after 2 years of age.

Speech and Language

The diagnosis of language impairment meant that the child's language development was deviant, not merely delayed. Many young children

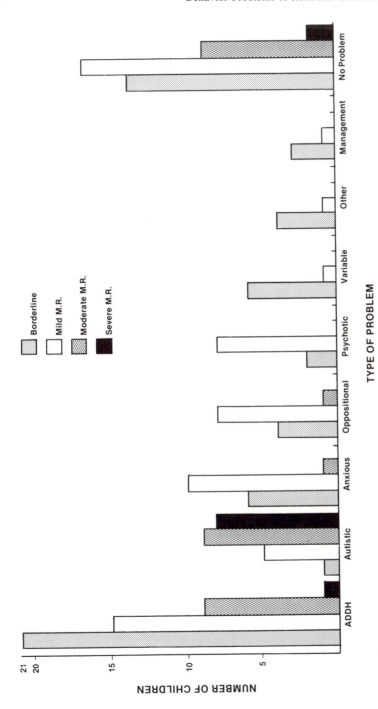

Figure 1.   Emotional and behavior problems in 167 retarded preschool children in relation to intelligence levels. *ADDH*-Attentional Deficit Disorder with Hyperactivity.

Table 1. Age and sex of 167 retarded children by behavior category

Behavior category	Age				Sex		Total
	2 years	3 years	4 years	5 years	Female	Male	
ADDH	6	13	19	8	12	34	46
Autism	10	5	6	2	4	19	23
Anxious	2	6	7	2	4	13	17
Oppositional	2	5	4	2	1	12	13
Psychotic	—	2	5	3	1	9	10
Variable	1	1	5	—	3	4	7
Other	—	—	1	4	2	3	5
Management	—	1	2	1	1	3	4
Subtotal—all problems	21	33	49	22	28	97	125
Total in category	31	50	63	23	47	120	167

of all levels of retardation have markedly lower language skills than performance skills on psychological testing. Some do not fulfill the criteria for language impairment, and others have such low language skills that the criteria are difficult to apply. In such cases we have simply described the language skills as being significantly lower than the performance ones, and included in this group children with no speech.

Sixty-four children were language impaired or speech and language impaired as diagnosed by a speech pathologist, or had verbal scores more than one standard deviation lower than performance on psychological testing; 75% of them (48 children) had emotional or behavior problems. Of these 48, 17 (35%) manifested autistic features and 13 (28%) had attentional deficits. Most of the remaining children had variable or oppositional behavior; only two were inhibited or anxious.

The above language-deficient group was compared to the 68 children whose language skills equaled or surpassed their performance skills. Of this group without speech or language problems, 47 (69%) had behavior problems, of which 26 (57%) were attentional difficulties, with the remainder divided among all the categories. Only four children (9%) had autistic features.

The distribution of intelligence levels in the groups with and without language deficits was similar except for an excess of severely retarded children among those with lower language skills. If all severely retarded children are excluded from the calculation, the percentage with autistic behavior is 24% (10/41) for the language-deficient group and 7% (3/45) in the group without speech or language problems.

Articulation problems unaccompanied by language impairment were noted in 23 children, of whom 18 (78%) had behavior problems. The behavioral deviations consisted of inhibited or anxious behavior in 47%, attentional deficits in 32%, and variable or oppositional behavior or management problems reported by the parent in the remaining 17%. None of these children manifested unrelated or psychotic behavior. The intellectual level of this group was higher than that of either of the above-mentioned groups, with half of the children in the mildly retarded range and the other half functioning in the borderline range.

Medical Diagnoses

Medical diagnoses presumed to be the cause of the mental retardation were identified in 74 children (44%) in the total sample of 167. In the group that had no behavior problems 55% (23 children) had medical diagnoses, whereas among those with problems the comparable figure was 41% (51 children). There was no association noted between particular medical and behavioral diagnoses.

DISCUSSION

Previous literature deals with various facets of, and approaches to, the study of behavior problems in mentally retarded children. Comparisons are hampered by differences in definition, classification, and interpretation of behavior problems. However, behavioral descriptions in previous studies are similar to each other and to our findings. Chess and Hassibi (1970) observed restlessness and excessive motor activity in all settings, as well as repetitive aimless motor activity, in a majority of the mildly retarded school-age children whom they studied. Obsessional behavior, stereotyped play activity, and unusual seeking of sensory experience was also noted in a substantial minority of this group. Based on his study of retarded preschool children, Webster (1963) stated that all of them manifested the "primary psychopathology of retardation" consisting of nonpsychotic autism, repetitiousness, inflexibility, passivity, and simplicity of emotional life.

Menolascino (1977) described the relationship between level of retardation and type of emotional disturbance. He reported that moderately and severely retarded children show many repetitive behaviors, and display "non-psychotic autism," and proneness to hyperactivity and impulsivity. We found autistic behaviors in 59% of the moderately and severely retarded children with emotional problems. The distinction between psychotic and nonpsychotic autism was difficult to make in these young children with significant retardation. Our therapeutic approach was not affected by this distinction because it consisted of referral to a preschool program for retarded children and parent guidance. Therapeutic programs rarely accept children with this level of retardation unless they doubt the test results. Unrelated behaviors were infrequent in the mildly retarded and borderline children, but more common than in the general population.

The DSM III states that a child with Attention Deficit Disorder "displays, for his or her mental and chronological age, signs of developmentally inappropriate inattention, impulsivity and hyperactivity." A specific caution is added that signs of the disorder may be absent in a new or one-to-one situation. In our experience with preschool children the attentional problems are usually evident in a clinic setting at each evaluation. ADDH is the most common behavioral problem seen in our retarded population. We found that this pattern was most characteristic of the mildly retarded and borderline children.

Richman et al. (1975) reported similar behaviors among unselected 3-year-olds found to have behavior problems based on parental questionnaires. The behaviors described in more than half the problem group were: overactive, poor concentration, attention seeking, tempers, difficult to control, unhappy mood, and poor peer relations. Until recently hyperactive and inattentive behaviors of school-age children were a major focus of research interest. However, these behaviors are seen also in the preschool years among children of average and retarded intelligence and present the parents with problems in child management. Further follow up of these groups are needed to clarify the prognostic significance of hyperactivity in young children.

The group of children labeled psychotic was a small and diagnostically puzzling one; all of them were mildly retarded or borderline intellectually and above 3 years of age, and only one was a girl. Of these 10 children one was diagnosed as schizophrenic. The other nine presented with early-onset disturbances in the development and use of language and in impulse control. They also manifested bizarre, atypical, and manneristic behaviors, but did not qualify for a diagnosis of autism, childhood-onset pervasive developmental disorder, or childhood schizophrenia. These children related too well to be called autistic, but related in inappropriate ways. They did not develop normally until the age of 30 months, did not hallucinate, and did not deteriorate from a previous level of functioning, thus making them ineligible for a diagnosis of schizophrenia. However, the combination of deficits outlined above results in functioning that appears to warrant a diagnosis of childhood psychosis. DSM III does not offer any clearly defined diagnostic category into which such children appear to fit. We have therefore begun to use the category of Atypical Pervasive Developmental Disorder for these children, whose symptomatology appears to be on a continuum between autism and schizophrenia (Levine and Demb, 1983).

Baker et al. (1980) used parent and teacher ratings to evaluate behavioral abnormalities among children ages $3\frac{1}{2}$ to $11\frac{1}{2}$ years with pure speech disorder compared to those with speech and language delay. Their results show that children whose language is impaired have more behavioral abnormalities, particularly hyperactive and developmentally immature behaviors, compared to the speech-impaired group.

In our population, which was younger and retarded, children with language deficits were overrepresented in the autistic group, although they were also found in many other categories, including the "no problem" group. The most frequent behavior problem among children without speech or language deficit was ADDH, whereas autistic behaviors were rare. Children with only articulation difficulty were disproportionately found in the anxious, inhibited group.

Multiaxial diagnostic formulation in terms of behavior, language, and medical findings, as well as intellect, permits clarification of patterns of dysfunction and their interrelationships.

ACKNOWLEDGMENT

The authors express appreciation to Howard Demb, M.D., consulting psychiatrist, for his valuable assistance.

REFERENCES

American Psychiatric Association. 1980. Diagnostic and Statistical Manual III. American Psychiatric Association, Washington, D.C.

Baker, L., Cantwell, D. P., and Mattison, R. E. 1980. Behavior problems in children with pure speech disorders and in children with combined speech and language disorders. J. Abnorm. Child Psychol. 8:245–256.

Chess, S., and Hassibi, M. 1970. Behavior deviations in mentally retarded children. J. Am. Acad. Child Psychiatry 9:282–297.

Earls, F. 1980. Prevalence of behavior problems in 3-year-old children: A cross-national replication. Arch. Gen. Psychiatry 37:1153–1157.

Kaminer, R., Jedrysek, E., and Soles, B. 1981. Intellectually limited parents. J. Develop. Behav. Pediatr. 2:39–43.

Levine, J., and Demb, H. 1983. Atypical pervasive developmental disorder, or the other early onset childhood psychosis. Paper presented at the 30th annual meeting of the American Academy of Child Psychiatry, San Francisco, California.

Menolascino, F. J. 1977. Challenges in Mental Retardation, pp. 121–180. Human Sciences Press, New York.

Richman, N., Stevenson, J. E., and Graham, P. J. 1975. Prevalence of behaviour problems in 3-year-old children: An epidemiological study in a London borough. J. Child Psychol. Psychiatry 16:277–287.

Webster, T. G. 1963. Problems of emotional development in young retarded children. Am. J. Psychiatry 120:37–43.

PERSPECTIVES AND PROGRESS IN MENTAL RETARDATION
Volume II—Biomedical Aspects
Edited by J. M. Berg
Copyright © 1984 by I.A.S.S.M.D.

BEHAVIORAL DISTURBANCE IN MENTALLY HANDICAPPED ADULTS

J. B. Frost

Pope John Paul Centre, Galway, Ireland

A controlled study involving 67 mentally handicapped adults was carried out with the object of examining factors that contribute to the development of behavioral disturbance in such persons. Information on early childhood experiences, including parental circumstances, pregnancy and neonatal health, intellectual functioning, and educational placements was obtained. Although the behaviorally disturbed and control groups had similar backgrounds and childhood experiences in many respects, including sibship size, ordinal position, general health, and additional physical disabilities, there was evidence that parental discord and disorganization occurred significantly more often in the families of the behaviorally disturbed individuals.

Increasing attention has been given in recent years to the diagnosis and treatment of psychiatric illness and behavioral disorder affecting mentally handicapped persons. Whereas most mentally handicapped individuals are free from additional emotional or behavioral problems, some are unable to benefit fully from continuing education and training because of such problems. Some of the behavioral disturbances are associated with the kinds of psychiatric illnesses that occur in the non-mentally handicapped population. In other cases, an association between the behavioral disturbance and chronic disorders of personality development can be recognized (Craft, 1959). There remain those whose disturbed behavior shows a relatively undifferentiated pattern and cannot satisfactorily be ascribed to any of the more familiar categories.

The extent to which mentally handicapped individuals are subject to behavioral disturbance is unclear, as are the reasons why most of them remain free from significant behavioral difficulties. Attempts have been made to estimate the absolute prevalence of psychiatric illness, including various forms of behavioral disturbance, within the mentally handicapped population. Penrose (1972) suggested that approximately one-third of the mentally handicapped had some form of mental disorder, the commonest being psychoneurosis. He noted that affective psychosis and schizophrenia also occurred in this population. Pollack (1944) found that psychosis was present in almost 40% of his 440 admissions of "dull individuals" to hospital and that 18% of this population suffered from schizophrenia. He concluded that the general rate of mental illness was higher among subnormal individuals and that the rate of mental disease appeared to decline as the degree of intelligence advanced. Craft (1959) emphasized the importance of personality disorders among the mentally handicapped. He estimated that 7% of the mentally handicapped population that he studied had a mental illness and that 33% of these individuals had a personality disorder, whereas true depressive illnesses were rare in that group. Corbett (1979) in his Camberwell study referred to the inadequacy of existing diagnostic criteria when used to describe and classify personality disorders in mentally handicapped adults. He estimated that 25% of his population had personality disorders.

The nature of the association between psychiatric illness and mental handicap is not fully understood. Rutter et al. (1970a) noted that children with organic brain dysfunction had a greatly increased susceptibility to psychiatric disorder. Corbett (1979) found that the rate of psychiatric disorder was high even in those intellectually retarded children who had no evidence of brain disorder. He also drew attention to the probable influence of social rejection on the development of psychiatric disorder in that group, suggesting that intellectually retarded children could be adversely influenced by the same kinds of family and social pathologies that are associated with such disorders in children of average ability. Parental instability, unsatisfactory discipline, and family discord might all lead to behavior disturbance. Forrest (1979) referred to the possibility that failure in training methods employed by parents could lead to a failure of impulse control and the absence of defense mechanisms to deal with aggression in some mildly handicapped individuals.

PRESENT STUDY

In the present study the case records of mentally handicapped adults admitted to the Kilcornan Training Center within a 5-year period were examined to see whether information was available that could contribute to an explanation of the association between mental handicap and behavioral disturbance. In addition, nursing staff were asked to indicate which of the individuals had manifested significant and serious behavioral disturbance in the 6-month period following admission. Behavioral disturbance was defined as behavior that might or might not be associated with recognizable psychiatric illness but that was seriously disruptive or damaging to the resident or others, was persistent or recurrent, or was relatively or absolutely unresponsive to normal social controls and interfered with ordinary social interaction and acceptance.

Sixty-seven mentally handicapped adults were included in the study, of whom 35 (26 males and nine females) were behaviorally disturbed. The control group was composed of 32 individuals (23 males and nine females), matched for age and sex. Subjects were included in the study when clinical interview and review of the case records indicated that they met the criteria outlined above. Inclusion of mentally handicapped adults within the disturbed group of subjects was based on a consensus between two diagnosticians who independently rated each patient on the basis of interviews and reviews of the case records.

Psychological assessments had been carried out on the majority of individuals. In addition, assessment of the home and family environment had been undertaken by community nurses and social workers prior to admission. In organizing the information recorded on the home circumstances of the mentally handicapped individuals, note was taken of whether either parent had had in- or outpatient treatment for psychiatric illness, whether involvement of other social agencies such as the Society for the Prevention of Cruelty to Children had been recorded, whether specific reference had been made to the presence of intellectual deficiency in either parent, and whether observations indicated that the attitude of the parents was positive and constructive. Although comments varied in detail, those that could be construed as representing specific parental concern and interest were recorded as being of a positive nature. In such cases parents were frequently described as being warm, caring, supportive, or interested. Attention also was directed toward information available on the health of the individuals during the perinatal period, the presence of additional physical disabilities, sibship size, and ordinal position.

Similar information was obtained on the control group of mentally handicapped adults who were not behaviorally disturbed.

RESULTS

There were no significant differences in sibship size between the behaviorally disturbed and behaviorally nondisturbed groups, nor was

Table 1. Complications of pregnancy, delivery, or early development recorded prior to admission

	Behaviorally disturbed group	Controls
Hemorrhage during pregnancy	3	7
Toxemia	0	2
Abnormal presentation	0	1
Prolonged labor	2	2
Prematurity	3	5
Encephalitis/meningitis	2	1
Pneumonia	2	2
Down's syndrome	1	7
Hydrocephalus	0	1
Occipital myelocele	0	1
No complications recorded	22	10

the ordinal position of the behaviorally disturbed adult significantly related to a higher risk of manifesting behavioral disturbance.

Early records of mentally handicapped adults are frequently incomplete because of a failure of recall by those reporting later on or absence of adequate notes made at the time. Information available may thus underrepresent the extent to which pre- and perinatal difficulties had been experienced. In this study, many behaviorally disturbed individuals were recorded as being the product of normal full-term pregnancies and deliveries without complications. Twenty-two behaviorally disturbed individuals had no evidence of perinatal difficulties, compared with only 10 of the control group (Table 1). The difficulties and complications that were recorded in each group are shown in this table. Other physical problems encountered are listed in Table 2; grand mal epilepsy was the most common of these.

Psychological assessment had been carried out utilizing the Stanford-Binet or Wechsler Adult Intelligence Scale (Table 3). The control group had 11 individuals whose mental handicap was of severe or pro-

Table 2. Additional physical disabilities recorded in case histories

	Behaviorally disturbed group	Controls
Epilepsy	10	9
Visual defects	2	13
Asthma	1	1
Cerebral palsy	4	4
Memory defects	1	1
Tuberculosis	1	1
Congenital heart disease	0	1
No additional physical disabilities	16	16

Table 3. Distribution of subjects by IQ

IQ	Behaviorally disturbed group	Controls
<20	0	1
20–34	6	10
35–49	11	13
50–70	15	7
70+	2	1
Unrecorded	1	0

found degree as compared to six in the behaviorally disturbed group. The settings in which the subjects in the study had been educated or trained had been recorded in most cases (Table 4). A comparison between the behaviorally disturbed and the control groups revealed that similar educational services had been provided to each group.

Comparison of the social class of the fathers did not reveal any marked differences between the two groups (Table 5). Classifications of social groupings in a rural area are distorted by the proportion of individuals who specify farming as their occupation. In this study 27 out of 67 families so described their activities. Among these it may be assumed that there is a range of income and activity such that some of the individuals could be more correctly included in the higher social classes and others in the lower.

The most marked differences between the two groups emerged when information on home circumstances was compared (Table 6). In 19 of the 35 homes with behaviorally disturbed members, serious domestic difficulties had been reported. In those homes, one of the parents had had treatment for psychiatric illness, violent behavior, addiction to alcohol, or mental handicap. In one of these homes both parents were regarded as being seriously disturbed. By contrast, in the control group only two parents were recorded as having significant

Table 4. Types of educational services utilized during developmental period

	Behaviorally disturbed group	Controls
National school	10	11
Special school (mild)	10	10
Special school (moderate)	2	4
Day care center	1	2
Residential center	16	10
Psychiatric hospital	2	0
Special class	0	2
No placement recorded	1	2

Table 5.   Social class as indicated by occupation of father

	Behaviorally disturbed group	Controls
Executive	0	0
Managerial	0	0
Semiprofessional	0	2
Clerical	5	2
Skilled and farmers	9	18
Semiskilled	3	2
Unskilled	2	0
Unrecorded	16	8

difficulties, one related to mental instability and the other to alcoholism.

When observations on the extent to which the families remained involved in the care and further training of their children were examined, it was notable that 18 of the control group had specific observations of a positive nature referring to the families' continuing concern and interest, whereas only two cases within the behaviorally disturbed group had specific references of this nature made. In two cases in the behaviorally disturbed group, the prevention of cruelty services had been involved; this had not occurred in the control group. Four of the individuals in the behaviorally disturbed group had had life-long institutional care.

The behaviorally disturbed group was reexamined in an attempt to distinguish those individuals whose disturbance was linked to recognizable psychiatric conditions. In 19 of the 35 cases it was possible to establish a diagnosis. There were 11 adults with conduct disorders,

Table 6.   Types of family difficulties recorded in social and medical histories completed prior to admission

	Behaviorally disturbed group	Controls
Maternal		
Instability	1	1
Psychiatric treatment	6	0
Violent behavior	2	0
Mental retardation	2	0
Paternal		
Alcoholism	3	1
Psychiatric treatment	1	0
Violent behavior	3	0
Mental retardation	1	0
Positive parental involvement reported	2	18

three with schizophrenia, three with affective psychosis, and two with neurosis. The remaining 16 individuals had mixed or undifferentiated behavioral difficulties.

DISCUSSION

It has been suggested that behavioral disturbance probably represents a complex interaction with only limited evidence on the relative importance of different mechanisms (Corbett, 1979). Behavioral disturbance may be associated with conditions such as schizophrenia, manic depressive psychosis, neurosis, personality disorders, and various forms of organic brain damage such as the Lesch Nyhan syndrome. However, its presence is not limited to individuals with clearly recognizable psychiatric illness. Although difficulties may arise in differentiating between age-appropriate behavior of severely handicapped individuals and the presence or coexistence of behavioral disturbance as such, it seems possible to distinguish a group of handicapped persons whose predominant difficulties are related to developmental delay alone. The behavior of this group would be abnormal if it was manifested in a non-mentally handicapped individual, but is understandable when seen in the light of serious intellectual deficiencies. However, there are handicapped individuals whose behavior is both immature and damaging to themselves and others. At times this behavior can be persistent and unresponsive to ordinary methods of intervention. Indeed, increased attention may inadvertently and unintentionally perpetuate behavioral disturbances, particularly if the complexity of the relationship between mental handicap, family stress, and behavioral problems is not appreciated.

Rutter et al. (1970b) noted the slight tendency for the eldest child in a family to have a greater likelihood of developing an emotional disorder and he also observed an association between family size and conduct disorder. He found that large families were twice as likely to have children who develop conduct disorders or become delinquent. The small sample size in the present study, together with the larger average family size in both sample and controls, may account for the fact that these associations were not evident.

The possible association between brain dysfunction resulting from perinatal complications and consequent behavioral problems was first introduced by Strauss and Lehtinen (1947). The work of Knobloch et al. (1956) suggested that factors associated with disturbed pregnancies or difficult deliveries could continue to influence a child's adjustment in infancy and childhood, possibly to the extent of producing disturbed behavior in adult life. The findings in this study indicate that the difficulties during pregnancy were not of significance in indicating an increased likelihood of behavioral disorder. These findings tend to confirm the work of McCord and McCord (1959), who found no significant relationship between prematurity, difficult birth, cesarean section, and later delinquency. Drillien (1968) also indicated that obstetric complications, although important in relation to later neurological defects, were not of major significance as regards mental handicap as such.

Suggestions have been made that brain damage in intellectually retarded children is in part responsible for the high rate of psychiatric disorder. However, in this study, organic brain damage as reflected by scores on standard intellectual assessment was more evident in the control group than in the behaviorally disturbed group. Seventeen of the behaviorally disturbed individuals had IQs of 50 or above compared to eight in the control group (Table 3).

A minority of the members of each of the groups examined had epilepsy, the numbers being approximately equal in each group (Table 2). This suggests that epilepsy is not of itself a significant factor in the development of persistent behavioral difficulty and confirms the observations of Chaudhry and Pond (1961) and Corbett et al. (1975) on the association between epilepsy and behavioral disturbance. The fact that only one individual with Down's syndrome was found in the behaviorally disturbed group (Table 1) is in keeping with observation that individuals with this condition are significantly less likely to be emotionally disturbed (Ellis and Beechley, 1950; Johnson and Abelson, 1969).

Educational placements that had been utilized by each group (Table 4) were similar and included state primary schools, special classes for the mentally handicapped, and special schools. However, the behaviorally disturbed group had more often been placed in long-term residential care during their early years, either in centers for the mentally handicapped or psychiatric hospitals. The increased utilization of long-term residential care may have been due to the absence of satisfactory alternatives for some children or to the early manifestation of behavioral disturbances. It is also possible that the acknowledged deficiencies of traditional residential care, in terms of personality development, may have led to the more marked association between behavioral disturbance and long-term care. Where emotional and behavioral disorders occur in non-mentally handicapped children, mental illness is frequently noted also in one or both parents. Buck and Laughton (1959), Kellner (1963), and Wolff and Acton (1968) found personality disorders to be twice as common in parents of children attending a psychiatric clinic as in parents of nonpatients.

There was a clear distinction between the quality of the family circumstances recorded in the case of the behaviorally disturbed group as compared to the control group. Craft's (1959) study on mentally defective individuals transferred to a maximum security state institution, because of dangerously aggressive behavior also noted that the distinctive features were not in the patients' physical or neurological abnormalities, but in the presence of disordered or broken homes and emotional deprivation in their early background. The present study suggests that the early childhood experiences of adult mentally handicapped individuals and the dynamics of the family home have a major and long-lasting impact. The freedom of the control group from additional behavioral problems further suggests that severe mental handicap with associated major physical disability does not of itself lead to behavioral disturbance if the home environment is satisfactory and parental interest is maintained in the child.

Within the behaviorally disturbed group there were some individuals who had identifiable psychiatric illnesses. These represented a minority of this group as a whole and were notably different in that they did not have family histories that suggested a major degree of familial disorganization. The remainder of the behaviorally disturbed group, consisting of those who had evident personality or conduct disorders or other difficulties, had the highest frequency of family problems.

CONCLUSIONS

The conclusion may be drawn from these observations that attention should be paid to the ways in which specific family difficulties influence the emotional development of the mentally handicapped. It is evident that psychiatric illness in one or both parents is of considerable importance. The precise way in which these disturbances affect the emotional and intellectual development of some mentally handicapped children needs closer examination. The assumption that severely mentally handicapped children will inevitably have some degree of behavioral difficulty when they reach adult life should be questioned.

The results of this study suggest that organic brain damage, as indicated by intellectual assessment, may be less significant than circumstances within the family and that family pathology is the major factor in the genesis of psychiatric disorder in the adult mentally handicapped population. If this is so, then greater attention should be paid to the quality of the home environment of the mentally handicapped child, together with vigorous treatment of any psychiatric illness that may exist in the family. This could make a significant contribution to a reduction in the distress caused by intractable behavioral disturbance in mentally handicapped adults.

REFERENCES

Buck, C., and Laughton, K. 1959. Family patterns of illness: The effects of psychoneuroses in the parent upon illness in the child. Acta Psychiatr. 34:165–175.

Chaudhry, M. R., and Pond, D. A. 1961. Mental deterioration in epileptic children. J. Neurol. Neurosurg. Psychiatry 24:213–219.

Corbett, J. A. 1979. Psychiatric morbidity and mental retardation. In: F. E. James and R. P. Snaith (eds.), Psychiatric Illness and Mental Handicap. Gaskell Press, London.

Corbett, J. A., Harris, E., and Robinson, R. 1975. Epilepsy. In: J. Wortis (ed.), Mental Retardation and Developmental Disabilities, Vol. VII, An Annual Review. Brunner/Mazel, New York.

Craft, M. 1959. Mental disorder in the defective: A psychiatric survey among in-patients. Am. J. Ment. Defic. 63:829–834.

Drillien, C. M. 1968. Obstetric factors and mental handicap. In: B. W. Richards (ed.), Proceedings of the First Congress of the International Association for the Scientific Study of Mental Deficiency, pp. 113–124. IASSMD, Larbert, Scotland.

Ellis, A., and Beechley, R. M. 1950. A comparison of matched groups of mongoloid and non-mongoloid feeble-minded children. Am. J. Ment. Defic. 54:464–468.

Forrest, A. D. 1979. Neurosis in the mentally handicapped. In: F. F. James and R. P. Snaith (eds.), Psychiatric Illness and Mental Handicap. Gaskell Press, London.

Johnson, R. C., and Abelson, R. B. 1969. The behavioral competence of mongoloid and non-mongoloid retardates. Am. J. Ment. Defic. 69:467–473.

Kellner, R. 1963. Family Ill Health: An Investigation in General Practice. Tavistock, London.

Knobloch, H., Rider, R., Harper, P., and Pasamanick, B. 1956. Neuropsychiatric sequelae of prematurity. JAMA 161:581–585.

McCord, W., and McCord, J. 1959. Origins of Crime. Columbia University Press, New York.

Penrose, L. S. 1972. The Biology of Mental Defect, 4th ed. Sidgwick and Jackson, London.

Pollack, H. M. 1944. Mental disease among mental defectives. Am. J. Psychiatry 101:361–363.

Rutter, M., Graham, P., and Yule, W. 1970a. A Neuropsychiatric Study in Childhood. Clinics in Developmental Medicine, Nos. 35/36. SIMP/Heinemann, London.

Rutter, M., Tizard, J., and Whitmore, K. (eds.), 1970b. Education, Health and Behaviour. Longman, London.

Strauss, A. A., and Lehtinen, L. E. 1947. Psychopathology and Education of the Brain Injured Child. Vol. I. Grune and Stratton, New York.

Wolf, S., and Acton, W. P. 1968. Characteristics of parents of disturbed children. Br. J. Psychiatry 114:593–601.

PERSPECTIVES AND PROGRESS IN MENTAL RETARDATION
Volume II—Biomedical Aspects
Edited by J. M. Berg
Copyright © 1984 by I.A.S.S.M.D.

DYNAMIC ANALYSIS OF AGGRESSION IN AN INSTITUTIONALIZED MENTALLY RETARDED POPULATION

J. W. Kessler,[1] V. A. Binzley,[2] R. Arendt,[2] P. Polomsky,[2] and P. Shah[2]

[1] *Department of Psychology, Case Western Reserve University, Cleveland, Ohio 44106*
[2] *Northeast Ohio Developmental Center, Warrensville Township, Ohio 44128*

Aggression, particularly in an institutionalized population, is always treated as a maladaptive behavior to be eliminated as rapidly as possible. Little thought is given to the idea that aggression may be developmentally appropriate, possibly even adaptive in some situations, and therefore should be responded to differently at different developmental levels. In order to test this hypothesis, observational data were collected over two 2-week intervals on the occurrence of aggression in three different mentally retarded populations: severe/profound, mild/moderate, and dual diagnosed, noting in each instance the situation, form of aggression, and effective intervention. Each instance was then categorized according to an aggression rating scale devised by Dr. Kessler and correlations were computed between developmental level and form of aggression. An obvious developmental trend was found, and suggestions are made for clinical interventions that would promote emotional growth and hence more age-appropriate expression of aggression.

Aggression is a major problem of residents in mental retardation (MR) institutions. Eyman and Call (1977) reported a much higher prevalence of behavior problems in institutions than in community placements, with various forms of aggression reported in 40–50% of the hospitalized individuals compared to approximately 20% of those in community placement. Only stereotypic behavior in profoundly retarded hospitalized persons loomed larger (61%). In a study using the American Association on Mental Deficiency's Adaptive Behavior Scale (ABS), Campbell et al. (1982) compared scores for MR individuals referred for institutionalization and those never referred, and found the greatest difference in the category of violent and destructive behavior.

It is clear that maladaptive behavior is a primary reason for institutionalization (Sternlicht and Deutsch, 1972; McGarver and Craig, 1974; Macmillan, 1977; Eyman and Borthwick, 1980), particularly for moderately and mildly retarded persons. Interestingly, in his study of behavioral correlates of levels of intelligence in 11,139 MR residents, Ross (1972) reported a greater occurrence of aggressive behavior at the higher measured intelligence levels. Although Ross suggested that the greater percentage of hyperactive and nonparticipating residents in the profoundly retarded groups should make the moderately and mildly retarded easier to work with, the evidence for changing aggressive behavior over time is not strong. Eyman et al. (1981) found no significant changes in maladaptive scores over a 2-year period for some 426 clients. They concluded that any maladaptive behavior that exists at the time of placement is likely to persist regardless of the client's age group, level of retardation, or community versus institutional residence.

Recently, a few studies have helped to clarify the dynamics of aggression in institutionalized MR populations. Cook (1980) reported on what provoked aggression, and Rago et al. (1978) and O'Neill and Paluck (1980) examined environmental changes that decreased aggression in select groups. Boe (1977) reported on some "economical procedures" for reducing aggression in a residential setting that simply involved noncontingent rewards given on a fixed time schedule to everyone present. Bott (1979) found improved ABS scores for aggressive behavior in 30 mildly and moderately retarded adults after twice-weekly treatment sessions involving either verbal discussion, relaxation, or combined treatment. However, in general, we are a long way from successful management of aggressive behavior problems in retarded populations.

The usual tool for assessment of aggressive behavior is Part II of the ABS. Of the 13 behavior domains included in Part II, two relate directly to aggression: Violent and Destructive Behavior and Rebelliousness. In their review of the measurement of adaptive behavior, Meyers et al. (1979) commented on the fact that social competency is assumed to be an age-related developmental attribute but that there is no such assumption in the case of the maladaptive behavior scales. Indeed, these scales represent a simple checklist of troublesome behaviors with no developmental sequencing. The behaviors used for assessment are not differentiated according to seriousness (other than frequency), although Clements et al. (1980) devised a system of "severity scores" based on clinical judgment. According to this system, Violent and Destructive Behavior, Sexually Aberrant Behavior, and

Self-Abusive Behavior had the highest mean severity scores. Briefly, aggressive behavior in all its manifestations is seen as "maladaptive" and therefore something to be suppressed or eliminated as rapidly as possible.

We think that this is not only an unrealistic goal but undesirable if one considers that aggression is a normal part of everyone's emotional makeup. Indeed, as Hartup and DeWit (1974) have noted, no one can survive, regardless of where he/she lives in our modern, Western society, without acquiring the ability to defend himself/herself and some capacity for coping with aggressive affect. Surely this is also true for the retarded person living in an institution.

In view of the size of the problem, the relative lack of therapeutic success, and the absence of any developmental frame of reference that would lead to progressive steps in intervention, it seemed worthwhile to reexamine the problem of assessment of aggressive behavior. Kessler proposed a new scale entitled Coping with Aggression that assumed both the ubiquitous nature of aggression and that the provocation and expression of aggression changes with age as the result of socialization experiences. At Level I (Pre-verbal and Infantile), rage reactions are immediate, uninhibited, and primitive-physical (e.g., biting). Behavior is likely to be unpredictable, with little discernible cause, not amenable to distraction, and with no concern for what happens to others or to self. At Level II (Typical Toddler), the expression of aggression may be similar but the causes are more apparent and related to external interference with a person's desire for autonomy. The person is more likely to be amenable to distraction by verbal reminders or promises and definitely more aware of the consequences of aggression—even to taking pleasure in the discomfort inflicted on others. Level III (Egocentric-verbal) is characterized by more purposeful aggression, often verbal but, if physical, usually restricted to hitting or pushing the offending person. The behavior is more organized with more justifiable reasons, even if the aggressive response is an overreaction. Persons in this stage are more aware of "doing wrong," although they usually can justify their behavior. Level IV (Threshold of Self-Control) is characterized by more restraint, particularly of physical action, so that the aggression is often verbal and there is some concern about doing wrong. If ignored, or talked with, persons at this level can often stop themselves. The provocation is usually justified and well established. Level V (Mature) is characterized by self-control, attempts to use alternative methods to solve interpersonal conflicts, and remorse after an aggressive explosion.

In summary, the general concept is that, in the process of socialization, one becomes more discriminating as to the stimuli that evoke aggression (antecedent conditions), more inhibited in the behavioral manifestation (shown in delay and the shift from physical to verbal forms), more concerned about the effects of aggression on others (as shown by after-response of anxiety and/or guilt), and in general less openly aggressive. There is also a corollary implication that aggressive responses under some circumstances are appropriate and adaptive.

Another aspect of the dynamic assessment of aggressive behavior is an evaluation of the external circumstances. To date, as noted, that has been limited to examination of physical space and the nature of programming. No attention has been paid to the quality of interpersonal relationships, both between staff and resident and between residents. Ideally, intervention should take into consideration the characteristic level of coping so that one can plan progress to the next step (i.e., the cognitive level and the social circumstances that surround the individual). The goal should be to teach alternative methods of conflict resolution.

In this study, the problem was approached by systematically examining aggression in institutionalized groups of various developmental levels to determine if the groups differ in amount and form of aggression, circumstance of occurrence, and effective intervention as suggested by the developmental levels of the Coping with Aggression scale. The study involved evaluation using naturalistic observations reported by direct care staff.

METHOD

The study sample consisted of five groups of residents, all living in one state residential facility for the mentally retarded in Northeastern Ohio. The five groups, each developmentally homogeneous, lived in separate cottages. All cottages are physically alike and were designed to be as homelike as possible. Age [both chronological (CA) and social (SA)], sex, functioning level, and psychiatric diagnosis were the primary criteria for placement in a particular cottage. The subgroups were: mild/moderate male adults ($n = 32$, mean CA 33, mean IQ 46.5, mean SA 8.4); mild/moderate coed adults ($n = 32$, mean CA 39, mean IQ 56, mean SA 11.7); severe/profound coed adults ($n = 32$, mean CA 30.5, mean IQ 26, mean SA 5); severe/profound children ($n = 32$, mean CA 14, mean IQ 23.9, mean SA 3.4); and dual diagnosed* coed adults ($n = 28$, mean CA 29, mean IQ 54, mean SA 9.3).

Incidents were reported over two 2-week periods. Aggressiveness was defined as deliberate physical or verbal behavior that is directed

---

* Dual diagnosed refers to a retarded person who has severe emotional problems in addition to limited intellectual ability. In each case this finding was made as a result of comprehensive evaluation by a multidisciplinary team.

toward an object or another person and that has the capacity to damage or injure (Hartup, 1977). An Aggressive Incident Report form was developed to record all relevant information concerning each aggressive event. The form required the observer to indicate which of several choices most closely described the aggressive act, the mental status of the involved residents, the cause, form and seriousness of the aggression, and the responses of staff. Observers included professional staff, direct care staff, and classroom and workshop instructors. Basic instruction on completing the forms was provided to each of the groups by the authors. The forms were designed to differentiate levels of aggression according to the scale developed by Kessler. (A copy of this scale and report form can be obtained from Dr. V. A. Binzley.)

The incident reports were collected by the experimenters and subsequently categorized according to Kessler's levels. A second blind categorization was done by an independent rater trained in behavioral observation. The overall agreement between the two ratings on the level of aggression was 47%. Considering the commonality of traits that spread over more than one level and the varying degrees of accuracy provided by the reporters of each aggressive incident, complete agreement between ratings could not be expected. However, when the agreement between ratings was extended to include differences of no more than one level, the agreement reached 97%.

Four 1-hour independent time sampling observations were done by the experimenters in each of the living units as a means of verifying the accuracy of the reports from the direct care staff. Results from these observations were inconclusive because only one aggressive incident was noted during these periods. We think that the presence of the observer provided enough attention and implicit supervision to suppress the aggressive behavior of the subjects.

RESULTS

The absolute number of aggressive incidents and the type of aggression were tabulated for each group and compared using chi-square analyses. These data are shown in Table 1. The dual diagnosed group was not included in any of the statistical analyses because the group size was different from that of the other groups. A comparison of the number of incidents produced a χ_3^2 of 21.06 ($P < 0.001$), indicating that the various groups differed in amount of aggression. The adult severe/profound group had fewer incidents than the other groups. This agrees with Ross's (1972) finding of greater amounts of aggression at higher measured intelligence levels.

Table 1.   Types of aggressive incidents

Groups	No. of incidents	Types of aggression		
		Verbal	Physical	Temper tantrums
Mild/moderate male adult	44	31	18	10
Mild/moderate coed adult	41	29	27	28
Severe/profound coed adult	10	3	9	2
Severe/profound child	36	0	32	4
Dual diagnosed coed adult	22	11	7	11
Totals	153	74	93	55

A chi-square in which the four groups were collapsed into two was done on the types of aggression. This resulted in a χ_2^2 of 39.35 ($P < 0.001$). The severe/profound group had fewer verbal, but more physical, aggressive outbursts than the mild/moderate group. This would be expected, given the lower functioning clients' lack of verbal skills. When victims of aggression were tabulated and compared for each group, it was found that the children attacked staff as frequently as their peers, whereas the three adult groups mainly sought out their peers ($\chi_3^2 = 8.25$, $P < 0.05$). An analysis of the situations in which aggression occurred also revealed a difference in the two developmental groups ($\chi_3^2 = 17.7$, $P < 0.001$). These data appear in Table 2.

The severe/profound group had fewer aggressive episodes during mealtime but more during other, mainly school, situations. These find-

Table 2.   Situations in which aggression occurred

Groups	Situation			
	Leisure	Skill training	Mealtime	Other
Mild/moderate male adult	20	3	18	3
Mild/moderate coed adult	19	1	9	12
Severe/profound coed adult	7	0	2	1
Severe/profound child	11	6	1	18 (school)
Dual diagnosed coed adult	8	0	7	7
Total	65	10	37	41

Table 3.   Individuals involved in incidents

Groups	Involvement			
	Aggressors	Victims	Both	Total
Mild/moderate male adult	7	3	8	18
Mild/moderate coed adult	6	7	4	17
Severe/profound coed adult	5	4	2	11
Severe/profound child	6	3	4	13
Dual diagnosed coed adult	9	2	1	12
Totals	33	19	19	71

ings would be expected, because mealtime is ordinarily a pleasurable experience, whereas the school situation is demanding and task oriented. On the other hand, the mild/moderate group had more aggressive episodes during mealtime, for them a social period allowing a greater opportunity for conflict.

A Pearson product-moment correlation of 0.67 was found, using the Vineland Social Age score of each aggressor and the aggression level rating, which indicates a developmental trend in the data; that is, the severe/profound group was more physical and less discriminating in its aggression than the mild/moderate group. The mean aggression level (AL) and social age for the five groups were: severe/profound children—AL 1.6, SA 2.61; severe/profound coed adults—AL 2.25, SA 7.19; mild/moderate male adults—AL 2.77, SA 8.59; dual diagnosed coed adults—AL 2.82, SA 8.85; and mild/moderate coed adults—AL 2.92, SA 11.7. The aggression scale had a range of 1 to 5, with 1 indicating the most primitive level and 5 the most developmentally advanced. Although a few incidents were rated at level 4, none was rated at 5. The range of scores was constricted, indicating that, although the mild/moderate group expressed their aggression more maturely than the profound/severe group, they were not as mature as their social age would lead one to expect.

The data were also examined for the numbers of individuals involved as either victims, aggressors, or both. Only 71 people (45% of the study sample) were involved in some way. The specific numbers and role they play are shown in Table 3.

Examination of the 138 aggressive incidents in which the kind of effective control was reported revealed that verbal and physical controls were each used the same amount of time (46%). Self-control was reported only 7% of the time and only in the mild/moderate and dual diagnosed groups. Group comparisons indicated physical control was used more often except in the mild/moderate male and the dual diagnosed groups. Effective control was not reported in all cases because some aggressive episodes ran their course without intervention being required.

DISCUSSION

The finding that the mildly/moderately retarded adult groups exhibited about four times the number of aggressive incidents exhibited by the severely/profoundly retarded groups concurs with the earlier observations of Ross (1972) and partially explains why these more cognitively capable individuals are residing in an institution. However, it is interesting that the severely/profoundly retarded children demonstrated almost as much aggression as the more capable adults. The relationship between social age and aggression level was about what would be expected. The central role of verbalization in coping with aggressive affect would logically lead to a correlation with IQ level.

The use of Kessler's Coping Scale to evaluate single incidents was not exactly in accord with the original purpose of the scale, which was to evaluate the person's characteristic style, but nonetheless it showed fair reliability. In reviewing the incident reports, the observers were precise in describing what happened, who was involved, where, and when, but their knowledge of why was limited. Thirty-three persons (about 21% of the total of 156 residents) were reported as aggressors, and of these 19 (about 60%) were at other times victims of aggression. It was clear from the incident reports that there were consistent dyads involved in repeated conflicts. The repetition of conflict showed that no solution had been achieved by the staff intervention.

Reported staff intervention was almost always admonition and removal. The most important feature was to assume control and remove any danger, which, of course, was paramount in the minds of direct care staff. However, there was no indication of other corrective steps. One could rarely determine if the aggressor felt any remorse—or resentment—over the incident. If one wants to achieve the goal of self-control, simple banishment probably is ineffective. The mild/moderate groups, except for the dual diagnosed, directed most of their aggression at each other during the course of daily living. Provocations reported by Cook (1980), and found in this study, included being ordered around or corrected, possessions stolen or lost, territorial disputes, disruptive behavior of others, and apparent misinterpretation of events. In the long run, this kind of aggression would be better dealt with by helping clients develop other strategies, perhaps deliberately teaching prosocial behaviors, or intervening on their behalf before aggression erupts. As with groups of young children, it is important to teach such social skills as "asking nicely," "waiting one's turn," "leaving other people's things alone," or even getting help from staff to adjudicate disputes. It is also important to distinguish between "just talk" and actually doing something aggressive. Verbal threats or nasty names are an in-between stage of self-control, and a staff response might include something like "I am glad you are just talking; perhaps I can help you." However, most of the time verbal aggression is treated like the real thing, which does not reward the small measure of control exhibited by the verbal behavior. It is perhaps here that one sees the value of a developmental approach to the treatment of aggressive behavior.

On the other hand, the severely/profoundly retarded as a group are responsible for very little of the aggression directed at peers. What is directed at peers might be controlled or at least reduced by environmental manipulations such as increased personal space (Rago et al., 1978) or making adults spatially available (Boe, 1977; O'Neill and Paluck, 1980). Most of the aggression in this group is directed at staff when they intrude and make performance demands. This kind of aggression is probably most efficiently dealt with by behavior modification methods.

This study, involving analysis of discrete incident reports, does not tell us what is going on to avoid aggression. The report that DRO (a behavior modification technique that differentially reinforces behavior that is incompatible with that targeted for elimination or reduction) is the most common treatment of aggressive behavior suggests that it is necessary to reinforce other nonaggressive behaviors. It is likely that the aggressor is more reinforced by attention—and perhaps by getting out of the situation by removal—than that the nonaggressor is reinforced for doing what is expected. In the normal course of events, young children fuse their aggressive feelings with love feelings and control themselves because they do not want to fall out of favor. Perhaps Boe's simple device of giving out candy on a noncontingent schedule served to defuse aggression and made staying in the company of the staff desirable.

Clearly, the next step should be a systematic program for reducing aggression following different lines for different developmental groups. Reinforcement contingencies should be reconsidered for the severely/profoundly retarded and alternative coping skills emphasizing peer relationships should be presented for the mildly/moderately retarded. To achieve this latter goal, one might consider working with pairs or small groups, making "getting along" a worthwhile goal for the pair or the group. The reinforcements would be planned as a group consequence and peer pressure might be utilized effectively. The technique of aggressive incident reports could be used to judge the effectiveness of intervention both in terms of frequency and change in the nature of the event. One would hope to give the aggressor more opportunity to exert self-control, to stop himself, and to offer restitution. The somewhat stereotyped method of dealing with aggression by direct care staff tends to infantilize the resident and preclude learning more mature ways of coping with aggressive affect and peer conflict.

ACKNOWLEDGMENTS

We wish to thank the staff and residents of the Northeast Ohio Developmental Center for their participation and to acknowledge the assistance of Dr. Detterman of Case Western Reserve University and his colleagues, David Caruso and Jack Meyer, for assistance with data analysis.

REFERENCES

Boe, R. B. 1977. Economical procedures for the reduction of aggression in a residential setting. Ment. Retard. 15:25–28.

Bott, L. 1979. An investigation of the use of verbal discussion and relaxation training to control aggression in mildly and moderately retarded adults. Diss. Abstr. Int. 50:1864-B.

Campbell, V., Smith, R., and Wool, R. 1982. Adaptive Behavior Scale differences in scores of mentally retarded individuals referred for institutionalization and those never referred. Am. J. Ment. Defic. 86:425–428.

Clements, P. R., Bost, L. W., Dubois, Y. G., and Turpin, W. P. 1980. Adaptive Behavior Scale part two: Relative severity of maladaptive behavior. Am. J. Ment. Defic. 84:465–478.

Cook, A. 1980. The expression of anger and aggression in an institutional setting. Diss. Abstr. Int. 40:5804-B.

Eyman, R. K., and Borthwick, S. A. 1980. Patterns of care for mentally retarded persons. Am. J. Ment. Defic. 18:63–66.

Eyman, R. K., Borthwick, S. A., and Miller, C. 1981. Trends in maladaptive behavior of mentally retarded persons placed in community and institutional settings. Am. J. Ment. Defic. 85:473–477.

Eyman, R. K., and Call, T. 1977. Maladaptive behavior and community placement of mentally retarded persons. Am. J. Ment. Defic. 82:137–144.

Hartup, W. 1977. Aggression in childhood: Developmental perspectives. In: E. Hetherington and R. Parke (eds.), Contemporary Readings in Child Psychology, pp. 243–249. McGraw-Hill Book Company, New York.

Hartup, W., and DeWit, J. 1974. The development of aggression: Problems and perspectives. In: W. Hartup and J. DeWit (eds.), Determinants and Origins of Aggressive Behavior, pp. 595–620. Mouton, The Hague.

McGarver, R. B., and Craig, E. M. 1974. Placement of the retarded in the community: Prognosis and outcome. In: N. R. Ellis (ed.), International Review of Research in Mental Retardation, Vol. 7. Academic Press, Inc., New York.

MacMillan, D. L. 1977. Mental Retardation in School and Society. Little, Brown & Company, Boston.

Meyers, C. E., Nihira, K., and Zetlin, A. 1979. The measurement of adaptive behavior. In: N. Ellis (ed.), Handbook of Mental Deficiency, Psychological Theory and Research, pp. 431–481. Lawrence Erlbaum Associates, Hillsdale, New Jersey.

O'Neill, S., and Paluck, R. 1980. Altering territoriality through reinforcement. In: Proceedings of the 81st Annual Convention of the American Psychological Association, Montreal, Canada, Vol. 8, pp. 901–902. American Psychological Association, Washington, D.C.

Rago, W., Parker, R., and Cleland, C. 1978. Effect of increased space on the social behavior of institutionalized profoundly retarded male adults. Am. J. Ment. Defic. 82:554–558.

Ross, R. 1972. Behavioral correlates of levels of intelligence. Am. J. Ment. Defic. 76:545–549.

Sternlicht, M., and Deutsch, M. R. 1972. Personality Development and Social Behavior in the Mentally Retarded. D. C. Heath, Lexington, Massachusetts.

SECTION VII
Preventive
and Therapeutic
Aspects

PERSPECTIVES AND PROGRESS IN MENTAL RETARDATION
Volume II—Biomedical Aspects
Edited by J. M. Berg
Copyright © 1984 by I.A.S.S.M.D.

IMPACT ON FAMILY PLANNING OF THE BIRTH OF A CHILD WITH 21 TRISOMY
The Effect of Genetic Counseling

G. Evers-Kiebooms,[1,2] R. Vlietinck,[2] J. P. Fryns,[2] and H. Van Den Berghe[2]
[1] *Population and Family Study Centre, Brussels, Belgium*
[2] *Division of Human Genetics, Minderbroedersstraat 12, 3000 Leuven, Belgium*

One hundred nineteen families with a firstborn or secondborn child with trisomy 21 (born in the period 1972–79) were interviewed at home by a social nurse to assess as completely as possible the total impact of a child with Down's syndrome. Results are reported on the impact of the birth of a child with trisomy 21 on subsequent reproductive plans. Specific attention is paid to the effects of genetic counseling on the knowledge and understanding of risks, as well as to the role of genetic counseling and the availability of prenatal diagnosis in the decision-making process concerning further pregnancies. A follow-up contact by mailed questionnaire allowed comparison of the proposed reproductive plans and the intention to use prenatal diagnosis with subsequent actualities.

Down's syndrome is probably the single most frequent disorder for which genetic counseling is requested. In the last two decades more than 1,000 patients with Down's syndrome were karyotyped in the Centre for Human Genetics in Leuven; in 94.8% of these standard trisomy 21 was found. Thirty-three percent of these children were firstborn and 23.7% were secondborn. Mean maternal age at birth of the Down's syndrome children decreased from 33.7 years in the period 1960–69 to 31.7 years after 1970. Mean paternal age decreased from 35.6 years to 33.3 years (Evers-Kiebooms et al., 1982).

We report results of a study on the impact of the birth of a child with trisomy 21 on subsequent reproductive plans. In this study specific attention was paid to the effects of genetic counseling on the knowledge and understanding of recurrence risks, as well as to the role of genetic counseling and the availability of prenatal diagnosis in the decision-making process concerning further pregnancies.

MATERIAL AND METHODS

Sample Composition

From the total group of families in which a child with standard trisomy 21 was born in the period 1972–79, we selected families who met two additional criteria: 1) parental age at birth of the child had to be ≤35 years, and 2) the child with Down's syndrome had to be the firstborn or secondborn. These criteria are essential for a study aimed at assessing the impact of the birth of a Down's syndrome child on family planning, because in industrialized countries about 95% of births occur before the mother is 35 years old and because, in general, the number of planned children is two or three (Cliquet and Schoenmaeckers, 1976).

A first group of 40 families received genetic counseling at the Centre for Human Genetics in Leuven; they had at least one, but usually two or more, counseling sessions. During these sessions physical examination of the child and cytogenetic studies were carried out, and developmental and other medical aspects of Down's syndrome as well as its natural history were discussed with both parents. When discussing the recurrence risk, the availability and procedure of prenatal diagnosis was outlined in detail. A second group of 40 families did not receive genetic counseling at the Centre for Human Genetics in Leuven. A third group consisted of 39 families with Down's syndrome children who had prenatal diagnosis performed in the period 1974–80; most families belonging to this group also attended counseling sessions at the Centre for Human Genetics in Leuven.

The most important demographic data of the 76 counseled and the 43 uncounseled families are summarized in Table 1. Although counseled families tend to have a higher educational level, there was nevertheless an important group of families with lower socioeconomic status who attended one or more genetic counseling sessions in the Centre. This is in contrast to the clientele of many other genetic counseling services (Sorenson et al., 1980). In the counseled families the proportion of firstborn Down's syndrome children was higher than in the uncounseled group. This may reflect the fact that, in Belgium, parents are more often referred to a genetic service when the problem child is firstborn.

Table 1. Age at interview, sex, and birth rank of proband; parental educational level, religion, and age at birth of proband

	Counseled[a] (n = 76)	Uncounseled[a] (n = 43)
Proband		
Age at interview		
≤2 years	23 (30)	21 (49)
3–5 years	30 (39)	14 (33)
>5 years	7 (9)	2 (5)
Deceased	16 (21)	6 (14)
Sex		
Male	43 (57)	21 (49)
Female	33 (43)	22 (51)
Birth rank		
Firstborn	51 (67)	21 (49)
Secondborn	25 (33)	22 (51)
Parents		
Educational level of mother		
<High school	36 (47)	32 (74)
High school	30 (39)	7 (16)
>High school	10 (13)	4 (9)
Educational level of father		
<High school	34 (45)	27 (63)
High school	20 (26)	11 (26)
>High school	22 (29)	5 (12)
Religion		
Roman Catholic, regular practice	20 (26)	14 (33)
Roman Catholic, irregular practice	27 (35)	12 (28)
No religion or nonpracticing	29 (38)	17 (39)
Maternal age at birth		
<25 years	22 (29)	13 (30)
25–30 years	34 (45)	17 (40)
>30 years	20 (26)	13 (30)
Paternal age at birth		
<25 years	14 (18)	5 (12)
25–30 years	36 (47)	22 (51)
>30 years	26 (34)	16 (37)

[a] Numbers in parentheses are percentage of total.

Methodology

As a first step, parents were contacted by letter asking for their collaboration in the postcounseling follow-up study. More than four-fifths of the couples agreed to be interviewed at home by a social nurse who was familiar with the problems occurring in families with Down's syndrome children. An exhaustive questionnaire* was used to guide the

* This questionnaire and that mentioned on page 326 (in Dutch) are too long for publication here; copies are available upon request from the authors.

interview and to assess as completely as possible the total impact of a child with Down's syndrome. This questionnaire comprised multiple choice questions as well as open-ended questions to allow the families to express their opinions as accurately as possible. The mean duration of the interviews was 2.5 hours (SD = 28 minutes). The interviews took place between 1978 and 1981. During 74 interviews both parents were present; 43 mothers were interviewed without the father and two fathers without the mother. In the latter cases part of the questionnaire was filled out afterward by the other partner and returned by mail.

All 119 families were contacted recently (1982) for a second follow-up. We used a detailed mailed questionnaire (see footnote p. 325) to gather data on the actual knowledge of recurrence risks, actual reproductive plans, the intention to use prenatal diagnosis, and reproduction during the period following the interview. The questionnaire was returned by 95 of the 119 families. The mean interval between the interview and the follow-up contact was 38 months (SD = 8 months).

RESULTS

Recall of the Risk Figures and Relevant Genetic Information

Before analyzing the impact of a child with standard 21 trisomy on further reproductive plans, it is necessary to investigate to what extent the parents are aware of the 1% recurrence risk of having another child with the anomaly. The correlation between the recall of risk figures on the one hand and several related variables on the other hand is shown in Table 2. The recall of the correct risk figure was better in the counseled group, but even in this group results were disappointing because 34% could not give a numerical risk figure and 21% had an explicit misconception. The preexisting reproductive plans appear to influence the knowledge of the risk figure: 58% of the group in which no further pregnancy was planned could not give a numerical risk figure; only 23% of this group was aware of the correct recurrence risk.

Parental educational level clearly affected the knowledge of the recurrence risk: only a quarter of the families belonging to a lower educational level were aware of the recurrence risk versus about half of the families belonging to higher education levels. In contrast, knowledge of the recurrence risk was similar in the families with a Down's syndrome child regardless of whether it was alive or deceased. When compared to women of the same age who did not give birth to a Down's syndrome child, only 23% of the families in the uncounseled group were aware of their increased risk versus 59% in the counseled group. The incidence of Down's syndrome at birth in the general population

Table 2.   Percentage of parents able to recall risk figures in relation to receiving genetic counseling, death of Down's syndrome child, reproductive plans at interview, maternal educational level, and paternal educational level

	Responses of parents				
	No risk or risk (<0.001)	About 1/700	About 1%	Between 5% and 90%	No numerical risk figure
Genetic counseling					
No counseling (n = 43)	12	9	21	5	54
Counseling (n = 76)	9	5	45	7	34
Death of Down's syndrome child					
Alive at interview (n = 97)	11	7	35	5	41
Dead before interview (n = 22)	5	5	41	9	41
Reproductive plans at interview					
No pregnancy planned (n = 48)	6	2	23	10	58
Pregnancy planned (n = 53)	11	11	43	4	30
Undecided (n = 16)	19	6	50	0	25
No answer (n = 2)					
Maternal educational level					
<High school (n = 68)	12	6	26	6	50
High school (n = 37)	8	5	57	5	24
>High school (n = 13)	8	8	31	8	46
Paternal educational level					
<High school (n = 61)	15	5	26	5	50
High school (n = 31)	3	10	48	3	36
>High school (n = 26)	8	4	46	12	31

was correctly given by 23% of the uncounseled families and by 50% of the counseled ones.

Before leaving the interviewed family, the social nurse always mentioned the correct risk figure and gave additional information to correct misconceptions. At the second follow-up contact, some years after the interview (mean interval 38 months), recall of the correct risk figure for the total group nevertheless was disappointing: only 34 of

Table 3.   Relationship between the risk recalled at interview and the risk recalled at a follow-up contact some years later

Risk recalled at second follow-up contact	Risk recalled at interview			
	Correct	No risk figure	Misconception	Totals
Correct	22	4	8	34
No risk figure	7	26	5	38
Misconception	4	12	7	23
Totals	33	42	20	95

the 95 families gave a correct answer. Comparison between recalling the risk figure at interview and some years later is given in Table 3. Although the overall level of knowledge was similar at both follow-up contacts, a relatively important number of shifts occurred from correct answers to poor knowledge and vice versa. It is important to note that only six of the 17 couples who planned a pregnancy at the second follow-up contact were aware of the correct recurrence risk.

Table 4 illustrates the complex relationship between the recalled numerical risk figure and the subjective evaluation of the risk. About half of the families felt the recurrence risk for Down's syndrome was high to very high. The fact that only nine of the 49 families who could not recall a numerical risk figure felt that the recurrence risk was low seems to suggest that the knowledge of the exact risk figure reassures a number of families.

Most families (110/119) were aware of the availability of amniocentesis before the interview. Only one counseled family did not remember that prenatal diagnosis was mentioned during the counseling session. In the uncounseled group, eight families never received any

Table 4.   Relationship between the recalled numerical risk figure and the subjective evaluation of the risk

	No risk/ risk < 0.001	About 1/700	About 1%	Between 5% and 90%	No numerical risk figure	Totals
High or very high risk	2	3	23	5	24	57
Medium	1	2	5	1	6	15
Low or very low	9	3	15	1	9	37
No subjective interpretation	0	0	0	0	10	10
Totals	12	8	43	7	49	119

information about the availability of amniocentesis until our social nurse visited them for the follow-up interview. In addition to these nine families, three families were only informed after one or more subsequent pregnancies. Altogether about 90% of the interviewed families were informed about the possibility of prenatal diagnosis before a subsequent pregnancy occurred, usually in the first half-year following the birth of the Down's syndrome child (one-fifth of this group was aware of the availability of this procedure before the birth of an affected child). In the counseled group, 33 families received this information from the geneticist and 25 from their general practitioner, pediatrician, or gynecologist. The remaining families had been informed via other sources, e.g., the news media. In the uncounseled group, half of the informed families got their information from their general practitioner or specialist, the others through the news media and other sources.

Decisions for Family Planning after the Birth of a Child with Down's Syndrome

Modification of the Initially Planned Number of Children   The initially planned number of children was decreased in 29.4% of the families, increased in 11.8%, and unchanged in 58.8%. The results were similar in the counseled and uncounseled groups. The principal reason for increasing the number of children was the wish to have at least one or two normal ones. The subjective recurrence risk, the age of the parents, and the burden of the child with Down's syndrome were the principal reasons for decreasing the initially planned number. Only nine out of the 15 families who wanted fewer children because of the subjective recurrence risk were aware of the 1% risk; five families could not give a numerical risk figure and one family underestimated the risk.

Impact of Genetic Counseling on Decision Making   The influence of genetic counseling on family planning decisions can only be assessed for the 66 mothers who were not pregnant at the first counseling session. Forty-five percent of the counseled families reported that the decision to have or not have more children was made prior to counseling. The influence of counseling on the positive decision to have more children in the remaining 55% was attributed to two factors: the information on the risk of having another affected child and the information concerning availability of amniocentesis. Nevertheless, only 13 of the 21 families who attributed the influence of genetic counseling to the information gained about the recurrence risk were aware of the exact risk figure.

About one-fifth of the families whose decision was influenced by counseling had decided to have no more children prior to counseling, but the information gained from the counseling sessions changed their decision. The influence of genetic counseling seemed to be independent of the educational level of the parents. There was general satisfaction with the genetic counseling sessions: 69 out of the 76 counseled families reported that the counseling was a very positive experience.

Role of Prenatal Diagnosis   Only 17% of the families had a partially or completely aversive reaction at the first information about amniocentesis. In 72% reactions were rather positive. The remaining 11% gave no clear answer on this topic. Data on the first reaction and on the impact of the availability of prenatal diagnosis on subsequent pregnancy planning were only collected if the families received the first information before the follow-up interview. [For more information see Evers-Kiebooms et al. (1980).] For half of these 110 families the availability of amniocentesis was an important factor in decision making on further pregnancies. Thirty-six families reported that the availability of amniocentesis positively influenced their decision to have more children. For 19 families (16% of the group informed about amniocentesis) it even was a condition sine qua non for having more children.

With regard to the intention to make use of prenatal diagnosis, for families in which no amniocentesis was performed before the interview, 62% of the mothers had intended to ask for prenatal diagnosis if they became pregnant, 34% rejected prenatal diagnosis, and 4% were undecided. The intention to use prenatal diagnosis was influenced by religion and religious practice of the parents: 85% of the parents who have no religion or who do not practice intended to undergo amniocentesis, versus 62% and 35% of those with rather irregular and very regular practicing, respectively. Parental educational level did not seem to affect the intention to use prenatal diagnosis. However, it is important to note that 11 of the 39 families who underwent amniocentesis before the interview were very regularly practicing Roman Catholics and that 22 of them had at least a high school education.

Intention to use prenatal diagnosis was checked with reality during the second follow-up contact some years later. In 39 of the 95 families who returned the questionnaire, at least one pregnancy occurred after the interview. Thirty mothers underwent amniocentesis during this pregnancy and another two intended to use it but had an earlier miscarriage. Twelve of these 32 mothers had undergone amniocentesis in the previous pregnancy and 15 planned an amniocentesis at the time of the interview. The remaining five mothers had not expressed the intention at interview to utilize prenatal diagnosis. At the second follow-up contact, 77 of 95 families reported that they planned an amniocentesis if a new pregnancy occurred. Only 42 of the 95 families knew the approximate time when amniocentesis can be performed; the others did not answer the question or were in error.

Table 5. Reproduction at the time of interview as a function of the time elapsed since the birth of the Down's syndrome child and the birth rank

Time between DS birth and interview	Birth rank 1 ($n = 72$)		Birth rank 2 ($n = 47$)	
	No pregnancy	At least one pregnancy[a]	No pregnancy	At least one pregnancy[a]
≤2 years	21	10	17	3
2–4 years	6	17	9	11
4–6 years	0	12	0	5
>6 years	0	6	1	1
Totals	27 (38%)	45 (62%)	27 (57%)	20 (43%)

[a] Women pregnant at the time of interview were included in this category.

knew the approximate time when amniocentesis can be performed; the others did not answer the question or were in error.

Reproduction after the Birth of a Child with Down's Syndrome

In Table 5, reproductive histories of the 119 parents before the first follow-up contact are given in relation to the time since the birth of the Down's syndrome child and to birth rank. Sixty-two percent of the parents attempted reproduction at least once after a firstborn Down's syndrome child and 43% after a secondborn Down's syndrome child. Because the mean maternal and paternal age at interview was 30 years and 31.2 years, respectively, additional pregnancies could be expected. In the 95 families who returned the questionnaire at the second follow-up contact, 81% attempted reproduction after a firstborn Down's syndrome child and 42% after a secondborn Down's syndrome child.

DISCUSSION

In this study the overall awareness of an increased risk after the birth of a child with standard 21 trisomy, and knowledge of the exact risk figure, was rather disappointing. Although the results in the counseled group were better, only 45% of the families attending one or more counseling sessions knew the 1% recurrence risk at interview. Antley and Hartlage (1973) also concluded that counseling improved the knowledge of recurrence risk. The data reported by Oetting and Steele (1982) did not reveal quantitative differences in knowledge of recurrence risk between counseled and uncounseled families. Their finding that about 60% of the counseled families did not know their correct recurrence risk is similar to our experience. Although the understanding of risk figures was correlated with the parental educational level, even in those families with a higher educational level less than one-half had the correct knowledge. These results may be attributed in part to insufficient understanding of mathematical probabilities, and partly to ill-defined psychological (defense) mechanisms influencing the transfer of information during genetic counseling.

The birth of the Down's syndrome child often modified the initially planned number of children. In 29.4% of the families the number of planned children was decreased, often because of the subjective recurrence risk. Fifty-five percent of the counseled families felt counseling positively influenced their decision to have more children. This clear impact of genetic counseling was much less apparent in the study of Oetting and Steele (1982).

The availability of amniocentesis was an important factor in decision making about further pregnancies. For 19 families it was a condition sine qua non for having more children. This does not confirm the statement of Black (1979) that amniocentesis may be of only limited benefit for mothers of affected children. The intention to use prenatal diagnosis is clearly influenced by the religious convictions of the parents. However, it is notable that 35% of the regularly practicing Roman Catholics in our series intended to undergo amniocentesis, and also that, of the families who attempted further reproduction between the interview and the second follow-up contact, 75% underwent amniocentesis. The use of prenatal diagnosis in our study is much higher than in the study of Oetting and Steele (1982). The fact that about half of our families felt that the recurrence risk was high to very high may explain why so many decided to have amniocentesis, but our data are insufficient to positively identify overestimated risk as the major motive for amniocentesis.

Updating the actual reproductive behavior of the 95 families who returned the second questionnaire revealed that 81% attempted another pregnancy after a firstborn Down's syndrome child and 42% after a secondborn Down's syndrome child. Carr (1975) and Gath (1978) concluded that the birth of a child with Down's syndrome usually does not seem to deter a couple that wishes to have more children. This conclusion is correct but incomplete. Our follow-up indicates that the birth of a child with 21 trisomy does not seem to deter a couple that wishes to have more children mainly because of the prospect of prenatal diagnosis. For more than half of the families the availability of amniocentesis was an important factor in decision making on further pregnancies.

ACKNOWLEDGMENTS

We are grateful to Mrs. Carmen Breugelmans-Meeus for doing the interview work and we thank the staff of the Population Genetics Unit of the Centre for Human Genetics for their invaluable assistance in the data analysis. Special gratitude is extended to the interviewed families.

REFERENCES

Antley, R. M. and Hartlage, L. C. 1973. The effects of genetic counseling for Down syndrome (abstract). Pediatr. Res. 7:345.
Black, R. B. 1979. The effects of diagnostic uncertainty and available opinions on perceptions of risk. In: C. J. Epstein, C. J. R. Curry, S. Packman, S. Sherman, and B. D. Hall (eds.), Risk, Communication and Decision Making in Genetic Counseling. Birth Defects 15:341–354.
Carr, J. 1975. Young Children with Down's Syndrome. Butterworth's, London.
Cliquet, R. L. and Schoenmaeckers, R. 1976. From incidental to planned parenthood. Population and Family in the Low Countries. N.I.D.I. C.B.G.S. Publications, Number 2. Population and Family Study Centre, Brussels.
Evers-Kiebooms, G., Fryns, J. P. and Van Den Berghe, H. 1980. Prenatal diagnosis and genetic counseling in 21 trisomy: Its impact on family planning. J. Genet. Hum. 28:147–159.
Evers-Kiebooms, G., Vlietinck, R., Fryns, J. P. and Van Den Berghe, H. 1982. Diverse parameters bij het syndroom van Down en andere trisomie ën in België (Down syndrome and other trisomies in Belgium). C.B.G.S. report 50. Population and Family Study Centre, Brussels.
Gath, A. 1978. Down Syndrome and the Family. Academic Press, London.
Oetting, L. A. and Steele, M. W. 1982. A controlled retrospective follow up study of the impact of genetic counseling on parental reproduction following the birth of a Down syndrome child. Clin. Genet. 21:7–13.
Sorenson, J. R., Swazey, J. P. and Scotch, N. A. 1980. Impact of genetic counseling: Results of a collaborative study. Paper presented at the Birth Defects Conference on Fetus and Newborn, New York.

PERSPECTIVES AND PROGRESS IN MENTAL RETARDATION
Volume II—Biomedical Aspects
Edited by J. M. Berg
Copyright © 1984 by I.A.S.S.M.D.

AMNIOCENTESIS
Its Practical and Psychological Consequences

J. Wahlström and F. Hagelbäck

Psychiatric Department III, Lillhagen Hospital, S-422 03 Hisings Backa, Sweden

Between 3 and 5 years after considering prenatal diagnosis, 257 women who had chosen to undergo amniocentesis and 57 who had preferred not to were questioned concerning psychological reactions before and after making their respective decisions. The women who had amniocentesis also described their experiences of the clinical procedure and their feelings during the period of waiting for the results of the chromosome examination. Most women reported anxiety about the risks of amniocentesis and the health of the expected child. In no case was the psychological strain severe enough to require treatment. The women who had amniocentesis reported feeling more at ease during pregnancy and delivery than those who did not elect to undergo the procedure.

The immediate risks of damage to the fetus or miscarriage caused by amniocentesis have been extensively discussed and are, in general, considered to be small. Injury to the fetus after amniocentesis has been found only in isolated cases (Cross and Maumenee, 1973; Broome et al., 1976; Rickwood, 1977; Young et al., 1977; Rehder and Weitzel, 1978). The risk of miscarriage, which in our experience is less than 0.5% (Bartsch et al., 1980), has been estimated to be between 0 and 1.5% (NICHD, 1976; Chayen, 1978). Children born after amniocentesis have been shown not to differ from controls with respect to pediatric and neurodevelopmental disorders (Gillberg et al., 1982).

However, the psychological consequences of amniocentesis for prenatal chromosome determination have received little attention. Complications in the form of increased anxiety, apprehension, and cri-

The study was supported by the Swedish Medical Research Council (Project No. 3921-09B).

sis reactions are possible in the pregnant woman in connection with most aspects of amniocentesis, not the least the clinical procedure per se. Considerable psychological strain may also be experienced by a woman declining the offer of prenatal diagnosis. She may have doubts or regrets about such a decision throughout the pregnancy, and, if the child should turn out to have congenital defects, the psychological impact is likely to be particularly severe.

Psychological reactions to amniocentesis and prenatal diagnosis are being studied at Psychiatric Department III, Lillhagen Hospital, Sweden, and some preliminary results are presented here.

MATERIAL AND METHODS

Women who 3 to 5 years earlier had considered amniocentesis were contacted by letter and asked to participate in a survey concerning their impressions of the information they had received about the method, any difficulties involved in deciding whether or not to undergo amniocentesis, and the effect this decision might have had on the continued pregnancy and delivery. Those who had chosen amniocentesis were also asked about their experiences of the sampling of amniotic fluid and their reactions to the results of the chromosome determination. Because the women who had amniocentesis had been given more detailed information than the women who did not undergo the procedure, direct comparisons between the two groups could not be made.

Women Who Had Amniocentesis

A questionnaire containing 17 items was sent to 257 women who had undergone amniocentesis for prenatal chromosome determination at the East Hospital in Gothenburg. The genetic counseling given before the amniocenteses had not been standardized, but had in every case included the following points:

Clinical procedure during the sampling of amniotic fluid.
Risk of a chromosome aberration in the expected child.
Risks involved in the sampling of amniotic fluid.
Normal waiting time for the results of the cytogenetic analysis.
No disorders other than chromosome aberrations would be detected (in cases with increased risk of metabolic hereditary disease or neural tube defect, additional information was given about the detection of such defects).
No treatment other than a legal abortion would be available if a fetus was found to have a chromosome aberration.
Amniocentesis should be performed during gestational weeks 15–17 and the results would not be known until about 2 weeks later,

Table 1.   Reasons for considering prenatal diagnosis in 257 women who
had amniocentesis and 57 who did not

Indication	Women who had amniocentesis		Women who did not have amniocentesis	
	Number	%	Number	%
Maternal age 35–39 years	102	39.7	30	52.6
Maternal age 40 years or more	47	18.3	11	19.3
Previous child or other relative with relevant disorder[a]	108	42.0	16	28.1

[a] Structural chromosome aberration, aneuploidy, metabolic hereditary disease, balanced translocation, mosaicism for trisomy 21, X-linked hereditary disease, or increased risk of neural tube defect.

which meant that any legal abortion would have to be performed at a late stage of the pregnancy with increased risks of physical and psychological complications.

Both parents of the expected child would be called for renewed counseling if any chromosome disorder was found in the fetus.

All the women in this group were informed by the same two genetic consultants. The amniocentesis and preceding ultrasound examinations were performed by the same two gynecologists.

Women Who Did Not Have Amniocentesis

A questionnaire containing 13 items was sent to 57 women who had considered amniocentesis and received some information about it, but decided against prenatal diagnosis.

RESULTS

Table 1 gives the indications for amniocentesis in both groups of women.

Women Who Had Amniocentesis

Of the 257 women who had amniocentesis, 239 responded to our survey. Some items in the questionnaire were not completed by all these women. The information given prior to the amniocentesis was considered fully satisfactory and sufficient as a basis for decision by 97% (230 out of 238) of the women. Almost 90% (214 out of 238) were of the opinion that the choice of whether or not to undergo amniocentesis had been left up to them and their husbands. Most of the 24 women who reported having been influenced in their decision felt that the personnel at the antenatal clinic had urged them to request amniocentesis. About 25% (58 out of 237) had been anxious about amniocentesis before receiving detailed information about it. Their worry had mainly concerned the risks of miscarriage or injury to the fetus.

Some pain during the sampling of amniotic fluid was reported by 10% (24 out of 239). Other types of discomfort, such as fear and worry, had been experienced by about 24% (53 out of 225). While waiting for the results of the chromosome determination, 46% (108 out of 235) of the women had felt increased anxiety about the health of the expected child.

At the time of this study, but not necessarily while considering amniocentesis, 85% (202 out of 235) of the women claimed that they would have elected to terminate the pregnancy if a chromosome aberration had been found in the fetus, 11% (27 out of 235) were uncertain, and 3% (6 out of 235) stated that they would have continued the pregnancy. More than 90% (214 out of 239) felt that the finding of normal chromosomes in the fetus had greatly facilitated the pregnancy and delivery. In the event of another pregnancy, 95% (222 out of 239) indicated that they would request amniocentesis again. In no case had psychological problems been severe enough to require professional treatment.

The frequency of complications was, in this as in previous studies, no greater in the children born after amniocentesis than in the general population. No chromosome abnormalities were found in any of the 257 fetuses analyzed. The frequency of spontaneous abortion or neonatal death in our material, 2.9% (7 cases), did not differ significantly from the expected rate after the 16th week of pregnancy (2–3%). Congenital abnormalities were found in 2.3% (six children: two with organic heart disease, one with anal atresia, one with talipes calcaneovalgus, one with epigastric hernia, and one with testicular hydrocele), which is also within the normal range.

Women Who Did Not Have Amniocentesis

Of the 57 women who were sent the questionnaire, 44 responded. About 75% (33 out of 44) of these women had known about amniocentesis before it was offered to them. Although information about the examination given to the women in this group had been less extensive than that received by the group who had amniocentesis, 65% (28 out of 43) considered it satisfactory as a basis for decision. The most common of the reasons for declining amniocentesis were the risk of miscarriage (31 out of 44) and the lack of guarantee that a healthy child would be born after examination (16 out of 44). Eleven women objected to abortion at a late stage of the pregnancy, and four had ethical objections to prenatal diagnosis. Six of the 44 women reported that they had been advised or persuaded not to undergo amniocentesis, three of them by the personnel at the antenatal clinic.

Increased anxiety during the continued pregnancy as a result of declining amniocentesis was reported by 27% (12 out of 44) of the women. During delivery, four women had felt severe anxiety about the condition of the child because prenatal diagnosis had not been undertaken. In the event of another pregnancy, 34% (16 out of 44) indicated that they would request amniocentesis. None of the women in this group required treatment for psychological problems during pregnancy.

CONCLUSIONS

Our preliminary results indicate that the psychological effects of amniocentesis are not severe enough to constitute a reason for limiting the application of the method. Although the majority had experienced anxiety about the sampling of amniotic fluid and considerable apprehension until the results of the chromosome analysis were known, the women who had amniocentesis reported feeling more at ease during the continued pregnancy and delivery than the women who had declined prenatal diagnosis. The importance of comprehensive genetic counseling was illustrated by the fact that the women who had received the more extensive information had felt more independent in their decision to undergo amniocentesis than the women who were less well informed and declined amniocentesis.

REFERENCES

Bartsch, F. K., Lundberg, J., and Wahlström, J. 1980. One thousand consecutive midtrimester amniocenteses. Obstet. Gynecol. 55:305–308.

Broome, D. L., Wilson, M. G., Weiss, B., and Kellog, B. 1976. Needle puncture of fetus: A complication of second trimester amniocentesis. Am. J. Obstet. Gynecol. 126:247–252.

Chayen, S. (ed.), 1978. An assessment of the hazards of amniocentesis. Br. J. Obstet. Gynaecol. 85:suppl. 2.

Cross, H. E., and Maumenee, A. E. 1973. Ocular trauma during amniocentesis. Ophthalmologica 90:303–304.

Gillberg, C., Rasmussen, P., and Wahlström, J. 1982. Long-term follow-up of children born after amniocentesis. Clin. Genet. 21:69–73.

NICHD National Registry for Amniocentesis Study Group 1976. Midtrimester amniocentesis for prenatal diagnosis. JAMA 236:1471–1476.

Rehder, H., and Weitzel, H. 1978. Intrauterine amputations after amniocentesis. Lancet 1:382. (letter)

Rickwood, A. M. K. 1977. A case of ileal atresia and ileocutaneous fistula caused by amniocentesis. J. Pediatr. 91:312.

Young, P. E., Matson, M. R., and Jones, O. W. 1977. Fetal exsanguination and other vascular injuries from mid-trimester amniocentesis. Am. J. Obstet. Gynecol. 129:21–24.

PERSPECTIVES AND PROGRESS IN MENTAL RETARDATION
Volume II—Biomedical Aspects
Edited by J. M. Berg

SURVEY OF ANTICONVULSANT AND NEUROLEPTIC DRUG USE IN A RESIDENTIAL MENTAL RETARDATION CENTER IN ONTARIO

C. W. Gowdey,[1] L. M. Coleman,[2] and E. M. H. Crawford[3]

[1] *Department of Pharmacology and Toxicology, Health Sciences Centre, The University of Western Ontario, London, Ontario N6A 5C1*
[2] *Psychiatric Services, Huronia Regional Centre, Orillia, Ontario, Canda*
[3] *Medical Services, Huronia Regional Centre, Orillia, Ontario, Canada*

Audits of all psychoactive drugs prescribed for residents of an Ontario regional center for the mentally retarded were done on four arbitrarily chosen days in 1977, 1980, 1981, and 1982. Results suggest that, although there were fewer residents at the end of this period, the complexity of their problems had not decreased. The percentage of residents taking anticonvulsants plateaued at around 37% and antipsychotic drugs were prescribed for some 30–35% of those on antiepileptics. About one-third of residents received more than one psychoactive agent. In spite of attempts to reduce the number of drugs, combinations of anticonvulsants are still required for some residents with epilepsy of long standing complicated by mental or physical handicaps.

One inevitable result of the continuing movement of mentally handicapped people back into the general community is that those remaining in residential mental retardation centers often present difficult problems of management. Part of the treatment of these residents involves the use of drugs to modify brain malfunction, behavioral disturbances, and sleep disorders. The present study is a survey of the use of psychoactive drugs in one such institution, the Huronia Regional Centre in Ontario, at intervals over the past 5 years.

Table 1.   Anticonvulsant drug use

Year	Total number of residents	Percentage taking anticonvulsants	Percentage on anticonvulsants given neuroleptics
1977	1250	30	41
1980	981	38	40
1981	967	37	31
1982	934	37	29

METHOD

The study focused on those drugs whose primary action is on the central nervous system and that were used regularly: anticonvulsants (antiepileptics), neuroleptics (antipsychotics), hypnotics, sedative-anxiolytics, antidepressants, and anti-Parkinsonism agents. From the medication records of every resident the Pharmacy Department prepared lists of all such drugs, and their doses, that had been prescribed for any resident on an arbitrarily chosen day on four different occasions. Residents were identified only by a code. Audits were carried out in June 1977, August 1980, August 1981, and May 1982. The data were classified, tabulated, analyzed, and summarized. Clinical information was obtained from the records and the attending physicians.

RESULTS

The total number of residents in the Centre decreased progressively over the 5-year period of analysis (Table 1). In the 1982 survey their ages varied between 12 and 83 years (in 1980 about 5% were under 13 years of age). Of the present population of residents 70% are severely or profoundly retarded, and this percentage has been rising. The table shows that the percentage of residents who were prescribed anticonvulsant medication increased sharply between 1977 and 1980 and has since remained around 37%. Inspection reveals that drugs in the anticonvulsant class have consistently represented between 53 and 58% of all the psychoactive agents prescribed over this period. In the 1982 analysis 83% of residents with a diagnosis of epilepsy regularly received anticonvulsant drugs, in spite of which 214 had had at least one seizure within the preceding 12 months.

A recent examination of records discloses that 165 residents have been identified as "dangerous to others." About one-third of the "dangerous" group have been diagnosed as epileptic, and in 64 residents (39%) evidence is recorded of a neurological component in addition to the psychiatric condition. For another 64 residents of this group neither

Table 2. Number of anticonvulsants taken by epileptic residents

Year	No. of residents on anticonvulsants	Percentage of residents on antiepileptics taking _____ anticonvulsants[a]				
		1	2	3	4	5
1977	369	33	45	17	5	0.3
1980	371	45	44	9	2	0
1981	361	49	42	9	0.3	0
1982	342	54	38	7	1	0.3

[a] Including diazepam in doses of 10 mg or more with another anticonvulsant, and phenobarbital in doses of 60 mg or more or with another anticonvulsant.

diagnosis has so far been recorded. The table shows that, of those on antiepileptic medication, the percentage who also received neuroleptic drugs decreased since 1977 from 41% to 29%. It is estimated that about two-thirds of all the present residents exhibit moderate to severe behavioral problems, including acts harmful to others and self-abuse.

The number of anticonvulsant drugs taken by epileptic residents is given in Table 2. This shows that, over the 5-year study period, the percentage of residents taking more than one anticonvulsant drug per day has gone down from 67% to 46%. Only four residents in 1982 received as many as four anticonvulsant drugs a day, whereas in 1977 the number was 17. Eleven of the residents who in 1977 were taking four anticonvulsant drugs per day are still in the Centre and on antiepileptic medication, but only one is still on four drugs. Seven of this original group are now taking only two anticonvulsants a day and three take three. The percentage of residents given three anticonvulsants per day is less than half of that in 1977, but of the original 1977 group, two have deteriorated—one now takes four and another five anticonvulsants.

In 1981, of a group of 21 female epileptic residents, nine were taking one anticonvulsant per day, nine took two, and three got three. By careful withdrawal 16 of them are now controlled on one drug; none requires three. Similarly, of 21 male epileptic residents in 1981, only three received one anticonvulsant, 16 were prescribed two, and two got three. One year later, 17 are controlled on one; one requires three. In other residents slow withdrawal of an anticonvulsant led to increases in seizure rate.

In Table 3 the pattern of use of anticonvulsants is depicted. Phenytoin is still the most widely prescribed antiepileptic drug in the Centre; three-fifths of those now taking anticonvulsants take phenytoin. Primidone and phenobarbital are now given to 39% and 19% respectively. Combinations of these three anticonvulsants continue to be commonly employed: in 1982 about one in seven of those residents taking phen-

Table 3.   Analysis of anticonvulsants used by residents

Anticonvulsant	Percentage on anticonvulsants taking:			
	1977 (n = 369)	1980 (n = 371)	1981 (n = 361)	1982 (n = 342)
Phenytoin	69	56	58	60
Primidone	58	45	40	39
Phenobarbital[a]	45	30	26	19
Carbamazepine	13	13	15	16
Valproic acid	0	12	11	13
Clonazepam	0.3	0.5	0.3	2
Diazepam[b]	—	0.5	1	2
Ethosuximide	10	7	5	6
Methosuximide	1	1	1	0.3
Phensuximide	7	2	1	0.3

[a] In doses of 60 mg or more, or with one or more other anticonvulsants.
[b] In doses of 10 mg or more with other anticonvulsants.

ytoin also got phenobarbital, and more than one in four (28%) taking phenytoin also received primidone. The table shows that the proportion of epileptic residents for whom carbamazepine was prescribed was about 13% in 1977, and changed little over the 5-year period. Valproic acid was used about as frequently in 1982 as it was in 1980. Closer examination showed that about one-third of those receiving valproic acid also got carbamazepine. Use of the succinimide derivatives has diminished; only one resident is taking methosuximide and one phensuximide. Ethosuximide was prescribed for 19 residents, seven of whom took it in combination with phenytoin or primidone and/or carbamazepine, clonazepam, or phenobarbital.

The pattern of use of psychoactive drugs other than those of the anticonvulsant class is summarized in Table 4. Neuroleptic (antipsychotic) drugs were prescribed for around 30% of all residents in each

Table 4.   Pattern of psychoactive drug use

Drug type	Percentage of residents taking drug			
	1977	1980	1981	1982
Some psychoactive agent	55	63	61	62
Neuroleptics[a]	32	35	30	30
Hypnotics	3	6	6	8
Sedative-Anxiolytics[b]	±5	4	6	6
Antidepressants	4	2	2	2
Anti-Parkinsonism drugs	4	7	3	3

[a] Phenothiazine or butyrophenone derivatives.
[b] Sedative-anxiolytics include phenobarbital in doses under 60 mg without another anticonvulsant, methylphenidate, and diazepam unless it was prescribed in doses of 15 mg or more together with another anticonvulsant.

Table 5. Pattern of neuroleptic drug use

Drug	Percentage of residents taking drug			
	1977	1980	1981	1982
Any neuroleptic	32	35	30	30
Methotrimeprazine	22	21	19	18
Thioridazine	3	4	5	4
Haloperidol	2	2	2	3
Chlorpromazine	2	3	3	2
Pericyazine	2	1	0.3	1
Mesoridazine	1	1	0.5	0.5
Trifluoperazine	0.6	1	0.7	0.5
Piperacetazine	0.3	2	1	1
Butaperazine	0.1	—	—	—

of the years surveyed. None was taking lithium in 1982. The use of nonbarbiturate hypnotic drugs has increased progressively over this period. In 1977 about 2.5% of the residents were taking these agents; in 1982 the number had risen to 8%. Inspection of the data reveals that use of chloral hydrate became increasingly common. It was prescribed for 1% of residents in 1977, 1.8% in 1980, 2.9% in 1981, and 5.7% in 1982 (which includes over two-thirds of those given hypnotic drugs). Methyprylon was not prescribed in 1982 records; oxazepam was administered to two residents.

In the sedative/minor tranquilizer/antianxiety group of drugs we have arbitrarily included hydroxyzine, promethazine, methylphenidate, phenobarbital in doses under 60 mg without another anticonvulsant, the benzodiazepines (except clonazepam), and diazepam in doses of 15 mg or more together with one of the anticonvulsants. About 6% of residents were prescribed drugs of this group.

An analysis of neuroleptic drug use is summarized in Table 5. Methotrimeprazine was by far the most widely prescribed neuroleptic over the whole 5-year period. In 1977 it was taken by 69% of the residents on neuroleptic medication and in 1982 by 60%. Thioridazine was the next most popular, representing 14% of neuroleptic use in 1982, followed by haloperidol and chlorpromazine. The newer neuroleptics were not often prescribed. Closer examination of the data discloses that in 1977 a total of 28 residents received two neuroleptic drugs per day, whereas in 1982 the number had decreased to six.

DISCUSSION

The survey shows that over recent years the number of residents requiring antiepileptic medication remained above 35%. This may partly reflect a successful return to the community of residents with less formidable handicaps. The percentage of residents taking more than one anticonvulsant drug fell markedly, and this finding is corroborated by the calculation that the mean number of anticonvulsant drugs per resident on antiepileptic medication decreased progressively over the 5-year period from 2.1 to 1.6. In a controlled trial of antiepileptic drugs and monitoring in Germany (Froescher et al., 1979), the patients received an average of 2.5 anticonvulsants. From a British audit, Cawthorne and Silas (1981) reported that more than one anticonvulsant was prescribed for 41% of 183 patients receiving phenytoin. In another recent review of the records of epileptic patients in a Saskatchewan hospital, Young et al. (1982) found that 43% were taking more than one anticonvulsant at the time of referral.

The decrease in numbers of anticonvulsants prescribed at this Centre is a response to the mounting evidence that interactions among the anticonvulsant drugs themselves (Richens, 1976), as well as with other psychotropic agents (van Praag, 1978), modify their metabolism. Availability of the means of monitoring the blood levels of anticonvulsant drugs in problem cases gives the physician a more rational basis for adjustment of dosages. However, there is great variability among subjects in their responses to anticonvulsant drugs. Viukari (1969) used close drug monitoring in an attempt to control seizures in 40 mentally retarded epileptics with phenytoin alone. He found that, although the mean effective serum level of phenytoin was 22 μg/ml, some subjects required as little as 12 for control and others as much as 34.

Shorvon et al. (1978) studied single-drug epilepsy control in a carefully selected series of adult patients with few associated handicaps. They reported that, although the frequency of attacks could be markedly reduced with either phenytoin or carbamazepine alone, 12% of their patients did have further seizures even with "optimal" blood levels of these anticonvulsant drugs. This finding is consistent with earlier reports that multiple neuropsychiatric handicaps generally mean a poor prognosis for control (Millichap, 1972; Pippenger et al., 1974). The recent paper by Young et al. (1982) reports that, of those patients who started on one drug initially, only 27% required more than one drug later. In their opinion withdrawal of anticonvulsant medication once started is more difficult than avoidance of polypharmacy in the first place. This view is borne out by experience at this Centre. Although in some residents careful withdrawal of an anticonvulsant can be accomplished without increasing the frequency of seizures, in others the attempt fails.

Our survey shows that, although the newer anticonvulsant agents are prescribed at this Centre, phenytoin, primidone, and phenobarbital continue to be popular. There is recent evidence (Oxley et al., 1979) that, although primidone is metabolized to phenobarbital and phenylethylmalonamide and all three have anticonvulsant activity, primidone is more effective in man than the others for controlling major seizures. In 1980, when phenytoin was prescribed for residents, it was given as the sole anticonvulsant in 23%; in 1982, 37% of residents taking this drug received no other anticonvulsant. Valproic acid was rarely used alone to control seizures. In 1980, 85% of residents taking valproic acid were also given another anticonvulsant; in 1982, 77% received it in combinations. Coulter et al. (1980) found in children that, although petit mal responded best to valproic acid, other types of seizures, even with associated mental and physical handicaps, responded well.

Many residents have been given neuroleptic agents along with anticonvulsant drugs. Seizure control is notoriously difficult to achieve in severe epileptic patients, in whom the difficulty in achieving adequate blood levels of anticonvulsants is compounded by the necessity of administering psychotropic drugs to control the psychiatric manifestations of the disease (Pippenger et al., 1974). Most neuroleptic drugs lower the convulsion threshold of some patients (Davis and Casper, 1977), and this makes selection of drugs and dosages even more complex. From attempts to minimize the possible interactions of these agents, this study suggests that disruptive behavior and abnormal sleep patterns can be reduced by the prescription of hypnotics and/or neuroleptics such as methotrimeprazine at bedtime.

ACKNOWLEDGMENTS

We are grateful to Mr. Charles Tai, Chief of Pharmacy, and Mrs. Betty Skinner, Records Office, Huronia Regional Centre, for their efforts in collecting the data used in this study.

REFERENCES

Cawthorne, I. F., and Silas, J. H. 1981. Impact of therapeutic audit on phenytoin prescribing. Br. Med. J. 282:1278.

Coulter, D. L., Wu, H., and Allen, R. J. 1980. Valproic acid therapy in childhood epilepsy. JAMA 244:785–788.

Davis, J. J., and Casper, R. 1977. Antipsychotic drugs: Clinical pharmacology and therapeutic use. Drugs 14:260–282.

Froescher, W., Eichelbaum, M., Gugler, R., Hildenbrand, G., and Penin, H. 1979. Report on a controlled trial on the significance of plasma antiepileptic monitoring. In: S. I. Johannessen, P. L. Morselli, C. E. Pippenger, and A. Richens (eds.), Antiepileptic Therapy: Advances in Drug Monitoring, pp. 263–268. Raven Press, New York.

Millichap, J. G. 1972. Clinical efficacy and use. In: D. M. Woodbury, J. K. Penry, and R. P. Schmidt (eds.), Antiepileptic Drugs pp. 97–101. Raven Press, New York.

Oxley, J., Hebdige, S., Laidlaw, J., Wadsworth, J., and Richens, A. 1979. A comparative study of phenobarbitone and primidone in the treatment of epilepsy. In: S. I. Johannessen, P. L. Morselli, C. E. Pippenger, and A. Richens (eds.), Antiepileptic Therapy: Advances in Drug Monitoring, pp. 237–242. Raven Press, New York.

Pippenger, C. E., Siris, J. H., Werner, W. L., and Masland, R. L. 1974. The effect of psychotropic drugs on serum anti-epileptic levels in psychiatric patients with seizure disorders. In: H. Schneider, D. Ianz, C. Gardner-Thrope, H. Meinardi, and A. L. Sherwin (eds.), Clinical Pharmacology of Anti-epileptic Drugs, pp. 135–144. Springer Verlag, Heidelberg.

Richens, A. 1976. Liver enzyme induction by antiepileptic drugs: Its clinical significance. In: A. Richens and F. P. Woodford (eds.), Anticonvulsant Drugs and Enzyme Induction, pp. 3–12. Associated Scientific Publishers, Amsterdam.

Shorvon, S. D., Chadwick, D., Galbraith A. W., and Reynolds, E. H. 1978. One drug for epilepsy. Br. Med. J. 1:474–476.

van Praag, M. 1978. Psychotropic Drugs, p. 130. Brunner/Mazel, New York.

Viukari, N. M. A. 1969. Diphenylhydantoin as an anticonvulsant: Evaluation of treatment in forty mentally subnormal epileptics. J. Ment. Defic. Res. 13:212–218.

Young, G. B., Ashenhurst, W. M., and Eder, S. 1982. Treating epilepsy: One drug or several. Can. Med. Assoc. J. 126:1134–1136.

PERSPECTIVES AND PROGRESS IN MENTAL RETARDATION
Volume II—Biomedical Aspects
Edited by J. M. Berg
Copyright © 1984 by I.A.S.S.M.D.

PSYCHOTROPIC MEDICATION NEEDS OF MENTALLY RETARDED ADULTS BEFORE AND AFTER TRANSFER FROM LARGE INSTITUTIONS TO NEW SMALL UNITS

H. Hemming

Department of Social Studies, Paisley College of Technology, High Street,
Paisley PA1 2BE, Scotland

Psychotropic drug prescriptions for 51 mentally handicapped adults transferred from large institutions to new small units, and 50 controls remaining in the institutions, were noted before the transfer date and at intervals of 4 months, 9 months, 1 year, and 2 years after that date. Contrary to a hypothesis predicting drug reduction after transfer, there was a significant increase in antipsychotic drug prescription for transferred residents compared with controls ($P < 0.02$) 4 months after transfer and a significant increase in night sedation 9 months and 1 year after transfer ($P < 0.02$). Subsequent (nonsignificant) differences were largely due to return to institutions of residents with the most maladaptive behavior. Antipsychotic drug prescription was associated with maladaptive behavior and multiple drug prescription was common.

Concern has been expressed about the amount of psychotropic medication prescribed for mentally retarded people. Lipman (1970), for instance, reported that 51% of residents in American institutions for the retarded were taking psychotropic drugs, mostly major (39.2%) and minor (8.1%) tranquillizers. The general rationale behind prescription of psychotropic drugs in such populations is that mentally retarded people display problem behavior similar to that of institutionalized mentally ill persons; drugs that effectively reduce problem behavior of the mentally ill should therefore reduce similar behavior of mentally retarded people. Kornetsky (1976) noted that psychotropic drug use for the mentally ill has resulted in sufficient behavioral improvement to allow patients to function outside the hospital. There has been no parallel reduction in the number of institutionalized mentally retarded people prescribed psychotropic drugs.

Paul et al. (1972) found that, in the early stages of treatment, drugs interfered with improvement in long-term mentally ill patients. Continued low-dosage maintenance chemotherapy failed to produce direct effects or improve responsiveness to the environmental programs. Several authors (e.g., Ellsworth, 1968) have suggested that drugs are not advantageous when a progressive social environment has been created. Kirman (1975) proposed that behavior problems in institutionalized mentally retarded populations would be reduced by a change in the role of the nurse from an emphasis on sick and basic nursing to that of substitute parent, organizer, teacher, group leader, and adviser. Consequently the need for psychotropic medication should be reduced.

The Welsh Office has implemented a policy of providing care staff to act as substitute parents instead of nurses in their new small units for mentally retarded adults in one health area. This policy has allowed Kirman's proposition to be tested: i.e., that small units with care staff acting as substitute parents would reduce prescription of psychotropic medication compared with institutions run on traditional nursing lines. An investigation in this regard is reported below.

METHOD

Design

Two experimental designs were used: 1) an "own control" before-and-after design, and 2) a "matched pairs" design. The set of independent variables was change in type of environment, and changes in drug prescriptions for residents was the set of dependent variables.

Subjects and Settings

Experimental subjects were 51 mentally retarded adults living in large institutions who had been selected on the basis of next-of-kins' residence. Fifty experimental subjects were matched with controls remaining in the large institutions. Primary matching criteria were sex, age, number of institutional years, and ability (see Table 1). Secondary matching criteria included individual and environmental characteristics. Two years after transfer, the experimental sample had been re-

Table 1. Characteristics of transferred residents and controls

	Transferred residents (n = 51)	Controls (n = 50)
Sex	37 male; 14 female	37 male; 13 female
Mean age	39.5 (SD = 14.5)	39.0 (SD = 18.7)
Mean years in institutions	20.4 (SD = 10.5)	20.7 (SD = 10.3)
Frequency of residents in 3 IQ groups[a]		
Obtaining an IQ	23[b] ($\bar{x}$ = 55.3, SD = 11.0)	22 ($\bar{x}$ = 55.4, SD = 11.1)
Obtaining a test score below age norms	7	13
Untestable on WAIS	20	15

[a] $\bar{x}$ = mean, SD = standard deviation, WAIS = Wechsler Adult Intelligence Scale.
[b] No IQ test for one unmatched resident of high ability.

duced to 38 and controls to 33. Two controls died, two controls became experimental subjects, and 13 experimental subjects were returned.

Subjects came from seven institutions for mentally retarded adults, having from 27 to 566 beds and run on traditional nursing lines. The two new units were managed by a coordinator and two deputy coordinators with nurse training. Direct care staff were "care assistants" without nurse training, who were to act as substitute parents. One unit had four bungalows for eight residents each and the second unit had three similar bungalows. Drug prescribing policy did not differ between the institutions and the new units because the same medical consultants were involved.

Measures

Medication and dosage were noted from medication records before transfer, and at each assessment after transfer, for experimental and control subjects. Assessments were completed 4 months, 9 months, 1 year and 2 years after transfer. Part of each assessment involved administration of the American Association on Mental Deficiency's Adaptive Behavior Scale (ABS; 1974 revised version) (Nihira et al, 1974). This allowed drug prescriptions and changes in prescriptions to be compared with adaptive and maladaptive behavior. Because ABS Part II does not give an adequate assessment of frequency of maladaptive behavior, an effort was made to rectify this omission by analyzing the records of disturbing incidents kept on each bungalow for the first year after opening of the units. Data were obtained for 43 residents between transfer and 4 months after transfer, for 39 residents between 4 and 9 months after transfer and for 35 residents between 9 months and 1 year after transfer.

Table 2.   Percentage frequencies of transferred residents and controls taking each type of drug at each assessment

	0	4 mos	9 mos	1 year	2 years
Transferred residents					
All psychotropic drugs	68.6^a	69.4^a	72.7^b	73.8^c	61.1
Antipsychotic drugs	33.3	$49.0^{c,d}$	40.9^e	39.6^e	33.3
Anticonvulsant drugs	23.5	24.5	27.3	25.6	19.4
Antianxiety drugs	29.4	28.6	25.0	23.3	22.2
Antidepressant drugs	7.8	6.1	13.6	14.0	11.1
Anti-Parkinsonism drugs	13.7	12.2	11.4	11.6	13.9
Other	7.8	8.2	6.8	4.7	5.6
Night sedatives	4.0	$14.2^{b,e}$	20.5^f	$18.6^{c,e}$	8.3
n	51	49	44	43	38
Controls					
All psychotropic drugs	50.0	52.1	51.2	45.0	50.0
Antipsychotic drugs	22.0	27.1	26.8	27.5	34.4
Anticonvulsant drugs	14.0	14.6	17.1	15.0	18.8
Antianxiety drugs	22.0	18.8	17.1	15.0	18.2
Antidepressant drugs	8.0	4.2	4.9	2.5	0.0
Anti-Parkinsonism drugs	6.0	12.5	9.8	7.5	12.5
Other	4.0	4.2	4.9	5.0	6.3
Night sedatives	0.0	2.1	2.4	2.5	0.0
n	50	47	41	40	33

[a] $P < 0.1$; matched pairs design (i.e., significant comparisons between transferred residents and controls).

[b] $P < 0.05$; matched pairs design.

[c] $P < 0.02$; matched pairs design.

[d] $P < 0.02$; own control design (i.e., significant comparisons of changes between baseline and subsequent assessments).

[e] $P < 0.1$; own control design.

[f] $P < 0.01$; matched pairs design.

RESULTS

Psychotropic drugs were classified as antipsychotic (AP), anticonvulsant (AC), antianxiety (AA), antidepressant (AD), anti-Parkinsonian (A. Park), other, and night sedatives. Percentage frequencies of transferred residents and controls taking each type of drug at each assessment are shown in Table 2. AP drugs were the majority of drugs prescribed (21.6% male and 51% female transferred residents; 18% male and 56% female controls). Drugs most frequently prescribed were chlorpromazine (15.7% transferred residents, 10% controls) and thioridazine (11.8% transferred residents, 6% controls).

Changes that occurred at greater than chance level applied to all psychotropic drugs taken together, AP drugs, and night sedatives. The greatest increase occurred immediately after transfer. The increase in night sedatives was closely associated with AP drug prescription. Ap-

Table 3.   Percentage frequency of individuals
prescribed 0, 1, 2, 3, or 4 different drugs
(excluding night sedation) before transfer

No. of drugs	Experimental group ($n = 51$)	Control group ($n = 50$)
0	31.3	50
1	29.4	24
2	17.7	12
3	11.8	8
4	9.8	6

proximately 80% of those prescribed night sedatives also received AP drugs. The apparent decrease in AP drug prescription is largely due to return of the most recalcitrant residents to the institutions; AP drugs had not controlled their behavior.

Multiple drug prescription was frequent both before (Table 3) and after transfer. There were no significant differences between transferred residents and controls in frequency of multiple drug prescription either before or after transfer. However, the matched pairs design indicated that transferred residents had a greater than chance number of changes in multiple prescription compared with controls. These were both increases and decreases. There was a greater than chance overall increase in multiple drug prescription for transferred residents compared with controls up to the 2-year assessment. Two years after transfer there were no differences in increased multiple prescription between transferred residents and controls.

Some multiple drug prescriptions involved drugs within the same group. These were usually AC and AP drugs (5.9% AC and 5.9% AP for transferred residents; 6% AC and 4% AP for controls). More often multiple drug prescriptions involved drugs from different groups. The most frequent drug combinations before transfer were AC/AA drugs (13.7% transferred residents, 6% controls) and AP/A.Park drugs (11.8% transferred residents, 6% controls). The drug combination that increased most in transferred residents 4 months after transfer was AP with AA drugs (8.2% increase). This combination did not differ from the baseline 2 years after transfer, but by this time AP with A.Park (8.3% increase) and AD with A.Park (2.8% increase) had increased.

Transferred residents could be divided into three groups on the basis of AP drug prescription before transfer (old drug group), AP drug prescription after transfer only (new drug group), and no AP drug prescription. The ABS Part I (adaptive behavior) did not distinguish these groups either before or after transfer. However, total ABS Part II (maladaptive behavior) scores were highest for the old drug group and lowest for the no drug group ($P < 0.001$). The new drug group had a greater than chance ($P < 0.025$) higher ABS Part II score than the no drug group and did not differ from the old drug group. Individual ABS Part II scales that discriminated the old drug group from the no drug group were:

I. Violent and Destructive Behavior ($P < 0.02$)
III. Rebellious Behavior ($P < 0.005$).
VII. Inappropriate Interpersonal Manners ($P < 0.005$)
VIII. Unacceptable Vocal Habits ($P < 0.05$)
XIII. Psychological Disturbance ($P < 0.002$)

Part II scales contributing to the difference between the new drug group and no drug group were:

VII. Inappropriate Interpersonal Manners ($P < 0.01$)
VIII. Unacceptable Vocal Habits ($P < 0.002$)

Similar results were obtained from the disturbance measures. Both the old and new drug groups had more disturbing incidents reported in the bungalows than the no drug group. When the first year was analyzed according to time periods between assessments, the old and new drug group accounted for most of the initial disturbance. Between 4 and 9 months after transfer, the old drug group maintained a high level of disturbance and the new drug group showed a reduced amount of disturbance. Between 9 months and 1 year after transfer, the most disturbing residents had been returned to the institutions and there were only chance differences between the drug groups (Table 4).

DISCUSSION

The increase in psychotropic drug prescription after transfer raises the following questions:

1. *Did the environment improve after transfer?* The new units did have manifest improvements in environment compared with the institutions (Hemming et al., 1981). Resident orientation and staff-resident interaction increased, care staff had a substitute parent role instead of a nursing orientation, and more habilitative programs were practiced. However, improvements fell short of Kirman's full recommendations, particularly in lack of daytime occupations for the majority of residents when first transferred.

2. *Did psychotropic medication differ from that found in other mentally retarded populations?* Frequency of psychotropic drug use was comparable to that noted in Lipman's study. Chlorpromazine

Table 4. Number of disturbing incidents between assessments during the first year after transfer

	0–4 mos	4–9 mos	9 mos–1 year
Old drug group[a]			
Mean	24.6[d]	33.0[f]	14.6
SD	21.4	32.5	15.0
Mean/month	6.2	6.6	4.9
Median/month	2.8	4.0	3.0
n	14	11 (3 returned)	10 (4 returned)
New drug group[b]			
Mean	23.7[e]	17.0	8.4
SD	17.4	14.0	7.1
Mean/month	5.9	3.4	2.8
Median/month	5.8	2.7	2.0
n	9	8 (1 late transfer)	5 (2 returned) (2 late transfer)
No drug group[c]			
Mean	6.1	11.3	6.2
SD	5.2	8.6	5.3
Mean/month	1.5	2.3	2.1
Median/month	1.1	2.4	1.7
n	20	20	20

[a] Residents prescribed antipsychotic drugs before transfer.
[b] Residents prescribed antipsychotic drugs only after transfer.
[c] Residents not prescribed antipsychotic drugs before or after transfer.
[d] $P < 0.01$ for Mann-Whitney U test with no-drug group.
[e] $P < 0.001$ for Mann-Whitney U test with no-drug group.
[f] $P < 0.1$ for Mann-Whitney U test with no drug group.

and thioridazine were most frequently and haloperidol least frequently prescribed. The high frequency of multiple drug prescription requires evaluation. Ayd (1975) suggested that needs can be met by the correct dosage of a single psychoactive drug.

3. *Was maladaptive behavior associated with psychotropic medication?* AP drug prescription was associated with high ABS Part II scores both before and after transfer and with high disturbance scores 4 months after transfer. Residents who were newly prescribed AP drugs had high scores on Inappropriate Interpersonal Manners and Unacceptable Vocal Habits. This suggests that there may have been less tolerance for these aspects of behavior in the new units than in the institutions.

4. *Were increases in psychotropic medication associated with decreases in maladaptive behavior?* ABS Part II scores indicated an increase in maladaptive behavior in the first 4 months and a subsequent improvement. This is paralleled by an initial increase in AP drug prescription followed by a later decline. These results can

be misleading if sample depletion due to returnees is not taken into account. Most residents returned to the institutions had been prescribed AP drugs, suggesting that these drugs had not adequately controlled their behavior. Only one resident in the new drug group had the AP drug prescription discontinued.

There is some evidence that transferred residents who were newly prescribed AP drugs reduced their maladaptive behavior. In this group, total ABS Part II scores and disturbing incidents declined after the first 4 months, and only two were returned to institutions. In contrast, transferred residents who had previously been prescribed AP drugs were either returned or maintained a comparatively high level of disturbance. The newly prescribed AP drug group showed a decrease on Psychological Disturbance 4 months after transfer. This scale includes items suggesting poor emotional control, paranoia, and hypochondria. This behavior is similar to that for which AP drugs are recommended and could account for their relative success in this group.

REFERENCES

Ayd, F. J. 1975. Psychotropic drug combinations: Good and bad. In: M. Greenblatt (ed.), Drugs in Combination with other Therapies. Grune & Stratton, New York.

Ellsworth, R. B. 1968. Nonprofessionals in Psychiatric Rehabilitation. Meredith, New York.

Hemming, H., Lavender, A., and Pill, R. 1981. Quality of life of mentally retarded adults transferred from large institutions to new small units. Am. J. Ment. Defic. 86:157–169.

Kirman, B. 1975. Drug therapy in mental handicap. Br. J. Psychiatry 127:545–549.

Kornetsky, C. 1976. Pharmacology: Drugs Affecting Behavior. John Wiley & Sons, Inc., New York.

Lipman, R. S. 1970. The use of psychopharmacological agents in residential facilities for the retarded. In: F. J. Menolascino (ed.), Psychiatric Approaches to Mental Retardation. Basic Books, Inc., New York.

Nihira, K., Foster, R., Shellhaus, M., and Leland, H. 1974. AAMD Adaptive Behavior Scale Manual, 1974 Revision. American Association on Mental Deficiency, Washington, D.C.

Paul, G. L., Tobias, L. L., and Holly, B. L. 1972. Maintenance psychotropic drugs in the presence of active treatment programs. Arch. Gen. Psychiatry 27:106–115.

PERSPECTIVES AND PROGRESS IN MENTAL RETARDATION
Volume II—Biomedical Aspects
Edited by J. M. Berg
Copyright © 1984 by I.A.S.S.M.D.

DIET REINSTITUTION IN PHENYLKETONURIA

G. Barabas,[1] W. S. Matthews,[1] D. Koch,[1] and L. T. Taft[2]

[1] *Department of Pediatrics, UMD-Rutgers Medical School, P. O. Box 101, Piscataway, New Jersey 08854*
[2] *Department of Pediatrics, UMD-Rutgers Medical School, Health Science Center, CN-19, New Brunswick, New Jersey 08903*

Evidence was reviewed regarding 1) possible adverse effects of discontinuation of a low-phenylalanine diet in phenylketonuria, 2) fetal damage associated with maternal phenylketonuria, and 3) anecdotally reported positive effects of diet reinstitution. This evidence, in conjunction with our observations of social and intellectual variability in a phenylketonuric clinic population, resulted in a systematic reinstitution of a low-phenylalanine diet in that population. This paper describes the format that was employed as well as some of the problems that were encountered.

Research evidence for the effectiveness of a low-phenylalanine diet in preventing mental retardation among children with phenylketonuria (PKU) continues to accumulate. There is uniform consensus concerning when the diet should be initiated (the earlier the better), but opinions as to when the diet should be terminated vary substantially. Most current literature seems to contrast with earlier studies, and suggests that the low-phenylalanine dietary regime should be maintained even after the age of 6.

As a result of 1) concerns expressed in the literature regarding possible adverse effects of diet discontinuation, 2) our own experience with deterioration in social and cognitive functioning in some PKU children, 3) mounting evidence for fetal damage associated with maternal PKU, and 4) anecdotal evidence of positive effects of diet reinstitution, we were prompted to alter our treatment policies. Parents of newly diagnosed PKU infants are now advised from the start that their children are to be maintained beyond the age of 6 on their low-phenylalanine diet, and those children whose dietary therapy had been discontinued are placed back on a low-phenylalanine diet. In the present report, we review the evidence underlying the decision to reinstitute dietary therapy in PKU and offer a format for use by clinics seeking to resume treatment of their school-age PKU patients.

REVIEW OF THE LITERATURE

Effects of Discontinuation of Dietary Therapy for Children with PKU

After the identification in the 1930s of PKU as an inherited metabolic disorder (Fölling, 1971) and the determination 20 years later of a therapeutic dietary regime beginning in the early weeks of life (Bickel et al., 1953), investigators began to turn their attention to the effects of discontinuing dietary therapy in later childhood.

Some researchers reported adverse effects of diet discontinuation. Koch et al. (1964) saw restlessness, irritability, sleeplessness, and the onset of psychomotor seizures in one of their patients and a general regression in another and concluded that "discontinuation of dietary therapy may be more hazardous than previously thought." Bickel and Gruter (1963) also noted "marked intellectual decline and convulsions." Langdell (1965) reported irritability, hyperactivity, destructiveness, and lowered frustration tolerance. Although he noted no change in performance on intelligence testing among his patients, he concluded that "dietary treatment may be necessary for a lifetime." Murphy (1969) noted in one patient "a steady drop in I.Q. with an increasing difference between verbal and performance tests." Although diet discontinuation did not appear to affect the intellectual functioning of her patient's similarly affected sibling, there was associated distractibility, short attention span, restlessness, and poor concentration.

Despite these anecdoctal reports, the bulk of the early research supported the discontinuation of dietary treatment in the preschool years. Horner et al. (1962) reported no change in growth pattern nor deterioration of mental function in three patients taken off restricted diets at approximately 4 years of age. Vandeman (1963) also observed "no significant deterioration" as measured psychometrically but, as others had, described a behavioral complex "characterized by hyperactivity, marked responsiveness to stimulation, brief attention span, and weakness in immediate memory."

The early studies were uniformly fraught with methodological difficulties. Sample sizes were small and consisted primarily of "late-treated" patients. Control groups were lacking. Long-term follow-ups were not yet forthcoming. Statistical analyses were inappropriate, even nonexistent. Case studies predominated, and neuropsychological indices were confined to intelligence tests scores and EEG readings. By the 1970s, methodologies began to improve: sample sizes grew; control groups appeared with increasing frequency; the statistical analysis of group differences began to be utilized, and the early detection procedure was then well enough established to allow for samples composed exclusively of early-treated subjects.

At this time, the evidence shifted toward the continued maintenance of the low-phenylalanine dietary regime. In a pilot study on the behavioral consequences of increased phenylalanine intake conducted by Frankenburg et al. (1973), the diet was altered in a double-blind procedure by which, for 25 days, 170 mg of L-phenylalanine was added to the Lofenalac of three out of seven patients. They found that, initially, administration of L-phenylalanine was associated with daily behavioral reports of increased lethargy, irritability, naughtiness, and low frustration tolerance; after approximately 10 days, however, the adverse behavioral changes gradually tended to diminish.

In 1976, Brown and Warner studied the intellectual development of 28 PKU children, 17 of whom remained on the diet and 11 of whom went off the diet at 6 years of age. They found that children who went off diet were "not developing as well mentally on the average as PKU children remaining on diet." Cabalska et al.'s (1977) study of the effects of termination of dietary treatment revealed a progressive fall in intelligence quotients in patients with classical PKU, difficulties in adaptation and school achievement, and the occurrence of EEG abnormalities after diet discontinuation. In a collaborative research effort by investigators at the Hospital for Sick Children in London and the Universität-Kinderklinik in Heidelberg, Smith et al. (1978) reported a significant fall of 5 to 9 points in London and a nonsignificant slowing of intellectual progress in Heidelberg. They stated that "it can now be argued that children with phenylketonuria should be kept on a strict diet for as long as they will accept the restrictions willingly."

The intellectual development and academic achievement of early-treated PKU children were monitored by Berry et al. (1979) and found to be lower among children whose diet was discontinued at age 4 than among those continuing treatment beyond that age. Underachievement in IQ scores was noted as well. They concluded that continuing the strict diet was necessary. In a progress note on the Collaborative Study of Children Treated for Phenylketonuria, which has been underway in 15 medical centers since 1967, follow-up data on 8-year-old PKU children revealed that those whose dietary therapy had been discontinued at the age of 6 had fallen a mean of 5 IQ points and were now functioning at a significantly lower level of intelligence than those who had been maintained on the low-phenylalanine diet (Williamson et al., 1979).

However, several recent studies have failed to find adverse effects of discontinuation. Kang et al. (1970) reported no significant deterioration in IQ scores of patients taken off diet. Koff et al. (1979) also found no statistically significant differences between prediscontinuation and postdiscontinuation scores.

In order to examine systematically the effects of dietary discontinuation in our own patients, we conducted a retrospective study involving 22 children who had been seen in our clinic over a period of approximately 15 years (Matthews and Barabas, 1981). Each child had been given a complete psychological test battery annually or biannually. The battery consisted of an intelligence test, a social maturity test, and a variety of miscellaneous measures.

The results of a 2 × 3 analysis of variance with repeated measures on one factor (subjects) indicated, first, a significant effect of dietary treatment on the child's serum phenylalanine levels. Following diet discontinuation, serum phenylalanine levels rose and continued to rise; levels on and off the therapeutic diet were significantly different, as were levels in the first 2 years compared to the third and fourth year following diet discontinuation. Second, a significant effect of diet discontinuation on the child's social maturity was noted. Social quotients, as measured by the Vineland Social Maturity Scale, fell following the discontinuation of the low-phenylalanine diet. Third, in addition to the presence or absence of dietary restrictions contributing to the large variations in blood levels and social quotients, the children themselves contributed a great deal to the variability of the results by their widely differing intelligence levels, social maturity, and degree of dietary control. Although no significant decreases were found in the intellectual functioning of this group of PKU children, we were impressed by the fact that a significant number of the patients did drop 5 or more points on the IQ tests.

Phenylalanine Levels and Maternal PKU

An additional consequence of diet discontinuation involves the effects of high levels of phenylalanine in PKU women of child-bearing age on their unborn children. The offspring of women with PKU may be mentally retarded (from 18 to 92%), microcephalic (as high as 73%), of low birthweight (13 to 56%), and have congenital heart disease (up to 11%) (Levy et al., 1981). The severity of these defects appears to be directly related to maternal blood phenylalanine levels during pregnancy.

Effects of Diet Reinstitution

Noting the risks of diet discontinuation in PKU, a number of investigators have attempted to reinstitute a therapeutic diet. Although no systematic study on the effects of diet reinstitution exists, we found

11 isolated case reports in the literature. For example. Vandeman (1963) reinstituted a low-phenylalanine diet in an early-treated, 3-year-old patient severely affected with eczema. After 6 months on a restricted diet, the eczema improved. The patient discontinued dietary therapy once the symptoms were alleviated.

Koch et al. (1964) resumed dietary therapy in a 5-year-old patient after noting a "rapid regression" in the child's behavior following diet discontinuation. The results of this treatment were not reported. However, in another report Koch (1964) described more fully a case of diet reinstitution in a 6-year, 10-month-old child who had been off diet for nearly 2 years and who had become irritable and restless at night, with sleepwalking and crying spells. Her EEG was abnormal, showing some seizure discharges. After approximately 1 year of diet reinstitution her EEG had improved, as had her behavior. She was reportedly doing better in school as well.

To counteract the destructiveness, irritability, drowsiness, hostility, and learning problems in a late-treated, retarded 9-year-old child following diet termination, Langdell (1965) reinstituted the low-phenylalanine diet after only 1 month. He reported that the child became less irritable, exhibited less disturbed behavior, and improved in learning. A 7-year-old patient of Hackney et al. (1968) exhibited a decrease in mental age, mental disorganization, short attention span, and regressed behavior 6 months after dietary discontinuation. Diet reinstitution reportedly was followed by an improved mental age and reduced behavior problems. A 5-year-old patient with an IQ of 105 described by McBean and Stephenson (1968) was found to regress behaviorally, to salivate, and to assume an abnormal posture and change in gait following diet termination. By $6\frac{1}{2}$ years of age, on a reinstituted diet, she "improved at once," with her IQ score rising to 114.

Murphy (1969) found that one of her patients, whose diet had been initiated at 2 weeks of age and terminated at 2 years 10 months, became "intoxicated," fidgety, restless, and unable to concentrate, and showed a decline in intellectual functioning from average to retarded following dietary termination. Reinstituting the diet at the age of 7 led to a calmer, less restless child whose motor activity decreased and whose IQ increased from 62 to 71. A previously well-behaved, early-treated $6\frac{1}{2}$-year-old was described by Robertson et al. (1976) as rough, aggressive, and difficult to manage $1\frac{1}{2}$ years after diet termination at age 5. His IQ had fallen from 101 to 75. Diet reinstitution was accompanied by marked improvement in behavior and a slight change in IQ to 83.

Wood (1976) reported on a 14-year-old patient placed on a liberalized diet at $13\frac{1}{2}$ years of age who developed progressive right-sided weakness, stumbling, clumsiness, and deterioration in behavior at home and at school. Although the patient had previously had no lo-comotion problems nor neurological abnormalities on examination, 10 months following diet termination he was barely able to walk and had increased deep tendon reflexes, clonus, and an extensor plantar response on the right side. The patient had epilepsy, which was treated with diphenylhydantoin and phenobarbital. The EEG showed mild background slowing prior to diet discontinuation. Following discontinuation, the EEG "deteriorated." After placing the child back on a restricted diet, Wood noted improved balance, no tremor, improved but difficult walking, and slightly improved EEG.

More recently, Schuett et al. (1980) treated with a low-phenylal-anine diet an adolescent who had been off-diet for 9 years and an 8-year-old who had been off-diet for 2 years. The adolescent had an abnormal EEG and bleeding eczema; the 8-year-old exhibited behavioral problems such as hyperactivity, short attention span, and aggressiveness, as well as a 20 point drop in IQ. Following diet reinstitution in both cases, the symptoms were reversed.

The patients discussed in these case reports are diverse. They include both early- and late-treated children whose dietary control ranged from good to poor, whose IQs ranged from average to severely retarded, whose previous therapy ranged from 1 to $13\frac{1}{2}$ years in duration, and whose diets had been terminated as early as 2 years 10 months of age and as late as 14 years 4 months of age. The diets were reinstituted for reasons ranging from eczema, behavioral abnormalities, and gait deterioration to paresis and deteriorating IQ. However, in every case the results of diet reinstitution were positive, sometimes dramatically so.

Considering the findings by ourselves and others of social and intellectual deterioration following dietary termination, the disastrous consequences of high levels of phenylalanine in infants born to phenylketonuric women, and the sketchy but encouraging reports on the effects of diet reinstitution, we were prompted to reinstitute a restricted, low-phenylalanine diet in all of our patients who had previously been placed on a liberalized diet. In doing so, we concur with Rosenberg (cited in Annexton, 1978), who said, "Wisdom is on the side of conservatism. . .and conservatism is on the side of returning to the diet."

REINSTITUTION PROCEDURE AT THE PKU OUTPATIENT CLINIC, THE BANCROFT SCHOOL, HADDONFIELD, NEW JERSEY

In order to assure optimal health status in our patients we reinstituted diet in the manner described below.

Step 1: Counseling

As patients were scheduled for their routine neurological examinations, they were advised of recent evidence pointing to the beneficial effects of a low-phenylalanine diet among even older children: those whose early diets had never been discontinued, and those whose diets had been reinstituted either to counteract adverse symptoms associated with high phenylalanine levels or to prepare for the conception of a child. All patients previously taken off their low-phenylalanine diet at age 5 were invited to resume the diet; all but one family were willing to attempt diet reinstitution.

Step 2: Establishing Baseline Data

Rather than devise a single low-phenylalanine diet for a group of children whose age, weight, and dietary habits varied considerably, we first requested a 2-week dietary history from which we could formulate an individually tailored plan for each child. Each family was instructed, at the time of the neurological examination, in the procedure for recording the dietary history and encouraged to be as accurate and honest as possible about their child's unrestricted dietary intake.

Following the completion of the dietary history, each child was scheduled for a return visit to the clinic. At the time of this return visit, each child was administered an extensive battery of psychological tests. Detailed data were obtained from parents about the child's current behavior. At the return visit, following psychological testing, a blood specimen was drawn for analyses in the state laboratory by the McCaman-Robins (1962) method.

Step 3: Dietary Format

A reinstituted diet was begun immediately following the return visit. The families were introduced to a 125% recommended daily allowance (RDA) for protein diet. The amount of protein was calculated from a standard RDA age and weight chart for protein. (An example of the computation involved in determining protein intake is as follows: a 12-year-old child weighing 37.3 kg would be permitted 1.3 g of protein per kilogram of weight, or 48.5 g total.) The precise form in which the child received protein was formulated for each family individually according to the participant's dietary routine.

Three months later, Phenyl-Free (Mead Johnson) was introduced, along with a 100% RDA for protein diet. Because Phenyl-Free has milk protein with the phenylalanine removed, the child was permitted to drink as much of this product as desired, although families were requested to keep a record of the amount of Phenyl-Free consumed.

Other protein sources in the child's diet provided the essential amino acid phenylalanine.

Six months following diet reinstitution, dietary adjustments were made such that the amount of protein from Phenyl-Free and other protein sources, together, met the 125% RDA for protein. For example, the 12-year-old weighing 37.7 kg who had been permitted 1.3 g/kg, or 48.5 g of protein to meet the requirements for the 100% RDA for protein diet could now consume 60.6 g (48.5 × 125% RDA) of protein. Because two cups of Phenyl-Free provide 20 g of protein, the child would need only 40.6 g of protein from other sources.

At this point, the diets were monitored to assure that sufficient phenylalanine was being obtained from other protein sources. The 12-year-old child on 40,600 mg of protein intake would be taking 2300 mg of phenylalanine (5% of his or her protein intake). Because 16 mg/kg are required, the child would need 37.5 kg × 16 mg/kg, or 596.8 mg, of phenylalanine, and would thus be well within the range of phenylalanine needed for optimal growth and neurological functioning.

Step 4: Monitoring Behavioral, Cognitive, and Affective Functioning

At 6 and again at 12 months following diet reinstitution, administration of the psychological test battery was repeated for each child.

Step 5: Monitoring Serum Levels

Serum phenylalanine levels were monitored at 3 months and 6 months. The goal was to reduce the serum phenylalanine levels to one-half of what they had been prior to diet reinstitution.

CONCLUSIONS

The reinstitution of low-phenylalanine diet in PKU children previously taken off the diet at approximately 5 years of age was systematically undertaken by our clinic. The most striking finding relative to the implementation of this medical procedure concerned the difficulty the patients and their families had in complying with the dietary restrictions. The families were unable to adjust to the newly required maintenance of dietary therapy, and accommodation at mealtimes to a single family member appeared to be nearly impossible. Outside of the family, the children had to contend with their peer group and general cultural preoccupation with precisely those foods that were most threatening to their health status (i.e., bacon and eggs, hotdogs, cupcakes). In addition, they seemed to lack full comprehension of the potential detrimental effects of high levels of serum phenylalanine and high levels of protein intake. Compounding this problem was the fact that these possible effects were neither immediate nor overtly obvious. Future work is necessary to understand what encourages compliance to medical regimes; this information must be integrated into any format for dietary reinstitution in PKU. This knowledge can also be applied to the maintenance of the diet from birth, because we have found that optimum maintenance of the phenylalanine diet is difficult over the years.

The effects of our reinstitution of a restricted low-phenylalanine diet on the behavioral, intellectual, and affective functioning in children with PKU are currently under study. Preliminary analyses are pending and will be reported elsewhere. In spite of the variability of our success in reinstituting the diet, both within and between subjects, the results are nevertheless encouraging thus far. Given the least hope for the achievement of more optimal levels of functioning in PKU children and given the difficulty in reinstituting diet once terminated, our policy at present is to maintain our younger children on the restricted diets indefinitely.

REFERENCES

Annexton, M. 1978. Diet termination for PKU: Yes or no? JAMA 240:1471–1472.

Berry, H. K., O'Grady, D. J., Perlmutter, L. J., and Bofinger, M. K. 1979. Intellectual development and academic achievement of children treated early for phenylketonuria. Dev. Med. Child Neurol. 21:311–320.

Bickel, H., Gerrard, J., and Hickmans, E. M. 1953. Influences of phenylalanine intake on phenylketonuria. Lancet 2:812–813.

Bickel, H., and Gruter, W. 1963. Management of phenylketonuria. In: F. L. Lyman (ed.), Phenylketonuria, pp. 136–172. Charles C Thomas Publisher, Springfield, Illinois.

Brown, E. S., and Warner, R. 1976. Mental development of phenylketonuric children on or off diet after the age of six. Psychol. Med. 6:287–296.

Cabalska, B., Duczynska, N., Borzymowsha, J., Zorska, K., Koslacz Folga, A., and Bozkowa, K. 1977. Termination of dietary treatment in phenylketonuria. Eur. J. Pediatr. 126:253–262.

Fölling, A. 1971. The original detection of phenylketonuria. In: H. Bickel, F. P. Hudson, and L. I. Woolf (eds.), Phenylketonuria and Some Other Inborn Errors of Metabolism, pp. 1–3. George Thieme Verlag, Stuttgart.

Frankenburg, W. K., Goldstein, A. D., and Olson, C. O. 1973. Behavioral consequences of increased phenylalanine intake by phenylketouric children: A pilot study describing a methodology. Am. J. Ment. Defic. 77:524–532.

Hackney, I. M., Hanley, W. B., Davidson, W., and Lindsao, L. 1968. Phenylketonuria: Mental development, behavior, and termination of low phenylalanine diet. J. Pediatr. 72:646–655.

Horner, F. A., Streamer, C. W., Alejandrino, L. L., Reed, L. H., and Ibbot, F. 1962. The termination of dietary treatment of phenylketonuria. N. Engl. J. Med. 266:79–81.

Kang, E. S., Sollee, N. D., and Gerald, R. S. 1970. Results of treatment and termination of the diet in phenylketonuria (PKU). Pediatrics 46:881–890.

Koch, R. 1964. Letter to Dr. Vandeman. Am. J. Dis. Child. 107:537–538.

Koch, R., Fishler, K., Schild, S., and Ragsdale N. 1964. Clinical aspects of phenylketonuria. Ment. Retard. 2:47–54.

Koff, W., Kammerer, B., Boyle, P., and Pueschel, S. M. 1979. Intelligence and phenylketonuria: Effects of diet termination. J. Pediatr. 94:534–537.

Langdell, J. I. 1965. Phenylketonuria—Eight year evaluation of treatment. Arch. Gen. Psychiatry 12:363–367.

Levy, H. L., Lenke, R. R., and Crocker, A. C. (eds.). 1981. Maternal PKU. Department of Health and Human Services, Rockville, Maryland.

Matthews, W. S., and Barabas, G. 1981. The effects of diet termination upon the intellectual and social functioning of children with PKU. Paper presented to the American Psychological Association meeting, Los Angeles.

McBean, M. S., and Stephenson, J. B. P. 1968. Treatment of classical phenylketonuria. Arch. Dis. Child. 43:1–7.

McCaman, M. W., and Robins, E. 1962. Fluorimetric method for the determination of phenylalanine in serum. J. Lab. Clin. Med. 59:885–890.

Murphy, D. 1969. Termination of dietary treatment of phenylketonuria. Ir. J. Med. Sci. 2:177–183.

Robertson, F., Hill, G. N., Bashel, K., Rooney, J., Brummit, R., and Pollard, A. C. 1976. Management of phenylketonuria. South Australian experience of 12 cases. Med. J. Aust. 1:647–650.

Schuett, V. E., Gurda, R. F., and Brown, E. 1980. Diet discontinuation policies and practices of PKU clinics in the United States. Am. J. Public Health 70:498–503.

Smith, I., Lobascher, M. E., Stevenson, J. E., Wolff, O. H., Schmidt, H., Grubel-Kaiser, S., and Bickel, H. 1978. Effect of stopping low-phenylalanine diet on intellectual progress of children with phenylketonuria. Br. Med. J. 2:723–726.

Vandeman, P. R. 1963. Termination of dietary treatment for phenylketonuria. Am. J. Dis. Child. 106:492–495.

Williamson, M., Koch, R., and Devlow, S. 1979. Diet discontinuation in phenylketonuria. Pediatrics 63:823–824.

Wood, B. 1976. Neurological disturbance in a PKU child after discontinuation of dietary treatment. Dev. Med. Child Neurol. 18:657–665.

PERSPECTIVES AND PROGRESS IN MENTAL RETARDATION
Volume II—Biomedical Aspects
Edited by J. M. Berg
Copyright © 1984 by I.A.S.S.M.D.

MANAGING THE DEVELOPMENTALLY DISABLED DYSPHAGIC

J. J. Sheppard,[1] L. J. Berman,[2] and R. M. F. Kratchman[2]

[1] *Department of Speech and Language Pathology and Audiology, Teachers College, Columbia University, New York, New York 10027*
[2] *Flower Hospital, 1249 Fifth Avenue, New York, New York 10029*

This paper discusses a feeding program for severely and profoundly retarded, dysphagic, institutionalized clients. A screening of clients for dysphagic symptoms revealed the amount of special care required because of their eating problems. Subsequently, comprehensive dysphagia evaluations were performed by speech-language pathologists. An interdisciplinary management team implemented the mealtime recommendations and the related therapy and educational programs. Mealtime management included attention to client positioning, utensils, diet, feeding techniques, and oral hygiene. Dysphagia therapy and education focused on improving severely deficient abilities. The program required extensive staff training. Special problems and impact on clients are reviewed.

Feeding problems in developmentally disabled individuals are frequently related to dysphagia, a condition that includes problems with ingestion of foods and with oral secretions (commonly known as drooling), difficulty in sucking, swallowing, and chewing, and choking (Palmer and Horn, 1978; Korabek et al., 1981). Dysphagia is associated with neuromuscular, anatomical, and psychomotor abnormalities that affect 1) the ability to maintain adequate body postures during eating, 2) oral and pharyngeal movement competencies, 3) oral reflexes, and 4) acquisition of chewing and cup-drinking skills. Palmer and Horn (1978) noted that prolonged subsistence on puréed food and delay in self-feeding were often secondary to the dysphagic involvement. In addition, Sheppard and Berman (1981) observed that behavioral problems such as bizarre food habits, multiple food dislikes, and mealtime tantrums occurred in response to dysphagic difficulties. In a review of 27 profoundly retarded dysphagics, Sheppard (1982, unpublished observations) found that dependent and independent eaters with dys-

368 Sheppard et al.

Table 1. Dysphagic symptoms in 146 severely
and profoundly retarded, institutionalized persons

Deficiency	Number of clients (%)
Drooling	84 (58)
Drinking	98 (67)
Eating nonchewables	67 (46)
Eating chewables	114 (78)

phagia exhibited mild problems, such as sloppy eating or drooling, to severe disabilities that affected nutrition, hydration, and respiration.

Management of dysphagic clients in institutional settings is complex, involving meals, medications, therapy, and education (Korabek et al., 1981; Sheppard and Berman, 1981). An effective program requires a working partnership between nurses, physicians, dieticians, direct caregivers, speech, physical, and occupational therapists, and educators. In addition, special support is often needed from orthotics and kitchen staffs.

This paper describes a feeding program in a residential institution for severely and profoundly retarded, multiply handicapped individuals that was started in 1978. The program aimed to reduce the impact of dysphagic disabilities on both client and caregivers through optimum mealtime management and client training.

POPULATION SURVEY

The institution population consisted of 146 individuals, ages 2 years 8 months to 36 years (mean = 15 years 4 months). Our survey revealed 142 (97%) with one or more symptoms of dysphagia (see Table 1). This high incidence was a function of the extremely severe handicaps of these clients. The survey revealed the number of clients needing special mealtime attention because of dysphagia, and also provided a general indication of the amount of care they required. Factors related to amount of care were client independence at meals; need for special diets, medication, chairs, and utensils; presence of disabilities, deformities, and behaviors that affected eating (e.g., blindness, seizures, tantrums, and sitting problems); need for special feeding techniques and procedures; and the amount of time required for eating a meal.

Speech pathologists evaluated the individual clients for patterns of dysphagic involvement. Body and oral postural control, oral structures and reflexes, breath control, control of oral secretions, and eating abilities were examined. Results of the evaluation and recommendations for mealtime management, therapy, and educational programs were discussed with the client's treatment team—the therapists, educators, caregivers, and nurses responsible for his care.

MEALTIME MANAGEMENT

The goals of the mealtime management program were: 1) to improve the ease and efficiency with which the client ate; 2) to minimize the incidence of choking and aspiration; and 3) to practice recently acquired eating abilities (Sheppard and Berman, 1981). Factors that influenced the client's eating performance—client position, eating utensils, diet, feeding techniques, and oral hygiene after meals—needed to be regulated in order to achieve these goals.

Chairs

Client positioning was a critical factor. Upright sitting was the optimum position for swallowing ease, effective protective reflexes, and adequate oral movements (Finnie, 1975). Seventy-five percent (106) of the dysphagic clients required adaptive seating equipment to maintain adequate postures during eating. Appropriate furniture and adaptive equipment, including specially designed chairs, lap trays, and seat belts, were selected in cooperation with physical and occupational therapists and constructed and maintained by the orthotics staff. Chair accessories, such as trays and bolsters, were stored in eating areas to be readily available for use during meals and snacks.

Utensils

Spoon size, shape, and coating and cup size, shape, and material were found to be significant for the ease and efficiency with which the dysphagic client could eat. Special utensils were needed by 87% (124) of the dysphagics. Utensils were recommended by the speech-language pathologist. The problems of keeping track of these small pieces of equipment and having them available when needed were solved by washing them in the dining area and storing them in plastic pouches attached to each client's chair.

Diet

Diet types were developed in cooperation with dieticians and kitchen administrators. Food texture is critical in influencing the ease with which a dysphagic can eat. Diets therefore ranged from nonchewable puréed and chopped solids to chewable cut-up and whole solids. Liquids were either thickened or of regular thickness. Clients' diets were reviewed monthly in meetings between dieticians, nurses, and speech-language pathologists. Among the dysphagic clients, 11% (16) were on chewable diets, 67% (96) on chopped diets, 21% (30) on purées, and 47% (66) were given thickened liquids.

Special Feeding Techniques

Dysphagics frequently need special feeding techniques or assistance during eating. Recommendations were made, based on the results of the evaluation, for pacing eating speed, for spooning, for finger feeding, for giving drinks, for maintaining good body and head positions, and for assisting more adequate oral movements. Special feeding techniques and timing were recommended for 77% (109) of the clients.

Oral Hygiene

Oral hygiene is especially important in such populations to minimize potential aspiration of unnoticed food residuals, and to maintain healthy teeth and gums. Rinsing out the mouth, brushing the teeth, and positioning clients after eating are important components of the mealtime routine.

DYSPHAGIA THERAPY

Mealtimes offered opportunities to practice recently acquired or partially developed eating abilities. In our experience, however, it was not an appropriate setting for developing new abilities or improving those that were severely deficient. Better results were realized from snacktime training during education and therapy programs. Treatment strategies to improve motor coordinations for eating and for control of oral secretions were developed by speech-language pathology, occupational therapy, and physical therapy staff. Education and recreation specialists provided additional training opportunities by incorporating these routines into their programs. As component eating behaviors improved, practice was carried over into mealtimes.

IN-SERVICE TRAINING

Our program drove home the important realization that feeding and treating the developmentally disabled dysphagic required substantial technical skills that are not commonly acquired by people working with this type of population. In-service training was therefore the keystone of the program. It consisted of:

1. Lecture and printed material for all new staff.
2. Assignment of new direct care staff to a speech-language pathologist for a feeding apprenticeship.

3. Periodic in-service workshops for professional and direct care workers.
4. Consultant advice, on referral, for especially difficult cases.
5. Feeding at mealtimes by professional staff to encourage observation and communication between professionals and direct care workers.
6. Supervision of evening meals by speech-language pathologists and other professionals.

DISCUSSION

Programming for dysphagics was not without its problems. In our experience the most resistant and complex problems concerned providing adequate and ongoing staff training and coordinating the support services involving food and equipment with treatment. However, once the program was in place positive results motivated staff to continue to work toward adequate solutions.

The results were readily apparent. All of the clients benefited from more thoughtful and careful positioning for eating and from consideration of food textures. Snacktime training and inclusion of eating skills in educational activities became regular features of client programs. Clients improved in functional mealtime skills, especially tolerance of upright sitting for eating, decreased coughing and choking, acquisition of cup-drinking and chewing skills, improved neatness, and generally improved ease of eating. The net effect has been more pleasant and efficient mealtimes for both clients and caregivers.

REFERENCES

Finnie, N. R. 1975. Handling the Young Cerebral Palsied Child at Home, 2nd ed., pp. 113–132. E. P. Dutton & Company, Inc. New York.

Korabek, C. A., Reid, D. H., and Ivancic, M. T. 1981. Improving needed food intake of profoundly handicapped children through effective supervision of institutional staff. Appl. Res. Ment. Retard. 2:69–88.

Palmer, S., and Horn, S. 1978. Feeding problems in children. In: S. Palmer and S. Ekvall (eds.), Pediatric Nutrition in Developmental Disorders, pp. 107–129. Charles C Thomas Publisher, Springfield, Illinois.

Sheppard, J. J., and Berman, L. 1981. Establishing a dysphagia program for developmentally disabled individuals. In: R. G. DiCuio and R. B. Kugel (eds.), Into the Light: Helping People with Handicaps at Flower Hospital, pp. 95–103. New York Medical Publishing Corp., New York.

PERSPECTIVES AND PROGRESS IN MENTAL RETARDATION
Volume II—Biomedical Aspects
Edited by J. M. Berg
Copyright © 1984 by I.A.S.S.M.D.

SURGICAL AND COGNITIVE INTERVENTION IN DOWN'S SYNDROME
A Critique

M. J. Begab

University Park Press, 300 North Charles Street, Baltimore, Maryland 21201

Surgical and cognitive intervention with Down's syndrome children is a promising, but as yet untested, method for their full integration and assimilation into the mainstream of society. The conceptual and theoretical implications of this approach are explored in the context of current knowledge about the specific learning capabilities and limitations of these individuals and the criteria to be applied in selecting candidates for these procedures.

Surgical procedures with Down's syndrome children, primarily for cosmetic purposes, but in lesser degree for corrective objectives as well, are not new to medical practice. By the same token, studies bearing on cognitive assessment, processes, and performance in Down's children have been going on for a long time and are replete in the literature. Intervention programs aimed at cognitive modification with this group are less extensive, reflecting in part the conventional wisdom—or lack of it—on the part of the behavioral sciences that little can be done to change the cognitive status of such children.

Despite the history of previous surgical and cognitive interventions with Down's children, experimental approaches combining these interventions are unique. Surgery in the past has been largely clinically, rather than scientifically, oriented, and there are no data on functional or psychological outcomes. Medicine and behavior have pursued independent goals. Never before have surgeons, physicians, educators, psychologists, and counselors combined talents in a scientific experiment of this magnitude.

The intervention program initiated by Dr. Reuven Feuerstein (of the Hadassah-Wizo-Canada Research Institute, Israel) in February 1982 is ambitious and comprehensive. It embraces cosmetic and corrective surgery, educational stimulation and guidance in problem solving, and informational and supportive services to the family. It is bold, challenging, and controversial. The goal of the program, to effect the social integration of Down's children and adolescents, might well be considered foolhardy. Yet there is sufficient evidence from research and clinical practice that such conclusions are not foregone. The theoretical implications and social significance of the Israeli study are far-reaching, extending well beyond this particular clinical syndrome, and are most deserving of serious scientific attention.

BIOMEDICAL INTERVENTION

Down's syndrome is the most common form of mental retardation of organic etiology. It accounts for a significant proportion of the retarded population, is highly associated with advanced maternal age (Hook, 1981) and is more minimally related to paternal age (Matsunaga et al., 1978). The causes remain obscure, but, with the advent of amniocentesis, prenatal diagnosis, and a ubiquitous drop in the proportion of older women having live births, the incidence of Down's syndrome has declined (Stein et al., 1977). Although incidence rates may be lower, the increased life expectancy of this group has kept prevalence rates high and added new service needs for Down's individuals well into adulthood.

Some prominent geneticists reject the view that nothing can be done to alter the status of a child with Down's syndrome after it is born. They believe that genetically controlled processes continue into adulthood and that pathological influences can be interrupted with proper therapeutic modalities. Effective modalities have not yet been discovered, although over the years extravagant, but unsubstantiated, claims have been foisted upon desperate, vulnerable parents: the sicca cell therapy of Niehans in the 1930s, the admixture of vitamins, hormones, and minerals recommended by Haubold, the U-series approach of Turkel, and the more recent use of dimethylsulfoxide (DMSO). None of these treatments has had any effect on the mental development, behavior, or academic achievement of Down's children. Controlled trials with the application of 5-HTP (hydroxytryptophan) as a precursor to serotonin have proved equally ineffective (Pueschel, 1981). Despite the failure of these treatments, they continue to be used in various parts of the world, moot testimony that in the hearts of parents of Down's children "hope springs eternal."

BEHAVIORAL INTERVENTION

Efforts to improve the cognitive abilities of these children through behavioral strategies are somewhat more encouraging, although the parameters and magnitude of possible change are still to be specified. Numerous investigations have demonstrated that the measured intelligence of Down's syndrome infants has little predictive validity and declines an average of 30 to 40 IQ points over the first 6 years of life (Dicks-Mireaux, 1972; Melyn and White, 1973). The reasons for the decline, which vary significantly among children, are not fully understood. Several explanations are tenable: 1) a true regression in development; 2) a statistical artifact of the tests used during infancy, which can measure only a limited repertoire of behaviors; or 3) deficiencies in parent/child interaction processes or mediated learning experiences that fail to sustain the infant's learning potential.

Down's syndrome children, despite the similarity in their physical appearance, are by no means a homogeneous population. Although most tend to score in the moderate range of mental retardation, the range embraces all levels of intellectual retardation. Borderline intelligence is the exception, not the rule, and normal intelligence is an extreme rarity. Much of this variation is probably due to individual differences in the same way that nonretarded persons vary in their biological endowment. Yet the environment plays an important contributory role too; children raised in a stimulating early home environment demonstrate better mental development than those in less salutary settings (Piper and Ramsey, 1980).

Omnibus tests of intelligence, such as the Stanford-Binet, offer limited information on the intellectual strengths or weaknesses of Down's syndrome individuals. When matched to other retarded persons on IQ, the Down's group performs better on figural content and visual motor ability. They are less capable in tasks involving semantic content, social intelligence, general comprehension, and/or judgment and reasoning (Silverstein et al., 1982). Of special significance, given the importance of language in the developmental process, is the marked delay in language development experienced by Down's children. This delay appears to be due to deficiencies in vocal imitation skills (Mahoney et al., 1981) and possibly to deficits in auditory processing.

Given the presumed "nature" of the Down's syndrome organism, what are the potentials for cognitive change? To what extent is social integration possible? How do existing behavioral theories bear upon the outcome of Feuerstein's daring intervention program?

BIOLOGY/ENVIRONMENT

The origins, nature, and determinants of intelligence are complex and controversial issues. Biology and environment, interacting, undoubtedly affect development, but the relative contributions of each remain a matter of dispute. However, most scientists would agree that, where brain abnormality or central nervous system pathology is manifest, environmental factors assume secondary importance. Thus, with Down's children biology may set the ceiling on intellectual capacity.

Biology notwithstanding, the quality of living conditions to which individuals are exposed in childhood will determine whether that ceiling is realized. In the intact organism, it has been estimated that a shift in life circumstances from the very worst to the best possible environment for the development of intelligence could result in a swing of 20–25 IQ points. In real life, such extreme changes seldom occur for the "normal" child. Such transitions in the quality of life experiences are not likely to occur serendipitously for handicapped children either. Yet these are the goals of this intervention program: to change not only the individual's appearance and behavior, but the behavior of his/her family as well, and by so doing to create an interactive process conducive to social acceptance and integration.

The educational intervention programs of the 1960s clearly demonstrated that mental growth could be accelerated. That IQ gains were not sustained over time could well be the results of "starting too late and stopping too soon" and returning children to the same depriving environment that presumably retarded their intellectual growth in the first place. Where the family environment is also modified and enriched experiences are provided into the school years, the gains appear greater and the impact of longer duration (Seitz et al., 1981).

The critical issue with Down's children is that we have very little information on their true ability to learn. Although some parents of these children may provide an optimal learning environment for them, the large majority are too devastated to adequately perform the parental role. The Down's infant is generally identified from the moment of birth. His stigmata are evident to his parents and to all who observe him, creating in the parents a sense of shame and embarrassment. The parent-child relationship under these stress conditions is negatively affected and communication patterns are distorted. It is not surprising that vocal imitation by the child is deficient and language development delayed.

The point to be made here is that, even with damaged children, environment matters. Few Down's children are privileged to live in the "best possible" setting for mental development. The positive correlation between the intellectual status of parents and their Down's child indirectly supports this proposition. Given the nature of affective relationships and the likelihood that parents would not provide the handicapped child with the range of mediated learning experiences essential for growth, is it reasonable to conclude that the basic capacities of the child—his learning potential—are greater than his measured intelligence? If so, meaningful cognitive change is clearly possible.

SURGICAL INTERVENTION: STIGMA, SELF-CONCEPT, LABELING

Of the two aspects of surgery—cosmetic and corrective— the latter may be more meaningful in influencing social acceptance of the Down's child. As noted earlier, these children, compared to others of similar developmental and mental age, are especially deficient in vocal imitation, language acquisition, and articulation skills. If shortening of the tongue improves articulation and at the same time eliminates drooling and decreases physical stigmata, such surgery could prove very beneficial to language development. Language, it is generally agreed, is the primary pathway to problem solving, learning, and cognitive growth.

The effect of cosmetic change on social acceptance is less clear. Similarity theory (Jones, 1974) postulates that interpersonal attraction is determined by an individual's perception of others as similar to himself. Personal attitudes, tastes, and beliefs are positively correlated with these perceptions. The most rewarding sense of self comes from associating with others like oneself. By this theory, the Down's child whose facial appearance has been altered to near-normality has a better self-image and a greater potential for evoking positive responses from his peers.

Physical appearance, however, is only one possible aspect of similarity. Intelligence, personality, and behavior are probably more critical. Most educable mentally retarded children have no physical stigmata, yet their mainstreaming in regular classes does not appreciably reduce their exposure to stigmatization. Their sociometric status is much lower than that of segregated children when rated by their normal peers (Shotel et al., 1972). Despite the proliferation of articles on the adverse effect of labeling, some of which is ideologically rather than empirically inspired, there is little support for the view that labels by themselves affect self-concept, peer rejection, family attitudes, teacher expectancies, or future vocational adjustment (MacMillan et al., 1974).

Labeling is a highly personal process. It takes place through interpersonal encounter, not formal procedures. Children and adults react to the retarded person's social competence and overt behavior rather than a label per se, although the label may create an initial mind set. For most mildly retarded children in regular classroom settings, academic failure and disruptive behavior are the basis for teacher rejection, peer ridicule, and the retarded child's sense of inferiority. Confronted with this negative "mirror-image," the retarded child in effect labels himself. Only as he is perceived to be more similar than different by his peers can this outcome be changed.

CONCLUSIONS

The aims of this surgical and cognitive intervention experiment are to achieve full social acceptance and integration of Down's syndrome individuals into the mainstream of society. There is a great deal of evidence that many individuals who test at the upper level of the retarded range (generally about 60 + IQ points) are able to meet the expectations and demands of society in major areas of life functions and responsibilities. They are part of the well-documented "disappearing retardate" phenomenon, often submarginal in the quality of their living experiences, but indistinguishable in most respects from the lower social class of which they are usually a part. Those within this IQ range who fail frequently demonstrate antisocial, aggressive, or other forms of maladaptive behavior.

Those Down's children and adults who already function at this level of intellectual performance or who can be helped to achieve this status through cognitive intervention and social competency training are excellent candidates for surgical intervention. Removing the barrier of physical stigmata and improving their articulatory skills could go a long way toward ensuring their self-confidence, social acceptance, and independence. There may be some unforeseen hazards in the surgery, as well. Will Down's women, by virtue of their more normal and attractive appearance, be more vulnerable to sexual exploitation? Will the deficiencies of this group be concealed and unrealistic expectations accordingly be imposed upon them? Will they be denied protections and considerations automatically afforded them before? These factors will need to be considered in preparing them for social living.

It should also be emphasized that these individuals seldom demonstrate the kind of maladaptive behavior characteristic of the mildly retarded from seriously disadvantaged families; also, because they come from every strata of society, they are more likely to have the family supports and social network resources essential to a successful transition from childhood to adulthood. The important consideration here is that both criteria for successful integration—physical and cognitive—must be achieved. Neither form of intervention can stand alone.

It must be recognized, however, that individuals with Down's syndrome vary widely phenotypically and, like any other group in the population, differ in their functional abilities and capacity for change. Some have multiple handicaps, such as congenital heart defect or impairment in hearing and vision. Often, these individuals are severely retarded and would be questionable candidates for intervention.

The advent of newer techniques for chromosome investigation supports the "gradation of clinical features" in Down's syndrome and the biological differences between individuals sharing this diagnosis. Information derived from these procedures, coupled with psychological assessments of learning potential, as well as performance, could enable the selection of individuals most likely to benefit from intervention.

The experiment referred to here is daring, exciting, and potentially of great social significance. It has theoretical import, too, not only for Down's individuals, but for others whose physical stigmata are a barrier to integration. Unquestionably, many parents will look to such programs as solutions to their problems. It may well prove the long sought for answer for some; for others, it could be another devastating disappointment in the continuing search for help. Clearly, we must await the outcomes of this experiment, currently in its very early phases, before the adoption of surgical procedures can be encouraged. The professional responsibility of the investigators and the comprehensiveness and scientific rigor of their research design and methodology assure that the proper cautions will be instituted.

Personally, I look forward with great enthusiasm and cautious optimism to the findings of this experiment. I am certain that the scientific and professional community and the many thousands of parents with Down's syndrome children also eagerly await the results.

REFERENCES

Dicks-Miraux, M. J. 1972. Mental development of infants with Down's syndrome. Am. J. Ment. Defic. 77:26–32.
Hook, E. B. 1981. Down syndrome: Frequency in human populations and factors pertinent to variation in rates. In: F. F. de la Cruz and P. Gerald (eds.), Trisomy 21 (Down Syndrome): Research Perspectives. University Park Press, Baltimore.
Jones, S. 1974. Psychology of interpersonal attraction. In: C. Nemeth (ed.), Social Psychology, Classic and Contemporary Integrations. Rand-McNally, Chicago.

Macmillan, D. L., Jones, R. L., and Aloia, G. F. 1974. The mentally retarded label: A theoretical analysis and review of research. Am. J. Ment. Defic. 79:241–261.

Mahoney, G., Glover, A., and Finger, I. 1981. Relationship between language and sensorimotor development of Down's syndrome and nonretarded children. Am. J. Ment. Defic. 86:21–27.

Matsunaga, E., Tonomura, A., Oishi, H., and Kakuchi, Y. 1978. Reexamination of paternal age effect in Down's syndrome. Hum. Genet. 40:259–268.

Melyn, M. A., and White, D. T. 1973. Mental and developmental milestones of noninstitutionalized Down's syndrome children. Pediatrics 52:542–545.

Piper, M. C., and Ramsay, M. K. 1980. Effects of early home environment on the mental development of Down's syndrome infants. Am. J. Ment. Defic. 85:39–44.

Pueschel, S. M. 1981. Therapeutic approaches in Down syndrome. In: F. F. de la Cruz and P. Gerald (eds.), Trisomy 21 (Down Syndrome): Research Perspectives. University Park Press, Baltimore.

Seitz, V., Appel, N. H., and Rosenbaum, L. K. 1981. Project Head Start and follow through: A longitudinal evaluation of adolescents. In: M. J. Begab, H. C. Haywood, and H. L. Garber (eds.), Psychosocial Influences in Retarded Performance, Vol. II. University Park Press, Baltimore.

Shotel, J. R., Iano, R. P., and McGettigan, J. F. 1972. Teacher attitudes associated with the integration of handicapped children. Except. Child. 38:677–683.

Silverstein, A. B., Legutki, G., Friedman, S. L., and Takayama, D. L. 1982. Performance of Down's syndrome individuals on the Stanford-Binet intelligence scale. Am. J. Ment. Defic. 86:548–550.

Stein, Z. A., Susser, M., Klein, J., and Warburton, D. 1977. Amniocentesis and selective abortion for trisomy 21 in the light of the natural history of pregnancy and fetal survival. In: E. B. Hook and J. H. Porter (eds.), Population Cytogenetics: Studies in Humans, pp. 257–274. Academic Press, Inc., New York.

PERSPECTIVES AND PROGRESS IN MENTAL RETARDATION
Volume II—Biomedical Aspects
Edited by J. M. Berg

EXPERIENCES WITH INDIVIDUAL RELATIONSHIP THERAPY WITHIN A THERAPEUTIC MILIEU FOR RETARDED CHILDREN WITH SEVERE EMOTIONAL DISORDERS

A. Došen

Center for the Observation of Children with Developmental Disorders,
"DE HONDSBERG", Hondsberg 5, 5062 JT Oisterwijk, The Netherlands

Clinical experience is reported concerning the application of relationship therapy within the framework of a therapeutic milieu for emotionally disturbed, mentally handicapped children. The theoretical background, method, and practical results are described. Individual psychotherapy was carried out by a well-trained, supervised nursing staff within the living group. The emphasis of therapy is on an individual, positive, affectionate bond with the child, through which he is helped to surmount his emotional conflicts and to gradually compensate for the lag in his emotional development. It is thought that the application of individual relationship therapy within a therapeutic milieu is especially suitable for mentally handicapped children, because of the specific interaction pattern of these children with their environment.

With the development of the idea of "normalizing" the lives of mentally handicapped children, an increased need to develop psychotherapeutic methods for the treatment of often simultaneously occurring behavioral problems and emotional disorders becomes evident. Because of the particular way in which a retarded child exists in his environment, relationship therapy as described by Allen (1942) and Moustakas (1959), is, in my opinion, often applicable to the severe emotional disorders of such children. Allen and Moustakas developed relationship therapy for treatment of intellectually normal emotionally disturbed children. We have adopted their method and combined it with a "therapeutic milieu" (Aichorn, 1925; Bettelheim, 1950; Redl and Wineman, 1951) for a residential treatment program for retarded children with behavioral problems. In this arrangement psychotherapy is carried out by a day-residential nursing staff under the constant, intensive guidance and supervision of qualified therapists.

CLINIC POPULATION

Each year, some 80 children are admitted to our observation clinic. All children are, or are presumed to be, mentally deficient. In about 80% of the cases, the reason for the child's admission is serious behavioral and functional problems at home or at school. The ages of these children vary from 3 to 16 years. Serious emotional disorders are found in 40–50% of them and, in these cases, relationship therapy is often used for treatment. During the average 6-month period of residential treatment efforts are made by means of this therapy to free a child of his emotional problems, and hence allow him to function adequately in his own environment. The parents, and sometimes the staff of kindergartens and schools, are involved in the treatment.

Examples of Treatment

Child A   Child A, a 4-year-old girl, is the older of twins and the second of three siblings. Her weight at birth was 3,500 g; no complications occurred during pregnancy or delivery. The child showed delayed psychomotor development: she began walking at the age of 3 years, and speech had not developed. Upon admission, she was averse to any attempt at contact. Her mood was variable and attacks of temper were frequent. She showed many stereotyped movements. On intelligence testing, severe retardation was found. The diagnosis was that of a severely handicapped child with serious social contact disturbances.

In the first phase of treatment, an attempt was made to familiarize the child with the space of the living environment. She chose a corner of the living room where she lay on the floor, denying all entrance to her territory. A nurse was assigned the task of giving her attention regularly, and trying to establish contact. This contact was not physical or verbal, but instead joining in play with her favorite objects. Initially, these forms of communication were repeated every 20 minutes, and never lasted longer than a few minutes. Eventually, the child showed that such contact was appreciated. For that reason, "contact play" was introduced using water, sand, and clay, during which her hands were touched and playfully moved by the nurse. Gradually, "contact play" was extended and the child was stroked, caressed, and lifted. She began to like being cuddled, and there came the moment when she spontaneously went to her nurse.

At this point, verbal communication was introduced. A limited number of words (with a positive meaning for the child) was repeated in the communication. After 6 months' treatment, the girl made marked progress in relating to her environment. She moved freely, explored the space of the department, and took the initiative in establishing physical contact with her nurse.

Our treatment was based on the concept that the child's development of "attachment" (Bowlby, 1969) was delayed. She had stagnated in the first phase of psychic development, when the personal bodily limits are not yet realized and there is as yet no concept of the objective world. We knew that her capacity for accepting external stimuli was very limited, so she was placed in a constant environment in which she was given her own place in the room, thereby reducing external stimuli. Within this space, she always received an offer for contact by the same nurse within a well-planned day program, with a constant dose of contact of constant daily frequency. The treatment was aimed at establishing contact with the child through her tactile senses. The guiding principle here was that tactile sense, proprioceptors, and kinesthesia are capable of adequately receiving external stimuli sooner than such senses as hearing and sight (Spitz, 1945).

Via such a structured approach, and through an optimal supply of physical contact, the primary contact with a "love-object" of the child was established. This was the condition for further progress toward self-differentiation and for her social and emotional development.

Child B   Child B is a 7-year-old boy, the older of two children. Pregnancy and delivery were uneventful. The child showed delayed psychomotor development: he began to walk at the age of 2 years, the first words were spoken at the age of $2\frac{1}{2}$, and he was toilet trained at the age of 5. Admission was due to delayed speech development, poor learning capacity, and a strange, inward-turned behavior. Upon admission, he was very anxious, withdrawn, and inactive. He spoke a few unconnected words, and preferred sterotyped actions involving a certain object. He was passive to the initiative of others. During psychological testing he functioned at a moderately retarded level; on physical examination no abnormalities were found. An electroencephalogram showed diffuse nonspecific abnormalities. The diagnosis in this case was atypical child psychosis; the child met the DSM-III (American Psychological Association, 1980) criteria for atypical pervasive developmental disorder.

In individual therapy, it was obvious that the child liked physical contact very much. This need for physical contact was therefore used as the starting point for therapy. The therapist was to give the child as much physical contact as he wanted. The consequence of this approach was that the child did not want to detach himself from the therapist. She had to keep him in her lap, carry him, feed him, and completely look after him. Bowel and bladder control were lost. The child regressed to an infantlike stage. This complete dependence on the nurse lasted for 2 months. Gradually, he began to increase spatial distance from the nurse. This was the second phase in his development: independence increased, but at the same time negative, stubborn, and provocative attitudes developed.

A few months later, the stubborn and negative trends became somewhat less marked and the child showed greater cooperation toward the nurse and greater creativity in handling materials. Slowly he began to show more interest in the other children in the group and, encouraged by the therapist, began to play actively with them. In this phase, he was placed in a class of the special school. During treatment, which lasted for 5 months, great progress was made in his initiative and speech development. He became more involved in reality and his behavior lost the characteristics of the psychosis diagnosed 5 months previously.

We assumed that this child had not established a confident relationship with his mother in the "symbiotic phase" (Mahler et al., 1975) of his development and had found no "basic trust" (Erikson, 1959). He had acquired the capacity to make known what he needed but, because of these needs, he repeatedly collided with regulations and prohibitions in the environment. These frustrations and anxieties kept him from true communication with the environment; accordingly, he preferred to withdraw into his own small world and to give his attention to inanimate objects rather than to the people around him. With relationship therapy, we tried to find a manner of communication through which the child could make satisfactory contact with his environment. In the course of the treatment, as the boy regressed to infantlike behavior, he found himself safe in a symbiotic contact with his nurse. The therapy emphasized repetition of the symbiotic phase of the child's development by which his basic trust could be enhanced. Once his safety was increased, he ventured to establish communication with reality, abandoning his psychotic behavior.

RELATIONSHIP THERAPY

During the last 3 years, 97 children have received relationship therapy at our clinic. These were children with severe contact disorders who were psychotic, depressed, and seriously neurotic (Došen, in preparation, in press). Treatment can be divided into three phases.

First Phase: Tolerance and Acceptance

In the first phase, the aim is to adapt the group to the child in such a manner that the child feels accepted by the group. An attempt is made to accept the child and all his actions in such a way that he finds his own place and role within the group. The symptoms of disturbed behavior are not combatted, but rather accepted as an aspect of the child's total existence. The initial task is to make the child feel at peace in the therapeutic milieu of the department, and at the same time to discover to what extent and in what way the child can be induced to communicate pleasantly.

Second Phase: Meeting and Growing Together

The second phase consists of the formation of a positive, affectionate relationship between the therapist and the child. Initially, the therapist tries to react positively to all forms of the child's behavior. By this positive approach, the therapist hopes to make the child realize that he is totally accepted. Once this realization has been established, the child is stimulated to develop his own initiative in communication and to express his wishes and feelings.

Third Phase: Reeducation

The third phase is that in which the therapist becomes somewhat more active in relation to the child. Based on the positive and trusting relationship already built, the therapist tries to relieve the child of his established behavior and to teach a new form of socially acceptable behavior. In this phase, the therapist introduces a pedagogic structure into the relationship, including "must" and "must not" clauses. The boundaries of social behavior are set. Within this pedagogic structure, the child receives social reinforcement, stimulating further learning of social behavior and creativity. In this phase, the therapist can also use other therapeutic techniques for some children, such as play therapy or "roleplay therapy." In such treatment, we maintain three principles: 1) structure in space, persons, and time; 2) diurnal rhythm; and 3) gradual emotional growth.

Principle 1 means that therapeutic activities must take place in surroundings to which the child is accustomed. The most familiar environment is that of daily life, so therapy should be included within this milieu. As much as possible, the therapy room should remain unaltered in design and furniture. Structure in respect to people means that a change in department personnel should be avoided if possible. The child should have a permanent therapist. The therapeutic activity should take place within a planned daily program, and should remain consistent with respect to time and duration.

Principle 2 means that activity and inactivity of the child should alternate regularly during the day. We consider this principle to be of great importance for work with mentally handicapped children because their mental powers of integration and regulation are often very weak. This mental capability should be individually determined, and the rhythm of activity and inactivity individually decided for each child on this basis. In this manner, we try to avoid a possible over- or under-stimulation of the child in the therapeutic process.

Principle 3 means that the therapist should be aware that, once communication with the child has been established, further development must be gradual. The therapist should be "developmentally oriented"; i.e., he should consecutively follow the growth phases every normal child experiences in normal emotional development. In concrete terms, this means that in a child with contact disturbances one should not try to establish material or verbal communication before contact via the skin and proprioceptors is possible. In the same manner, for a negative and destructive child, one should not try to induce structure within the group before the child has reached a structure and positive and familiar bond with an adult.

In this way, we wish to accentuate the developmental approach (Berlin, 1978; Greenspan et al., 1979; Greenspan and Lourie, 1981). Developmental diagnosis of a child's ego functioning is made, and his developmental needs are defined. During treatment, the therapist stimulates the child to grow from one developmental phase to another.

RESULTS

On average, therapy lasted for 6 months. Forty-one percent of the children showed an improvement comparable with the two children described above. They were discharged free of the symptoms with which they were admitted. In another 41%, there was insufficient improvement; these children required further treatment. Eighteen percent showed no improvement. The children with contact disorders and psychotic children showed the most improvement.

DISCUSSION

During relationship therapy, a child learns to solve his problems in the immediate environment in cooperation with the therapist. In this therapeutic process, he goes through phases of emotional growth (Moustakas, 1959). "Therapy emerges from an experience in living within a relationship with another from whom the patient can eventually differentiate himself as he comes to perceive and accept his own self as separate and distinct" (Allen, 1942).

We assume that at some point a mentally handicapped child begins his postnatal development, in respect to relationships, like a normal child does, and that further development occurs in the same phases as it does for an intellectually normal child. However, these phases have different timing than those of a normal child. Mentally handicapped children have a weaker organic potential and thus a weaker power of adaptation. Such a child does not activate his surroundings according to his needs, and so from the outset may be doomed to neglect and social deprivation. According to various authors (Gunzburg, 1974; La Vietes, 1978; Bernstein, 1979; Bicknell, 1979; Forrest, 1979), a consistent relationship can have a powerful therapeutic effect on behavioral and psychiatric disorders in these children.

After establishing a psychopathological and developmental diagnosis, and after determining the child's developmental needs, the therapist attempts to adapt his approach to the child's emotional and intellectual level, thus giving the child a "meeting point." The therapist tries to "give the child a hand" on the difficult path to his development; assisted by the therapist, the child conquers his fears and emotional conflicts. The child is not taught to become aware of his old emotional conflicts and processes, but rather is stimulated on the basis of the immediate situation. He is taught to adopt an adequate attitude in communicating with the therapist, and to cope with conflicts in communication here and now.

Our technique for psychotherapeutic treatment is applied by a trained and supervised nursing staff within the living group. By activating the nursing staff, the positive aspects of a therapeutic milieu can be well combined with the advantages of individual therapy. Important aspects in psychotherapy of the mentally handicapped, such as constancy in space, time, and people and the rhythm of the activities, can thus also be maintained. In this manner, the child has the opportunity of receiving more attention and affection from the therapist. In order to maintain the therapeutic "know-how" at a high level, the delegated staff need intensive coaching, support, and supervision. This support requires much time and effort from qualified therapists.

It is important that the atmosphere of the therapeutic milieu be characterized by optimism and acceptance. Such an atmosphere can be attained only if the members in charge of guidance and supervision display this optimism for the children. The nursing staff together with their supervisors must create a coherent group. Not only professional guidance, but good interpersonal relationships between the supervisor and nursing staff and among the nursing staff themselves, is very important. In this kind of psychotherapy, this is a very sensitive point. Often we have realized that, because of unfavorable interpersonal relationships within the departmental nursing staff, therapeutic efforts were insufficent and results bad.

Besides being of use in residential treatment, the method of relationship therapy is, in our opinion, applicable to the home training of mothers with retarded children. In this manner, the mothers can also take an active part in therapy to prevent emotional disorders in their children. Further research regarding indications and more detailed techniques for this therapeutic approach are needed. Investigations in this field could be important for the protection of the retarded child's mental health.

REFERENCES

Aichorn, A. 1925. Verwahrloste Jugend Wien. Int. Psychoanalyt. Verlag.

Allen, F. H. 1942. Psychotherapy with Children, p. 49. W. W. Norton & Company, Inc., New York.

American Psychological Association. 1980. Diagnostic and Statistical Manual of Mental Disorders, 3rd ed. American Psychological Association, Washington, D.C.

Berlin, J. N. 1978. Developmental issues in the psychiatric hospitalization of children. Am. J. Psychiatry 135:1044–1048.

Bernstein, N. R. 1979. Mental retardation. In: J. D. Noshpitz (ed.), Basic Handbook of Child Psychiatry, Vol. III. Basic Books, Inc., New York.

Bettelheim, B. 1950. Love is Not Enough. The Free Press, Glencoe, Illinois.

Bicknell, D. J. 1979. Treatment and management of disturbed mentally handicapped patients. In: F. F. James and R. P. Snaith (eds.), Psychiatric and Mental Handicap. Gaskell Press, London.

Bowlby, J. 1969. Attachment and Loss, Vol. I: Attachment. Basic Books, Inc., New York.

Došen, A. Disorders of social contact in mentally deficient children—Autism, psychosis or effect of social deprivation. (in preparation)

Došen, A. Depressive conditions in mentally handicapped children. (in press)

Erikson, E. H. 1959. Identity and the Life Cycle: Selected Papers. International Universities Press, Inc., New York.

Forrest, A. D. 1979. Neurosis in the mentally handicapped. In: F. F. James and R. P. Snaith (eds.), Psychiatric Illness and Mental Handicap. Gaskell Press, London.

Greenspan, S. I., and Lourie, R. S. 1981. Developmental structural approach; Infancy and early childhood. Am J. Psychiatry 138:725–735.

Greenspan, S. I., Lourie, R. S., and Nover, R. A. 1979. A developmental approach to the classification of psychopathology in infancy and early childhood. In: J. D. Noshpitz, Basic Handbook of Child Psychiatry, Vol. II. Basic Books, Inc., New York.

Gunzburg, H. C. 1974. Psychotherapy. In: A. M. Clarke and A. B. D. Clarke (eds.), Mental Deficiency: The Changing Outlook, pp. 708–728. Methuen & Co. Ltd., London.

La Vietes, R. 1978. Mental retardation: Psychological treatment. In: B. B. Wolman and J. E. A. O. Ross (eds.), Handbook of Treatment of Mental Disorders in Childhood and Adolescence. Prentice-Hall, Inc., Englewood Cliffs, New Jersey.

Mahler, M. S., Pine, F., and Bergman, A. 1975. The Psychological Birth of the Human Infant. Basic Books, Inc., New York.

Moustakas, C. I. 1959. Psychotherapy with Children: The Living Relationship. Harper & Row Pubs., Inc., New York.

Redl, F., and Wineman, D. 1951. Children Who Hate. The Free Press, Glencoe, Illinois.

Spitz, R. A. 1945. Hospitalism: Psycho-analytic Study of the Child. International Universities Press, Inc., New York.

AUTHOR INDEX

SUBJECT INDEX